Reading STREET

Program Authors

Peter Afflerbach

Camille Blachowicz

Candy Dawson Boyd

Elena Izquierdo

Connie Juel

Edward Kame'enui

Donald Leu

Jeanne R. Paratore

P. David Pearson

Sam Sebesta

Deborah Simmons

Alfred Tatum

Sharon Vaughn

Susan Watts Taffe

Karen Kring Wixson

PEARSON

Glenview, Illinois • Boston, Massachusetts • Chandler, Arizona
Upper Saddle River, New Jersey

We dedicate Reading Street to
Peter Jovanovich.

His wisdom, courage,
and passion for education
are an inspiration to us all.

ISBN-13: 978-0-328-47028-0
ISBN-10:   0-328-47028-7
2 3 4 5 6 7 8 9 10 V064 14 13 12 11 10
CC1

Any Path, Any Pace

Reading STREET

CALLE de la Lectura

"Welcome to
Reading Street!
Bienvenidos too."

PEARSON

Find Your Place on Reading Street!

Who said so?

The Leading Researchers,

Program Authors

Peter Afflerbach, Ph.D.
Professor
Department of Curriculum
and Instruction
University of Maryland
at College Park

Camille L. Z. Blachowicz, Ph.D.
Professor of Education
National-Louis University

Candy Dawson Boyd, Ph.D.
Professor
School of Education
Saint Mary's College of California

Elena Izquierdo, Ph.D.
Associate Professor
University of Texas at El Paso

Connie Juel, Ph.D.
Professor of Education
School of Education
Stanford University

Edward J. Kame'enui, Ph.D.
*Dean-Knight Professor of
Education and Director*
Institute for the Development of
Educational Achievement and
the Center on Teaching and Learning
College of Education
University of Oregon

Donald J. Leu, Ph.D.
*John and Maria Neag Endowed
Chair in Literacy and Technology
Director, The New Literacies
Research Lab*
University of Connecticut

Jeanne R. Paratore, Ed.D.
Associate Professor of Education
Department of Literacy and
Language Development
Boston University

P. David Pearson, Ph.D.
Professor and Dean
Graduate School of Education
University of California, Berkeley

Sam L. Sebesta, Ed.D.
Professor Emeritus
College of Education
University of Washington, Seattle

Deborah Simmons, Ph.D.
Professor
College of Education and
Human Development
Texas A&M University

Alfred W. Tatum, Ph.D.
*Associate Professor and Director
of the UIC Reading Clinic*
University of Illinois at Chicago

Sharon Vaughn, Ph.D.
*H. E. Hartfelder/Southland
Corporation Regents Professor
Director, Meadows Center for
Preventing Educational Risk*
University of Texas

Susan Watts Taffe, Ph.D.
Associate Professor in Literacy
Division of Teacher Education
University of Cincinnati

Karen Kring Wixson, Ph.D.
Professor of Education
University of Michigan

Consulting Authors

Jeff Anderson, M.Ed.
Author and Consultant
San Antonio, Texas

Jim Cummins, Ph.D.
Professor
Department of Curriculum,
Teaching and Learning
University of Toronto

Lily Wong Fillmore, Ph.D.
Professor Emerita
Graduate School of Education
University of California, Berkeley

Georgia Earnest García, Ph.D.
Professor
Language and Literacy Division
Department of Curriculum
and Instruction
University of Illinois at
Urbana-Champaign

George A. González, Ph.D.
Professor (Retired)
School of Education
University of Texas-Pan American,
Edinburg

Valerie Ooka Pang, Ph.D.
Professor
School of Teacher Education
San Diego State University

Sally M. Reis, Ph.D.
*Board of Trustees Distinguished
Professor*
Department of Educational
Psychology
University of Connecticut

Jon Scieszka, M.F.A.
*Children's Book Author
Founder of GUYS READ
Named First National Ambassador
for Young People's Literature 2008*

Grant Wiggins, Ed.D.
Educational Consultant
Authentic Education
Concept Development

Lee Wright, M.Ed.
Pearland, Texas

Practitioners, and Authors.

Consultant

Sharroky Hollie, Ph.D.
Assistant Professor
California State University
Dominguez Hills, CA

Teacher Reviewers

Dr. Bettyann Brugger
Educational Support Coordinator—
Reading Office
Milwaukee Public Schools
Milwaukee, WI

Kathleen Burke
K–12 Reading Coordinator
Peoria Public Schools, Peoria, IL

Darci Burns, M.S.Ed.
University of Oregon

Bridget Cantrell
District Intervention Specialist
Blackburn Elementary School
Independence, MO

Tahira DuPree Chase,
M.A., M.S.Ed.
Administrator of Elementary
English Language Arts
Mount Vernon City School District
Mount Vernon, NY

Michele Conner
Director, Elementary Education
Aiken County School District
Aiken, SC

Georgia Coulombe
K–6 Regional Trainer/
Literacy Specialist
Regional Center for Training and
Learning (RCTL), Reno, NV

Kelly Dalmas
Third Grade Teacher
Avery's Creek Elementary, Arden, NC

Seely Dillard
First Grade Teacher
Laurel Hill Primary School
Mt. Pleasant, SC

Jodi Dodds-Kinner
Director of Elementary Reading
Chicago Public Schools, Chicago, IL

Dr. Ann Wild Evenson
District Instructional Coach
Osseo Area Schools, Maple Grove, MN

Stephanie Fascitelli
Principal
Apache Elementary, Albuquerque
Public Schools, Albuquerque, NM

Alice Franklin
Elementary Coordinator, Language
Arts & Reading
Spokane Public Schools, Spokane, WA

Laureen Fromberg
Assistant Principal
PS 100 Queens, NY

Kimberly Gibson
First Grade Teacher
Edgar B. Davis Community School
Brockton, MA

Kristen Gray
Lead Teacher
A.T. Allen Elementary School
Concord, NC

Mary Ellen Hazen
State Pre-K Teacher
Rockford Public Schools #205
Rockford, IL

Patrick M. Johnson
Elementary Instructional Director
Seattle Public Schools, Seattle, WA

Theresa Jaramillo Jones
Principal
Highland Elementary School
Las Cruces, NM

Sophie Kowzun
Program Supervisor, Reading/
Language Arts, PreK–5
Montgomery County Public Schools
Rockville, MD

David W. Matthews
Sixth Grade Teacher
Easton Area Middle School
Easton, PA

Ana Nuncio
Editor and Independent Publisher
Salem, MA

Joseph Peila
Principal
Chappell Elementary School
Chicago, IL

Ivana Reimer
Literacy Coordinator
PS 100 Queens, NY

Sally Riley
Curriculum Coordinator
Rochester Public Schools
Rochester, NH

Dyan M. Smiley
Independent Educational Consultant

Michael J. Swiatowiec
Lead Literacy Teacher
Graham Elementary School
Chicago, IL

Dr. Helen Taylor
Director of English Education
Portsmouth City Public Schools
Portsmouth, VA

Carol Thompson
Teaching and Learning Coach
Independence School District
Independence, MO

Erinn Zeitlin
Kindergarten Teacher
Carderock Springs Elementary School
Bethesda, MD

Any Path, Any Pace

UNIT 5

Cultures

In this Teacher's Edition Unit 5, Volume 2

WEEK 4 • Jalapeño Bagels

WEEK 5 • Me and Uncle Romie

WEEK 6 • Interactive Review

What happens when two ways of life come together?

In the **First Stop** on Reading Street

 GO Digital!

See It!

- **Big Question Video**
- **Concept Talk Video**
- **Interactive Sound-Spelling Cards**
- **Envision It! Animations**

Hear It!

- **eSelections**
- **eReaders**
- **Grammar Jammer**
- **Leveled Reader Database**

Do It!

- **Vocabulary Activities**
- **Story Sort**
- **21st Century Skills Activities**
- **Online Assessment**
- **Letter Tile Drag and Drop**

Living and Learning

Key
SI Strategic Intervention
OL On-Level
A Advanced
ELL ELL

Volume 1

Volume 2

UNIT 2

Smart Solutions

Key
- **SI** Strategic Intervention
- **OL** On-Level
- **A** Advanced
- **ELL** ELL

Volume 1

WEEK 1 • Penguin Chick Expository Text 200a–231q
Plants: Fitting into Their World Photo Essay

Differentiated Instruction SI OL A ELL ....DI•1–DI•25

WEEK 2 • I Wanna Iguana Realistic Fiction.............232a–265q
The Big Soccer Game E-Mail

Differentiated Instruction SI OL A ELL ....DI•26–DI•50

WEEK 3 • Prudy's Problem and How She Solved It Fantasy..............266a–299q
Meeting the Challenge of Collecting Interview

Differentiated Instruction SI OL A ELL ....DI•51–DI•75

Volume 2

WEEK 4 • Tops & Bottoms Animal Fantasy 300a–333q
The Hare and the Tortoise Fable

Differentiated Instruction SI OL A ELL ....DI•76–DI•100

WEEK 5 • Amazing Bird Nests Expository Text....334a–363q
Extra! Extra! Fairy-Tale News from Hidden Forest Fairy Tale

Differentiated Instruction SI OL A ELL ....DI•101–DI•125

WEEK 6 • Interactive Review ....IR•1–IR•60
What are some smart ways that problems are solved?
Unit 2 Reading Poetry...364–367a

Customize Writing ....CW•1–CW•20
Customize Literacy...CL•1–CL•47
Let's Learn Amazing Words ....OV•1–OV•3

UNIT 3

People and Nature

Volume 1

WEEK 1 • How Do You Raise a Raisin?
Expository Text...370a–403q
Worms at Work Procedural Text

Differentiated Instruction SI OL A ELL ....DI•1–DI•25

WEEK 2 • Pushing Up the Sky   Drama.................404a–437q
Catch It and Run! Myth

Differentiated Instruction SI OL A ELL ....DI•26–DI•50

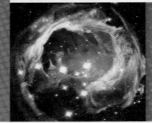

WEEK 3 • Seeing Stars   Expository Text 438a–467q
Scien-Trickery: Riddles in Science Poetry

Differentiated Instruction SI OL A ELL ....DI•51–DI•75

Volume 2

WEEK 4 • A Symphony of Whales   Fiction.......468a–501q
He Listens to Whales Magazine Article

Differentiated Instruction SI OL A ELL ....DI•76–DI•100

WEEK 5 • Around One Cactus
Narrative Nonfiction 502a–537q
The Water Cycle Search Engines

Differentiated Instruction SI OL A ELL ....DI•101–DI•125

WEEK 6 • Interactive Review ....IR•1–IR•60
How are people and nature connected?
Unit 3 Reading Poetry 538–541a

Customize Writing .... CW•1–CW•20
Customize Literacy..CL•1–CL•47
Let's Learn Amazing Words ....OV•1–OV•3

UNIT 4

One of a Kind

Volume 1

Volume 2

UNIT 5

Cultures

Volume 1

Volume 2

UNIT 6

Freedom

Volume 1

Volume 2

Skills Overview

UNIT 5

Key

T Tested Skill

🎯 Target Skill

	WEEK 1	WEEK 2
	Suki's Kimono Realistic Fiction, pp. 198–211 **Clothes: Bringing Cultures Together** Expository Text, pp. 216–219	**I Love Saturdays y domingos** Realistic Fiction, pp. 230–245 **Communities Celebrate Cultures** Textbook, pp. 250–251
Question of the Week	How does culture influence the clothes we wear?	How are cultures alike and different?
Amazing Words	*fabric, traditional, fret, scarves, acceptable, inspire, robe, drape, stylish, elegant*	*belief, dwelling, settler, chant, clan, barbecue, concentrate, headdress, procession, shield*
Phonics	T 🎯 Syllable Pattern CV/VC	T 🎯 Homophones
Literary Terms	Word Choice	Point of View
Story Structure/ Text Features	Resolution	Rising Action
Comprehension	T 🎯 **Skill** Compare and Contrast 🎯 **Strategy** Visualize Review **Skill** Cause and Effect	T 🎯 **Skill** Main Idea and Details 🎯 **Strategy** Inferring Review **Skill** Compare and Contrast
Vocabulary	T 🎯 **Skill** Synonyms	T 🎯 **Skill** Homophones
Fluency	Rate	Accuracy
Writing	Letter to the Editor Trait: Organization	Poetry Trait: Word Choice
Conventions	Adjectives and Articles	Comparative and Superlative Adjectives
Spelling	Syllable Pattern CV/VC	Homophones
Speaking/Listening	Introduction	Drama
Research Skills	Newletter	Maps

Get Ready to Read

Read and Comprehend

Language Arts

The Big Question

What happens when two ways of life come together?

WEEK **3**	WEEK **4**	WEEK **5**	WEEK **6**
Good-Bye, 382 Shin Dang Dong Realistic Fiction, pp. 262–279 **Sing a Song of People** Poetry, pp. 284–285	**Jalapeño Bagels** Realistic Fiction, pp. 296–309 **Foods of Mexico: A Delicious Blend** Expository Text, pp. 314–317	**Me and Uncle Romie** Realistic Fiction, pp. 328–349 **Country to City** Online Reference Sources, pp. 354–357	**Interactive Review**
Why is it hard to adapt to a new culture?	How can different cultures contribute to the foods we eat?	How does city life compare to life in the country?	Connect the Question of the Week to the Big Question
native, homeland, advantage, aspect, sponsor, habit, impolite, manner, conscious, insult	*nutrition, flavor, calorie, spice, nutmeg, grumble, allergic, wholesome, grate, agent*	*scamper, scurry, skyscraper, taxicab, vendor, hurl, meager, gutter, bitter, ramble*	Review Amazing Words for Unit 5
T Vowel Patterns for /ò/	T Vowel Patterns *ei, eigh*	T Suffixes *-y, -ish, -hood, -ment*	
Mood	Dialogue and Narration	Onomatopoeia	
Rising Action	Climax	Conflict	
T **Skill** Sequence **Strategy** Monitor and Clarify Review **Skill** Draw Conclusions	T **Skill** Draw Conclusions **Strategy** Summarize Review **Skill** Sequence	T **Skill** Author's Purpose **Strategy** Background Knowledge Review **Skill** Draw Conclusions	Review Unit 5 Target Comprehension Skills
T **Skill** Compound Words	T **Skill** Unfamiliar Words	T **Skill** Homonyms	Review Unit 5 Target Vocabulary Skills
Expression/Punctuation Cues	Accuracy	Appropriate Phrasing	Review Unit 5 Fluency Skills
Poetry Trait: Word Choice	Invitation Trait: Focus/ Ideas	Book Review Trait: Conventions	Quick Write for Fluency
Adverbs	Comparative and Superlative Adverbs	Conjunctions	Review Conventions
Vowel Patterns *au, augh, ou, ough*	Vowel Patterns *ei, eigh*	Suffixes *-y, -ish, -hood, -ment*	Review Spelling patterns
Song or Poem	Media Literacy: Radio Advertisement	Retelling	
Atlas	Outlining	Electronic Text	

UNIT 5
Monitor Progress

Don't Wait Until Friday!

SUCCESS PREDICTOR	WEEK 1	WEEK 2	WEEK 3	WEEK 4
Word Reading / **Phonics**	T Syllable Pattern CV/VC	T Homophones	T Vowel Patterns for /ò/	T Vowel Patterns *ei, eigh*
WCPM / **Fluency**	Rate 102–112 WCPM	Accuracy 102–112 WCPM	Expression/Punctuation Cues 102–112 WCPM	Accuracy 102–112 WCPM
Vocabulary / **Oral Vocabulary/ Concept Development** (assessed informally)	fabric traditional fret scarves acceptable inspire robe drape stylish elegant	belief dwelling settler chant clan barbecue concentrate headdress procession shield	native homeland advantage aspect sponsor habit impolite manner conscious insult	nutrition flavor calorie spice nutmeg grumble allergic wholesome grate agent
Lesson Vocabulary	T festival T snug T rhythm T paces T graceful T pale T cotton T handkerchief	T circus T nibbling T bouquet T difficult T pier T swallow T soars	T homesick T airport T raindrops T memories T farewell T curious T described T delicious T cellar	T bakery T ingredients T batch T mixture T dough T braided T boils
Retelling / **Text Comprehension**	T Skill Compare and Contrast Strategy Visualize	T Skill Main Idea and Details Strategy Inferring	T Skill Sequence Strategy Monitor and Clarify	T Skill Draw Conclusions Strategy Summarize

Key

T Tested Skill

◉ Target Skill

WEEK 5	WEEK 6
T ◉ Suffixes *-y, -ish, -hood, -ment*	R E V I E W
Appropriate Phrasing 102–112 WCPM	
scamper scurry skyscraper taxicab vendor hurl meager gutter bitter ramble	
T flights T stoops T ruined T fierce T treasure T feast T cardboard T pitcher	
T ◉ **Skill** Author's Purpose ◉ **Strategy** Background Knowledge	

Online Classroom

Manage Data

- Assign the Unit 5 Benchmark Test for students to take online.

- Online Assessment records results and generates reports by school, grade, classroom, or student.

- Use reports to disaggregate and aggregate Unit 5 skills and standards data to monitor progress.

- Based on class lists created to support the categories important for AYP (gender, ethnicity, migrant education, English proficiency, disabilities, economic status), reports let you track adequate yearly progress every six weeks.

Group

- Use results from Unit 5 Benchmark Tests taken online through Online Assessment to measure whether students have mastered the English-Language Arts Content Standards taught in this unit.

- Reports in Online Assessment suggest whether students need Extra Support or Intervention.

Individualized Instruction

- Tests are correlated to Unit 5 tested skills and standards so that prescriptions for individual teaching and learning plans can be created.

- Individualized prescriptions target instruction and accelerate student progress toward learning outcome goals.

- Prescriptions include remediation activities and resources to reteach Unit 5 skills and standards.

UNIT 5

Assessment and Grouping
for Data-Driven Instruction

4-Step Plan for Assessment
1 Diagnose and Differentiate
2 Monitor Progress
3 Assess and Regroup
4 Summative Assessment

Baseline Group Tests

 STEP 1 Diagnose and Differentiate

Diagnose

To make initial grouping decisions, use the Baseline Group Test, the *Texas Primary Reading Inventory (TPRI)*, or another initial placement test. Depending on student's ability levels, you may have more than one of each group.

Differentiate

If... student performance is then... use the regular instruction and the daily **Strategic Intervention** small group lessons.

If... student performance is then... use the regular instruction and the daily On-Level small group lessons.

If... student performance is then... use the regular instruction and the daily **Advanced** small group lessons.

Small Group Time

SI Strategic Intervention

- Daily small group lessons provide more intensive instruction, more scaffolding, more practice, and more opportunities to respond.
- Reteach lessons in the *First Stop on Reading Street* provide more instruction with target skills.
- Leveled readers build background and provide practice for target skills and vocabulary.

OL On-Level

- Explicit instructional routines teach core skills and strategies.
- Daily On-Level lessons provide more practice and more opportunities to respond.
- Independent activities provide practice for core skills and extension and enrichment options.
- Leveled readers provide additional reading and practice for core skills and vocabulary.

A Advanced

- Daily Advanced lessons provide instruction for accelerated learning.
- Leveled readers provide additional reading tied to lesson concepts and skills.

Additional Differentiated Learning Options

Reading Street Response to Intervention Kit
- Focused intervention lessons on the five critical areas of reading: phonemic awareness, phonics, vocabulary, comprehension, and fluency

My Sidewalks on Reading Street
- Intensive intervention for struggling readers

STEP 2 Monitor Progress

Use these tools during lesson teaching to **monitor student progress.**

- **Skill and Strategy** instruction during reading

- **Don't Wait Until Friday** boxes to check word reading, retelling, fluency, and oral vocabulary

- **Weekly Assessment** on Day 5 checks comprehension and fluency

- **Reader's and Writer's Notebook** pages at point of use

- **Weekly Tests** assess target skills for the week

- **Fresh Reads** for Fluency and Comprehension

Weekly Tests

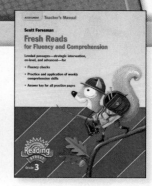

Fresh Reads for Fluency and Comprehension

STEP 3 Assess and Regroup

Use these tools during lesson teaching to **assess and regroup.**

- **Weekly Assessments** Record results of weekly assessments in retelling, comprehension, and fluency to track student progress.

- **Unit Benchmark Tests** Administer this assessment to check mastery of unit skills.

- **Regroup** We recommend the first regrouping to be at the end of Unit 2. Use weekly assessment information and Unit Benchmark Test performance to inform regrouping decisions. Then regroup at the end of each subsequent unit.

Unit Assessment Charts in First Stop

Group

Baseline Group Test → Regroup Units 1 and 2 → Regroup Unit 3 → Regroup Unit 4 → Regroup Unit 5 → End of Year

| Weeks 1-6 | Weeks 7-12 | Weeks 13-18 | Weeks 19-24 | Weeks 25-30 | Weeks 31-36 |

Outside assessments, such as *TPRI, DRA,* and *DIBELS,* may recommend regrouping at other times during the year.

STEP 4 Summative Assessment

Use these tools after lesson teaching to **assess students.**

- **Unit Benchmark Tests** Use to measure a student's mastery of each unit's skills.

- **End-of-Year Benchmark Test** Use to measure a student's mastery of program skills covered in all six units.

Unit and End-of-Year Benchmark Tests

Concept Launch

Understanding By Design

Grant Wiggins, Ed. D.
Reading Street Author

"We need to go beyond questions answerable by unit facts to questions that burst through the boundaries of the topic. Deep and transferable understandings depend upon framing work around such questions."

Cultures

Reading Street Online

www.ReadingStreet.com
• Big Question Video
• eSelections
• Envision It! Animations
• Story Sort

THE BIG ?

What happens when two ways of life come together?

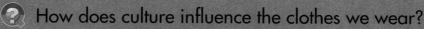

UNIT 5

Small Group Time
Flexible Pacing Plans

SI OL A

5 Day Plan

DAY 1	• Reinforce the Concept • Read Leveled Readers Concept Literacy Below-Level
DAY 2	• Comprehension Skill • Comprehension Strategy • Revisit Main Selection
DAY 3	• Vocabulary Skill • Revisit Main Selection
DAY 4	• Practice Retelling • Read/Revisit Paired Selection
DAY 5	• Reread for Fluency • Reread Leveled Readers

4 Day Plan

DAY 1	• Reinforce the Concept • Read Leveled Readers Concept Literacy Below-Level
DAY 2	• Comprehension Skill • Comprehension Strategy • Revisit Main Selection
DAY 3	• Vocabulary Skill • Revisit Main Selection
DAY 4	• Practice Retelling • Read/Revisit Paired Selection • Reread for Fluency • Reread Leveled Readers

3 Day Plan

DAY 1	• Reinforce the Concept • Read Leveled Readers Concept Literacy Below-Level
DAY 2	• Comprehension Skill • Comprehension Strategy • Revisit Main Selection
DAY 3	• Practice Retelling • Read/Revisit Paired Selection • Reread for Fluency • Reread Leveled Readers

ELL

5 Day Plan

DAY 1	• Frontload Concept • Preteach Skills • Conventions/Writing
DAY 2	• Review Concept/Skills • Frontload and Read Main Selection • Conventions/Writing
DAY 3	• Review Concept/Skills • Reread Main Selection • Conventions/Writing
DAY 4	• Review Concept/Skills • Read ELL or ELD Reader • Conventions/Writing
DAY 5	• Review Concept/Skills • Reread ELL or ELD Reader • Conventions/Writing

4 Day Plan

DAY 1	• Frontload Concept • Preteach Skills • Conventions/Writing
DAY 2	• Review Concept/Skills • Frontload and Read Main Selection • Conventions/Writing
DAY 3	• Review Concept/Skills • Reread Main Selection • Conventions/Writing
DAY 4	• Review Concept/Skills • Read ELL or ELD Reader • Conventions/Writing

3 Day Plan

DAY 1	• Frontload Concept • Preteach Skills • Conventions/Writing
DAY 2	• Review Concept/Skills • Frontload and Read Main Selection • Conventions/Writing
DAY 3	• Review Concept/Skills • Read ELL or ELD Reader • Conventions/Writing

This Week's ELL Overview

ELL Handbook

- Maximize Literacy and Cognitive Engagement
- Research Into Practice
- Full Weekly Support for Every Selection

Jalapeño Bagels
- Multi-Lingual Summaries in Five Languages
- Selection-Specific Vocabulary Word Cards
- Frontloading/Reteaching for Comprehension Skill Lessons
- ELD and ELL Reader Study Guides

- Transfer Activities
- Professional Development

Daily Leveled ELL Notes

ELL notes appear throughout this week's instruction and ELL Support is on the DI pages of your Teacher's Edition. The following is a sample of an ELL note from this week.

English Language Learners

Beginning Write several words with the vowel sound /ē/ from the Decodable Reader on the board, such as *either, ceiling,* and *receive.* Point to each word as you say it aloud. Then underline the letters that represent the spelling pattern for /ē/ in each word. Have students repeat the words with you. Repeat the procedure for the sound /ā/, using word such as *weight, eight, neigh,* and *neighbor.*

Intermediate After reading, have students find pairs of rhyming words with the vowel sound /ā/. For example: *weight, eight, freight.*

Advanced Have students tell how each of the following words was used in the story: *Heidi, neigh, neighbor, eight,* and *freight.*

Advanced High After reading the story, have students choose four or five words with the vowel sounds /ā/ or /ē/ spelled *ei* or *eigh* and write a sentence for each word.

ELL by Strand

The ELL lessons on this week's Support for English Language Learners pages are organized by strand. They offer additional scaffolding for the core curriculum. Leveled support notes on these pages address the different proficiency levels in your class. See pages DI•91–DI•100.

ELL Guy
Dr. Jim Cummins

The Three Pillars of ELL Instruction

ELL Strands	Activate Prior Knowledge	Access Content	Extend Language
Vocabulary pp. DI•92–DI•93	Preteach	Reteach	Leveled Writing Activities
Reading Comprehension p. DI•97	Frontloading	Sheltered Reading	After Reading
Phonics, Spelling, and Word Analysis p. DI•95	Preteach and Model	Practice	Leveled Practice Activities
Listening Comprehension p. DI•94	Prepare for the Read Aloud	First Listening	Second Listening
Conventions and Writing pp. DI•99–DI•100	Preteach/Introduce	Practice	Leveled Practice Activities/ Leveled Writing Activities
Concept Development p. DI•91	Prior Knowledge	Discuss Concept	Daily Concept and Vocabulary Development

This Week's Practice Stations Overview

Six Weekly Practice Stations with Leveled Activities can be found at the beginning of each week of instruction. For this week's Practice Stations, see pp. 288h–288i.

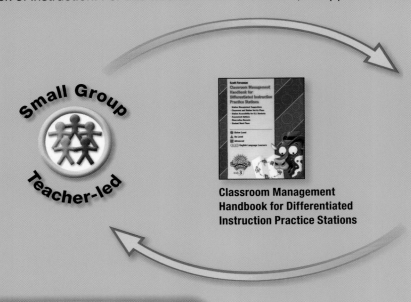

Practice Stations

Classroom Management Handbook for Differentiated Instruction Practice Stations

Daily Leveled Center Activities

- ⬤ Below
- ◻ Advanced
- △ On-Level
- Ⓔ Ⓛ Ⓛ

Practice Stations Flip Charts

	Word Wise	Word Work	Words to Know	Let's Write	Read For Meaning	Get Fluent

Objectives	• Spell words with vowel patterns *a, au, aw, al, augh, ough.*	• Identify and pronounce words with vowel patterns *a, au, aw, al, augh, ough.*	• Identify the meanings of compound words.	• Write free-verse poetry.	• Identify a sequence of events.	• Read aloud with appropriate expression and attention to punctuation cues.
Materials	• *Word Wise* Flip Chart Activity 24 • Teacher-made word cards • paper • pencils	• *Word Work* Flip Chart Activity 24 • Teacher-made word cards • paper • pencils	• *Words to Know* Flip Chart Activity 24 • Teacher-made word cards • paper • pencils	• *Let's Write* Flip Chart Activity 24 • paper • pencils	• *Read for Meaning* Flip Chart Activity 24 • Leveled Readers • paper • pencils	• *Get Fluent* Flip Chart Activity 24 • Leveled Readers

This Week on **Reading Street!**

 Question of the Week

How can different cultures contribute to the foods we eat?

Cultures

Daily Plan

Don't Wait Until Friday

Whole Group

- ◉ Draw Conclusions
- ◉ Unfamiliar Words
- • Fluency/Accuracy
- • Writing/Conventions
- • Research and Inquiry

MONITOR PROGRESS | **Success Predictor**

Day 1	Day 2	Day 3	Day 4	Day 5
Check Oral Vocabulary	Check Word Reading	Check Retelling	Check Fluency	Check Oral Vocabulary

Small Group

Teacher Led

- • Reading Support
- • Skill Support
- • Fluency Practice

Practice Stations

Independent Activities

Customize Literacy More support for a balanced literacy appoach, see pp. CL•1–CL•45

Customize Writing More support for a customized writing approach, see pp. CW•11–CW•20

Whole Group

- • Writing: Invitation
- • Conventions: Comparative and Superlative Adverbs
- • Spelling: Vowel Patterns *ei, eigh*

Assessment

- • Weekly Tests
- • Day 5 Assessment
- • Fresh Reads

You Are Here!
Unit 5
Week 4

This Week's Reading Selections

Main Selection
Genre: **Realistic Fiction**

Paired Selection
Genre: **Expository Text**

Decodable Readers

Leveled Readers

ELL and ELD Readers

Resources on Reading Street!

	Build Concepts	Phonics	Comprehension
Whole Group	 Let's Talk About pp. 288–289	 Phonics Skill Lesson pp. 290–291 — Decodable Readers — Sound-Spelling Cards	 Envision It! Skills/ Strategies — Comprehension Skill Lesson pp. 292–293
Go Digital	• Concept Talk Video	• Interactive Sound-Spelling Cards • Decodable eReaders	• Envision It! Animations • eSelections
Small Group and Independent Practice	 Jalapeño Bagels pp. 296–309 ELL and ELD Readers Leveled Readers Decodable Readers	 Decodable Readers — Practice Station Flip Chart	 Jalapeño Bagels pp. 296–309 ELL and ELD Readers Leveled Readers  Envision It! Skills/ Strategies Reader's and Writer's Notebook Practice Station Flip Chart
Go Digital	• eReaders • eSelections • Decodable eReaders	• Letter Tile Drag and Drop • Decodable eReaders	• Envision It! Animations • eSelections • eReaders
Customize Literacy	• Leveled Readers • Decodable Readers	• Decodable Readers	• Envision It! Skills/Strategies Handbook • Leveled Readers
Go Digital	• Concept Talk Video • Decodable eReaders • eReaders	• Decodable eReaders	• Envision It! Animations • eReaders • Decodable eReaders

Question of the Week
How can different cultures contribute to the foods we eat?

Vocabulary	Fluency	Conventions and Writing
Envision It! Vocabulary Cards  Vocabulary Skill Lesson pp. 294–295	Let's Learn It! pp. 318–319  Decodable and Leveled Readers	Let's Write It! pp. 312–313 Decodable Readers
• Envision It! Vocabulary Cards • Vocabulary Activities	• eSelection • Decodable eReades • eReaders	• Grammar Jammer
Envision It! Vocabulary Cards Jalapeño Bagels pp. 296–309  Practice Station Flip Chart Words! Reader's and Writer's Notebook	Jalapeño Bagels pp. 296–309 Practice Station Flip Chart Leveled Readers ELL and ELD Readers	Reader's and Writer's Notebook Jalapeño Bagels pp. 296–309 Practice Station Flip Chart
• Envision It! Vocabulary Cards • Vocabulary Activities • eSelection	• eSelection • eReaders	• Grammar Jammer
• Envision It! Vocabulary Cards	• Leveled Readers • Decodable Readers	• Reader's and Writer's Notebook
• Vocabulary Activities	• eReaders • Decodable eReaders	• Grammar Jammer

Week 4

You Are Here! Unit 5 Week 4

My 5-Day Planner for Reading Street!

MONITOR PROGRESS — Don't Wait Until Friday

	Check Oral Vocabulary **Day 1** pages 288j–293f	Check Word Reading **Day 2** pages 294a–303e

Get Ready to Read	**Concept Talk,** 288j–289
	Oral Vocabulary, 289a
	  nutrition, calorie, flavor
	Listening Comprehension, Read Aloud, 289b
	Phonics/Word Analysis, 290a–291b
	  ◉ Vowel Patterns *ei, eigh*
	READ Decodable Practice Reader, 291a–291b
		Concept Talk, 294a
		Oral Vocabulary, 294b
		  spice, nutmeg
		Phonics/Word Analysis, 294c
		  ◉ Vowel Patterns *ei, eigh*
		Literary Terms, 294d
		  Dialogue and Narration
		Story Structure, 294d
		  Climax

Read and Comprehend	**Comprehension Skill,**
	  ◉ Draw conclusions, 292a
	Comprehension Strategy,
	  ◉ Summarize, 292a
	READ Comprehension, 292–293
	Model Fluency, Accuracy, 292–293
	Introduce Lesson Vocabulary, 293a
	  bakery, ingredients, batch, mixture, dough, braided, boils
		Vocabulary Skill, ◉ Unfamiliar words, 294e
		Vocabulary Strategy, Context Clues, 294e
		Lesson Vocabulary, 294–295
		  bakery, ingredients, batch, mixture, dough, braided, boils
		READ Vocabulary, 294–295
		Model Fluency, Accuracy, 294–295
		READ Main Selection, *Jalapeño Bagels,* 296–303a

Language Arts	**Research and Inquiry,** Identify Questions, 293b **Spelling,** Vowel Patterns *ei, eigh,* 293c **Conventions,** Comparative and Superlative Adverbs, 293d **Handwriting,** Cursive Letters *N, M, U,* 293d **Writing,** Invitation, Introduce, 293e–293f	**Research and Inquiry,** Navigate/Search, 303b **Conventions,** Comparative and Superlative Adverbs, 303c **Spelling,** Vowel Patterns *ei, eigh,* 303c **Writing,** Invitation, Focus/Ideas, 303d–303e

You Are Here! Unit 5 Week 4

Question of the Week

How can different cultures contribute to the foods we eat?

Check Retelling	Check Fluency	Check Oral Vocabulary
Day 3 pages 304a–313c	**Day 4** pages 314a–319e	**Day 5** pages 319f–319q

Concept Talk, 304a
Oral Vocabulary, 304b
  grumble, allergic
Phonics/Word Analysis, 304c–304d
  ◉ Vowel Patterns *ei, eigh*
Decodable Story, 304d
Comprehension Check, 304e
Check Retelling, 304f
	Concept Talk, 314a
	Oral Vocabulary, 314b
	  wholesome, grate, agent
	Phonics/Word Analysis, 314c–314f
	  Review Vowel Patterns for /ò/
	Decodable Story, 314f
	Genre: Expository Text, 314g
		Concept Wrap Up, 319f
		Check Oral Vocabulary, 319g
		  nutrition, calorie, flavor, spice,
		  nutmeg, grumble, allergic,
		  wholesome, grate, agent
		Amazing Ideas, 319g
		  Review ◉ **Draw Conclusions,** 319h
		  Review ◉ **Unfamiliar Words,** 319h
		  Review ◉ **Vowel Patterns** *ei, eigh,*
		  319i
		  Review **Literary Terms,** 319i

READ Main Selection,
  Jalapeño Bagels, 304–309a
Retelling, 310–311
Think Critically, 311a
Model Fluency, Accuracy, 311b
Research and Study Skills, Outlining,
  311c
	READ Paired Selection,
	  "Foods of Mexico: a Delicious
	  Blend," 314–317
	Let's Learn It! 318–319a
	  Fluency: Accuracy
	  Vocabulary: ◉ Unfamiliar
	  Words
	  Media Literacy: Radio
	  Advertisement
		Fluency Assessment,
		  WCPM, 319j–319k
		Comprehension Assessment,
		  ◉ Draw Conclusions, 319l–319m

Research and Inquiry, Analyze, 311d
Conventions, Comparative and
  Superlative Adverbs, 311e
Spelling, Vowel Patterns *ei, eigh,*
  311e
Let's Write It! Invitation, 312–313
Writing, Invitation, Purpose,
  313a–313c
	Research and Inquiry,
	  Synthesize, 319b
	Conventions, Comparative and
	  Superlative Adverbs, 319c
	Spelling, Vowel Patterns *ei, eigh,*
	  319c
	Writing, Invitation, Revising,
	  319d–319e
		Research and Inquiry, Communicate,
		  319n
		Conventions, Comparative and
		  Superlative Adverbs, 319o
		Spelling Tests, Vowel Patterns *ei, eigh,*
		  319o
		Writing, Invitation, Adverbs,
		  319p–319q
		Quick Write for Fluency, 319q

Week 4

Grouping Options for Differentiated Instruction
Turn the page for the small group time lesson plan.

Planning Small Group Time on Reading Street!

SMALL GROUP TIME RESOURCES

Look for this Small Group Time box each day to help meet the individual needs of all your children. Differentiated Instruction lessons appear on the DI pages at the end of each week.

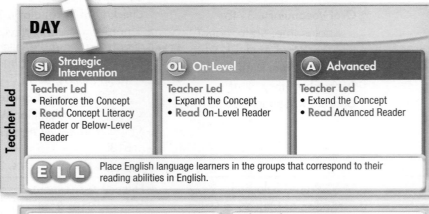

DAY 1

Teacher Led

SI Strategic Intervention	**OL On-Level**	**A Advanced**
Teacher Led	**Teacher Led**	**Teacher Led**
• Reinforce the Concept	• Expand the Concept	• Extend the Concept
• **Read** Concept Literacy Reader or Below-Level Reader	• **Read** On-Level Reader	• **Read** Advanced Reader

ELL Place English language learners in the groups that correspond to their reading abilities in English.

Practice Stations
• Read for Meaning
• Get Fluent
• Word Work

Independent Activities
• Concept Talk Video
• *Reader's and Writer's Notebook*
• Research and Inquiry

ELL

ELL Reader
Advanced
Advanced High

ELD Reader
Beginning
Intermediate

ELL Poster

Day 1

SI Strategic Intervention	**Reinforce the Concept,** DI•76– DI•77 **Read Decodable Reader** and **Concept Literacy Reader** or **Below-Level Reader**
OL On-Level	**Expand the Concept,** DI•82 **Read On-Level Reader**
A Advanced	**Extend the Concept,** DI•87 **Read Advanced Reader**
ELL English Language Learners	DI•91–DI•100 **Frontload Concept Preteach Skills Writing**

You Are Here! Unit 5 Week 4

Reading Street
Response to
Intervention Kit

Reading Street
Practice Stations Kit

SI Strategic Intervention

The World of Bread!
by Patricia West

Below-Level
Reader

Bread!
by Meish Goldish

Concept Literacy Reader

OL On-Level

KAPUAPUA'S MAGIC SHELL

On-Level Reader

A Advanced

Mixing, Kneading, and Baking: The Baker's Art
by Francelia Sevin

Advanced
Reader

Decodable Practice Readers Units 4-6
• Practice phonics skills
• Blending practice
• Reread for fluency

Decodable
Readers

Jalapeño Bagels pp. 296–309

Foods of Mexico: a Delicious Blend pp. 314–315

Small Group Weekly Plan

Week 4

Day 2	Day 3	Day 4	Day 5
Reinforce Comprehension, DI•78 **Revisit Main Selection**	**Reinforce Vocabulary,** DI•79 **Read/Revisit Main Selection**	**Reinforce Comprehension,** Practice Retelling, DI•80 Genre Focus **Read/Revisit Paired Selection**	**Practice Fluency,** DI•81 **Reread Concept Literacy Reader** or **Below-Level Reader**
Expand Comprehension, DI•83 **Revisit Main Selection**	**Expand Vocabulary,** DI•84 **Read/Revisit Main Selection**	**Expand Comprehension,** Practice Retelling, DI•85 Genre Focus **Read/Revisit Paired Selection**	**Practice Fluency,** DI•86 **Reread On-Level Reader**
Extend Comprehension, DI•88 **Revisit Main Selection**	**Extend Vocabulary,** DI•89 **Read/Revisit Main Selection**	**Extend Comprehension,** Genre Focus, DI•90 **Read/Revisit Paired Selection**	**Practice Fluency,** DI•90 **Reread Advanced Reader**
DI•91–DI•100 **Review Concept/Skills** **Frontload Main Selection** **Practice**	DI•91–DI•100 **Review Concept/Skills** **Reread Main Selection** **Practice**	DI•91–DI•100 **Review Concept** **Read ELL/ELD Readers** **Practice**	DI•91–DI•100 **Review Concept/Skills** **Reread ELL/ELD Reader** **Writing**

Practice Stations for Everyone on Reading Street!

Word Wise
Vowel patterns *a*, *au*, *aw*, *al*, *augh*, *ough*

Objectives
• Spell words with vowel patterns *a*, *au*, *aw*, *al*, *augh*, *ough*.

Materials
• *Word Wise* Flip Chart Activity 24
• Teacher-made word cards
• paper   • pencils

Differentiated Activities

⬤ Choose five word cards. Write the words. Underline the vowel pattern. Add other words you know with vowel patterns *a*, *au*, *aw*, *al*, *augh*, and *ough* to your list.

▲ Choose seven word cards, and list your words. Write sentences using each of your words. Add other words you know with vowel patterns *a*, *au*, *aw*, *al*, *augh*, and *ough* to your list.

◼ Choose nine word cards, and write the words. Write sentences using each of the words. Think of other words with vowel patterns *a*, *au*, *aw*, *al*, *augh*, *ough*. Add them to your list.

Technology
• Online Dictionary

Word Work
Vowel patterns *a*, *au*, *aw*, *al*, *augh*, *ough*

Objectives
• Identify and pronounce words with vowel patterns *a*, *au*, *aw*, *al*, *augh*, *ough*.

Materials
• *Word Work* Flip Chart Activity 24
• Teacher-made word cards
• paper   • pencils

Differentiated Activities

⬤ Choose eight word cards. Say each word. Write rhyming words. Write a silly, four-line rhyming poem. Use as many of the words as you can.

▲ Choose ten word cards, and say each word. Write the words. Write a silly, four- or eight-line rhyming poem using as many of the words as you can.

◼ Choose twelve word cards, and say each word. Write the words. Write a silly, eight-line rhyming poem that uses as many of the words as you can.

Technology
• Modeled Pronunciation Audio CD

Words to Know
Compound words

Objectives
• Identify the meanings of compound words.

Materials
• *Words to Know* Flip Chart Activity 24
• Teacher-made word cards
• paper   • pencils

Differentiated Activities

⬤ Choose five word cards. Write the words. Circle the two words that form each compound word. Use a dictionary to find each word's meaning. Write sentences using the words.

▲ Choose seven word cards, and write the words. Circle the two words that form each compound word. Use a dictionary to find each word's meaning. Write sentences using the words.

◼ Choose ten word cards. Write the words, and use a dictionary to find each word's meaning. Circle the two words that form each compound word. Write sentences using each word.

Technology
• Online Dictionary

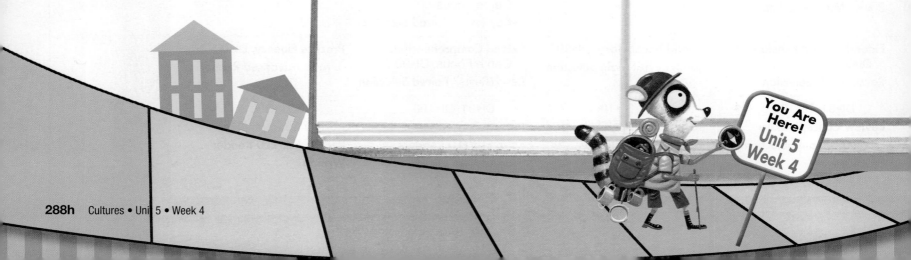

You Are Here!
Unit 5
Week 4

Use this week's materials from the
Reading Street Leveled Practice Stations
Kit to organize this week's stations.

Key
- 🔵 Below-Level Activities
- 🔺 On-Level Activities
- 🟥 Advanced Activities

Practice Station Flip Chart

Let's Write!
Free-verse poetry

Objectives
• Write free-verse poetry.

Materials
• *Let's Write!* Flip Chart Activity 24
• paper   • pencils

Differentiated Activities

🔵 Think about your first time at a new place. Write a free-verse poem that tells your feelings about this time. Choose words that will help your readers imagine the experience and understand how you felt.

🔺 Write a free-verse poem that tells about your first time at a new place. Choose words to help your readers understand how you felt. Include details that will help them imagine they are there.

🟥 Write a free-verse poem telling about your experience in a new situation. Use figurative language to help readers understand how you felt. Include details to help readers imagine the experience.

Technology
• Online Graphic Organizers

Read for Meaning
Sequence of events

Objectives
• Identify a sequence of events.

Materials
• *Read for Meaning* Flip Chart Activity 24
• Leveled Readers
• paper   • pencils

Differentiated Activities

🔵 Choose a book from those your teacher provides. Think about the story's order of events. Write three sentences that tell the order of these events. Use words such first, next, and finally to show the order.

🔺 Read one of the books your teacher provides and think about the story's sequence of events. Write four sentences that tell the sequence of events.

🟥 Choose and read a leveled reader. As you read your book, think about the story's sequence of events. Write a short paragraph that tells the sequence of important story events.

Technology
• Leveled Reader Database

Get Fluent
Expression and punctuation cues

Objectives
• Read aloud with appropriate expression and attention to punctuation cues.

Materials
• *Get Fluent* Flip Chart Activity 24
• Leveled Readers

Differentiated Activities

🔵 Work with a partner. Choose a Concept Literacy Reader or Below-Level Reader. Take turns reading a page from the book. Use the readers to practice correct expression and punctuation cues. Provide feedback as needed.

🔺 Work with a partner. Choose an On-Level Reader. Take turns reading a page from the book. Use the reader to practice correct expression and punctuation cues. Provide feedback as needed.

🟥 Work with a partner. Choose an Advanced Reader. Take turns reading a page from the book. Use the reader to practice correct expression and punctuation cues. Provide feedback as needed.

Technology
• Leveled Reader Database
• Reading Street Readers CD-ROM

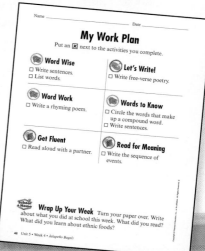

Name _____ Date _____

My Work Plan
Put an ☒ next to the activities you complete.

Word Wise
☐ Write sentences.
☐ List words.

Let's Write!
☐ Write free-verse poetry.

Word Work
☐ Write a rhyming poem.

Words to Know
☐ Circle the words that make up a compound word.
☐ Write sentences.

Get Fluent
☐ Read aloud with a partner.

Read for Meaning
☐ Write the sequence of events.

Wrap Up Your Week Turn your paper over. Write about what you did at school this week. What did you read? What did you learn about ethnic foods?

48 Unit 5 • Week 4 • Jalapeño Bagels

My Weekly Work Plan

Week 4

Objectives
- Introduce the weekly concept.
- Develop oral vocabulary.

Today at a Glance

Oral Vocabulary
nutrition, calorie, flavor

Phonics/Word Analysis
◎ Vowel patterns *ei, eigh*

Comprehension
◎ Draw conclusions
◎ Summarize

Reading
"What Does a Baker Do?"

Fluency
Accuracy

Lesson Vocabulary
Tested vocabulary

Research and Inquiry
Identify questions

Spelling
Vowel patterns *ei* and *eigh*

Conventions
Comparative and superlative adverbs

Handwriting
Cursive letters *N, M, U*

Writing
Invitation

Concept Talk

Question of the Week

How can different cultures contribute to the foods we eat?

Introduce the concept

To further explore the unit concept of Cultures, this week students will read, write, and talk about how different cultures contribute to the foods we eat. Write the Question of the Week on the board.

> **ROUTINE** **Activate Prior Knowledge** **Team Talk**
>
> **Think** Have students think about foods they eat that come from different cultures.
>
> **Pair** Have pairs of students discuss the Question of the Week.
>
> **Share** Call on a few students to share their ideas and comments with the group. Guide the discussion and encourage elaboration with prompts such as:
>
> - What is your favorite food? What culture is it from?
> - Have you been to a festival where cultural foods were served?

Routines Flip Chart

Anchored Talk

Develop oral vocabulary

Have students turn to pp. 288–289 in their Student Editions. Look at each of the photos. Then, use the prompts to guide discussion and create the *How different cultures contribute to the foods we eat* concept map. Remind students to make pertinent comments and answer questions with appropriate detail.

- What type of food is shown on page 289? **(Mexican food)** Mexican foods include hot peppers and *spices* that give the food *flavor.* Let's add *flavors* to our concept map.

- What are the woman and the girl doing? **(They are eating turkey and stuffing to celebrate Thanksgiving.)** Different cultures celebrate traditions, such as holidays, with special foods. Let's add *traditions* to the map.

Oral Vocabulary

Let's **Talk** About

Foods We Eat
• Share ideas about foods that come from different cultures.
• Ask relevant questions about foods unique to specific cultures.
• Pose and answer questions about the foods we eat.

READING STREET ONLINE
CONCEPT TALK VIDEO
www.ReadingStreet.com

You've learned **2 2 6** Amazing Words so far this year!

288

289

Student Edition pp. 288–289

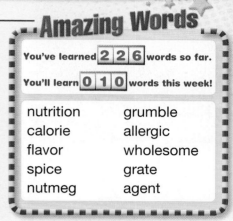

Amazing Words

You've learned **2 2 6** words so far.

You'll learn **0 1 0** words this week!

nutrition	grumble
calorie	allergic
flavor	wholesome
spice	grate
nutmeg	agent

Writing on Demand

Writing Fluency
Ask students to respond to the photos on pp. 288–289 by writing as well as they can and as much as they can about how different cultures contribute to the foods we eat.

• Why else is it good for us to eat different foods? (They make us healthy.) We get *nutrition* from our food. Let's add *Nutrition* to the map.

• After discussing all the photos, ask: How can different cultures contribute to the foods we eat?

How different cultures contribute to the foods we eat

| Flavors | Nutrition | Traditions |

Connect to reading
Tell students that this week they will be reading about foods from different cultures. Encourage students to add concept-related words to this week's concept map.

E L L **Preteach Concepts** Use the Day 1 instruction on ELL Poster 24 to assess and build background knowledge, develop concepts, and build oral vocabulary.

E L L

English Language Learners
ELL support Additional ELL support and modified instruction is provided in the *ELL Handbook* and in the ELL Support lessons on pp. DI•91–DI•100

Listening comprehension
English learners will benefit from additional visual support to understand the key terms in the concept map. Use the pictures on pp. 288–289 to scaffold understanding.

Frontload for Read Aloud Use the modified Read Aloud on p. DI•94 of the *ELL Support* lessons to prepare students to listen to "Quentin's Complaint" (p. 289b).

Objectives
- Develop listening comprehension.
- Build oral vocabulary.

Check Oral Vocabulary
SUCCESS PREDICTOR

Oral Vocabulary
Amazing Words

Introduce Amazing Words

"Quentin's Complaint" on p. 289b is about a boy who learns that the foods we eat come from many different countries. Tell students to listen for this week's Amazing Words—*nutrition, calorie,* and *flavor*—as you read.

Model fluency

As you read "Quentin's Complaint," model accuracy with smooth, fluent reading.

Teach Amazing Words

Amazing Words — Oral Vocabulary Routine

nutrition
calorie
flavor

① **Introduce** Write the word *flavor* on the board. Have students say the word aloud with you. In "Quentin's Complaint," Quentin says that foods from other countries have different flavors. Does the text include any context clues about the meaning of *flavor*? Supply a student-friendly definition.

② **Demonstrate** Have students answer questions with appropriate detail to demonstrate understanding. What kind of *flavor* is in chili? Do you like foods with a salty *flavor*?

③ **Apply** Ask students to tell what *flavor* they like the best.

See p. OV•1 to teach *nutrition* and *calorie.*

Routines Flip Chart

Apply Amazing Words

To build oral language, lead the class in a discussion about the meanings of the Amazing Words.

MONITOR PROGRESS Check Oral Vocabulary

During discussion, listen for students' use of the Amazing Words.

If... students are unable to use the Amazing Words to discuss the concept,

then... use Oral Vocabulary Routine in the Routines Flip Chart to demonstrate words in different contexts.

Day 1	Day 2	Day 3	Day 4	Day 5
Check Oral Vocabulary	Check Word Reading	Check Retelling	Check Fluency	Check Oral Vocabulary

Read Aloud

Quentin's Complaint

Quentin bounded through the front door and listened for the screen door to slam shut behind him.

"I'm ho-ome!" he called out.

"I'm here in the kitchen," his mother called back. When he came around the corner, there she was, grating onions.

"What's for dinner?" Quentin asked. All of a sudden, he felt hungry. His stomach was grumbling.

"Well, hi to you too!" His mother laughed. "I thought we'd have meat loaf and potatoes. You could help me make a salad," she added.

The expression on Quentin's face changed. "How come we never have anything interesting to eat?" he blurted.

Quentin's mother stopped grating and gave him a puzzled look. "Interesting? Our meals are always delicious," she pointed out. "I make sure we have good nutrition. And we look at the calorie count."

"I know," Quentin said. "But other kids get to eat things from other countries! Their food has a different flavor from ours. Everything we eat is so *American*."

Quentin's mother got that little smile on her face that always told him she knew something he didn't.

"American?" she answered. "Give me an example."

Quentin thought for a moment. Then he pointed to the three red potatoes resting on the kitchen counter. "Potatoes," he said.

"The first potatoes came from South America," his mother said. "Try again."

Quentin pointed to the red tomato waiting to be sliced into the salad. "Tomatoes," he said.

"Tomatoes also came from South America," his mother said. "Centuries ago, Spanish explorers found them growing there. They took some back to Europe. Later, Europeans brought tomatoes back across the ocean when they emigrated here."

Quentin wrinkled his forehead. He remembered what they had had for dinner the night before. "What about noodles?" he asked.

"Long before United States was a country, people were eating noodles in China and Italy," his mother said.

Quentin was feeling desperate. Finally, he thought of chocolate.

"It came from Mexico and Central America," his mother said.

Quentin could see he had lost the argument, but he didn't really mind. "I never knew those foods came from other parts of the world," he admitted. "I guess they aren't so boring after all."

Oral Vocabulary

Success Predictor

Objectives
◎ Blend and read words with vowel sounds /ā/, /ē/, or /ī/ spelled *ei* and *eigh.*

◎ Associate the vowel sounds /ā/ and /ē/ with *ei* and *eigh,* and the vowel sounds /ā/ and /ī/ with *eigh.*

Skills Trace
◎ **Vowel Patterns *ei, eigh***
Introduce U5W4D1
Practice U5W4D3; U5W4D4
Reteach/Review U5W4D5; U5W5D4
Assess/Test Weekly Test U5W4
Benchmark Test U5
Key: U = Unit, W = Week, D = Day

Phonics
↻ Vowel Patterns *ei, eigh*

Sound-Spelling Card 64

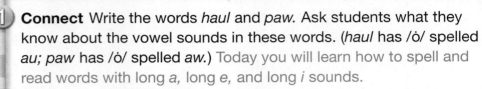

Blending Strategy

1 Connect Write the words *haul* and *paw.* Ask students what they know about the vowel sounds in these words. (*haul* has /ȯ/ spelled *au; paw* has /ȯ/ spelled *aw.*) Today you will learn how to spell and read words with long *a,* long *e,* and long *i* sounds.

2 Use Sound-Spelling Cards Display Card 64. Point to *ei.* The sound /ē/ can be spelled *ei.* Have students say /ē/ several times as you point to *ei.* Follow the same procedure with Card 65, the sound /ā/, spelled *eigh* and Card 66, the sound /ī/ spelled *eigh.*

3 Model Write *weigh.* In this word, the letters e-i-g-h stand for the sound /ā/. Point to each spelling as you say its sound. Then blend the word: /w/ /ā/, *weigh.* Follow this procedure to model *height* and *receive.*

Sound-Spelling Card 65

4 Guide Practice Continue the process in step 3. This time have students blend with you. Remind students that *ei* can stand for the sounds /ā/ or /ē/ and *eigh* can stand for the sounds /ā/ or /ī/. Tell them that, in certain words, *ei* can stand for the sound /ī/.

sleigh	veiled	weight	either	ceiling
neighbors	reins	neither	vein	height

5 Review What do you know about reading these words? When you see the spelling *ei* in a word, try the sounds /ā/ or /ē/. When you see the spelling *eigh* in a word, try the sounds /ā/ or /ī/.

Routines Flip Chart

Model | Have students turn to p. 290 in their Student Editions. Each word on this page has the vowel sound /ā/, /ē/, or /ī/. The first word is *either.* I hear /ē/ in the first syllable. In *either,* /ē/ is spelled *ei.* When I say *eight,* I hear /ā/. In *eight,* /ā/ is spelled *eigh.*

Guide practice | For each word in Words I Can Blend, ask for the sound of each letter or group of letters. Make sure that students identify the correct sounds for the vowel syllabication patterns *ei* and *eigh.* Then have them blend the words.

Corrective feedback | **If...** students have difficulty blending a word, **then...** model blending the word, then ask students to blend it with you.

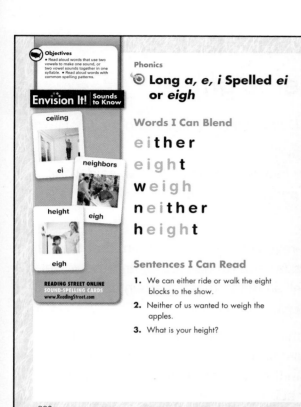

Student Edition pp. 290–291

Differentiated Instruction

SI Strategic Intervention

Read words with vowel patterns *ei, eigh* If students have difficulty reading multi-syllabic words, then use the Multisyllabic Word Strategy Routine on the Routines Flip Chart to practice blending decodable words.

Vocabulary Support

You may wish to explain the meaning of these words.

either one or the other

neither not one or the other

sleigh a horse-drawn sled

vein tube-like body part that carries blood

ELL

English Language Learners

Language transfer The English sound /ē/ is rare in other languages. English learners may have difficulty distinguishing between /ē/ and /ā/. Provide practice by pronouncing word pairs such as *may/me* and *say/see* and having students echo your pronunciation.

Blend and Read

Read words independent of context

After students can successfully segment and blend the words on p. 290 in their Student Editions, point to words in random order and ask students to read them naturally.

Read words in context

Have students read each of the sentences on p. 290. Have them identify words in the sentences that have the vowel sounds /ā/, /ē/, and /ī/ spelled *ei* or *eigh*.

(Team Talk) Pair students and have them take turns reading each of the sentences aloud.

Chorally read the I Can Read! passage on p. 291 with the students. Then have them read the passage aloud to themselves.

On their own

For additional practice, use the *Reader's and Writer's Notebook* p. 349.

Reader's and Writer's Notebook p. 349

Objectives

- Apply knowledge of sound-spellings to decode unknown multisyllabic words when reading.
- ◎ Decode and read words with the vowel patterns *ei* and *eigh*.
- Practice fluency with oral rereading.

Decodable Practice Reader 24A
↺ Vowel Patterns *ei, eigh*

Read words independent of context

Read high-frequency words

Have students turn to page 97 in *Decodable Practice Readers 3.2*. Have students read each word.

Have students read the high-frequency words *was, clothes, said, your, you, from, would, one,* and *laugh* on the first page.

Preview Decodable Practice Reader

Have students read the title and preview the story. Tell them that they will read words with the vowel sounds /ā/ and /ē/ spelled *ei,* and the vowel sounds /ā/ and /ī/ spelled *eigh.* Tell students that in certain cases, the vowel sound /ī/ is spelled *ei,* as in *Heidi* and *heist.*

Read words in context

Pair students for reading and listen as they read. One student begins. Students read the entire story, switching readers after each page. Partners reread the story. This time the other student begins. Make sure that students are monitoring their accuracy when they decode.

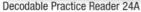

Decodable Practice Reader 24A

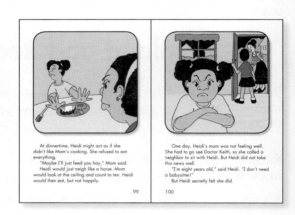

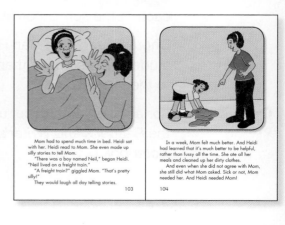

Corrective feedback

If... students have difficulty reading a word, **then...** refer them to the Sound-Spelling Cards to identify the sounds in the word. Then prompt them to blend the word.

- What is the new word?
- Is the new word a word you know?
- Does it make sense in the story?

Check decoding and comprehension

Have students retell the story to include characters, setting, and events. Then have students find words in the story that have /ā/, /ē/, or /ī/ spelled with the syllabication pattern *ei* or *eigh*. Students should supply *Heidi, eight, either, neither, neigh, ceiling, Keith, neighbor, receive, weight, Neil,* and *freight.*

Reread for Fluency

Have students reread Decodable Practice Reader 24A to develop automaticity decoding words that have /ā/, /ē/, or /ī/ spelled *ei* or *eigh.*

ROUTINE **Oral Rereading**

 Read Have students read the entire book orally.

 Reread To achieve optimal fluency, students should reread the text three or four times.

 Corrective Feedback Listen as students read. Provide corrective feedback regarding their fluency and decoding.

Routines Flip Chart

E L L

English Language Learners
Beginning Write several words with the vowel sound /ē/ from the Decodable Reader on the board, such as *either, ceiling,* and *receive.* Point to each word as you say it aloud. Then underline the letters that spell the sound /ē/ in each word. Have students repeat the words with you. Repeat the procedure for the sound /ā/, using words such as *weight, eight, neigh,* and *neighbor.*

Intermediate After reading, have students find pairs of rhyming words with the vowel sound /ā/. For example: *weight, eight, freight.*

Advanced/Advanced High After reading the story, have students choose 4 or 5 words with the vowel sounds /ā/ or /ē/ spelled *ei* or *eigh* and write a sentence for each word.

Objectives

◎ Draw conclusions to aid comprehension.

◎ Summarize information to aid comprehension.

• Read grade-level appropriate text with accuracy.

Skills Trace

◎ **Draw Conclusions**

Introduce U2W3D1; U3W1D1; U5W4D1

Practice U2W3D2; U2W3D3; U2W5D2; U3W1D2; U3W1D3; U3W4D2; U4W5D3; U5W3D2; U5W4D2; U5W4D3; U5W5D2

Reteach/Review U2W3D5; U3W1D5; U5W4D5

Assess/Test Weekly Tests U2W3; U3W1; U5W4

Benchmark Tests U3

Key: U = Unit, W = Week, D = Day

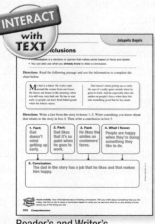

Reader's and Writer's Notebook p. 350

Skill ↔ Strategy
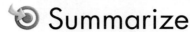
Draw Conclusions
Summarize

Introduce draw conclusions

Envision It!

When you draw conclusions, you use facts and details to make decisions about characters or events as you read. If you know that someone likes to draw pictures of football players, what can you conclude if you see that person drawing? **(The person is probably drawing football players.)** Have students turn to p. EI•6 in the Student Edition to review draw conclusions. Then read "What Does a Baker Do?" with students.

Student Edition p. EI•6

Model the skill

Think Aloud

Today we're going to read about what bakers do. **Have students follow along as you read the first three paragraphs of "What Does a Baker Do?"** The third paragraph of "What Does a Baker Do?" explains that bakers need to know what kinds of treats their customers like best. I am going to think about the facts that were given and use common sense to draw conclusions about how bakers know what baked goods their customers like best. I think they can ask customers and they can see what sells the most.

Guide practice

Have students finish reading "What Does a Baker Do?" on their own. After they read, have them use a graphic organizer like the one on p. 292 and draw conclusions about why practicing with experienced bakers is a good way for new bakers to learn.

Strategy check

Summarize Remind students that active readers often summarize as they read to help them understand the text and to draw conclusions about what they have read.

Model the strategy

Think Aloud

When I read, I often stop and summarize what has happened to recall important ideas. When I reread the first two paragraphs of "What Does a Baker Do?" I notice that bakers make many things and that they have to get up early. I will draw conclusions and summarize by saying that bakers work very hard. **Have students review the strategy of summarizing on p. EI•25 of the Student Edition.**

Envision It!

On their own

Use p. 350 in the *Reader's and Writer's Notebook* for additional practice with drawing conclusions.

Student Edition p. EI•25

Objectives
- Examine and make judgments from the facts in the article, and support your conclusions with evidence.
- Summarize information in a text.

Envision It! | Skill Strategy

Skill

Draw Conclusions

Strategy

Summarize

READING STREET ONLINE
ENVISION IT! ANIMATIONS
www.ReadingStreet.com

292

Comprehension Skill

Draw Conclusions

- You draw conclusions when you use facts and details to make decisions about characters or events.
- Think about what you already know to help you draw conclusions.
- Use what you learned about drawing conclusions and a graphic organizer like the one below as you read "What Does a Baker Do?" Then use your conclusion as the topic sentence for a paragraph that tells what a baker does.

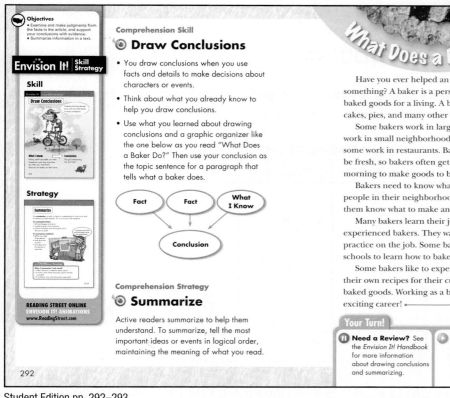

Fact → Conclusion ← Fact
What I Know → Conclusion

Comprehension Strategy

Summarize

Active readers summarize to help them understand. To summarize, tell the most important ideas or events in logical order, maintaining the meaning of what you read.

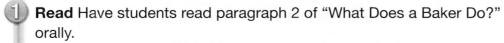

What Does a Baker Do?

Have you ever helped an adult bake something? A baker is a person who makes baked goods for a living. A baker makes bread, cakes, pies, and many other treats!

Some bakers work in large stores, some work in small neighborhood bakeries, and some work in restaurants. Baked goods must be fresh, so bakers often get up early in the morning to make goods to be sold that day.

Bakers need to know what kinds of treats people in their neighborhood like. This helps them know what to make and how much.

Many bakers learn their job by working with experienced bakers. They watch, listen, and practice on the job. Some bakers go to special schools to learn how to bake.

Some bakers like to experiment and create their own recipes for their customers' favorite baked goods. Working as a baker can be an exciting career!

Skill What can you conclude about the other treats a baker makes?

Skill How do bakers find out what customers want?

Strategy Summarize the selection. Include why the author concludes that being a baker is an exciting career.

Your Turn!

Need a Review? See the *Envision It! Handbook* for more information about drawing conclusions and summarizing.

Ready to Try It? As you read *Jalapeño Bagels*, use what you've learned about drawing conclusions and summarizing to understand the text.

293

Student Edition pp. 292–293

Skill The treats are different from bread, cakes, and pies.

Skill They might ask customers what they like.

Strategy A baker bakes bread and other treats. They can work in large stores, neighborhood bakeries, and restaurants. They have to get up early to bake food and sell it the same day. They learn their job by watching other bakers or by going to a special school. Some bakers like to experiment and create their own recipes. Baking food that people like is what makes this career exciting.

Model Fluency
Accuracy

Model fluent reading

Have students listen as you read paragraph 4 of "What Does a Baker Do?" with accuracy. Explain that to read accurately, you read carefully so you don't skip words or say the wrong word.

ROUTINE Oral Rereading

1. **Read** Have students read paragraph 2 of "What Does a Baker Do?" orally.

2. **Reread** To achieve optimal fluency, students should reread the text three or four times.

3. **Corrective Feedback** Have students read aloud without you. Provide feedback about their accuracy and encourage them to take their time to read each word correctly.

Routines Flip Chart

ELL

English Language Learners
Draw conclusions Some students may interpret "draw conclusions" literally and assume the skill involves drawing a picture. Clarify for students that when you draw a conclusion, you think about facts and what you already know and make a decision. Then provide oral practice by having students draw conclusions about foods. For example: My favorite snacks are apples, pears, and oranges. What conclusion can you draw about my favorite type of food?

Objectives
• Activate prior knowledge of words.
• Identify questions for research.

Vocabulary
Tested Vocabulary

Lesson vocabulary

Have students create a word rating chart using the categories *Know, Have Seen,* and *Don't Know.*

Activate prior knowledge

Word Rating Chart

Word	Know	Have Seen	Don't Know
bakery	✔		
batch		✔	
boils			✔
braided		✔	
dough	✔		
ingredients			
mixture			

Read each word to students and have them rate their knowledge of the word by placing a checkmark in one of the three columns: *Know* (know and can use); *Have Seen* (have seen or heard the word; don't know the meaning); *Don't Know* (don't know the word).

Have students provide sentences for words they checked in the "Know" column. By the end of the week, have them revise their charts and demonstrate their understanding by using each word in a sentence.

Preteach academic vocabulary

ELL **Academic Vocabulary** Write the following terms on the board:

advertisement	**invitation**
comparative adverb	**superlative adverb**
climax	**narration**

Have students share what they know about this week's Academic Vocabulary. Use the students' responses to assess their prior knowledge. Preteach the Academic Vocabulary by providing a student-friendly description, explanation, or example that clarifies the meaning of each term. Then ask students to restate the meaning of the Academic Vocabulary term in their own words.

Research and Inquiry
Identify Questions

Teach

Discuss the Question of the Week: *How can different cultures contribute to the foods we eat?* Tell students they will research foods from different cultures. They will write an article to present to the class on Day 5.

Model

Think Aloud I'll start by brainstorming a list of questions about foods from different cultures. I know that special foods are part of celebrating holidays or certain traditions in various cultures. For example, Americans celebrate Thanksgiving with turkey dinners. Some possible questions could be *In what holidays and traditions do foods play an important role? What types of food do people in various cultures cook to celebrate holidays? What are the traditional foods in different cultures?*

Guide practice

After students have brainstormed inquiry questions, explain that tomorrow they will conduct research using their questions. Help students identify keywords that will guide their search.

On their own

Have students work individually, in pairs, or in small groups to write an inquiry question.

INTERNET GUY
Don Leu

21st Century Skills

Weekly Inquiry Project
Day 1 Identify Questions
Day 2 Navigate/Search
Day 3 Analyze
Day 4 Synthesize
Day 5 Communicate

Small Group Time

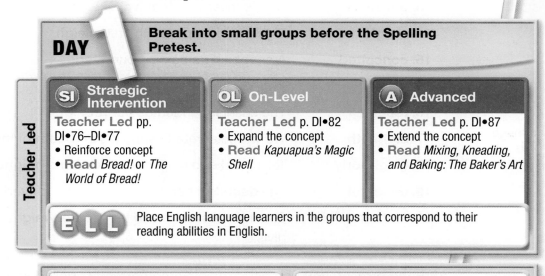

DAY 1

Break into small groups before the Spelling Pretest.

Teacher Led

(SI) Strategic Intervention
Teacher Led pp. DI•76–DI•77
• Reinforce concept
• **Read** *Bread!* or *The World of Bread!*

(OL) On-Level
Teacher Led p. DI•82
• Expand the concept
• **Read** *Kapuapua's Magic Shell*

(A) Advanced
Teacher Led p. DI•87
• Extend the concept
• **Read** *Mixing, Kneading, and Baking: The Baker's Art*

ELL Place English language learners in the groups that correspond to their reading abilities in English.

Practice Stations
• Read for Meaning
• Get Fluent
• Word Work

Independent Activities
• Concept Talk Video
• *Reader's and Writer's Notebook*
• Vocabulary Activities

ELL

English Language Learners
Multilingual vocabulary
Students can apply knowledge of their home languages to acquire new English vocabulary by using the Multilingual Vocabulary Lists (*ELL Handbook*, pp. 433–444).

Objectives
- Spell words with vowel patterns *ei* and *eigh*.
- Use and understand comparative and superlative adverbs.
- Write cursive capital letters *N, M,* and *U.*

Spelling Pretest
Vowel Patterns *ei* and *eigh*

Introduce
Tell students to think of words with the vowel patterns *ei (vein)* and *eigh (eight).* This week we will spell words with vowel patterns *ei* and *eigh.* As you spell these words, remember to think about letter sounds.

Pretest
Use these sentences to administer the spelling pretest. Say each word, read the sentence, and repeat the word.

1. ceiling	The party favors hung from the **ceiling.**
2. neighbor	The person who lives next door is my **neighbor.**
3. either	I will go to **either** the mountains or the beach.
4. eighteen	**Eighteen** is one more than seventeen.
5. height	My dad's **height** is 5 feet, 11 inches.
6. neither	**Neither** of those two chairs is the right size.
7. weight	The nurse used the scale to measure our **weight.**
8. leisure	Shooting hoops is a fun **leisure** activity.
9. protein	Milk is an important source of **protein.**
10. freight	There is cargo on the **freight** train.
11. receive	When will we **receive** your invitation?
12. weigh	The packages **weigh** five pounds each.
13. deceive	A lie is meant to **deceive.**
14. sleigh	Eight reindeer pulled the red **sleigh.**
15. conceited	A snobbish person is **conceited.**

Challenge words

16. receipt	The cashier handed us our **receipt.**
17. eightieth	We will celebrate Grandma's **eightieth** birthday.
18. neighborly	Taking cake to neighbors is kind and **neighborly.**
19. deceitful	The **deceitful** person was not to be trusted.
20. featherweight	Smaller wrestlers are in the **featherweight** division.

Self-correct
After the pretest, you can either display the correctly spelled words or spell them orally. Have students self-correct their pretests by rewriting misspelled words correctly.

On their own
For additional practice, use *Let's Practice It!* page 319 on the *Teacher Resources DVD-ROM.*

Let's Practice It!
TR DVD•319

 Go Digital! **Grammar Jammer**

Conventions
Comparative and Superlative Adverbs

Teach — Display Grammar Transparency 24, and read aloud the explanation and examples in the box. Point out that some adverbs compare actions, and the adverbs *higher* and *more slowly* are used to compare two actions. *Highest* and *most slowly* are used to compare three or more actions.

Model — Model underlining the adverb that compares in item 1. Point out that *harder* ends in *-er* because it compares two things: how Mrs. Sanchez works and how everyone else at the bakery works.

Guide practice — Guide students to complete items 2–5. Remind them to look for adverbs that end in *-er* or *-est* or adverbs that use *more* and *most* to compare. Record the correct responses on the transparency.

Daily Fix-It — Use Daily Fix-It numbers 1 and 2 in the right margin.

Connect to oral language — Have students read sentences 6–10 on the transparency and circle the correct adverb to correctly complete each sentence.

Handwriting
Cursive Letters N, M, U

Model letter formation — Display capital letters *N, M,* and *U.* Follow the stroke instructions pictured to model letter formation.

Model adjusting letters to fit space — Explain that writing legibly involves making adjustments to the size of handwriting to make sure it fits the available space. Draw write-on lines on the board and model writing this sentence: *Nick moved from New Mexico to Utah.* Demonstrate adjusting the size of your handwriting to fit the space of the write-on lines.

Guide practice — Provide write-on lines for students and have them write these sentences: *Mañuelo is from the Northeast. Nina lives in Uruguay.* Remind students to capitalize geographical names and places. Circulate around the room, guiding students.

Academic Vocabulary

Comparative adverbs compare two people, places, or things. Add *-er* to most adverbs to make them comparative. Use *more* with adverbs that end in *-ly.*

Superlative adverbs compare three or more people, places, or things. Add *-est* to most adverbs to make them superlative. Use *most* with adverbs that end in *-ly.*

Grammar Transparency 24, TR DVD

Daily Fix-It

1. Marias mom tought her to bake bread. *(Maria's; taught)*
2. Her flower was sifted more sooner than mine. *(flour; sifted sooner)*

ELL

English Language Learners
Language production: Comparative and superlative adverbs Write on the board a list of adverbs, such as *quickly, slow, carefully, warm, fun,* and *soon.* Have students read the words and determine whether to use *-er* and *-est* or *more* and *most.* Then use some of the adverbs incorrectly in sentences. For example, say: Cheetahs run the most fast of all the animals. Call on students to say the sentence with the correct form.

Objectives
• Understand and identify the features of an invitation.

MINI-LESSON

5 Day Planner
Guide to Mini-Lessons

DAY 1	Read Like a Writer
DAY 2	Organize Your Ideas
DAY 3	Establish a Purpose When Writing
DAY 4	Revising Strategy: Adding
DAY 5	Proofread for Adverbs

Writing—Invitation
Introduce

MINI-LESSON

Read Like a Writer

Reader's and Writer's Notebook p. 351

■ **Introduce** An **invitation** is a written request for someone to come to a party or other special event. If you wanted to invite people to a party, would you write an invitation or a short story? This week you will write an invitation.

Prompt   Invite a friend over for dinner, using specific details.

Trait   Focus/Ideas

Mode   Expository

■ **Examine Model Text** Let's read an example of an invitation. Have students read "Monday Night Party!" on p. 351 of their *Reader's and Writer's Notebook.*

■ **Key Features A good invitation offers a reason for the special event.** It tells readers why they are being invited to the event and what they will be celebrating. Guide students in identifying the reason for Lila's pizza party. Have them underline the words that tell them.

Invitations tell the date, time, and location of the event. Ask students what might happen if an invitation was missing one of these important details.

Invitations provide contact information so readers can ask questions about the event or tell the host whether they will attend. What type of contact information does Lila include in her invitation? (her telephone number) Have students role-play calling Lila to tell her whether they will attend her pizza party.

Invitations are often decorated with pictures or drawings. These get the reader's attention.

Review key features Review the key features of an invitation with students. You might want to post the key features in the classroom for students to reference as they work on their invitations.

Key Features of an Invitation

- gives the reason for the invitation
- provides a date, time, and location
- includes contact information if a reply is needed
- often uses creative pictures or drawings

ROUTINE Quick Write for Fluency **Team Talk**

1. **Talk** Have pairs take a few minutes to discuss the importance of providing contact information in an invitation.

2. **Write** Each student writes three sentences summarizing his or her ideas.

3. **Share** Partners read one another's sentences.

Routines Flip Chart

Wrap Up Your Day

- ✔ **Build Concepts** How do different cultures contribute to the foods we eat?

- ✔ **Oral Vocabulary** Have students use the Amazing Words they learned in context sentences.

- ✔ Homework Send home this week's Family Times newsletter, *Let's Practice It!* pages 320–321 on the *Teacher Resources DVD-ROM.*

Let's Practice It!
TR DVD•320–321

Write Guy
Jeff Anderson

Let Me Check My List

Encourage students to keep lists of words they come across that are exciting or interesting to them. This is a great way to improve vocabulary and word choice.

Academic Vocabulary

An **invitation** is a written request for someone to come to a party or other special event.

English Language Learners
Activate prior knowledge
Read aloud the writing model on p. 313 of the Student Edition and help students understand it. Ask students to tell about a time they sent or received an invitation. Provide sentence frames, such as the following, to help spark discussion:

I was invited to _____.
The party was held at _____.
The day of the party was _____.

Preview DAY 2

Tell students that tomorrow they will read about Pablo and his parents' bakery.

Objectives
- Expand the weekly concept.
- Develop oral vocabulary.

Today at a Glance

Oral Vocabulary
spice, nutmeg

Phonics/Word Analysis
◉ Vowel patterns *ei, eigh*

Literary Terms
Dialogue and Narration

Story Structure
Climax

Lesson Vocabulary
◉ Unfamiliar words

Reading
"Biscuits for Breakfast"
Jalapeño Bagels

Fluency
Accuracy

Research and Inquiry
Navigate/Search

Conventions
Comparative and superlative adverbs

Spelling
Vowel patterns *ei* and *eigh*

Writing
Invitation

Concept Talk

Question of the Week

How can different cultures contribute to the foods we eat?

Expand the concept

Remind students of the Question of the Week. Tell students that today they will begin reading *Jalapeño Bagels.* As they read, encourage students to think about how different cultures contribute to the foods we eat.

Anchored Talk

Develop oral vocabulary

Use the photos on pp. 288–289 and the Read Aloud, "Quentin's Complaint," to talk about the Amazing Words: *nutrition, calorie,* and *flavor.* Add those and other concept-related words to the concept map to develop students' knowledge of the topic. Discuss the following questions. Remind students to make pertinent comments and answer questions with appropriate detail during a discussion.

- How can foods from different cultures affect our *nutrition*?
- Name a food that is high in *calories.* Do you know what culture the food is from?
- Why might foods from different cultures have different *flavors*?

Oral Vocabulary
Amazing Words

Amazing Words

nutrition	grumble
calorie	allergic
flavor	wholesome
spice	grate
nutmeg	agent

Teach Amazing Words

Amazing Words — Oral Vocabulary Routine

1 **Introduce** Write the Amazing Word *spice* on the board. Have students say it aloud with you. Relate *spice* to the photographs on pp. 288–289 and "Quentin's Complaint." Why do cooks use *spices* in food? What kinds of *spices* are used in Mexican food? Have students determine the definition of the word. A *spice* is a seasoning from a plant used to flavor food.

2 **Demonstrate** Have students answer questions to demonstrate understanding. Why might you find different *spices* in foods from different cultures? What flavors do *spices* add to food?

3 **Apply** Have students apply their understanding. How do your family members use *spices* in their cooking?

See p. OV•1 to teach *nutmeg*.

Routines Flip Chart

Apply Amazing Words

As students read "Biscuits for Breakfast" on p. 295, have them think about how *spices* might be used in baking biscuits, and what baked goods might include *nutmeg*.

Connect to reading

Explain that today students will read about a boy who helps his parents cook at their bakery. As they read, they should think about the Question of the Week, and how the Amazing Words *spice* and *nutmeg* apply to preparing baked goods.

ELL Reinforce Vocabulary Use the Day 2 instruction on ELL Poster 24 to teach lesson vocabulary and the lesson concept.

ELL Poster 24

DAY 2 Get Ready to Read

Objectives

◎ Read words with vowel patterns *ei, eigh.*

• Apply knowledge of letter-sound correspondences and syllable patterns to decode words in context and independent of context.

Check Word Reading

🖑 **SUCCESS PREDICTOR**

Phonics
 Vowel Patterns *ei, eigh*

Review

Review the /ā/, /ē/, and /ī/ vowel syllabication patterns *ei* and *eigh* using Sound-Spelling Cards 64, 65, and 66.

Read words independent of context

Display these words. Have the class blend the words. Then point to the words in random order and ask students to read them quickly.

sleigh	reins	veil	weight
neigh	height	freight	neither

Corrective feedback

Model blending decodable words and then ask students to blend them with you.

Read words in context

Display these sentences. Have the class read the sentences.

Team Talk Have pairs take turns reading the sentences naturally.

> The king's evil **reign** lasted for **eight** years.
> The robbers appeared to get away with the **heist**.
> After the girl **received** her crown, she was full of **conceit**.

Don't Wait Until Friday

MONITOR PROGRESS **Words with Vowel Patterns *ei, eigh***

Write the following words and have the class read them. Notice which words students miss during the group reading. Call on individuals to read some of the words.

ceiling	leisure	neigh	either	**Spiral Review** Row 2 reviews words with prefixes and suffixes.
unhappy	usable	hopeless	return	Row 3 contrasts words with prefixes and suffixes and words with vowel patterns *ei, eigh.*
neighed	freighter	unveiled	weightless	

If... students cannot read words with vowel patterns *ei* and *eigh* at this point,

then... use the Day 1 Blending Strategy routine on p. 290a to reteach vowel patterns *ei* and *eigh*. Use words from the Decodable Practice Passages (or Reader). Continue to monitor students' progress using other instructional opportunities during the week. See the Skills Trace on p. 290a.

Day 1	Day 2	Day 3	Day 4	Day 5
Check Oral Vocabulary	**Check Word Reading**	Check Retelling	Check Fluency	Check Oral Vocabulary

Literary Terms
Dialogue and Narration

Teach narration

Tell students that dialogue is a conversation in a book, movie, play, or TV show. Narration is the recounting of an event or a series of events with accompanying description. A reader experiences the events through the eyes, mind, and voice of the storyteller, called the narrator or speaker.

Model narration

Think Aloud Let's look at "What Does a Baker Do?" How is narration used in the passage? (It gives information about bakers.) Narration can be used in nonfiction to provide a description. What does the narrator describe in the passage? (what bakers cook and where they work)

Guide practice

Have students find examples of narration in *Jalapeño Bagels.* Be sure to point out that dialogue, the conversation between two or more people, is often combined with narration to tell a story.

On their own

Have students look for examples of dialogue and narration in other selections of their Student Edition.

Story Structure
Climax

Teach climax

A plot, or storyline, is a series of related events in a story that shows the characters in action. One of the elements of a plot is the **climax,** the turning point at which the character takes the decisive action that will bring about the conclusion.

Model the strategy

Think Aloud The climax is the turning point in the plot where the character makes a decision that brings about the conclusion. To identify the climax of the story, I'll look for the point where a main character makes an important decision.

Guide practice

Help students identify the climax in *Jalapeño Bagels* after they finish reading the selection. (Pablo decides what food to take to school for International Day.) Be sure to point out that recognizing the climax helps students understand the story.

On their own

Have students look for other examples of climax in their Student Editions.

Academic Vocabulary

narration the recounting by a storyteller of an event or series of events with accompanying description

Word Reading

Success Predictor

Objectives

◎ Use context clues to determine the meanings of unfamiliar words.

• Read grade-level text with accuracy.

Vocabulary Strategy for
🔊 Unfamiliar Words

Context Clues

Student Edition p. W•7

Teach unfamiliar words

Envision It!

Tell students that they can use the strategy of context clues to determine the meanings of unfamiliar words. Context clues are the words before and after a word that help define the word. When they see a word they don't know they can read the words and sentences around the word to find clues that help them figure out the meaning of the word. Refer students to *Words!* on p. W•7 in the Students Edition for additional practice.

Model the strategy

 Think Aloud

Write on the board: *I like to shop with my mother at the bakery. Everything smells good. We buy bread there every week. Sometimes we buy cakes or cinnamon rolls.* If I were not sure of the meaning of *bakery,* I would continue reading the next sentences to determine the context around the word. When I read the sentences, they tell me that a bakery has baked goods such as bread, cakes, and cinnamon rolls. I know from the first sentence that a bakery is also a place where people buy things. I can use those context clues to determine that a bakery must be a store that sells baked goods.

Guide practice

Write these sentences from "Biscuits for Breakfast" on the board: *Use a fork to add the shortening to the flour, baking powder, and salt. The mixture should look like fine crumbs.* Have students use context clues to determine the meaning of *mixture.* For additional support, use *Envision It! Pictured Vocabulary Cards* or *Tested Vocabulary Cards.*

On their own

Read "Biscuits for Breakfast" on p. 295. Have students use context clues to understand the meanings for the lesson vocabulary. Encourage them to test the meanings in the sentences. For additional practice, use the *Reader's and Writer's Notebook* p. 352.

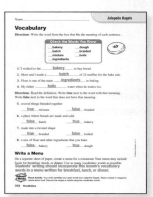

Reader's and Writer's Notebook p. 352

Objectives
- Use context clues to figure out words you don't know or words that have more than one meaning. • Find and use information by following and explaining a set of written directions with many steps.

Envision It! Words to Know

bakery

batch

dough

boils
braided
ingredients
mixture

READING STREET ONLINE
VOCABULARY ACTIVITIES
www.ReadingStreet.com

Vocabulary Strategy for
☺ Unfamiliar Words

Context Clues Sometimes you come across an unfamiliar word. How can you figure out what the word means? Look at the context, or the words and sentences around the word. You might find clues that can help you figure out the meaning of the word.

1. Read the words and sentences around the word you don't know. Sometimes the author tells you what the word means.

2. If not, use the words and sentences to predict a meaning for the word.

3. Try that meaning in the sentence. Does it make sense?

Read "Biscuits for Breakfast" on page 295. As you read, use context clues to help you understand the meanings of the Words to Know and other unfamiliar words.

Words to Write Reread "Biscuits for Breakfast." Write the directions explaining how to make your favorite breakfast food. Be sure to include the ingredients and the steps. Use words from the Words to Know list.

294

Biscuits for Breakfast

Would you like something for breakfast that you will not find in a bakery? Make biscuits! You'll need only a few ingredients to make one batch.

⅓ cup shortening
1 ¾ cups flour
2 ½ teaspoons baking powder
¾ teaspoon salt
¾ cup milk

Use a fork to add the shortening to the flour, baking powder, and salt. The mixture should look like fine crumbs. Add enough milk so that the dough rounds into a ball. Put the dough on a floured board. Knead it 10 times and only 10 times.

Roll the dough flat, about ½ inch thick. Cut out round circles using a biscuit cutter or an overturned glass. Place the circles on a baking sheet. Do not let the circles touch one another. Bake at 350° for 10 to 12 minutes or until the biscuits are light brown on top. Serve them with butter and honey.

Forget about braided coffee cakes. When the water boils for your morning tea and you are looking for something to go with it, grab a hot, fresh biscuit.

Your Turn!

⏸ **Need a Review?** For additional help with unfamiliar words, see *Words!*

▶ **Ready to Try It?** Read *Jalapeño Bagels* on pp. 296–309.

295

Student Edition pp. 294–295

Reread for Fluency
Accuracy

Model fluent reading

Read aloud paragraph 3 of "Biscuits for Breakfast" clearly and accurately. Tell students that you are reading the paragraph carefully and without skipping words. Explain the correct terms for reading the fraction, temperature, and numbers in the paragraph.

ROUTINE | **Oral Rereading**

1. **Read** Have students read paragraph 3 of "Biscuits for Breakfast" orally.

2. **Reread** To achieve optimal fluency, students should reread the text three or four times.

3. **Corrective Feedback** Have students read aloud without you. Provide feedback about their accuracy. Listen for correct pronunciation and make sure they do not skip any words.

Routines Flip Chart

Lesson Vocabulary

bakery a place where bread and cake are made and sold

batch something made one at a time

boils to heat a liquid until it starts to bubble and give off steam

braided three or four strands woven together

dough flour and liquid mixed together to make bread, biscuits, and pastry

ingredients items that something is made from

mixture the combination of things mixed or blended together

Differentiated Instruction

SI **Strategic Intervention**

Context Clues Have students work in pairs to identify context clues that help them figure out the meanings of the lesson vocabulary. Have partners take turns testing their meanings by reading the sentence aloud and substituting the meaning for the word.

ELL

English Language Learners

Build Academic Vocabulary
Use the lesson vocabulary pictured on p. 294 to teach the meanings of *bakery, batch,* and *dough.* Call on pairs to write the words on sticky notes and use them to label images of the words on the ELL poster.

Objectives

- Understand key features of realistic fiction.
- Use story title and illustrations to preview and predict.
- Set a purpose for reading.

Jalapeño Bagels

by Natasha Wing
illustrated by Antonio L. Castro

Question of the Week
How can different cultures contribute to the foods we eat?

Genre **Realistic fiction** is a made-up story that can be set in a real place. What is the setting of this story?

296

297

Student Edition pp. 296–297

Build Background

Discuss foods from different cultures

Team Talk Have students turn to a partner and discuss the Question of the Week and these questions about foods from different cultures.

- Think of your favorite food. What culture is it from?
- What other foods from different cultures do you eat?
- Why do you think food is an important part of many cultures?

Connect to selection

Have students discuss their answers with the class. Possible responses: My favorite food is spaghetti and meatballs. Spaghetti and meatballs is from Italy. I also eat Mexican food, such as enchiladas, and Indian food, such as Tandoori chicken. People need food to live. Cooking and eating brings people together. For additional opportunities to build background, use the Background Building Audio.

Prereading Strategies

Genre
Remind students that **realistic fiction** tells a made-up story with characters, settings, and events that seem real. Characters' actions and story endings are reasonable and believable. The key features of realistic fiction are realistic characters, realistic settings, and a believable plot.

Preview and predict
Have students read the title of the selection and the names of the author and illustrator. Have them preview the illustrations for *Jalapeño Bagels* and identify the characters and setting they see. Have them use the title and the illustrations to predict what the story will be about.

Set purpose
Prior to reading, have students set their own purposes for reading this selection. To help students set a purpose, ask them to think about how different cultures influence the foods we eat.

Strategy Response Log

 INTERACT with TEXT

Have students use p. 30 in the *Reader's and Writer's Notebook* to review and use the strategy of summarizing.

Small Group Time

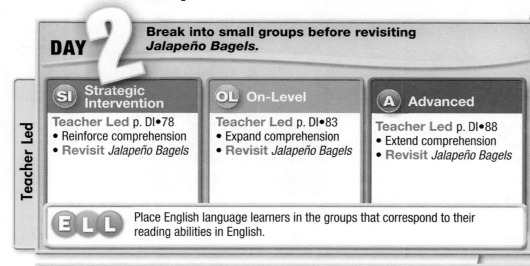

DAY 2

Break into small groups before revisiting *Jalapeño Bagels.*

Teacher Led

SI Strategic Intervention
Teacher Led p. DI•78
• Reinforce comprehension
• **Revisit** *Jalapeño Bagels*

OL On-Level
Teacher Led p. DI•83
• Expand comprehension
• **Revisit** *Jalapeño Bagels*

A Advanced
Teacher Led p. DI•88
• Extend comprehension
• **Revisit** *Jalapeño Bagels*

ELL Place English language learners in the groups that correspond to their reading abilities in English.

Practice Stations
• Words to Know
• Get Fluent
• Word Wise

Independent Activities
• Background Building Audio
• *Reader's and Writer's Notebook*
• Research and Inquiry

Differentiated Instruction

SI **Strategic Intervention**
Author's craft Work with students to set a purpose for reading or, if time permits, have students work with partners to set purposes.

A **Advanced**
Text to self Have students find out how their favorite bread, bagel, or pastry is made.

Double Day Reado **Multidraft Reading**

For **Whole Group** instruction, choose one of the reading options below. For each reading, have students set the purpose indicated.

Option 1
Day 2 Read the selection. Use Guide Comprehension to monitor and clarify understanding.
Day 3 Reread the selection. Use Extend Thinking to develop higher-order thinking skills.

Option 2
Day 2 Read the first half of the selection, using both Guide Comprehension and Extend Thinking instruction.
Day 3 Read the second half of the selection, using both Guide Comprehension and Extend Thinking instruction.

ELL

English Language Learners
Build background To build background, review the selection summary in English (*ELL Handbook* p. 169). Use the Retelling Cards to provide visual support for the summary.

Objectives

◎ Draw conclusions from information presented in text.

OPTION 1 Guide Comprehension Skills and Strategies

Teach Draw Conclusions

Draw Conclusions Tell students that when you draw conclusions, you make decisions that make sense about the characters or events in a story. You use what you know and the details in what you read to form conclusions. Ask students to draw a conclusion to answer the following question: *Where do Pablo and his parents live in relationship to the bakery?* (They live down the street from the bakery.)

Corrective Feedback

If... students are unable to draw a conclusion to answer the question, **then...** model how to draw conclusions.

Let's Practice It!
TR DVD•322

Model the Skill

Think Aloud The story doesn't say where Pablo's family lives, but it does give clues. In the last paragraph, Pablo's mother awakens Pablo early to go to work.

"**W**hat should I bring to school on Monday for International Day?" I ask my mother. "My teacher told us to bring something from our culture."

"You can bring a treat from the *panaderia*," she suggests. Panaderia is what Mama calls our bakery. "Help us bake on Sunday—then you can pick out whatever you want."

"It's a deal," I tell her. I like helping at the bakery. It's warm there, and everything smells so good.

Early Sunday morning, when it is still dark, my mother wakes me up.

"Pablo, it's time to go to work," she says.

298

Student Edition pp. 298–299

OPTION 2 Extend Thinking Think Critically

Higher-Order Thinking Skills

Draw Conclusions • Synthesis How can you figure out who runs the bakery? Possible response: I can draw the conclusion that Pablo's parents run the bakery because they open it and are the only people working there.

Dialogue and Narration • Analysis What do we learn about the story from the use of dialogue and narration on page 298? Possible response: The dialogue sets up the characters and gives us an idea of what they are like. We know what Pablo sounds like and the kinds of questions he asks. The narration adds details. It tells us that a *panaderia* is a bakery and that it is warm and smells good.

The next sentence says that they walk down the street to the bakery. So, I draw the conclusion that the bakery is just down the street from their home.

We walk down the street to the bakery. My father turns on the lights. My mother turns on the ovens. She gets out the pans and ingredients for *pan dulce*. Pan dulce is Mexican sweet bread.

I help my mother mix and knead the dough. She shapes rolls and loaves of bread and slides them into the oven. People tell her she makes the best pan dulce in town.

"Maybe I'll bring pan dulce to school," I tell her.

299

Genre • Evaluation Could this story happen in real life? What information supports your answer? Possible response: This is a realistic story because it includes realistic characters, a realistic setting, and a believable plot. A family like Pablo's could run a bakery in real life.

On Their Own

Have students reread pp. 298–299 and draw a conclusion about Pablo's relationship with his parents. For additional practice, use *Let's Practice It!* page 322 on the *Teacher Resources DVD-ROM.*

Differentiated Instruction

SI Strategic Intervention

Unfamiliar words Explain that some words in the story, such as *panaderia* and *pan dulce,* may be unfamiliar. Explain that there are clues in the text to help the reader understand what these words mean. Point out that Pablo tells us that Mama calls their bakery the *panade-ria.* He also tells us that *pan dulce* is "Mexican sweet bread."

Connect to Social Studies

Discuss with students how a neighborhood bakery helps the owners and the residents of the community. For example, by providing food, the bakery helps the residents. The residents, in return, put their money back into the community by helping people, such as the owners, who live there.

ELL

English Language Learners
Activate prior knowledge Create a content web to record students' prior knowledge of bakeries. We are going to read about foods that are made in a bakery. What foods can you find at a bakery? Record students' answers on the web, and add to the web as students read the selection.

OPTION 1   Skills and Strategies, continued

Teach Unfamiliar Words

🔄 **Unfamiliar Words** Have students use context clues to determine the meaning of *empanadas de calabaza* on the top of p. 300.

Corrective Feedback

If... students are unable to figure out the meaning of *empanadas de calabaza*,

then... model using context clues to figure out the unfamiliar word.

Reader's and Writer's Notebook p. 356

Model the Skill

Think Aloud The term *empanadas de calabaza* is unfamiliar because it comes from another language. Do you know what language the term is from? (Spanish)

Next we make *empanadas de calabaza*—pumpkin turnovers. I'm in charge of spooning the pumpkin filling. Mama folds the dough in half and presses the edges with a fork. She bakes them until they are flaky and golden brown. Some customers come to our bakery just for her turnovers.

300

Student Edition pp. 300–301

OPTION 2   Think Critically, continued

Higher-Order Thinking Skills

🔄 **Unfamiliar Words • Analysis** Use context clues to figure out the meaning of *chango bars* on page 301. Possible response: I see that there are clues in the text that will help me figure out the meaning. Pablo explains that *chango* means "monkey man." So *chango bars* means "monkey man bars." Pablo and his mother have been making sweets and pastries, so *chango bars* is probably a nickname for another type of pastry or dessert.

Author's Purpose • Analysis Why does the author include the Spanish names for the baked goods that Pablo is making with his mama? Possible response: The author includes the Spanish names for the baked goods to tell the reader that the foods are from the Mexican and Spanish cultures.

There are clues in the text that will help me figure out the meaning. I see that Pablo explains that *empanadas de calabaza* are pumpkin turnovers. We also find out that the turnovers have a filling and are baked until the dough is brown and flaky.

"Maybe I'll bring empanadas de calabaza instead."

"You'll figure it out," she says. "Ready to make *chango* bars?" Chango means "monkey man."

301

Inferring • Synthesis What culture is Pablo's mother from? How do you know? Possible response: Pablo's mother is from a Spanish-speaking culture. I can tell because she shows Pablo how to bake foods from Spanish and Mexican cultures.

On Their Own

Have students reread p. 300 and use context clues to figure out further information about the meaning of *empanadas de calabaza.* For additional practice with unfamiliar words, use *Reader's and Writer's Notebook* p. 356.

Differentiated Instruction

A **Advanced**

Vocabulary Have students tell the names of their favorite baked goods. Have them use English dictionaries and foreign language dictionaries to find out the meanings and origins of the names.

Connect to Social Studies

Have a volunteer point out the country of Mexico on a world map. Explain that most people in Mexico speak Spanish. Then point out other countries where the Spanish language is spoken, such as Panama, Argentina, Costa Rica, and Spain.

ELL

English Language Learners
Vocabulary: Expression Focus students' attention on the expression "figure it out" in the second paragraph on p. 301. *Figure out* is an idiom that means "to think out." People might use this idiom when they are trying to make a decision or to understand something. Ask students to share a time when they had to "figure out" something.

Summarize Read aloud the paragraph on p. 300. What do Pablo and his mother do to prepare the empanadas de calabaza? Have students work in pairs to paraphrase the steps. Then record students' responses on the board.

Objectives

◎ Summarize the plot's main events, maintaining meaning and logical order.

OPTION 1

Skills and Strategies, continued

Teach Summarizing

⊙ **Summarize** After students finish reading pp. 302–303, ask them to summarize how Pablo helps his mother. (At his parents' bakery, he helps his mother mix and knead the dough for *pan dulce*. He spoons filling into *empanandas de calabaza* and adds chocolate chips and nuts to the *chango* bars mix.)

Corrective Feedback

If... students are unable to summarize,

then... model how to summarize how Pablo helps his mother.

Student Edition pp. 302–303

Model the Strategy

Think Aloud When I read, I often stop to summarize what has happened so far. When I summarize, I go back over the story in my head to recall the main events in the story.

Mama lets me pour in the chocolate chips and nuts. When she's not looking, I pour in more chocolate chips.

"I could bring chango bars. They're my favorite dessert."

"Mine, too," says Mama. "This batch should be especially good. I put in extra chips."

302

OPTION 2

Think Critically, continued

Higher-Order Thinking Skills

⊙ **Summarize • Analysis** Why does Pablo help his parents at the bakery? How does he help them? **Possible response:** Pablo needs to choose a food from his culture to bring to International Day. His parents tell him he can bring something from their bakery if he helps them bake on Sunday. Pablo helps his mother bake pastries and sweets from Spanish culture. He helps his father make bagels.

Background Knowledge • Synthesis • Text to Self Has a family member ever taught you how to cook something? How do you think Pablo's father learned how to make bagels? **Possible response:** My grandmother taught me how to make lemon squares. Pablo's father probably learned how to make bagels from his mother, Pablo's *bubbe*.

I remember that first Pablo helped his mother knead dough for *pan dulce*. I need to see what happened next. I can go back and reread the story to see. I want to be sure it makes sense and follows a logical order.

My father calls from the back room. "Pablo! Come help me with the bagels!" Papa speaks English and Yiddish. He learned Yiddish from his family in New York City. I know some words too. *Bubbe* means "grandmother." He uses my bubbe's recipe to make the bagels.

First he makes the dough in a big metal bowl. Then he rolls it out into a long rope shape. He cuts off pieces and shows me how to connect the ends in a circle. We put the circles on trays where they sit and rise.

303

On Their Own

Have students reread p. 303 and summarize the events on the page, maintaining meaning and logical order.

Predict • Synthesis Based on what you have read so far, how do you think the story will develop? Possible response: I see from the illustrations that Pablo helps his parents make many different baked goods. I predict that Pablo will help make more baked goods and will try to decide what to take to school for International Day.

Check Predictions Have students look back at the predictions they made earlier and discuss whether they were accurate. Then have students preview the rest of the selection and either adjust their predictions accordingly or make new predictions.

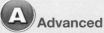

Differentiated Instruction

SI Strategic Intervention

Setting Have students work in pairs to discuss the setting shown in the illustrations. Ask them to describe the clues in the illustrations that indicate the setting is a bakery.

A Advanced

Vocabulary Explain that Yiddish is a language that comes from German. It is spoken by some Jewish people. Have students find more information about Yiddish and the people who speak it.

ELL

English Language Learners

Vocabulary List the names of the baked goods Pablo and his parents make: *pan dulce, empanadas de calabaza, chango bars, bagels.* Add to the list the names of students' favorite baked goods. Discuss the languages the names come from.

If you want to teach this selection in two sessions, stop here.

Objectives

- Find pertinent information from online sources.
- Recognize and correctly use comparative and superlative adverbs.
- Practice correctly spelling words with vowel patterns *ei* and *eigh*.

Research and Inquiry
Navigate/Search

Teach

Have students generate a research plan for gathering relevant information about their topic. Have students review their inquiry questions and decide on the best sources for answers to their questions: online sources, print sources, or expert sources. Remind students to take notes as they gather information. Then encourage students to improve the focus of their research by interviewing a local expert on the topic. Help students to use online directories to locate expert sources to contact.

Model

Think Aloud When looking for information about traditional foods, I found: *Challah is a loaf of bread that is traditionally eaten by Jewish people on the Sabbath, holidays, and other ceremonial occasions.* I will use keywords from this information, such as *traditional* and *bread*, to find more specific information about traditional breads from other cultures. I will also search for local bakers that I might interview about breads from various cultures.

Guide practice

Have students continue their review of Web sites they identified. Show them how to bookmark Web sites. Explain that bookmarks allow students to go on to a Web site immediately, instead of typing in the complete address.

On their own

Have students continue to research their topic. Encourage them to interview family or friends as expert sources about different cultures.

Conventions
Comparative and Superlative Adverbs

Teach
Write these sentences: *The turtle is slow. The snail is slower. The sloth is slowest of the three.* Underline *slower* and *slowest.* To compare actions or amounts of time, add *-er* to most adverbs. To compare three or more things, add *-est* to most adverbs. Then write sentences using the phrases *more slowly* and *most slowly.* Explain that we usually use *-er* and *-est* with one-syllable adverbs and *more* and *most* with longer adverbs. Adverbs that end in the suffix *-ly* usually use *more* and *most* to make comparisons.

Guide practice
Write the following adverbs of manner: *quickly, softly, soon,* and *early* on the board. Point out that the suffixes *-er* and *-est* are used with *early* because *-ly* is not a suffix in *early.* Guide students in changing each adverb to the appropriate comparative and superlative forms.

Daily Fix-It
Use Daily Fix-It numbers 3 and 4 in the right margin.

Connect to oral language
Provide students with this sentence about the selection: *Pablo twisted the dough the quickest.* Have students write other sentences about the story using comparative and superlative adverbs and read them aloud.

On their own
For more practice, use *Reader's and Writer's Notebook* p. 353.

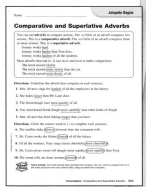
Reader's and Writer's Notebook p. 353

Spelling
Vowel Patterns *ei* and *eigh*

Teach
Remind students that their spelling words have vowel patterns *ei* and *eigh.* Point out that *ei* often stands for the long *e* sound, as in *ceiling* or *deceive.* Then point out that *eigh* can stand for long *a,* as in *weight,* or long *i,* as in *height.*

Guide practice
Have students write each spelling word and underline the vowel pattern. Remember to segment the words in your mind and think about letter sounds, word parts, and syllables. Call on students to correctly pronounce each word.

On their own
For more practice, use *Reader's and Writer's Notebook* p. 354.

Daily Fix-It
3. Blake and her put walnut in the banana bread. *(she; walnuts)*
4. A glass of Milk is a good source of protien. *(milk; protein)*

English Language Learners
Conventions To provide students with practice on comparative and superlative adverbs, use the modified grammar lessons in the *ELL Handbook* and Grammar Jammer online at: www.ReadingStreet.com

Reader's and Writer's Notebook p. 354

Objectives
• Organize ideas to prepare for writing.

Writing—Invitation
Writing Trait: Focus/Ideas

Introduce the prompt

Review the key features of an invitation with students. Remind students that an invitation should offer a reason for the special event and include important details, such as the event's date, location, and time. Have students think about these features as they plan their writing. Then explain that today they will begin the writing process for an invitation. Read aloud the writing prompt.

Writing Prompt

Invite a friend over for dinner, using specific details.

Select a topic

Think Aloud The first part of the writing process is selecting a topic. I know I will write an invitation to invite a friend to dinner, but I need to include a reason for the special event. Let's make a web and list reasons why we might invite someone over to dinner. **Display a concept web. Write *Reasons for a Dinner Party* in the center oval and model listing ideas.** One reason I might have a dinner party is to welcome someone back from a trip. **List the idea and continue brainstorming aloud with students.**

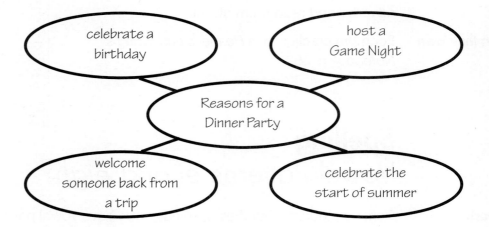

Have students complete a web of their own. Remind students that at this point they are only brainstorming. They will need to make a final decision about the focus of their invitation a little later.

Corrective feedback

As students fill in their webs, move around the room and confer briefly with struggling students. Suggest that these students generate ideas by brainstorming with a partner, drawing pictures, or remembering times they have had friends over for dinner.

MINI-LESSON

Organize Your Ideas

■ A four-column chart helps you organize ideas and create a focus for your writing. Write heads for each column and fill in details below. **Write the first column head:** *What.* To describe the event, I'll write *What* as my first head. I can fill in specific details about the dinner party in this column. **Fill in details, such as** *outdoor barbecue to celebrate the start of summer.*

■ Next, I will write *When* and *Where* as the heads of the next two columns. I can use these columns to list the date, time, and location of my dinner party. **Write the heads and fill in party details, such as** *Saturday, June 24th, 5:00 PM,* and *Horner Park.*

■ Finally, I will write RSVP as my head for the final column. I will use this column to include my contact information.

Have students begin a four-column chart for their own invitation using the form on p. 355 of their *Reader's and Writer's Notebook.*

ROUTINE — Quick Write for Fluency — Team Talk

1. **Talk** Have pairs discuss how the four-column chart helped them focus their ideas.

2. **Write** Each student writes a paragraph summarizing the steps he or she took to plan a draft.

3. **Share** Partners read their paragraphs to one another and share with other groups.

Routines Flip Chart

Wrap Up Your Day

✔ **Build Concepts** What did you learn about the different cultures where the foods Pablo's parents made come from?

✔ **Draw Conclusions** How were you able to draw conclusions about how Pablo felt about helping in the bakery?

✔ **Summarize** How did summarizing the story help you remember what had happened?

Differentiated Instruction

 Advanced

Evaluate Have students brainstorm other sources of contact information for their RSVP column, such as a home address, e-mail, and cell phone number. Have partners discuss and evaluate these different sources to determine which would work best for an invitation. Call on students to share their ideas with the class.

Reader's and Writer's Notebook p. 355

Teacher Tip

Do a periodic check of students' Quick Writes to make sure they are on task and communicating effectively with their partners.

Preview DAY 3

Tell students that tomorrow they will read about what Pablo decides to bring to International Day.

Objectives
- Expand the weekly concept.
- Develop oral vocabulary.

Today at a Glance

Oral Vocabulary
grumble, allergic

Phonics/Word Analysis
⊚ Vowel patterns *ei, eigh*

Comprehension Check/Retelling
Discuss questions

Reading
Jalapeño Bagels

Think Critically
Retelling

Fluency
Accuracy

Research and Study Skills
Outlining

Research and Inquiry
Analyze

Conventions
Comparative and superlative adverbs

Spelling
Vowel patterns *ei* and *eigh*

Writing
Invitation

Concept Talk

Question of the Week

How can different cultures contribute to the foods we eat?

Expand the concept

Remind students of the Question of the Week. Discuss how the question relates to how foods from different cultures can be combined to make something new. Tell students that today they will read about the foods Pablo bakes with his father, and about one special food that Pablo makes with both his parents. Encourage students to think about the spices, such as nutmeg, that bakeries use.

Anchored Talk

Develop oral vocabulary

Use illustrations to review pp. 296–303 of *Jalapeño Bagels.* Discuss the Amazing Words *spice* and *nutmeg.* Add these and other concept-related words to the concept map. Use the following questions to develop students' understanding of the concept. Remind students to make pertinent comments and answer questions with appropriate detail.

- Pablo and his mother add many ingredients to the pastries to give them flavor, such as pumpkin filling and chocolate chips. Think about ingredients we use to flavor food. How are *spices* used to flavor food?

- What types of foods might *nutmeg* be used to flavor?

Oral Vocabulary
Amazing Words

Amazing Words

nutrition	grumble
calorie	allergic
flavor	wholesome
spice	grate
nutmeg	agent

Teach Amazing Words

Amazing Words **Oral Vocabulary Routine**

1 **Introduce** Write the word *grumble* on the board. Have students say it with you. Yesterday we read about pastries and sweets that Pablo baked with his mother. Reading about the foods may have made you feel hungry. Sometimes our stomachs *grumble* when we feel hungry. Have students determine a definition for *grumble.* (When something *grumbles*, it makes a low, heavy sound like thunder.)

2 **Demonstrate** Have students answer questions to demonstrate understanding. What is another thing that might *grumble*? (A very heavy truck driving on an uneven street could make a grumbling noise.)

3 **Apply** Have students apply their understanding. When has your stomach *grumbled*?

See p. OV•1 to teach *allergic.*

Routines Flip Chart

Apply Amazing Words

As students read pp. 304–309 of *Jalapeño Bagels,* have them consider how the Amazing Words *grumble and allergic* apply to the foods we eat, and the products that bakers make.

Connect to reading

Explain that today students will read about more foods that Pablo helps his parents cook to sell at their bakery. As they read, students should think about how the Question of the Week and the Amazing Words *grumble* and *allergic* apply to foods that bakers and chefs make.

ELL Expand Vocabulary Use the Day 3 instruction on ELL Poster 24 to help students expand vocabulary.

ELL Poster 24

Jalapeño Bagels **304b**

Phonics
Sort Words

Model word sorting

Write *Long a, Long e,* and *Long i* as heads in a three-column chart. Now we are going to sort words that have the syllabication patterns *ei* and *eigh*. We'll put words with the long *a* vowel sound in the first column. Words with the long *e* vowel sound will go in the second column. Words with the long *i* sound will go in the third column. I will start. Write *weight* and model how to read it, using the Blending Strategy on p. 290a. I hear the vowel sound /ā/ in *weight,* so I will write the word in the first column. I will underline the letters that spell the long *a* sound in *weight: e-i-g-h.* Model reading *either* and *reins* in the same way.

Guide practice

Use the practice words from the activity on p. 294c and other words for the word sort. Point to a word. Have students read the word, identify the vowel sound, and tell where it belongs on the chart. Then have them identify the letters that stand for the vowel sound in the word.

Corrective feedback

For corrective feedback, model blending the word to read it.

Long *a*	Long *e*	Long *i*
w<u>eigh</u>t	<u>ei</u>ther	h<u>eigh</u>t
r<u>ei</u>ns	n<u>ei</u>ther	
sl<u>eigh</u>	c<u>ei</u>ling	
n<u>eigh</u>bor		
v<u>ei</u>led		
v<u>ei</u>n		

Fluent Word Reading

Model

Write *eight.* I know the sounds for *eigh* and *t.* Blend them and read the word *eight.*

Guide practice

Write the words below. Say the sounds in your head for each spelling you see. When I point to the word, we'll read it together. Allow one second per sound previewing time for the first reading.

neigh	**deceive**	**reindeer**	**receive**	**eighty**	**freight**

On their own

Have students read the list above three or four times, until they can read one word per second.

Decode and Read

Read words independent of context

Have students turn to p. 105 in *Decodable Practice Readers 3.2* and find the first list of words. Each word in this list has long *a,* long *e,* or long *i* spelled *ei* or *eigh.* Be sure that students correctly pronounce the long vowel sound in each word.

Next, have students read the high-frequency words.

Preview Decodable Practice Passage

Have students read the title and preview the story. Tell them that they will read words that have long *a,* long *e,* or long *i* spelled *ei* or *eigh.*

Read words in context

Chorally read the story along with the students. Have students identify words in the story that have long *a,* long *e,* or long *i* spelled *ei* or *eigh.* Make sure that students are monitoring their accuracy when they decode.

 Team Talk Pair students and have them take turns reading the story aloud to each other. Monitor students as they read to check for proper pronunciation and appropriate pacing.

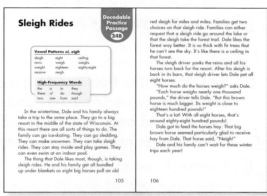

Decodable Practice Passage 24B

Differentiated Instruction

SI Strategic Intervention

Segment and blend If students have difficulty decoding multi-syllabic words, have them practice segmenting the sounds, then blending the sounds to pronounce the entire word.

A Advanced

Write sentences Have students choose three or four words from the story and write a sentence that uses each word.

English Language Learners

Pronunciation Have students practice pronouncing words with long *a* spelled *ei* or *eigh* by playing telephone. Have one student whisper the phrase *Eight sleighs and eighteen reindeer* to another student. The second student passes the words along to another, and so on.

Objectives

◉ Draw conclusions to aid comprehension.

◉ Summarize information to aid comprehension.

◉ Use context clues to determine the meanings of unfamiliar words.

Comprehension Check

Have students discuss each question with a partner. Ask several pairs to share their responses.

☑ **Genre • Analysis**

What details tell you that the story is realistic fiction? **Possible response: The story has realistic characters, realistic settings, and a believable plot. The main characters are a family. They work in a bakery, which is a real business. The foods they make exist in real life.**

☑ **Draw Conclusions • Synthesis**

Why do Pablo and his parents have to wake up early in the morning when it is still dark to bake? **Possible response: The family wakes up early to bake because it takes time to make all the pastries and breads. The baked goods need to be ready in the morning when the bakery opens and many customers will want to buy them.**

☑ **Summarize • Analysis**

Summarize what Pablo has made so far. How can you keep track of all the items? **Possible response: I can make a list of each thing he baked in the order it is mentioned in the story:** *pan dulce, empanadas de calabaza, chango* **bars, bagels,** *jalapeño* **bagels.**

☑ **Unfamiliar Words • Analysis**

Use context clues to figure out the meaning of *batch* on page 302. What context clues did you use? **Possible response: The story so far tells me that Pablo and his mother are making a certain amount of different types of baked goods. They make one mixture and bake everything at once. I can conclude that a** *batch* **is a certain quantity of baked goods made in one baking.**

☑ **Connect text to self**

Does your family bake things or visit a bakery to buy baked goods? What is your favorite treat? What would you choose to buy at Pablo's family's bakery? **Possible response: My favorite treat is chocolate brownies. I bake them with my grandmother. Since I like chocolate, I would buy the** *chango* **bars at Pablo's family's bakery.**

Strategy Response Log

Have students revisit the text and use p. 30 in the *Reader's and Writer's Notebook* to summarize the first half of *Jalapeño Bagels*.

INTERACT with TEXT

Check Retelling

Have students retell the part of *Jalapeño Bagels* that they read yesterday.

Corrective feedback

If... the students leave out important details,
then... have students look back through the illustrations in the selection.

Small Group Time

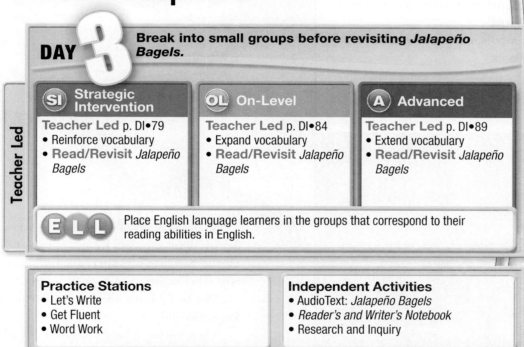

DAY 3

Break into small groups before revisiting *Jalapeño Bagels*.

Teacher Led

SI Strategic Intervention

Teacher Led p. DI•79
- Reinforce vocabulary
- **Read/Revisit** *Jalapeño Bagels*

OL On-Level

Teacher Led p. DI•84
- Expand vocabulary
- **Read/Revisit** *Jalapeño Bagels*

A Advanced

Teacher Led p. DI•89
- Extend vocabulary
- **Read/Revisit** *Jalapeño Bagels*

ELL Place English language learners in the groups that correspond to their reading abilities in English.

Practice Stations
- Let's Write
- Get Fluent
- Word Work

Independent Activities
- AudioText: *Jalapeño Bagels*
- *Reader's and Writer's Notebook*
- Research and Inquiry

ELL

English Language Learners

Check retelling To support retelling, review the multilingual summary for *Jalapeño Bagels* with the appropriate Retelling Card/s to scaffold understanding.

Objectives

◎ Summarize information and the main events in a text.

OPTION 1 **Skills and Strategies, continued**

Teach Summarizing

Summarize Explain that a summary is a brief statement that tells what happened in a story. After students finish reading pp. 304–305, ask them to summarize the story so far, maintaining meaning and logical order. (Pablo is helping his parents bake. He helps his mother make pumpkin turnovers and *chango* bars. Then he helps his father make bagels and *challah*.)

Corrective Feedback

If... students are unable to summarize story events,
then... model summarizing the plot's main events.

 **Multidraft Reading**

If you chose . . .

Option 1 Return to the Extend Thinking instruction starting on p. 299a.

Option 2 Read pp. 304–309. Use the Guide Comprehension and Extend Thinking instruction.

Student Edition pp. 304–305

OPTION 2 **Think Critically, continued**

Higher-Order Thinking Skills

Summarize • Synthesis Look at pp. 303–304. Why do Pablo and his father have time to make the *challah* and the bagels at the same time? When do they make the *challah*? What happens next? Pablo and his father have time to make the *challah* while the bagel dough rises. When the bagel dough has risen, Papa boils the bagels and Pablo sprinkles them with poppy seeds and sesame seeds. Then the bagels go in the oven.

Model the Strategy

Think Aloud Summarizing is a strategy that good readers use during reading to check their understanding of a selection. When I summarize, I tell the most important ideas or the main events in a story.

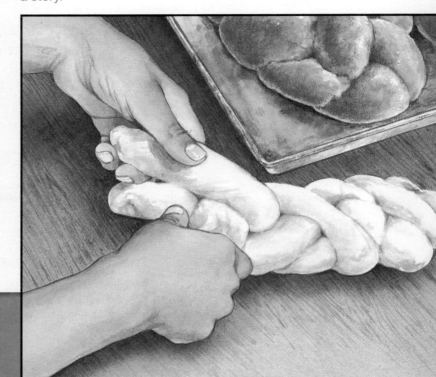

While we are waiting my father makes *challah*, Jewish braided bread. He lets me practice braiding challah dough at my own counter. It's a lot like braiding hair. The customers say it is almost too beautiful to eat.

"Maybe I'll bring a loaf of challah to school," I tell Papa. He smiles.

When the bagel dough has risen, he boils the bagels in a huge pot of water and fishes them out with a long slotted spoon. I sprinkle on poppy seeds and sesame seeds, and then they go in the oven.

304

Fact and Opinion • Evaluation Is it a fact or an opinion to say, "The customers say it is almost too beautiful to eat?" Why? It is a fact that they make the statement because you can prove whether the customers say that or not. The statement, "It is almost too beautiful to eat" is an opinion.

So far, I know that Pablo's parents own a bakery and that he helps them make delicious things to eat. Why is Pablo helping his parents? (He's helping them so that he can decide what to bring to International Day.) What foods do they bake? (*pan dulce,* pumpkin turnovers, *chango* bars, *challah,* bagels)

"Maybe I could bring sesame-seed bagels with cream cheese."

"No *lox?*" Lox is smoked salmon. My father's favorite bagel is pumpernickel with a smear of cream cheese and lox.

I crinkle my nose. "Lox tastes like fish. Jam is better."

305

Inferring • Synthesis Why does Papa smile when Pablo says he might bring a loaf of *challah* to school? Papa is proud that Pablo would like to bring something from Papa's culture to International Day.

On Their Own

Have pairs of students review pp. 304–305 of *Jalapeño Bagels* and list important events. Have them share the main events with the class.

Draw Conclusions • Analysis Does Pablo like *lox*? How can you tell? No, Pablo does not like *lox.* I know because Pablo crinkles his nose when his father mentions it.

Differentiated Instruction

SI Strategic Intervention

Build background Explain that pumpernickel is a coarse, dark brown bread made of unsifted rye flour. Pumpernickel bagels with cream cheese and lox are a favorite food among some Jewish people. Have students brainstorm types of bagels and the spreads and toppings that people put on them.

Connect to Social Studies

Tell students that *challah* is traditionally eaten by Jewish people on the Sabbath, holidays, and other ceremonial occasions.

ELL

English Language Learners
Graphic organizer Have students create a word log to help them remember food names and keep track of events in the story. Students list the names of the foods Pablo and his parents make, their meanings, and sample sentences. Students should list the names in the order they appear in the story, and use the log to summarize important events in the story.

Objectives

◎ Draw conclusions from facts presented in text.

OPTION 1 Skills and Strategies, continued

Teach Draw Conclusions

Draw Conclusions Explain that readers draw conclusions based on what they read and their own experiences. Ask students to draw a conclusion to answer the question: *Does Pablo like the food from one culture more than another? Why do you think so?* (No, he likes the food from his mother's culture as well as the food from his father's culture.)

Corrective Feedback

If... students are unable to draw a conclusion to answer the question, **then...** model how to draw conclusions.

Model the Skill

Think Aloud We often draw conclusions in daily life based on our experience and prior knowledge. Can you think of an example? When reading, a conclusion is a decision you reach that makes sense after you think about details or facts in what you read.

My mother joins us and helps my father make another batch of bagels—*jalapeño* bagels. My parents use their own special recipe. While Papa kneads the dough, Mama chops the jalapeño *chiles*. She tosses them into the dough and adds dried red peppers. We roll, cut, make circles, and let them rise. I can't wait until they are done because I am getting hungry.

306

Student Edition pp. 306–307

OPTION 2 Think Critically, continued

Higher-Order Thinking Skills

Draw Conclusions • Evaluation Do you think that Pablo's parents' bakery is a successful business? Why do you think so? I can draw the conclusion that the bakery is successful because Pablo's mother says that their customers buy everything up.

Compare and Contrast • Analysis How are the jalapeño bagels similar to the other bagels Pablo and his father make? What is different about the jalapeño bagels? The jalapeño bagels include the same basic ingredients as the poppy seed and sesame seed bagels. All the bagels are cooked and prepared the same way. However, the jalapeño bagels include jalapeño *chiles* and red peppers instead of seeds.

As I read, I think about the details that tell me whether Pablo likes certain foods. I know that Pablo likes all the foods he bakes because he considers bringing all of them to school.

"Have you decided what you're going to bring to school?" asks Mama.

"It's hard to choose. Everything is so good," I tell her. I look at Papa. "Except for lox."

"You should decide before we open," warns Mama, "or else our customers will buy everything up."

307

Predict • Evaluation What do you think Pablo will take to International Day? Why do you think that? Pablo seems most interested in the jalapeño bagels. From the illustration, it seems like he's having the fun making the jalapeño bagels because his mother and father make them together. Also, the title of the story is *Jalapeño Bagels.* I predict that he'll bring the jalapeño bagels to school.

On Their Own

Have students reread pp. 306–307 and draw a conclusion about how Pablo's parents created the special recipe for jalapeño bagels.

Connect to Social Studies

Explain that Americans began eating bagels in the early 1900s in New York after Eastern European Jews brought the food to the United States. Have students name foods from different cultures that they have tried and liked. Discuss how many foods that we eat regularly originally came from other cultures.

E L L

English Language Learners

Language transfer: Quotation marks Students may have difficulty distinguishing dialogue from the rest of a sentence. Tell them that quotation marks are used at the beginning and the end of dialogue. Explain that words such as *said* or *replied* usually are found just before or after dialogue. Make sure students can identify the dialogue on p. 307. Point out that the words *asks, tell,* and *warns* all indicate dialogue.

Objectives

• Sequence the plot's main events.

OPTION 1

Skills and Strategies, continued

Teach Sequence

Review **Sequence** Remind students that sequence means the order things happen in a story—what happens first, next, and last. Have students tell the sequence of the main events in *Jalapeño Bagels*. Prompt them by asking: *What baked goods do Pablo and his parents make? What does Pablo decide at the end of the story?*

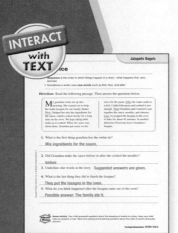

Corrective Feedback

If... students are unable to sequence the plot's main events,

then... model telling the order of events.

Let's Practice It!
TR DVD•323

Model the Skill

Think Aloud It's important to keep track of the sequence in this story to understand how Pablo decides what to bring for International Day. First he bakes *pan dulce,* pumpkin turnovers, and *chango* bars with his mother.

> I walk past all the sweet breads, chango bars, and bagels.
>
> I think about my mother and my father and all the different things they make in the bakery. And suddenly I know exactly what I'm going to bring.
>
> "Jalapeño bagels," I tell my parents. "And I'll spread them with cream cheese and jam."
>
> "Why jalapeño bagels?" asks Papa.
>
> "Because they are a mixture of both of you. Just like me!"

308

Student Edition pp. 308–309

Inferring • Analysis How are the jalapeño bagels a mixture of both Mama and Papa? Bagels come from Papa's Jewish culture. The recipe for jalapeño bagels includes jalapeño *chiles* and red peppers from Mama's Mexican culture.

OPTION 2

Think Critically, continued

Higher-Order Thinking Skills

Review **Sequence • Analysis** Recall the order of steps that Pablo and his father followed to prepare and bake bagels. How is the order of steps in the recipe on page 309 similar to the sequence they followed? First, Pablo and his father make the dough. Then they roll it into long rope shapes and connect the ends to make circles. Then they let the dough rise. Next they boil the bagels. Finally, they bake the bagels in the oven. The recipe follows the same sequence of steps.

Then he bakes bagels and *challah* with his father. Finally they all make jalapeño bagels. Pablo sees that jalapeño bagels are a mixture of both his parents' cultures.

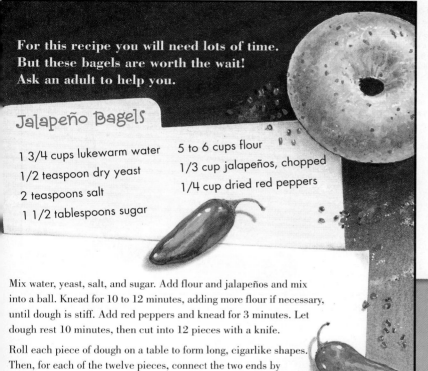

For this recipe you will need lots of time. But these bagels are worth the wait! Ask an adult to help you.

Jalapeño Bagels

1 3/4 cups lukewarm water

1/2 teaspoon dry yeast

2 teaspoons salt

1 1/2 tablespoons sugar

5 to 6 cups flour

1/3 cup jalapeños, chopped

1/4 cup dried red peppers

Mix water, yeast, salt, and sugar. Add flour and jalapeños and mix into a ball. Knead for 10 to 12 minutes, adding more flour if necessary, until dough is stiff. Add red peppers and knead for 3 minutes. Let dough rest 10 minutes, then cut into 12 pieces with a knife.

Roll each piece of dough on a table to form long, cigarlike shapes. Then, for each of the twelve pieces, connect the two ends by overlapping them about 3/4 of an inch and rolling the ends together to make a ring shape. Make sure each joint is secure, or it will come apart while boiling.

Cover with a damp towel and let rise 1 to 1 1/2 hours in a warm spot. In a large pot, bring 1 to 2 gallons of water to a rolling boil. Place bagels in boiling water and boil until they float (15 to 30 seconds). Remove with a slotted spoon and place on a lightly greased cookie sheet. Bake at 400 degrees for 10 to 15 minutes or until golden brown.

Note: A bakery uses dry malt instead of sugar, and high-gluten flour, which you may be able to get at a bakery or pizza parlor. For a milder bagel, reduce the quantities of the peppers.

309

On Their Own

Have pairs of students reread *Jalapeño Bagels* and create a sequence ladder to show the plot's main events. For additional practice, use *Let's Practice It!* page 323 on the *Teacher Resources DVD-ROM*.

Comprehension Check

Spiral Review

Visualize • Synthesis Think about all the words in the story that appeal to the senses. How do you think it feels to walk into Pablo's family's bakery? Give examples. **Possible response:** It smells wonderful. There are cases filled with beautiful pastries. The turnovers are "flaky and golden brown." The *challah* is "too beautiful to eat."

Author's Purpose • Evaluation The author wrote the story from Pablo's point of view. Why do you think she did this? **Possible response:** The author wrote the story from Pablo's point of view so that the reader could experience what he learns about foods from his cultures through his eyes and thoughts.

Check Predictions Have students return to the predictions they made earlier and confirm whether they were accurate.

Objectives

◎ Draw conclusions from facts presented in text.

◎ Summarize the plot's main events.

— Check Retelling

SUCCESS PREDICTOR

Plan to Assess Retelling

☑ **Week 1** Assess Strategic Intervention students.

☑ **Week 2** Assess Advanced students.

☑ **Week 3** Assess Strategic Intervention students.

☑ **This week assess On-Level students.**

☐ **Week 5** Assess any students you have not yet checked during this unit.

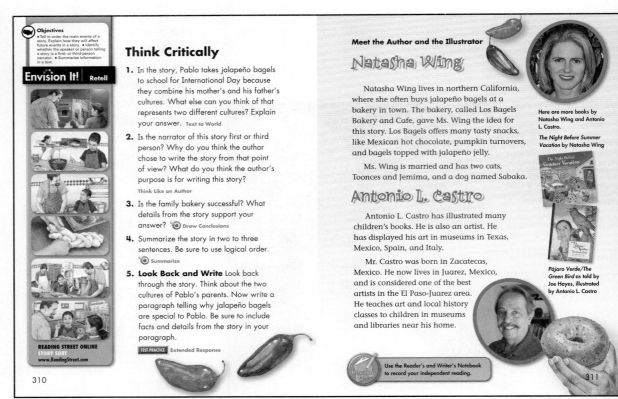

Student Edition pp. 310–311

Retelling

Envision It!

Have students work in pairs to retell the selection, using the Envision It! Retelling Cards as prompts. Remind students that they should accurately describe the main topic and important ideas and use key vocabulary in their retellings. Monitor students' retellings.

Scoring rubric

Top-Score Response A top-score response makes connections beyond the text, describes the main topic and important ideas using accurate information, and draws conclusions from the text.

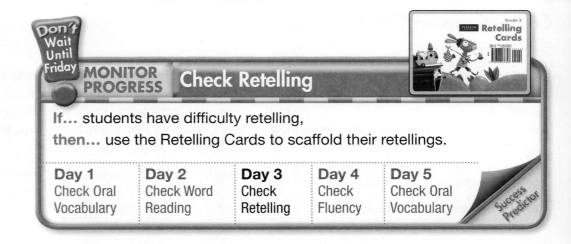

MONITOR PROGRESS   Check Retelling

If... students have difficulty retelling,

then... use the Retelling Cards to scaffold their retellings.

Day 1	Day 2	Day 3	Day 4	Day 5
Check Oral Vocabulary	Check Word Reading	Check Retelling	Check Fluency	Check Oral Vocabulary

Think Critically

Text to world

1. Possible response: A Mexican pizza represents Mexican and Italian heritages. Pizza is a food that came from Italy. The toppings on a Mexican pizza, such as beans and chili peppers, are foods from Mexico.

Think like an author

2. The narrator is first person. I think the author chose to tell the story from Pablo's point of view because it is a personal story and we understand him better that way. I believe the author's purpose is to entertain but also to show how different cultures can influence the foods we cook and eat.

Draw conclusions

3. Pablo's family's bakery is successful. I can draw this conclusion because Pablo says that people tell his mother she makes the best *pan dulce* in town. At the end of the story, Pablo's parents encourage him to choose a food to take to school before the customers buy everything up.

Summarize

4. Pablo helps his parents at the bakery so he can choose a food to bring to school for International Day. Pablo and his parents bake pastries, sweets, breads, and bagels using recipes from his parents' Mexican and Jewish cultures. Pablo decides to take jalapeño bagels to school because they represent both his parents' heritages.

5. **Look Back and Write** To build writing fluency, assign a 10–15 minute time limit.

Suggest that students use a prewriting strategy, such as brainstorming or using a graphic organizer, to organize their ideas. Remind them to establish a topic sentence and support it with facts, details, or explanations. As students finish, encourage them to reread their responses, revise for organization and support, and proofread for errors in grammar and conventions.

Scoring rubric

> **Top-Score Response** A top score response uses details to tell why jalapeño bagels are special to Pablo.
>
> **A top-score response should include:**
>
> - Pablo learns how to make *pan dulce, empanadas de calabaza,* and *chango* bars from his mother's Mexican culture.
>
> - Pablo learns how to make bagels and *challah* from his father's Jewish culture.
>
> - Jalapeño bagels use ingredients from both of Pablo's cultures.

Differentiated Instruction

 Strategic Intervention

Have students work in pairs to brainstorm a list of reasons why jalapeño bagels are important to Pablo.

Meet the Author and Illustrator

Have students read about the author Natasha Wing and the illustrator Antonio L. Castro on p. 311. Ask them how the bakery Ms. Wing goes to and the one she writes about are similar. Ask what Mr. Castro teaches.

Independent Reading

After students enter their independent reading information into their Reading Logs or a journal, have them paraphrase a portion of the text they have just read. Remind students that when we paraphrase, we express the meaning of a passage, using other words and maintaining logical order.

ELL

English Language Learners

Retelling Use the retelling cards to discuss the selection with students. Place the cards in an incorrect order and have volunteers correct the mistake. Then have students explain where each card should go as they describe the sequence of the story.

Check Retelling

Success Predictor

Objectives

- Read grade-level text with accuracy.
- Reread for fluency.
- Sort information into categories to form a simple outline.

Model Fluency
Accuracy

Model fluency reading

Have students turn to p. 304 in *Jalapeño Bagels.* Have students follow along as you read this page. Remind them that when you read accurately, you don't skip words or say the wrong word. Explain that you are going to read carefully and concentrate on saying each word correctly as you read about the special bagels Pablo makes with his parents. Point out that Pablo uses two words from the Spanish language in his description—*jalapeño* and *chiles.* Have students listen as you read slowly and pronounce the words correctly.

Guide practice

Have students follow along as you read the page again. Then have them reread the page as a group, without you, until they read accurately without mispronouncing or skipping any words. Ask questions to be sure students comprehend the text. Continue in the same way on p. 305.

Reread for Fluency

Corrective feedback

If... students are having difficulty reading with accuracy, **then...** prompt:

- Where do you see periods, dashes, and commas?
- What should you do when you see these marks?
- Read the sentence again. Pause when you see these marks.

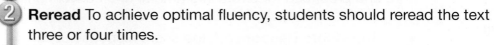

ROUTINE Oral Rereading

1. **Read** Have students read p. 306 of *Jalapeño Bagels.*
2. **Reread** To achieve optimal fluency, students should reread the text three or four times.
3. **Corrective Feedback** Have students read aloud without you. Provide feedback about their accuracy and assist with correct pronunciation as necessary. Encourage them to take their time to read each word correctly.

Routines Flip Chart

Research and Study Skills
Outlining

Teach

Discuss with students that outlining is a way to organize information before writing. Tell students that when they read, they need to take simple notes. Encourage them to look at distinguishing text features to help them find the important information. They can then organize their notes into categories which can become their outline. Using the example below, demonstrate writing a topic outline, which uses phrases to organize information from two or more sources.

Foods from Mexico

I. Main Dishes
      A. *frijoles* and *tortillas*
      B. *bolillos*
      C. *torta de tamal*

II. Desserts
      A. *pan dulce*
      B. *empanadas de calabaza*
      C. *chango bars*

Explain to students that an outline helps identify the most important points in research, and how the points are related to each other.

Guide practice

Discuss these questions:

How does the outline organize information about foods from Mexico? (The outline organizes the foods into the categories *main dishes* and *desserts*.)

How does outlining help you better understand and remember important points from your research? (An outline helps me organize important points into groups. When I group information into categories, it is easier to remember.)

As students work, make sure they are taking notes and sorting evidence into categories.

On their own

Have students review the instructions and complete p. 357 in the *Reader's and Writer's Notebook*.

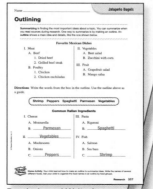

Reader's and Writer's Notebook p. 357

ELL

English Language Learners
Build Academic Vocabulary
Supply meanings for the supporting academic vocabulary as needed. For example:

A **category** is a group of things that are alike in some way.

An **outline** is a list that shows a general plan.

Objectives
- Analyze data for usefulness.
- Identify and correctly use comparative and superlative adverbs.
- Spell frequently misspelled words.

Research and Inquiry
Analyze

Teach

Tell students that today they will analyze their research findings. Have students sort the information from their notes into an outline. Remind students that an outline is a plan for writing. Then explain that students may have to improve the focus of their research by consulting additional sources, including experts.

Model

Think Aloud Originally I thought that just a few foods were used to celebrate holidays and traditions in various cultures. My online research tells me that many, many different foods are part of traditions in various cultures. In addition, part of my research was to ask a local expert about the topic. I talked with the owner of the bakery near my house, and she gave me information about traditional breads and pastries from different cultures. I will refocus my inquiry question to include information from my expert and from my online research. Now my inquiry question is *What types of breads and pastries do people in various cultures bake to celebrate holidays and traditions?*

Guide practice

Have students analyze their findings. They may need to refocus their inquiry question to better fit the information they found. Remind students that if they have difficulty improving their focus they can ask a reference librarian or the local expert for guidance.

Have students continue to take notes and sort the information they gather into the categories within their outline.

On their own

Have partners share their outlines and summarize the information they have gathered. Partners should discuss whether they need to collect additional information to answer the inquiry question.

Conventions
Comparative and Superlative Adverbs

Review Remind students that this week they learned about adverbs that compare.

- Comparative adverbs compare two people, places, or things. Add -er to most adverbs to make them comparative. Use *more* with adverbs that end in the suffix -ly.

- Superlative adverbs compare three or more people, places, or things. Add -est to most adverbs to make them superlative. Use *most* with adverbs that end in the suffix -ly.

Daily Fix-It Use Daily Fix-It numbers 5 and 6 in the right margin.

Connect to oral language Have the class complete this sentence frame orally.

> **Her voice is loud.**
>
> **The radio is _____ than her voice.**

On their own For additional support, use *Let's Practice It!* page 324 on the *Teacher Resources DVD-ROM*.

Let's Practice It!
TR DVD•324

Spelling
Vowel Patterns *ei* and *eigh*

Frequently misspelled words The words *believe* and *friend* are words that students often misspell. The words *either* and *receive* from your spelling list are also difficult to spell. I'm going to read a sentence. Choose the correct word to complete the sentence and then write it correctly.

> 1. I will order _____ the taco plate or the fajitas. (either)
>
> 2. Liam does not _____ your lie. (believe)
>
> 3. Karen is my best _____. (friend)
>
> 4. You will _____ the package next Friday. (receive)

On their own For additional support, use *Reader's and Writer's Notebook* p. 358.

Differentiated Instruction

SI Strategic Intervention

Conventions To practice writing comparative and superlative adverbs, have students work in small groups to write three sentences about cooking. They should write one with -er to compare two actions, one with -est to compare three or more actions, and one using *more* or *most* with an adverb ending in -ly.

Daily Fix-It

5. The students is having blue berry muffins for a snack. *(are; blueberry)*

6. I can finnish mine fastest than you. *(finish; faster)*

Reader's and Writer's
Notebook p. 358

Objectives

• Understand the criteria for writing an effective invitation.

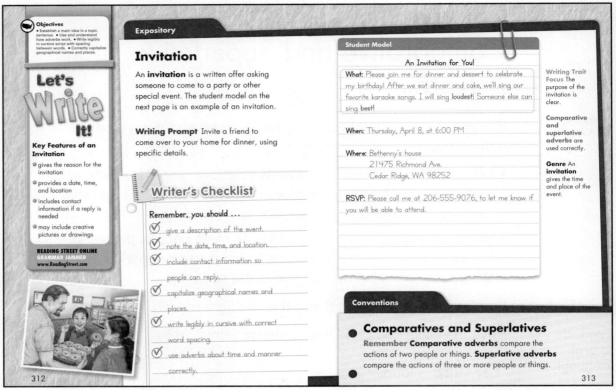

Student Edition pp. 312–313

Let's Write It!
Invitation

Teach

Use pp. 312–313 in the Student Edition. Direct students to read the key features of an invitation that appear on p. 312. Remind students that they can refer to the information in the Writer's Checklist as they write their own invitation.

Read the student model on p. 313. Point out the date, location, and time in the model, as well as Bethenny's contact information.

Connect to conventions

Remind students that most adverbs that compare three or more actions are formed by adding -*est*. Point out the correct use of the adverb *loudest* in the model.

Writing—Invitation
Writing Trait: Purpose

Display rubric

Display Scoring Rubric 24 from the *Teacher Resources DVD-ROM* and review the criteria for each trait under each score. Then, using the model in the Student Edition, choose students to explain why the model should score a 4 for one of the traits. If a student offers that the model should score below 4 for a particular trait, the student should support that response. Remind students that this is the rubric that will be used to evaluate the invitation they write.

Scoring Rubric: Invitation

	④	③	②	①
Focus/Ideas	Clear focus and purpose for invitation	Fairly clear focus and purpose for invitation	Unclear focus and purpose for invitation	No attempt made to offer a reason for the event
Organization	Clearly organized details, such as date, time, and location of party	Able to follow details, such as date, time, and location of party	Effort to include details, such as date, time, and location; details for party are unclear	No effort made to include party details, such as date, time, and location
Voice	Writer achieves an animated voice and makes the party sound enticing	Some evidence of animated voice and inviting tone	Attempts an animated voice and inviting tone	No attempt at an animated voice or inviting tone
Word Choice	Strong use of vivid words	Adequate use of vivid words	Weak use of vivid words	No use of vivid words
Sentences	Clear sentences of various lengths and types	Sentences of a few lengths and types	No sentences; little attempt at various lengths and types of sentences	No attempt at sentences; no attempt at various lengths and types of sentences
Conventions	Few, if any, errors; correct use of comparative and superlative adverbs	Several minor errors; mostly correct use of comparative and superlative adverbs	Many errors; inaccurate use of comparative and superlative adverbs	Numerous errors; no use of comparative and superlative adverbs

Four-column chart

Have students get out the four-column charts that they worked on yesterday. If their charts are not complete, allow students a few minutes of class time to add details for their invitation.

Write

You will use your four-column chart as you write the first draft of your invitation. When you are drafting, don't worry if the invitation does not sound exactly how you want it. You will have a chance to revise it later.

Differentiated Instruction

 Advanced

Generating alternatives Have students brainstorm alternative ways to organize the details in the student model on p. 313. Encourage students to make an outline for each idea. Have partners exchange outlines and check each other's work for inclusion of date, time, location, and contact information. Allow students to use their alternative outlines when drafting their own invitations.

ELL

English Language Learners
Invitation Have pairs of students use a four-column chart to organize the date, time, location, and contact information of the student model on p. 313.

Objectives
- Write a first draft of an invitation.
- Establish a purpose when writing.

Writing, continued
Writing Trait: Purpose

MINI-LESSON

Establish a Purpose When Writing

■ **Introduce** Discuss the importance of purpose in writing. Explain that there are four common reasons authors write: to persuade, inform, entertain, and express a mood or feeling. Discuss the purpose for writing an invitation. Guide students to understand that the purpose for writing an invitation is to inform readers of a special event. Invitations may also be written to persuade guests to attend the event.

Let's Grill!

What: Please join my family in an outdoor barbecue to celebrate the beginning of summer! We will have plenty of hamburgers and hot dogs for everyone. After dinner, we will play games. The three-legged race should be the funnest of all! Prizes will be given to the teams that run most fastest.

When: Saturday, June 24th, at 5:00 PM

Where: Meet us at the picnic tables at former Park.

R.S.V.P. Please call Mario Ortiz at 309-555-8428 to let me know if you will join us. Hope you can make it!

Unit 5 Jalapeño Bagels   Writing: Model 24A

Writing Transparency 24A,
TR DVD

Drafting Tips

✔ To get started, review your four-column chart.

✔ Make sure to include specific details to inform the reader of your special event.

✔ Focus on getting your ideas down. Don't worry about grammar and mechanics while writing your first draft.

Think Aloud Now I will write my draft. I will use the details from my four-column chart to help organize my ideas. First, I will write a title for my invitation. Because my invitation is for an outside barbecue, I will title it *Let's Grill!* Then I will write details about the barbecue to let my reader know when and where it will take place. Because I want to persuade my reader to attend the event, I will also try to make the event sound fun and exciting. I will not worry about grammar and mechanics until I get to the proofreading stage.

Direct students to use the drafting tips to guide them in developing their drafts. Remind them to keep in mind the overall purpose of an invitation to inform and persuade as they write.

ROUTINE — Quick Write for Fluency — Team Talk

1) **Talk** Have pairs discuss how they made their special event sound fun and exciting.

2) **Write** Each student writes a sentence about his or her event using a comparative adverb.

3) **Share** Partners read one another's writing and check for correct use of adverbs.

Routines Flip Chart

Wrap Up Your Day

✔ **Build Concepts** What did you learn about how Pablo's parents were able to combine their cultures into one food?

✔ **Draw Conclusions** What clues did you use to help you conclude why Pablo chose to bring jalapeño bagels?

✔ **Summarize** How did summarizing the events in the story help you draw conclusions about Pablo's decision?

Differentiated Instruction

 Advanced

Author's purpose Have groups of three or four students discuss and determine the author's purpose for writing *Jalapeño Bagels.* After arriving at a consensus, have each group member find a sentence from the story that supports his or her conclusion.

Preview DAY 4

Tell students that tomorrow they will read about foods from Mexico.

Objectives
- Expand the weekly concept.
- Develop oral vocabulary.

Today at a Glance

Oral Vocabulary
wholesome, grate, agent

Phonics/Word Analysis
Vowel patterns for /ò/

Genre
Expository text

Reading
"Foods of Mexico: a Delicious Blend"

Let's Learn It!
Fluency: Accuracy
Vocabulary: ⓦ Unfamiliar words
Media literacy: Radio advertisement

Research and Inquiry
Synthesize

Conventions
Comparative and superlative adverbs

Spelling
Vowel patterns *ei* and *eigh*

Writing
Invitation

Concept Talk

 Question of the Week
How can different cultures contribute to the foods we eat?

Expand the concept

Remind students that this week they have read about baked goods that come from different cultures. Tell students that today they will read about how native foods and foods from Europe, Asia, and Africa have shaped Mexican cuisine.

Anchored Talk

Develop oral vocabulary

Use the illustrations to review pp. 304–309 of *Jalapeño Bagels.* Discuss the Amazing Words *grumble* and *allergic* and add these and other concept-related words to the concept map. Use the following questions to develop students' understanding of the concept. Remind students to ask and answer questions with appropriate detail and to build on other students' answers.

- What is our body telling us when our stomach *grumbles*? What types of foods make your stomach *grumble*? What cultures are they from?

- What might happen to someone who is *allergic* to a particular food?

 *Strategy Response Log*

Have students complete p. 30 in the *Reader's and Writer's Notebook*. Then have students work in pairs to summarize "Foods of Mexico: a Delicious Blend."

Oral Vocabulary
Amazing Words

Amazing Words

nutrition	grumble
calorie	allergic
flavor	wholesome
spice	grate
nutmeg	agent

Amazing Words — **Oral Vocabulary Routine**

Teach Amazing Words

1 Introduce Write the word *wholesome* on the board. Have students say it with you. Yesterday we read about bread and bagels that Pablo made with his parents. In appropriate servings, bread is a *wholesome* food. Discuss how whole grains and bread can be part of healthy nutrition. Then have students use context to determine a definition for *wholesome*. (A *wholesome* food is a food that is good for your health.)

2 Demonstrate Have students answer questions to demonstrate understanding. What are examples of other *wholesome* foods? (fruits, vegetables, fish, meat)

3 Apply Have students apply their understanding. What is an antonym for *wholesome*? (unhealthy)

See p. OV•1 teach *grate* and *agent*.

Routines Flip Chart

Apply Amazing Words

As students read "Foods of Mexico: a Delicious Blend," have them think about the *agents* that make Mexican foods *wholesome*, and what cooks might *grate* in order to prepare Mexican foods.

Connect to reading

Explain that today students will read about foods that have shaped Mexican cuisine. As they read, students should think about how the Question of the Week and the Amazing Words *wholesome, grate,* and *agent* apply to Mexican foods.

E L L Produce Oral Language Use the Day 4 instruction on ELL Poster 24 to extend and enrich language.

E L L Poster 24

Phonics Review
Vowel Patterns for /o̯/

Review sound-spellings

To review last week's phonics skill, write *paw, ball, caught, talk,* and *bought.* You studied words like these last week. What do you know about the vowel sound in these words? (Each word has /o̯/, but the sound has different spelling patterns.) Have students identify the spelling pattern in each word. What letters spell the /o̯/ sound in *paw*? (*aw*) In *ball*? (*a*) Continue in the same way for /o̯/ in *caught* (*augh*) and *bought* (*ough*).

Corrective feedback

If students are unable to answer the questions about /o̯/ spelling patterns, refer them to Sound-Spelling Cards 56, 57, 58, 97, 105, and 106.

Guide practice

Draw a six-column chart. When I say a word, think about the letters that spell the vowel sound /o̯/. Say *walk. Walk* is spelled *w-a-l-k.* The letters *al* stand for /o̯/. I'll write *walk* in the fourth column. Write each word in the appropriate column. Then have students read the words and ask volunteers to underline the letters that stand for /o̯/ in each word.

a	au	aw	al	augh	ough
ball	cause	fawn	walk	taught	brought
stall	fault	raw	stalk	daughter	thought
	because	dawn			

On their own

For additional practice, use *Let's Practice It!* page 325 on the *Teacher Resources DVD-ROM.*

Let's Practice It!
TR DVD•325

Fluent Word Reading
Spiral Review

Read words independent of context

Display these words. Tell students that they can decode some words on this list. Explain that they should know other words because they appear often in reading.

Have students read the list three or four times until they can read at the rate of two to three seconds per word.

Word Reading

annual	rows	very	seen	violets
watched	videos	quiet	their	have
scene	unusual	tail	created	tale
people	giant	many	rose	two

Corrective feedback

If... students have difficulty reading whole words,
then... have them use sound-by-sound blending for decodable words or chunking for words that have word parts, or have them say and spell high-frequency words.

If... students cannot read fluently at a rate of two to three seconds per word,
then... have pairs practice the list until they can read it fluently.

Differentiated Instruction

SI **Strategic Intervention**

/ȯ/ Vowel patterns To assist students having difficulty with identifying vowel patterns for the sound /ȯ/, focus on two patterns at a time. For example, write words with /ȯ/ spelled *au* and *aw*, such as *cause, fault, haunt, paws, fawn, straw.* Read the words; then have students read the words and identify the letters that spell /ȯ/.

Spiral Review

These activities review:

- previously taught high-frequency words *have, many, people, their, two, very, watched.*

- homophones; syllable pattern CV/VC.

ELL

English Language Learners
Fluent word reading Have students listen to a more fluent reader say the words. Then have them repeat the words.

Objectives

- Read words fluently in context.
- Apply knowledge of sound-spellings to decode unknown words when reading.
- Practice fluency with oral rereading.

Read words in context

Display these sentences. Call on individuals to read a sentence. Then randomly point to review words and have students read them. To help you monitor word reading, high-frequency words are underlined and decodable words are italicized.

MONITOR PROGRESS | **Sentence Reading**

Dad read a *tale* about a <u>very</u> *quiet giant.*

Her garden has *rows* of *violets* and <u>two</u> *rose* bushes.

<u>Have</u> you ever *seen* a horse with such an *unusual tail?*

<u>Their</u> yard was the *scene* of our *annual* picnic.

<u>Many</u> <u>people</u> <u>watched</u> the *videos* we *created.*

If... students are unable to read an underlined high-frequency word,

then... read the word for them and spell it, having them echo you.

If... students have difficulty reading an italicized decodable word,

then... guide them in using sound-by-sound blending or chunking.

Reread for Fluency

Have students reread the sentences to develop automaticity decoding words.

ROUTINE | **Oral Rereading**

 Read Have students read all the sentences orally.

 Reread To achieve optimal fluency, students should reread the sentences three or four times.

 Corrective Feedback Listen as students read. Provide corrective feedback regarding their fluency and decoding.

Routines Flip Chart

Blend and Read

Read words independent of context

Have students turn to p. 107 in *Decodable Practice Readers 3.2* and find the first list of words. Each word in this list has long *a,* long *e,* or long *i* spelled *ei* or *eigh.* Let's blend and read these words. Be sure that students identify the correct vowel sound in each word.

Next, have students read the high-frequency words.

Preview Decodable Practice Passage

Have students read the title and preview the story. Tell them that they will read words with long *a,* long *e,* and long *i* spelled *ei* and *eigh.*

Read words in context

Chorally read the story along with the students. Have students identify words in the story that have long *a,* long *e,* and long *i* spelled *ei* or *eigh.* Make sure that students are monitoring their accuracy when they decode.

Team Talk Pair students and have them take turns reading the story aloud to each other. Monitor students as they read to check for proper pronunciation and appropriate pacing.

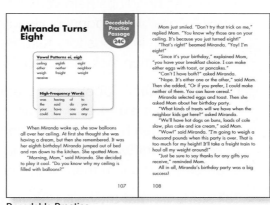

Decodable Practice
Passage 24C

Differentiated Instruction

 Advanced

Decodable words Have students write their own sentences using some of the decodable words found in the sentences on p. 314e.

Let's Think About Genre
Expository Text

Introduce the genre

Explain to students that what we read is structured differently depending on the author's reasons for writing and what kind of information he/she wishes to convey. Different types of texts are called genres. Tell them that expository text is one type of genre.

Discuss the genre

Remind students that they have read many types of expository text this year, including a photo essay and a magazine article. Review the elements and characteristics of expository text to activate student's prior knowledge. Ask the following questions:

- What is the purpose of expository text? Possible response: The purpose of expository text is to give information about something or to explain the nature of an object, idea, or theme.

- What are some text features that you might find in expository text? Possible responses: Expository text can include photos or graphics and text features such as diagrams, maps, a table of contents, headings, or an index.

- How can headings help you understand the information in expository text? Possible responses: Headings organize and categorize the information in expository text. Headings give a general preview of the information included in a section.

Guide practice

Use the questions above and students' detailed responses to lead a discussion about expository text and the elements it includes, especially headings. Then have students look at sample texts in the class or library to see different ways headings may be used. Encourage them to list their examples and share them with the class.

Connect to reading

Tell students that they will now read an expository text that tells about the cultures and foods that have blended to form Mexican cuisine. Have the class think about how the headings organize the information in the text.

Small Group Time

DAY 4

Break into small groups before reading or revisiting "Foods of Mexico: a Delicious Blend."

Teacher Led

SI Strategic Intervention

Teacher Led p. DI•80
- Practice retelling
- Genre focus
- **Read/Revisit** "Foods of Mexico"

OL On-Level

Teacher Led p. DI•85
- Practice retelling
- Genre focus
- **Read/Revisit** "Foods of Mexico"

A Advanced

Teacher Led p. DI•90
- Genre focus
- **Read/Revisit** "Foods of Mexico"

Place English language learners in the groups that correspond to their reading abilities in English.

Practice Stations
- Read for Meaning
- Get Fluent
- Words to Know

Independent Activities
- AudioText: "Foods of Mexico"
- *Reader's and Writer's Notebook*
- Research and Inquiry

English Language Learners

Graphic organizer Discuss with students how a graphic organizer such as a 5-column chart can organize information and make it easier to understand and remember. Review the elements of a chart: headings, rows, and columns. Then have students work in pairs to create a 3-column chart that shows their favorite foods for breakfast, lunch, and dinner, including foods from their native cultures.

Objectives
• Understand expository text.

Student Edition pp. 314–315

Objectives
• Identify the topic and find the author's purposes for writing. • Make connections between literary and informational texts with similar ideas and support your ideas with details from the texts.

Social Studies in Reading

Genre
Expository Text

• Expository text explains or describes the main idea about a topic, using facts and details.

• Graphic sources show the information visually.

• Text features, such as headings, italicized words, and captions help readers to predict, locate, and verify the information.

• As you read "Foods of Mexico," use the text features to predict, locate, and verify information about the topic.

Foods of Mexico
a Delicious Blend

From *Viva Mexico! The Foods*
by George Ancona

Panza llena, corazón contento is an old Mexican proverb that means "a full belly makes for a happy heart." The foods of Mexico are a treat to see, smell, taste, and eat.

Native Foods

The early people of Mexico developed maize (corn) from a small wild plant. They grew many varieties of maize: white, red, yellow, black, and other color combinations.

Between rows of corn they planted tomatoes, beans, chiles, pumpkins, sweet potatoes, and squash. They also raised avocados and amaranth, a nutritious grain that was ground into flour for tortillas and bread. Fields and forests supplied fruits, peanuts, cacao (cocoa) beans, honey, and mushrooms.

Chiles — Tuna — Nopal — Cacao beans — Beans — Jiotilla — Avocado — Amaranth — Peanuts — Guayaba — Chayote — Tomatoes — Sweet potatoes — Honey — Squash

Let's Think About
According to the title, what is the topic going to be? How does the proverb help introduce the main idea about the topic? **Expository Text**
1

Let's Think About
What facts and details that support the main idea can you learn from the photos and captions? **Expository Text**
2

314

315

Guide Comprehension

Teach the genre

Genre: Expository Text Have students preview "Foods of Mexico: a Delicious Blend (from *Viva Mexico! The Foods*)" on pp. 314–317. Tell them that the selection is expository text. Expository text is writing that explains the nature of an object, an idea, or a theme. Then ask: What do you think this expository text will be about? How do you know?

Corrective feedback

If... students are unable to predict what the text will be about, then... use the model to guide students in skimming and scanning.

Model the skill

Think Aloud

In expository text, there are often headings that tell what different parts of the text are about. I can read the headings to determine what it will be about.

On their own

Have students work in pairs to read the headings and preview the text in "Foods of Mexico: a Delicious Blend." Have them write what they think the text will be about.

Extend Thinking
Think Critically

Higher-order thinking skills

Graphic Sources • Analysis Why did the author include the labeled photograph on page 315? Possible response: It helps readers understand the text. They might recognize some of the foods and not have known their names.

 Draw Conclusions • Evaluation Do you think that the early people of Mexico were skilled farmers? Why do you think so? Possible response: The early people of Mexico were skilled farmers because they knew how to grow many types of plants. They also developed many varieties of maize.

Let's Think About...

1 Possible responses: The title tells me that the topic is going to be the delicious foods of Mexico. The proverb is a good introduction to the topic because it is also from Mexican culture and let's the reader know that the text will be about food.

2 Possible response: The photos show me what each food looks like and the captions tell me the name of each food.

Differentiated Instruction

SI Strategic Intervention

Graphic sources Discuss the photograph on p. 315. Have students list the foods in a T-chart and tell what they know about the foods (e.g., uses, taste, texture).

A Advanced

Recipe Have students use a cookbook or online sources to find a recipe that contains at least one of the native Mexican foods discussed on p. 315.

English Language Learners

Access content Have students preview the text by reading the title and looking at the photographs and other graphic aids. Ask them what the main topic of the article is. (food) Next, have students read the photograph labels aloud. If students recognize a word, have them share that what they know about it.

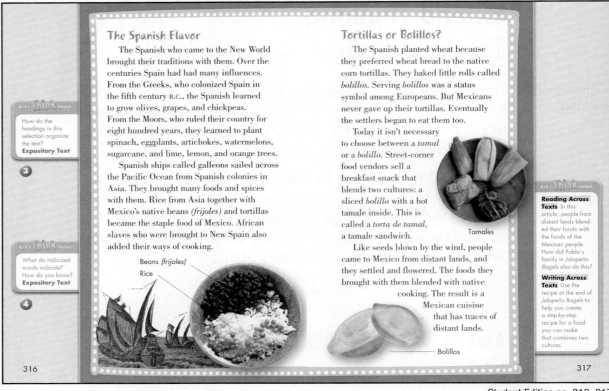

The Spanish Flavor

The Spanish who came to the New World brought their traditions with them. Over the centuries Spain had had many influences. From the Greeks, who colonized Spain in the fifth century B.C., the Spanish learned to grow olives, grapes, and chickpeas. From the Moors, who ruled their country for eight hundred years, they learned to plant spinach, eggplants, artichokes, watermelons, sugarcane, and lime, lemon, and orange trees.

Spanish ships called galleons sailed across the Pacific Ocean from Spanish colonies in Asia. They brought many foods and spices with them. Rice from Asia together with Mexico's native beans (frijoles) and tortillas became the staple food of Mexico. African slaves who were brought to New Spain also added their ways of cooking.

Beans (frijoles)
Rice

Let's Think About...

How do the headings in this selection organize the text?
Expository Text

❸

Let's Think About...

What do italicized words indicate? How do you know?
Expository Text

❹

Tortillas or Bolillos?

The Spanish planted wheat because they preferred wheat bread to the native corn tortillas. They baked little rolls called *bolillos*. Serving *bolillos* was a status symbol among Europeans. But Mexicans never gave up their tortillas. Eventually the settlers began to eat them too.

Today it isn't necessary to choose between a *tamal* or a *bolillo*. Street-corner food vendors sell a breakfast snack that blends two cultures: a sliced *bolillo* with a hot tamale inside. This is called a *torta de tamal*, a tamale sandwich.

Like seeds blown by the wind, people came to Mexico from distant lands, and they settled and flowered. The foods they brought with them blended with native cooking. The result is a Mexican cuisine that has traces of distant lands.

Tamales

Bolillos

Let's Think About...

Reading Across Texts In this article, people from distant lands blended their foods with the foods of the Mexican people. How did Pablo's family in *Jalapeño Bagels* also do this?

Writing Across Texts Use the recipe at the end of *Jalapeño Bagels* to help you create a step-by-step recipe for a food you can make that combines two cultures.

316

317

Student Edition pp. 316–317

Guide Comprehension

Teach the genre

Genre: Expository Text Remind students that expository text can include photos or graphics and text features such as diagrams, maps, a table of contents, headings, or an index. Have them discuss how text features help them understand information in expository text. Then ask: What do headings tell you about the information that will be presented in the text?

Corrective feedback

If... students are unable to explain how headings help preview the text, then... use the model to guide students to use headings to preview text.

Model the skill

Think Aloud I know that expository text can include graphics and text features such as headings. Headings organize the information presented and also give a quick preview of ideas or topics in the text. The headings in this text tell me that foods native to Mexico and Spanish foods will be discussed in the text.

On their own

Have students work in pairs to write three headings that might appear in an expository text about their favorite type of food.

Extend Thinking

Higher-order thinking skills

Compare and Contrast • Analysis How was the development of Spanish and Mexican cuisines similar? Possible response: Spanish and Mexican cuisines are both blends of foods from different cultures. Spanish cuisine includes foods from the Greeks and the Moors. Mexican cuisine includes native foods and foods from Spain, including those the Spanish adopted from other countries.

Text features • Evaluation Why is the heading on page 317 "Tortillas or Bolillos"? Possible response: The heading tells the reader that people choose between *tortillas* and *bolillos.* It leads the reader to expect to learn what is different about these foods.

Let's Think About...

3 Possible response: The headings in the text organize the information into sections about native foods of Mexico, the Spanish influence on Mexican cuisine, and how the two cultures blend.

4 Possible response: The italicized words are the Spanish words for different kinds of food. I know this because the words are defined in the text.

Reading Across Texts

Have students create a T-chart to record information about how Pablo's family blended foods together, and how Mexican cuisine blends foods together.

Writing Across Texts

Have students list steps to include when writing a recipe, based on the recipe on p. 309, such as "list ingredients and measurements" and "give directions." Then have them follow the steps to write their own recipe.

Connect to Social Studies

Even though people think of tomato sauce and pasta being native to Italian cuisine, the tomato was imported back to Europe after explorers arrived in the Americas. Also, the pasta noodle made from flour, water, and sometimes egg, has been found in ancient cuisines from China to Syria.

Differentiated Instruction

SI Strategic Intervention

Main idea Have pairs reread pp. 316–317 and write the main idea for each page. Then have them compare their main idea to the heading on the page.

A Advanced

Headings Have students think of alternate headings that might be used on pp. 316–317.

ELL

English Language Learners

Professional development: make personal and cultural connections "We should constantly search for ways to link academic content with what students already know or what is familiar to them from their family or cultural experiences. This not only validates children's sense of identity, but it also makes the learning more meaningful." —Dr. Jim Cummins

Cultural connections Have students work in small groups to discuss foods from their cultures and whether they recognize any of the foods native to their cultures in American cuisine.

Objectives

- Read with fluency and comprehension.
- ⊙ Use context clues to determine the meanings of unfamiliar words.
- Present a radio advertisement.

Check Fluency WCPM

🏆 **SUCCESS PREDICTOR**

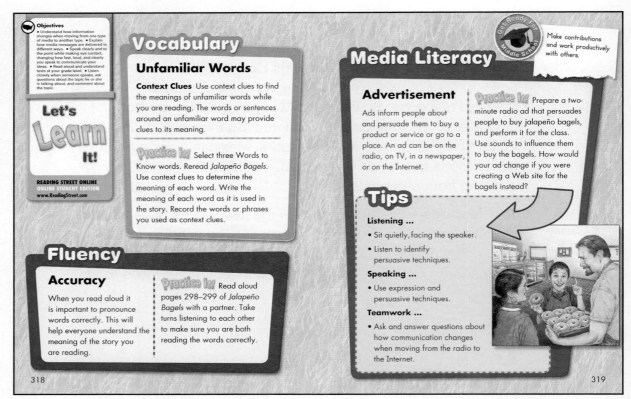

Objectives
- Understand how information changes when moving from one type of media to another type. • Explain how media messages are delivered in different ways. • Speak clearly and to the point while making eye contact, changing how fast, loud, and clearly you speak to communicate your ideas. • Read aloud and understand texts at your grade level. • Listen closely when someone speaks, ask questions about the topic he or she is talking about, and comment about the topic.

Let's
Learn It!

READING STREET ONLINE
ONLINE STUDENT EDITION
www.ReadingStreet.com

Vocabulary

Unfamiliar Words

Context Clues Use context clues to find the meanings of unfamiliar words while you are reading. The words or sentences around an unfamiliar word may provide clues to its meaning.

Practice It! Select three Words to Know words. Reread *Jalapeño Bagels*. Use context clues to determine the meaning of each word. Write the meaning of each word as it is used in the story. Record the words or phrases you used as context clues.

Fluency

Accuracy

When you read aloud it is important to pronounce words correctly. This will help everyone understand the meaning of the story you are reading.

Practice It! Read aloud pages 298–299 of *Jalapeño Bagels* with a partner. Take turns listening to each other to make sure you are both reading the words correctly.

Media Literacy

Make contributions and work productively with others.

Advertisement

Ads inform people about and persuade them to buy a product or service or go to a place. An ad can be on the radio, on TV, in a newspaper, or on the Internet.

Practice It! Prepare a two-minute radio ad that persuades people to buy jalapeño bagels, and perform it for the class. Use sounds to influence them to buy the bagels. How would your ad change if you were creating a Web site for the bagels instead?

Tips

Listening ...
- Sit quietly, facing the speaker.
- Listen to identify persuasive techniques.

Speaking ...
- Use expression and persuasive techniques.

Teamwork ...
- Ask and answer questions about how communication changes when moving from the radio to the Internet.

318   319

Student Edition pp. 318–319

Fluency
Accuracy

Guide practice

Use the Student Edition activity as an assessment tool. Make sure the reading passage is at least 200 words in length. As students read aloud with partners, walk around to make sure they read with accuracy, without omissions, substitutions, or errors in word identification.

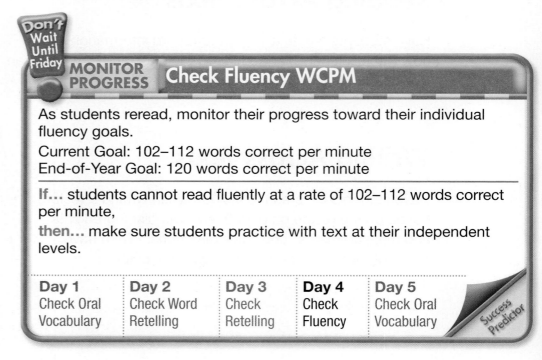

Don't Wait Until Friday

MONITOR PROGRESS Check Fluency WCPM

As students reread, monitor their progress toward their individual fluency goals.

Current Goal: 102–112 words correct per minute
End-of-Year Goal: 120 words correct per minute

If... students cannot read fluently at a rate of 102–112 words correct per minute,

then... make sure students practice with text at their independent levels.

Day 1	**Day 2**	**Day 3**	**Day 4**	**Day 5**	
Check Oral Vocabulary	Check Word Retelling	Check Retelling	Check Fluency	Check Oral Vocabulary	Success Predictor

Vocabulary

Unfamiliar Words

Teach unfamiliar words

Context Clues Tell students that sometimes when they read they will come across words they don't know. Remind them to use context clues to determine the meaning of unfamiliar words. They should look at the context, or the words and sentences around the word, for clues to the meaning of the unfamiliar word.

Guide practice

Write *boils* on the board. Have a volunteer read aloud the last paragraph on p. 304 of *Jalapeño Bagels.* Then say this sentence aloud and write it on the board: *As soon as the water boils, you can put the pasta in.* Guide students to use the context clues in the paragraph and sentence to determine the meaning of *boils.*

On their own

Walk around the room as students work in small groups to determine the meaning of three unfamiliar words in *Jalapeño Bagels.* Check that students record the words and phrases they are using as clues to figure out the meaning of each word.

Media Literacy
Radio Advertisement

Teach

Discuss advertising with students. Ask them to describe ads that they have seen or heard on the radio, in newspapers and magazines, on television, and on Web sites. Discuss the techniques used to communicate the message (Print uses text and images, radio uses spoken words and sounds, and Web sites and television use spoken words and images.) Point out that radio commercials use engaging, conversational language and repeat information to reinforce the message. They also include sounds that attract listeners' attention and entice them to want the product.

Guide practice

Give students time to prepare their radio advertisements. Be sure that students communicate the main message more than once. Remind them to use expression and convey excitement.

On their own

Have students perform their commercials for the class. Remind them to speak coherently at an appropriate rate and volume and employ eye contact.

Advertisement

Explain that a good advertisement presents a persuasive argument to buy a product. Tell students that a persuasive presentation states a clear position and provides relevant support. Students can use relevant facts, details, examples, quotations, statistics, stories, and anecdotes to support their arguments. They can also use persuasive language to influence others.

Academic Vocabulary

advertisement a written display or oral announcement meant to sell a product or service

ELL

English Language Learners
Vocabulary: Context Clues
Provide students with additional contextualized definitions for unfamiliar words. Demonstrate any words that can be acted out, and use illustrations and other visuals to clarify the relevant meanings of words. Have students illustrate the meaning of the word to confirm understanding.

Fluency

Success Predictor

Research and Inquiry
Synthesize

Teach

Have students synthesize their research findings and results. Remind them that when they synthesize, they integrate important information and relevant ideas from various sources to create an answer to their inquiry questions. Remind students that they can sort the information they gather into categories in an outline. Explain that their outline will help them synthesize and organize the information for their article and presentation.

Guide practice

Have students use a word processing program to prepare an outline for their articles and presentations on Day 5. Check to see that students' outlines organize the most important points from their research and include details to support each main point.

On their own

Have students write their articles, making sure to include details to support their main ideas. Then have them practice their presentations.

Conventions
Comparative and Superlative Adverbs

Test practice
Remind students that grammar skills, such as using comparative and superlative adverbs to discuss time and manner, are often assessed on important tests. Remind students to add *-er* to most adverbs to make them comparative. Add *-est* to make most adverbs superlative. Use *more* and *most* with adverbs that end in the suffix *-ly.*

Daily Fix-It
Use Daily Fix-It numbers 7 and 8 in the right margin.

On their own
For additional practice, use *Reader's and Writer's Notebook* p. 359.

Reader's and Writer's
Notebook p. 359

Spelling
Vowel Patterns *ei* and *eigh*

Practice spelling strategy
Write the words from the spelling list on the board. Have students read and spell each word chorally. Have students work with a partner to use each word in a sentence. Ask several pairs to share their sentences. Remind students to segment words by letter sounds, syllables, and word parts, when applicable.

On their own
For additional practice, use *Let's Practice It!* page 326 on the *Teacher Resources DVD-ROM.*

Let's Practice It!
TR DVD•326

7. Charles had went to school more earlier than Ms. Lawrence. *(gone; earlier)*

8. There are seven or aieght bagels left in the bassket. *(eight; basket)*

Objectives
- Revise draft of an invitation.
- Apply revising strategy of adding.
- Include specific details to better inform readers.

Writing—Invitation
Revising Strategy

MINI-LESSON

Revising Strategy: Adding

Writing Transparency 24B, TR DVD

■ Yesterday we wrote an invitation inviting a friend over to dinner. Today we will revise our drafts. The goal is to make our writing clearer, more interesting, and more informative.

■ Display Writing Transparency 24B. Remind students that revising does not include corrections to grammar and mechanics. Then introduce the revising strategy of adding.

■ As you revise, ask yourself whether your invitation includes enough specific details to inform your reader about the event. For example, our outdoor barbecue invitation tells readers to meet us at the picnic tables at a park. We can add the detail *the southwest corner of Horner Park* to help readers find the exact location of the party. Have students read their invitations and look for places to add specific details about their event.

Tell students that in addition to adding informative details, they should also look for places to replace non-descriptive language with more vivid words.

Revising Tips

✔ Check that details are well-organized and specific enough to inform your readers.

✔ Review writing for varied sentence types and lengths.

✔ Make sure that your tone is friendly and engaging.

Peer conferencing

Peer Revision Have pairs of students exchange papers for peer revision. After partners have read each other's invitations, have the reader summarize the details of the invitation to see whether they are what the writer intended. Have partners tell where they would add information to improve the invitations. Remind students to begin their critique with a compliment or strength of the invitation.

Have students revise their invitations using the key features of an invitation as well as the suggestions offered by their partner during Peer Revision. Be sure students are using the revising strategy of adding.

Corrective feedback

Circulate around the room to monitor students and confer with them as they revise. Remind students correcting errors that they will have time to edit tomorrow. They should be working on content and organization today.

Write Guy
Jeff Anderson

Focus Your Revising

In the revising process, students can easily get bogged down by everything that needs to be fixed. Revising one aspect at a time helps students focus their efforts and concentrate on one task, while making it easier for you as a teacher to fully explain for you as a teacher to fully explain and reteach the concept, moving students toward correctness. Sometimes less really is more.

ROUTINE — Quick Write for Fluency — Team Talk

 Talk Have pairs discuss what a dinner party with Pablo and his family from *Jalapeño Bagels* might be like.

 Write Each student writes a paragraph describing the event.

 Share Partners read each other's paragraphs and check for specific details about the event.

Routines Flip Chart

Wrap Up Your Day

✔ **Build Concepts** Have students discuss what they learned about Mexican food.

✔ **Oral Vocabulary** Monitor students' use of oral vocabulary as they respond to this question: Do you think the spices in the foods from Mexico make them wholesome and full of nutrition?

✔ **Story Structure** Discuss how dialogue between the characters helps students understand text.

ELL
English Language Learners
Peer revision Provide students with sentence starters to use during peer conferencing, such as: *I liked the way you _____,* and *Can you add details to explain _____?*

Preview DAY 5

Remind students to think about how foods can come from more than one culture.

Objectives
- Review the weekly concept.
- Review oral vocabulary.

Today at a Glance

Oral Vocabulary

Comprehension
◉ Draw conclusions

Lesson Vocabulary
◉ Unfamiliar Words

Phonics
◉ Vowel patterns *ei, eigh*

Literary Terms
Dialogue and Narration

Assessment
Fluency
Comprehension

Research and Inquiry
Communicate

Spelling
Vowel patterns *ei* and *eigh*

Conventions
Comparative and superlative adverbs

Writing
Invitation

Check Oral Vocabulary
SUCCESS PREDICTOR

Concept Wrap Up

Question of the Week

How can different cultures contribute to the foods we eat?

Review the concept

Have students look back at the reading selections to find examples that demonstrate how different cultures contribute to the foods we eat.

Review Amazing Words

Display and review this week's concept map. Remind students that this week they have learned ten Amazing Words related to foods from different cultures. Have students use the Amazing Words and the concept map to answer the Question of the Week *How can different cultures contribute to the foods we eat?*

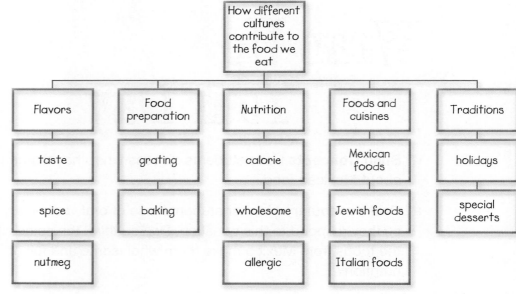

Concept map:

How different cultures contribute to the food we eat

Flavors	Food preparation	Nutrition	Foods and cuisines	Traditions
taste	grating	calorie	Mexican foods	holidays
spice	baking	wholesome	Jewish foods	special desserts
nutmeg		allergic	Italian foods	

ELL Check Concepts and Language Use the Day 5 instruction on ELL Poster 24 to monitor students' understanding of the lesson concept.

ELL Poster 24

Amazing Ideas

<aside>**Connect to the Big Question**</aside>

Have pairs of students discuss how the Question of the Week connects to the Big Question: *What happens when two ways of life come together?* Tell students to use the concept map and what they have learned in this week's Anchored Talks and reading selections to form an Amazing Idea—a realization or "big idea" about Cultures. Tell students to provide suggestions that build upon the ideas of their partner. Then ask each pair to share its Amazing Idea with the class.

Amazing Ideas might include these key concepts:

- People can blend foods from different cultures to create new dishes and cuisines.

- Foods from different cultures may contribute new flavors to the foods we eat.

- Different cultures may contribute new methods for preparing and cooking food.

- Foods from different cultures contribute to the nutritional value of the foods we eat.

<aside>**Write about it**</aside>

Have students write a few sentences about their Amazing Idea, beginning with "This week I learned…" They should support their Amazing Idea with facts, details, or explanations.

Amazing Words

nutrition	grumble
calorie	allergic
flavor	wholesome
spice	grate
nutmeg	agent

 It's Friday

MONITOR PROGRESS | **Check Oral Vocabulary**

Have individual's use this week's Amazing Words to describe foods from different cultures. Monitor students' abilities to use the Amazing Words and note which words you need to reteach.

If… students have difficulty using the Amazing Words,

then… reteach using the Oral Vocabulary Routine, pp. 289a, 294b, 304b, 314b, OV•1.

Day 1	**Day 2**	**Day 3**	**Day 4**	**Day 5**
Check Oral Vocabulary	Check Word Retelling	Check Retelling	Check Fluency	Check Oral Vocabulary

Success Predictor

ELL

English Language Learners
Concept Map Work with students to add new words to the concept map.

Oral Vocabulary

Success Predictor

Objectives
◎ Review draw conclusions.
◎ Review unfamiliar words.
◎ Review vowel patterns *ei, eigh.*
• Review dialogue and narration.

Comprehension Review
Draw Conclusions

Student Edition p. EI•6

Teach draw conclusions

Envision It!

Review the definition of draw conclusions on p. 292. Remind students that you draw conclusions when you use facts and details to make decisions about characters or events. For additional support, have students review p. EI•6 on draw conclusions.

Guide practice

Have student pairs give an example of a conclusion they can draw about information in the story *Jalapeño Bagels.* Then have pairs tell the facts and details from the story and the information they already know that they used to draw the conclusion.

On their own

For additional practice with draw conclusions, use *Let's Practice It!* page 327 on the *Teacher Resources DVD-ROM.*

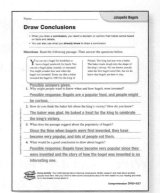

Let's Practice It!
TR DVD•327

Vocabulary Review
Unfamiliar Words

Teach unfamiliar words

Remind students that sometimes they can use context clues, the words and phrases around the word, to determine the meanings of unfamiliar words.

Guide practice

Review with students how to use context clues to determine the meaning of *braided* on p. 304. Remind them to use context clues to predict a meaning for the word, and then try the meaning in the sentence.

On their own

Have students practice using context clues to figure out the meanings of the words *ingredients* and *mixture* on p. 295. Ask them to record the words and phrases they use to determine the meanings.

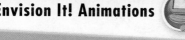
Phonics Review
 Vowel Patterns *ei, eigh*

Teach vowel patterns ei, eigh

Write the following sentences on the board. Have students read each one, first quietly to themselves and then aloud as you track the print.

> 1. Neither of our neighbors received today's newspaper.
> 2. The school nurse measured our height and weight.
> 3. My father painted the ceiling in his leisure time.
> 4. The freight was sent either by truck or train.
> 5. My eighteen-year-old brother is conceited.

Team Talk Have students discuss with a partner which words have the vowel sounds /ā/, /ē/, and /ī/ spelled *ei* or *eigh*. Ask them to identify the letters that spell the vowel sound in each word. Then call on individuals to share with the class.

Literary Terms Review
Dialogue and Narration

Teach

Have students reread pp. 302–306 of *Jalapeño Bagels.* Remind students that narration is the telling of a story or recounting of events in fiction or nonfiction. When people in the story speak, they use dialogue.

Guide practice

Discuss how narration is used to tell the story in *Jalapeño Bagels.* Ask students to say why the author tells the story through the eyes, mind, and voice of Pablo, the narrator. Have students point out examples of narration and dialogue from the section and discuss.

On their own

Have students make a T-chart with the headings *narration* and *dialogue.* Remind them that dialogue, the conversation between two or more people, is often combined with narration to tell a story. Have students list the events and information they learn from the narration under *narration* and what they learn from the dialogue under *dialogue.*

Lesson Vocabulary

bakery a place where bread and cake are made and sold

batch something made one at a time

boils to heat a liquid until it starts to bubble and give off steam

braided three or four strands woven together

dough flour and liquid mixed together to make bread, biscuits, and pastry

ingredients items that something is made from

mixture the combination of things mixed or blended together

ELL

English Language Learners

Articulation tip If students have trouble pronouncing words with long vowel spelling patterns *ei* or *eigh,* demonstrate how to pronounce them by slowly repeating words. Have students practice saying the words until they develop confidence.

Objectives
• Read grade-level text with fluency.

Plan to Assess Fluency

☑ **Week 1** Assess Advanced students.

☑ **Week 2** Assess Strategic Intervention students.

☑ **Week 3** Assess On-Level students.

☑ **This week assess Strategic Intervention students.**

☐ **Week 5** Assess any students you have not yet checked during this unit.

Set individual goals for students to enable them to reach the year-end goal.

• Current Goal: 102–112 WCPM

• Year-End Goal: 120 WCPM

Assessment

Check words corrected per minute

Fluency Make two copies of the fluency passage on p. 319k. As the student reads the text aloud, mark mistakes on your copy. Also mark where the student is at the end of one minute. To check the student's comprehension of the passage, have him or her retell you what was read. To figure words correct per minute (WCPM), subtract the number of mistakes from the total number of words read in one minute.

WCPM

Corrective feedback

If... students cannot read fluently at a rate of 102–112 WCPM,

then... make sure they practice with text at their independent reading level. Provide additional fluency practice by pairing nonfluent readers with fluent readers.

If... students already read at 120 WCPM,

then... have them read a book of their choice independently.

Small Group Time

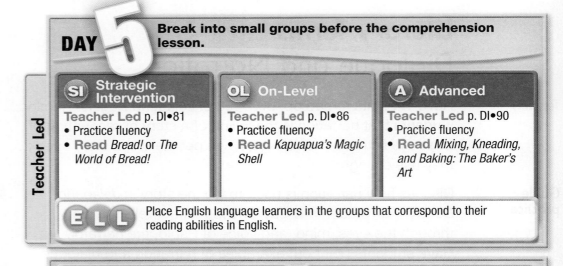

DAY 5 Break into small groups before the comprehension lesson.

Teacher Led

SI Strategic Intervention	**OL On-Level**	**A Advanced**
Teacher Led p. DI•81 • Practice fluency • Read *Bread!* or *The World of Bread!*	Teacher Led p. DI•86 • Practice fluency • Read *Kapuapua's Magic Shell*	Teacher Led p. DI•90 • Practice fluency • Read *Mixing, Kneading, and Baking: The Baker's Art*

ELL Place English language learners in the groups that correspond to their reading abilities in English.

Practice Stations	**Independent Activities**
• Words to Know • Get Fluent • Read for Meaning	• Grammar Jammer • Concept Talk Video • Vocabulary Activities

Making Challah

Making challah bread for the Sabbath is a tradition in many Jewish   12

families. The Sabbath is a day of rest. Many families share a special   25

dinner and spend time playing with family members. Challah may be   36

bought at a bakery. But many sons and daughters learn to make it from   50

an old family recipe. Some families have used the same one for many   63

generations.   64

First, the best bread ingredients are sought: flour, yeast, sugar,   74

salt, and eggs. The ingredients are mixed together. They are kneaded,   85

squeezing the dough between flour-covered hands until it is smooth. The   96

dough is left to rise in a warm place. After the first rising, the mixture   111

is punched down and left to rest for a few minutes. Then the dough is   126

separated into three pieces and braided into one long loaf. The bread is   139

set out to rise a second time.   146

Some people put poppy seeds or sesame seeds on top of the loaf.   159

Most people brush the uncooked dough with raw egg to give the crust a   173

glossy brown color when it is done baking.   181

Family recipes for challah may be different, but most families agree   192

that it is important to make bread for your family with loving thoughts.   205

MONITOR PROGRESS   • Check Fluency

Assessment

Check draw conclusions

Draw Conclusions Use "Arnie's Idea" on p. 319m to check students' understanding of drawing conclusions.

1. What was Arnie's idea? (Arnie's idea was to bake pizzas with foods from many different cultures.)

2. Why do you think people at the fair wanted to try more than one kind of pizza? (I can draw the conclusion that people enjoyed the pizzas and were curious to try the different ingredients.)

3. Why did Tess say that Arnie's idea was a great idea? (Tess thought Arnie's idea was a great idea because the third graders handed out all of the pizzas and their booth was very popular at the fair.)

Corrective feedback

If... students are unable to answer the comprehension questions, **then...** use the Reteach lesson in the *First Stop* book.

Arnie's Idea

The neighborhood public school was planning an International Fair. Kids and adults would display crafts, jewelry, and costumes from all over the world.

Mrs. Lanning's third graders wanted to do something really special to demonstrate that Americans eat foods from many different countries.

"How about making pizza?" suggested Arnie.

"That isn't such a good idea because pizza is just an Italian-American food," said Tess. "What about other countries?"

"Well, I meant we should bake pizzas in a special way," explained Arnie.

Then Arnie described his idea to the class.

On the evening of the fair, the third grade class had a large, colorful booth. Across the top, a sign said "Pizzas of the World." The class made little pizzas using ideas from all around the world. The Mexican pizza had taco sauce, cheese, and ground beef on it. The Chinese pizza had vegetables and little shrimp. The kids also made Jamaican pizza, German pizza, Indian pizza, Vietnamese pizza, and more.

Mrs. Lanning baked little pizza after pizza in an oven. The third graders served little pizzas to a long line of kids, parents, and teachers. Most people wanted to try more than one kind.

Tess, Arnie, and all the third graders were busy the whole evening of the fair. When it was finally over, the third grade class had no pizza left!

As the class cleaned up, Tess looked at Arnie and said, "Hey, Arnie, I told you this wasn't such a good idea."

Then she added, "It was a great idea!"

MONITOR PROGRESS   • **Draw conclusions**

Objectives
- Communicate inquiry results.
- Administer spelling test.
- Review compartive and superlative adverbs.

Research and Inquiry
Communicate

Present ideas   Have students share their inquiry results by presenting their articles and giving a brief talk on their research. Have students use the outline that they created on Day 3 to guide their talk.

Listening and speaking   Remind students how to be good speakers and how to communicate effectively with their audience.

- Respond to relevant questions with appropriate details.
- Speak clearly and loudly.
- Keep eye contact with audience members.
- Speak at an appropriate rate so that audience members can easily understand the ideas communicated.

Remind students of these tips for being a good listener.

- Wait until the speaker has finished before raising your hand to ask a relevant question.
- Be polite, even if you disagree.

Spelling Test
Vowel Patterns *ei* and *eigh*

Spelling test

To administer the spelling test, refer to the directions, words, and sentences on p. 293c.

Conventions
Extra Practice

Teach

Remind students that comparative adverbs compare two people, places, or things and often end in *-er.* Superlative adverbs compare three or more people, places, or things and often end in *-est.* Comparative and superlative adverbs that end in the suffix *-ly* use *more* and *most.*

Guide practice

Have students think of holidays to complete the sentence stems orally.

> _____ is soon.
>
> _____ is sooner.
>
> _____ is soonest.

Daily Fix-It

Use Daily Fix-It numbers 9 and 10 in the right margin.

On their own

Write these sentences on the board. Have students read aloud each sentence and replace the underlined phrase with the correct form of the adverb. Students should complete *Let's Practice It!* page 328 on the *Teacher Resources DVD-ROM.*

1. **The rolls bake <u>more quicker</u> than the bread.** (quicker)

2. **The cheetah runs the <u>most fastest</u> of any animal.** (fastest)

3. **The bus traveled <u>slowly</u> than yesterday.** (more slowly)

4. **My phone rings <u>most quietly</u> than Sara's.** (more quietly)

5. **The tacos taste <u>spiciest</u> than the soup.** (spicier)

Daily Fix-It

9. Matt creted a knew recipe for muffins. *(created; new)*

10. The muffins has strawberrys inside. *(have; strawberries)*

Let's Practice It!
TR DVD•328

Objectives
- Proofread revised draft of invitation, including correct use of comparative and superlative adverbs.
- Create and present final draft.

Writing—Invitation
Adverbs

Review
Revising

Remind students that yesterday they revised their invitations, paying particular attention to adding details to better inform their reader. Today they will proofread their invitations.

MINI-LESSON

Proofread for Adverbs

Writing Transparency 24C, TR DVD

■ **Teach** When we proofread, we look closely at our work, searching for errors in mechanics. Today we will focus on making sure we have used comparative and superlative adverbs correctly.

■ **Model** Display Writing Transparency 24C. Let's look at a sentence from the invitation we started yesterday. I see a problem in the fifth sentence with the phrase *most fastest.* To form most superlative adverbs, you add *-est.* For adverbs that end in the suffix *-ly,* you use the word *most.* You do not use *most* with adverbs that use the *-est* form. Because *fastest* ends with *-est,* I will take out the word *most.* Have students reread their invitations and check for correct use of comparative and superlative adverbs. Then explain to students that they should reread their invitations several times, each time looking for different types of errors: spelling, punctuation, capitalization, and grammar. Have students pay particular attention to the time of their event, checking for proper use of the colon.

Proofread

Display the Proofreading Tips. Ask students to proofread their compositions, using the Proofreading Tips and paying particular attention to comparative and superlative adverbs. Circulate around the room answering students' questions. When students have finished editing their own work, have pairs proofread one another's invitations.

Proofreading Tips

✔ Be sure that all adverbs are used correctly.

✔ Check for correct use of the colon when writing times (e.g. 5:00).

✔ Remember to capitalize geographical names and places.

Present Have students incorporate revisions and proofreading edits into their invitations to create a final draft.

Remind students that invitations often include creative drawings or illustrations. Have students copy their invitations on a folded sheet of cardstock and illustrate the final draft. Alternatively, students can use an invitation template from a desktop publishing program or the Internet. Have students type their final draft into the template. Then have them add photographs or relevant clip art or print the invitation and add their own illustrations.

ROUTINE   Quick Write for Fluency   Team Talk

1. **Talk** Have pairs discuss what they learned about writing invitations this week.

2. **Write** Each student writes a paragraph comparing the features of an invitation and the features of a friendly letter.

3. **Share** Partners read their paragraphs to each other.

Routines Flip Chart

Teacher Note

Writing self-evaluation Make copies of the Writing Self-Evaluation Guide on p. 39 of the *Reader's and Writer's Notebook* and hand out to students.

ELL

English Language Learners

Support editing Have students circle any adverbs in their invitations that end in *-er* or *-est*. Remind students that adverbs with these endings will not use the words *more* or *most*. Have students underline the word before each circle and delete it if it is *more* or *most*.

Poster preview Prepare students for next week by using Week 25, ELL Poster 25. Read the poster Talk-Through to introduce the concept and vocabulary. Ask students to identify and describe objects and actions in the art.

Selection summary Send home the summary of *Me and Uncle Romie* in English and in the students' home languages, if available. Students can read the summary with family members.

Preview NEXT WEEK

How does city life compare to life in the country? Tell students that next week they will read about a boy who travels from North Carolina to spend the summer in New York City.

DAY 5 Assessment Checkpoints for the Week

Weekly Assessment

Use pp. 169–174 of *Weekly Tests* to check:

✔ **Phonics** Vowel Patterns *ei, eigh*

✔ **Comprehension Skill** Draw Conclusions

✔ **Lesson Vocabulary**

✔ Review **Comprehension Skill** Sequence of Events

bakery	dough
batch	ingredients
boils	mixture
braided	

Weekly Tests

A Advanced

OL On-Level

SI Strategic Intervention

Differentiated Assessment

Use pp. 139–144 of *Fresh Reads for Fluency and Comprehension* to check:

✔ **Comprehension Skill** Draw Conclusions

✔ Review **Comprehension Skill** Sequence

✔ **Fluency** Words Correct Per Minute

Fresh Reads for Fluency and Comprehension

Managing Assessment

Use *Assessment Handbook* for:

✔ **Weekly Assessment Blackline Masters for Monitoring Progress**

✔ **Observation Checklists**

✔ **Record-Keeping Forms**

✔ **Portfolio Assessment**

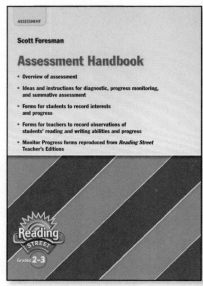

Assessment Handbook

Teacher Notes

Small Group Time

Pacing Small Group Instruction

15–20 min

5-Day Plan

DAY 1	• Reinforce the concept
	• Read Leveled Readers
	  Concept Literacy
	  Below Level

DAY 2	• ◉ Draw Conclusions • ◉ Summarize • Revisit Student Edition pp. 296–303
DAY 3	• ◉ Unfamiliar Words • Revisit Student Edition pp. 304–309
DAY 4	• Practice Retelling • Read/Revisit Student Edition pp. 314–317
DAY 5	• Reread for fluency • Reread Leveled Readers

3- or 4-Day Plan

DAY 1	• Reinforce the concept • Read Leveled Readers
DAY 2	• ◉ Draw Conclusions • ◉ Summarize • Revisit Student Edition pp. 296–303
DAY 3	• ◉ Unfamiliar Words • Revisit Student Edition pp. 304–309

DAY 4	• Practice Retelling
	• Read/Revisit Student
	  Edition pp. 314–317
	• Reread for fluency
	• Reread Leveled
	  Readers

3-Day Plan: Eliminate the shaded box.

SI *Strategic Intervention*

DAY 1

Build Background

■ **Reinforce the Concept** Talk about the weekly question *How can different cultures contribute to the foods we eat?* What kinds of ethnic foods have you eaten? What kinds can you name? Guide students' discussion of different foods based on what restaurants and grocery stores offer in your area. Pizza was invented in Italy. The British made fish and chips popular. Some Chinese foods came from China, but others—such as fortune cookies—were invented in the United States. French fries come from France, but people all over the world consider them an American food. Foods from different cultures can blend into delicious combinations, as we will learn in this week's selection, *Jalapeño Bagels.* Then have students add new words to the concept map.

Preview Decodable Practice Reader 24A

■ **Before Reading** Review the words on p. 97 of Decodable Practice Reader 24A. Then have students blend these words from the text: *eight, either, ceiling, neighbor, receive, weight,* and *freight.* Be sure students understand the meaning of such words as *neighbor* and *receive.* Guide students through the text by doing a picture walk.

Objectives
• Participate in teacher-led discussions by answering questions with appropriate detail.

SI Strategic Intervention DAY 1

For a complete literacy instructional plan and additional practice with this week's target skills and strategies, see the **Leveled Reader Teaching Guide.**

Concept Literacy Reader

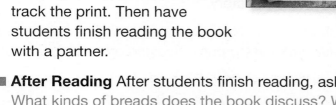

- **Read** *Bread!*
- **Before Reading** Preview the book with students, focusing on key concepts and vocabulary. Then help students set a purpose for reading.
- **During Reading** Read the first two pages aloud while students track the print. Then have students finish reading the book with a partner.
- **After Reading** After students finish reading, ask: What kinds of breads does the book discuss? Where do those breads come from? *(bagels from Poland, tortillas from Mexico, pita from Israel, pizza from Italy, roti from India)*

Below-Level Reader

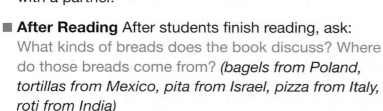

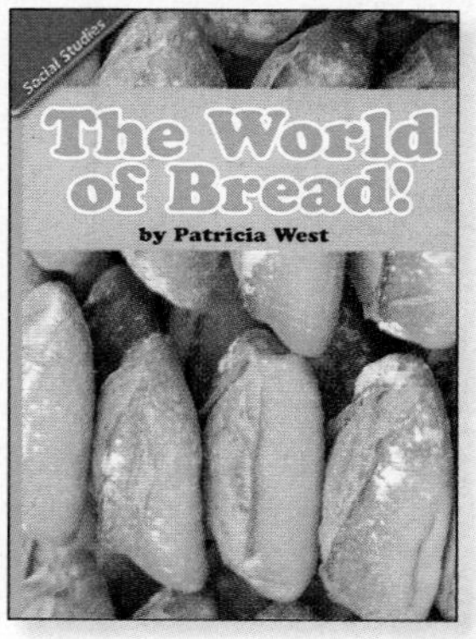

- **Read** *The World of Bread!*
- **Before Reading** Help students use the photographs to preview the book. Then help them set a purpose for reading.
- **During Reading** Read the first two pages aloud. Then do a choral reading of the next three pages. If students are able, have them read and discuss the remainder of the book with a partner. Ask: What are the basic ingredients in bread? *(flour and water)*
- **After Reading** Ask students to look at and discuss the concept map. Connect the Below-Level Reader to the weekly question *How can different cultures contribute to the foods we eat?* Ask: How did Polish newcomers to the United States add to the breads we eat? *(They brought the recipe for bagels.)* If you eat engera bread at home, to what culture does your family probably belong? *(Ethiopian)*

MONITOR PROGRESS

If... students have difficulty reading the selection with a partner,
then... have them follow along as they listen to the Leveled Readers DVD-ROM.

If... students have trouble understanding the different breads described,
then... review the glossary on p. 12 and help them locate each word in the text.

Objectives

- Participate in teacher-led discussions by answering questions with appropriate detail

DAY 2

Reinforce Comprehension

More Reading

Use additional Leveled Readers or other texts at students' instructional levels to reinforce this week's skills and strategies. For text suggestions, see the Leveled Reader Database or the Leveled Readers Skills Chart on pp. CL22–CL27.

◉ **Skill Draw Conclusions** Review with students *Envision It!* p. El•6 on Draw Conclusions. Then use p. 292 to review the skill. What does it mean to draw a conclusion?

◉ **Strategy Summarize** Review the definition of *summarize*. Remind students to pause regularly as they read and to summarize events in a sentence or two. For additional support, refer students to *Envision It!* p. El•25.

Revisit *Jalapeño Bagels* on pp. 296–303. As partners read, have them apply the comprehension skill and the strategy to the story.

- What are Pablo's mother's cultural roots? How do you know? *(She is Mexican. She speaks Spanish and is skilled at making* pan dulce *and other Mexican baked goods.)*

- What are Pablo's father's cultural roots? How do you know? *(He is Jewish. He speaks Yiddish and is skilled at making the Jewish bread* challah *and bagels.)*

- How would you summarize the story so far? *(Pablo helps his parents at their bakery and tries to decide what food to bring to school for International Day.)*

- What conclusion can you draw about how well Pablo gets along with his parents? Think about what they talk about and how they treat one another. *(Pablo helps his parents. They let him pick out a treat to bring to school to share with his classmates. Pablo and his parents have friendly conversations. Therefore, the reader can conclude that he and his parents get along well.)*

Use the During Reading Differentiated Instruction for additional support for struggling readers.

MONITOR PROGRESS

If... students have difficulty reading along with the group,

then... have them follow along as they listen to the AudioText.

Objectives
- Draw and support logical conclusions about text.
- Summarize the plot's main events.

 SI Strategic Intervention

DAY **3**

Reinforce Vocabulary

■ **Reread for Fluency** Use Decodable Practice Reader 24A.

■ **Decoding Multisyllabic Words** Write *slotted* and model how to look for meaningful parts in the word to read it. First I notice the ending *-ed* and see that the *t* was doubled when *-ed* was added. I cover the ending and read the base word: *slot. Slot* means "a narrow opening." Then I blend the two parts of the word: *slot ted, slotted.* The ending *-ed* shows the past tense of verbs or makes verb into adjectives. This word means "having a slot" or "having slots."

◉ **Unfamiliar Words/Context Clues** Write the word *Yiddish* on the board. From context clues I can tell this is a language. On p. 303, Pablo says his father "speaks English and Yiddish." *Yiddish* is capitalized the way the names of languages are. I am not sure exactly what kind of language it is. In the dictionary I discover that it is a language spoken by Jewish people whose cultural roots are in Eastern Europe.

■ **Revisit** *Jalapeño Bagels* on pp. 304–309. Review *Words!* on p. W•7. Encourage students to use context clues to figure out the meaning of unfamiliar words. When Pablo says that his father *fishes* the bagels out of a pot, what is he talking about? Is he referring to the animals called fish? *(The author does not mention fish until later in the story. At this point, Pablo's father is talking about an action that looks like fishing because it has to do with pulling something out of the water.)*

Use the During Reading Differentiated Instruction for additional support for struggling readers.

Student Edition p. W•7

More Reading

Use additional Leveled Readers or other texts at students' instructional levels to reinforce this week's skills and strategies. For text suggestions, see the Leveled Reader Database or the Leveled Readers Skills Chart on pp. CL22–CL27.

> **MONITOR PROGRESS**
>
> **If...** students need more practice with the lesson vocabulary,
> **then...** use *Envision It! Pictured Vocabulary Cards*.

Objectives
• Use context to determine the relevant meaning of unfamiliar words.

Small Group Time

Practice Retelling

■ **Retell** Guide students in using the Retelling Cards to list story events in sequence. In a few sentences, what is this story about? *(Pablo's dad is Jewish, and his mom is Mexican. He helps his parents at their bakery. He decides to share jalapeño bagels with his classmates because the bagels are a mixture of Jewish and Mexican cultures, like him.)*

If students struggle, model a fluent retelling.

Genre Focus

■ **Before Reading or Revisiting** "Foods of Mexico: A Delicious Blend" on pp. 314–317, read aloud the genre information about expository text on p. 314. Recall the Leveled Reader *The World of Bread,* rereading portions as needed. *The World of Bread* is also expository text. How does it give information about bread? *(It gives a photograph and a paragraph or two about each kind of bread.)* Then have students scan the pages for headings, photographs, and captions.

■ **During Reading or Revisiting** Have students perform a choral reading of the selection. Stop to discuss Spanish words, other unfamiliar words, and proper nouns.

■ **After Reading or Revisiting** Have students share their reactions to the paired selection. Then guide them through the Reading Across Texts and Writing Across Texts activities.

- When did the Spanish learn about rice? *(when they established colonies in Asia)*

- What did you learn about Mexican food from reading this book? *(Mexican food is the result of a blending of Native American and Spanish influences.)*

MONITOR PROGRESS

If... students have difficulty retelling the selection,
then... have them review the story using the illustrations.

Objectives
• Identify the topic of the text.

For a complete literacy instructional plan and additional practice with this week's target skills and strategies, see the **Leveled Reader Teaching Guide.**

Concept Literacy Reader

Bread!

■ **Model** Model the fluency skill of accuracy for students. Ask students to listen carefully as you read aloud the first two pages of *Bread!* Have students note that you read all the words that are on the page without leaving out any words, putting in other words, or substituting one word for another.

■ **Fluency Routine**

1. Have students reread passages from *Bread!* with a partner.

2. For optimal fluency, students should reread three to four times.

3. As students read, monitor fluency and provide corrective feedback. Have students work slowly at first to make sure they read accurately and then speed up as they become more familiar with the text.

See *Routines Flip Chart* for more help with fluency.

■ **Retell** Have students retell *Bread!* Prompt as necessary.

Below-Level Reader

The World of Bread!

■ **Model** Ask students to listen carefully as you read aloud the first two pages of *The World of Bread,* emphasizing accurate reading.

■ **Fluency Routine**

1. Have students reread passages from *The World of Bread* with a partner or individually.

2. For optimal fluency, students should reread three to four times.

3. As students read, monitor fluency and provide corrective feedback. Discuss how taking care to read accurately helps to ensure that you understand what the author wrote.

See *Routines Flip Chart* for more help with fluency.

■ **Retell** For additional practice, have students retell *The World of Bread* page by page, using the illustrations. Prompt students as necessary.

• What are some kinds of flat bread? *(tortilla, chapati, pita, engera, pizza)*

• How do French baguettes differ from flat breads? *(Baguettes are made with yeast.)*

MONITOR PROGRESS

If... students have difficulty reading fluently,

then... provide additional fluency practice by pairing nonfluent readers with fluent ones.

Objectives
• Read aloud grade-level appropriate text with fluency.

Small Group Time

Pacing Small Group Instruction

15–20 min

5-Day Plan

DAY 1	• Expand the concept • Read On-Level Reader
DAY 2	• Draw Conclusions • Summarize • Revisit Student Edition pp. 296–303
DAY 3	• Unfamiliar Words • Revisit Student Edition pp. 304–309
DAY 4	• Practice Retelling • Read/Revisit Student Edition pp. 314–317
DAY 5	• Reread for fluency • Reread On-Level Reader

3- or 4-Day Plan

DAY 1	• Expand the concept • Read On-Level Reader
DAY 2	• Draw Conclusions • Summarize • Revisit Student Edition pp. 296–303
DAY 3	• Unfamiliar Words • Revisit Student Edition pp. 304–309
DAY 4	• Practice Retelling • Read/Revisit Student Edition pp. 314–317 • Reread for fluency • Reread On-Level Reader

3-Day Plan: Eliminate the shaded box.

OL — On-Level

DAY 1

Build Background

■ **Expand the Concept** Connect to the weekly question *How can different cultures contribute to the foods we eat?* and expand the concept. Some foods are eaten mostly during celebrations instead of at everyday meals. You are about to read a story about foods associated with a Hawaiian party called a *luau.* Add new words to the concept map.

On-Level Reader

For a complete literacy instructional plan and additional practice with this week's target skills and strategies, see the **Leveled Reader Teaching Guide.**

■ **Before Reading** *Kapuapua's Magic Shell,* have students preview the On-Level Reader by looking at the title, cover, and pictures in the book. Ask them to start a concept web about the story that will be constructed around a center oval labeled *Luau.* You are going to read about a delicious Hawaiian feast called a luau. As you read, add the foods and ingredients you encounter in your story to your concept web.

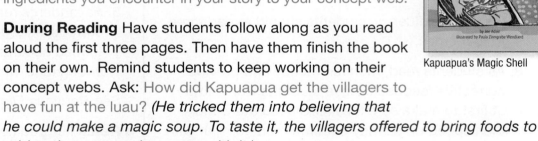

Kapuapua's Magic Shell

■ **During Reading** Have students follow along as you read aloud the first three pages. Then have them finish the book on their own. Remind students to keep working on their concept webs. Ask: How did Kapuapua get the villagers to have fun at the luau? *(He tricked them into believing that he could make a magic soup. To taste it, the villagers offered to bring foods to add to the soup and to serve with it.)*

■ **After Reading** Have students form pairs and compare their webs.

• How does this story help you to understand Hawaiian culture? *(It gives you an idea of what kinds of foods you would find at a Hawaiian luau and also explains what a traditional Hawaiian celebration might be like.)*

• Which food on your concept web would you most like to taste? Why?

Objectives
• Participate in teacher-led discussions by answering questions with appropriate detail.

 OL On-Level DAY 2

Expand Comprehension

Skill Draw Conclusions Use p. 292 to review the definition of draw conclusions. For additional review, see Draw Conclusions in *Envision It!* p. EI•6. One way to approach drawing conclusions is to think of yourself as a detective, noticing all of the clues in a story and trying to figure out what they mean. You can combine pieces of evidence and use them to draw a conclusion—a general idea about a character, place, or event.

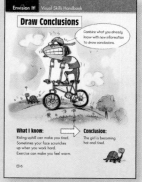

Student Edition p. EI•6

Strategy Summarize Review the definition of *summarize.* For additional support, use the Extend Thinking questions during reading or refer students to p. EI•25 of *Envision It!*

Revisit *Jalapeño Bagels* on pp. 296–303. Ask students to draw conclusions and summarize ideas based on the details in the story.

- At the beginning of the story, why do you think Pablo's mother tells him to help out in the bakery rather than just giving him whatever he wants? *(Some students may conclude that she wants him to learn responsibility, so she offers the food treats as payment in exchange for work. Other students may conclude that the mother enjoys having her son nearby and invites him to the bakery so that she can talk with him.)*

- Pablo describes the pumpkin turnovers as "flaky and golden brown." He also mentions that some customers visit the bakery just for the turnovers. What can you conclude about the turnovers based on this information? *(They are tasty and popular.)*

- How do you think the chango bars will turn out? Why? *(They will taste delicious because Pablo and his mother both added extra chocolate chips.)*

More Reading

Use additional Leveled Readers or other texts at students' instructional levels to reinforce this week's skills and strategies. For text suggestions, see the Leveled Reader Database or the Leveled Readers Skills Chart on pp. CL22–CL27.

Objectives
- Draw and support logical conclusions about text.
- Summarize the plot's main events.

On-Level

DAY 3

Expand Vocabulary

Student Edition p. W•7

More Reading

Use additional Leveled Readers or other texts at students' instructional levels to reinforce this week's skills and strategies. For text suggestions, see the Leveled Reader Database or the Leveled Readers Skills Chart on pp. CL22–CL27.

Unfamiliar Words/Context Clues Remind students that almost any reading assignment they complete for school will have at least some unfamiliar words in it.

- What are some ways to figure out the meaning of an unfamiliar word? *(break it into parts; use context clues; check a dictionary or glossary; ask someone for help.)*

- How can you use context clues to understand unfamiliar words? *(look at the words and phrases around the unfamiliar word and think about what other words might make sense.)*

- This selection includes many unfamiliar words in Spanish and Yiddish. What clues does the author give you so you can figure them out? *(Sometimes the author explains the terms in the text, as in "Panaderia is what Mama calls our bakery." At other times the author includes a dash between the term and the definition, as in "Next we make empanadas de calabaza—pumpkin turnovers.")*

Revisit *Jalapeño Bagels* on pp. 304–309. Encourage students to use context clues throughout the selection and as they read other stories and nonfiction texts. Write the word *turnover* as you say it aloud. Then ask:

- Look at the picture and read the description of the turnovers early in the story. What do these context clues suggest about how this pastry got its name? *(It is called that because you fold—or turn—the dough over the filling inside.)*

- Based on the description, what do you think a pumpkin turnover is like? *(Possibly it is like a single-serving pumpkin pie.)*

Objectives
- Use context to determine the relevant meaning of unfamiliar words.

 DAY 4

Practice Retelling

■ **Retell** To assess students' comprehension, use the Retelling Cards. Monitor retelling and prompt students as needed.

Genre Focus

■ **Before Reading or Revisiting** "Foods of Mexico: A Delicious Blend" on pp. 314–317, read aloud the genre information about expository text on p. 314. Remind students that the purpose of expository text is to explain a topic. Have students preview "Foods of Mexico: A Delicious Blend" and set a purpose for reading. Ask:

• How do the photos help to explain the topic? *(The photographs have labels identifying the foods they show.)*

• Why are some words in italic (slanted) type? *(This identifies them as coming from languages other than English.)*

■ **During Reading or Revisiting** Have students read with you. Ask:

• What is covered in the section titled "Native Foods"? *(foods of the Native American people of Mexico)*

• What is covered in the section titled "The Spanish Flavor"? *(foods brought to Mexico from Spain)*

• What is covered in the last section? *(a combination of a Native American food and a European food)*

■ **After Reading or Revisiting** Have students share their reactions to "Foods of Mexico: A Delicious Blend." Then have them write a paragraph describing their favorite food and what culture or cultures they think it comes from.

Objectives
• Identify the topic of the text.

Small Group Time

On-Level Reader

■ **Model** Read aloud the first two pages of the On-Level Reader *Kapuapua's Magic Shell,* emphasizing accuracy. If you wish, read a few passages poorly by skipping a word or two or by substituting one word for another, such as *sell* for *shell.* Talk about how inaccurate reading makes it difficult or impossible for the reader and the listener to understand what the author meant.

Kapuapua's Magic Shell

■ **Fluency Routine**

1. Have students reread passages from *Kapuapua's Magic Shell* with a partner.

2. For optimal fluency, students should reread passages three to four times.

3. As students read, monitor fluency and provide corrective feedback. If they stumble over words, have them work slowly at first and then speed up. Discuss how reading accurately ensures that you understand what the author wrote.

See *Routines Flip Chart* for more help with fluency.

■ **Retell** For additional practice, have students use the illustrations as a guide to retell *Kapuapua's Magic Shell.* Prompt as necessary.

• What does Kapuapua look like? *(He has white hair, a gentle smile, and a big belly.)*

• Who seem to be Kapuapua's first friends among the islanders? *(the children)*

• How does Kapuapua get the idea to make the magic seashell soup? *(A coconut falls on his head.)*

Objectives
• Read aloud grade-level appropriate text with fluency.

DAY 1

Build Background

■ **Extend the Concept** Lead a discussion about the weekly question *How can different cultures contribute to the foods we eat?* What are some special occasions when members of different ethnic groups might gather and eat foods from their cultures? *(Answers might include patriotic holidays, religious festivals, sports events, arts festivals, and neighborhood social gatherings.)*

Advanced Reader

For a complete literacy instructional plan and additional practice with this week's target skills and strategies, see the **Leveled Reader Teaching Guide.**

■ **Before Reading** *Mixing, Kneading, and Baking: The Baker's Art,* ask students to look at the illustrations and use them to consider what the book will be about. Then have students set a purpose for reading.

■ **During Reading** Have students read the Advanced Reader independently and encourage them to think critically.

• Which description of the bread-making process did you like better, the detailed narrative in Chapter 1 or the step-by-step chart in Table 2? Why? *(Some students will prefer the longer, descriptive version, while others will like the visual summary that the chart provides.)*

• Why do you think Claudia says that patience in baking is just as important as fresh ingredients? *(because making a good loaf of bread involves many steps and also a lot of time waiting for the yeast to rise)*

■ **After Reading** Have students review the Advanced Reader to find four unfamiliar words. Ask students to decide on a likely meaning by using context clues and then confirm their guesses by using a dictionary. Then ask students to write statements or questions that include the words they chose and context clues hinting at each word's meaning. Discuss the book and the statements or questions students wrote.

■ **Now Try This** Assign "Now Try This" at the end of the Advanced Reader.

Objectives
• Participate in teacher-led discussions by answering questions with appropriate detail.

Pacing Small Group Instruction

15–20 min

5-Day Plan

DAY 1	• Extend the concept • Read Advanced Reader
DAY 2	• Draw Conclusions • Summarize • Revisit Student Edition pp. 296–303
DAY 3	• Unfamiliar Words • Revisit Student Edition pp. 304–309
DAY 4	• Expository Text • Read/Revisit Student Edition pp. 314–317
DAY 5	• Reread for fluency • Reread Advanced Reader

3- or 4-Day Plan

DAY 1	• Extend the concept • Read Advanced Reader
DAY 2	• Draw Conclusions • Summarize • Revisit Student Edition pp. 296–303
DAY 3	• Unfamiliar Words • Revisit Student Edition pp. 304–309
DAY 4	• Expository Text • Read/Revisit Student Edition pp. 314–317 • Reread for fluency • Reread Advanced Reader

3-Day Plan: Eliminate the shaded box.

More Reading

Use additional Leveled Readers or other texts at students' instructional levels to reinforce this week's skills and strategies. For text suggestions, see the Leveled Reader Database or the Leveled Readers Skills Chart on pp. CL22–CL27.

Extend Comprehension

Skill Draw Conclusions Point out to students that the narrative nonfiction that they studied the day before, *Mixing, Kneading, and Baking: The Baker's Art,* will provide valuable background for the realistic fiction selection they are about to read, *Jalapeño Bagels.* What conclusions might you draw before you even start reading when I tell you that the characters in this book operate a small family bakery? *(Students might conclude that the characters must be quite hard-working and that they bake many kinds of bread.)*

Strategy Summarize Review the definition of the strategy. Remind students to pause occasionally as they read to summarize what has happened in the story so far.

Revisit *Jalapeño Bagels* on pp. 296–303. Have students draw conclusions and summarize as they read about this family and their bakery.

- After reading p. 298, what can you conclude about the narrator and his experiences with the bakery? *(He has worked there often, but it is not a job he is expected to do on Sundays because he gets to choose whether to go in or not.)*

- Summarize the information on p. 300. *(Pablo and his mother make* empanadas de calabaza, *which are pumpkin turnovers.)*

- What conclusions can you make about the author based on what you have read so far? *(She probably loves bread! She describes how to make many kinds of baked goods, so she must believe that this information is interesting and important. She knows some things about Mexican cooking, such as what the different baked goods are called and how they are made.)*

During reading, use the Extend Thinking questions and the During Reading Differentiated Instruction for additional support.

Objectives

- Draw and support logical conclusions about text.
- Summarize the plot's main events.

Extend Vocabulary

Unfamiliar Words/Context Clues Read passages from the Advanced Reader and help students understand unfamiliar words.

- "Yeast is a tiny, live organism. It eats the sugars that are part of the dough." **Ask:** If you use context clues, what would you say the word *organism* means? *(a living thing)* How did you figure that out? *(The text explains that yeast is an organism and that yeast is a living thing that eats.)*

- "Loaves can take two hours to cool. Once again, Claudia must be patient." **Ask:** What does *patient* mean? *(willing to wait)* How do you know? *(The words "can take two hours to cool" and "once again" suggest that* patient *means "willing to wait".)*

Revisit *Jalapeño Bagels* on pp. 304–309. Remind students to use a dictionary when context clues are insufficient to determine the meaning of any unfamiliar words.

- How did you figure out the Spanish and Yiddish words in this selection? *(They are in italic—slanted—type, so they are easy to notice. Sometimes the author uses the word* is *or* means *or a dash before the explanation of the term.)*

- How can you use what you have learned by reading this selection to help you read other texts? *(Students may say that reading unfamiliar terms will give them confidence as they read textbooks.)*

■ **Critical Thinking/Creative Thinking** Encourage students to think about what they have read.

- Pablo says he likes jalapeño bagels because "they are a mixture of both of you—just like me!" What does he mean by this? *(His parents are bakers. His father speaks Yiddish and his mother speaks Spanish. Jalapeño bagels are a Spanish-Yiddish baked good.)*

- What food do you think best represents your family's culture? Why?

More Reading

Use additional Leveled Readers or other texts at students' instructional levels to reinforce this week's skills and strategies. For text suggestions, see the Leveled Reader Database or the Leveled Readers Skills Chart on pp. CL22–CL27.

Objectives
- Use context to determine the relevant meaning of unfamiliar words.

A — Advanced

Genre Focus

"Foods of Mexico: A Delicious Blend"

■ **Before Reading or Revisiting** "Foods of Mexico: A Delicious Blend" on pp. 314–317, review the panel information on expository text. Then have students use the text features to set a purpose for reading.

■ **During Reading or Revisiting** Encourage students to think critically and creatively. For example, ask:

- What main idea do you think the author wants you to understand? *(Mexican cuisine is a blend of Native American and European cultures.)*

- How do the details in the section titled "Tortillas or Bolillos?" support this main idea? *(Mexicans blend native and European traditions in the* torta de tamal, *or tamale sandwich.)*

- Which of the foods would you most like to try? Why?

■ **After Reading or Revisiting** Guide students through the Reading Across Texts and Writing Across Texts activities.

Objectives
- Identify the topic of the text.

A — Advanced

■ **Reread for Fluency** Have students silently reread passages from the Advanced Reader. Then have them reread aloud with a partner or individually. As students read, monitor fluency and provide corrective feedback. If students read fluently on the first reading, they do not need to reread three to four times.

■ **Retell** Ask students to summarize the main idea and key details from the Advanced Reader *Mixing, Kneading, and Baking: The Baker's Art.*

■ **Now Try This** Have partners complete their research projects from "Now Try This" at the end of the Advanced Reader.

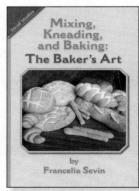

Mixing, Kneading, and Baking: The Baker's Art

Objectives
- Read aloud grade-level appropriate text with fluency.

 English Language Learners

The ELL lessons are organized by strands. Use them to scaffold the weekly curriculum of lessons or during small group time instruction.

Academic Language

Students will hear or read the following academic language in this week's core instruction. As students encounter the vocabulary, provide a simple definition or concrete example. Then ask students to suggest an example or synonym of the word and identify available cognates.

Skill Words	conclusion (*conclusion*) comparative (*comparativo*) summarize	superlative (*superlativo*) adverb (*adverbio*) unfamiliar words
Concept Words	culture (*culture*) contribute (*contribuir*)	recipe (*receta*)

*Spanish cognates in parentheses

Concept Development

How can different cultures contribute to the foods we eat?

■ **Preteach Concept**

- **Prior Knowledge** Have students turn to pp. 288–289 in the Student Edition. Call attention to the pictures of food and have students express ideas about different kinds of food. What are the names of the different kinds of food in these pictures? Do the pictures show any food that you like? Which ones?

- **Discuss Concept** Have students' express ideas about how different cultures contribute to the foods we eat. Do you like tacos? Do know where tacos came from? Why do we now eat tacos in the United States? Can you think of other foods that we eat that come from other cultures? Supply background information as needed.

- **Poster Talk-Through** Read aloud the Poster Talk-Through on ELL Poster 24 and work through the Day 1 activities.

■ **Daily Concept and Vocabulary Development** Use the daily activities on ELL Poster 24 to build concept and vocabulary knowledge.

Objectives
• Use prior knowledge and experiences to understand meanings in English.

Content Objectives

• Use concept vocabulary related to how different cultures can contribute to the foods we eat.

Language Objectives

• Express ideas in response to art and discussion.

Daily Planner

DAY 1	• **Frontload Concept** • **Preteach** Comprehension Skill, Vocabulary, Phonics/Spelling, Conventions • **Writing**
DAY 2	• **Review** Concept, Vocabulary, Comprehension Skill • **Frontload Main Selection** • **Practice** Phonics/Spelling, Conventions/Writing
DAY 3	• **Review** Concept, Comprehension Skill, Vocabulary, Conventions/Writing • **Reread Main Selection** • **Practice** Phonics/Spelling
DAY 4	• **Review Concept** • **Read ELL/ELD Readers** • **Practice** Phonics/Spelling, Conventions/Writing
DAY 5	• **Review** Concept, Vocabulary, Comprehension Skill, Phonics/Spelling, Conventions • **Reread ELL/ELD Readers** • **Writing**

*See the ELL Handbook for ELL Workshops with targeted instruction.

Concept Talk Video

Use the Concept Talk Video Routine (*ELL Handbook,* p. 477) to build background knowledge about food from different cultures. For more listening practice, see Use Classroom Resources (*ELL Handbook,* pp. 406–407).

Support for English Language Learners

Language Objectives

- Understand and use basic vocabulary.
- Learn meanings of grade-level vocabulary.

Basic Vocabulary

■ **High-Frequency Words** Use the ELL Vocabulary Routine on p. 471 of the *ELL Handbook* to systematically teach newcomers the first 300 sight words in English. Students who began learning ten words per week at the beginning of the year are now learning words 231–240 (*ELL Handbook,* p. 454). Page 446 of the handbook contains a bank of strategies that you can use to ensure students' mastery of high-frequency words.

Lesson Vocabulary

■ **Preteach** Use the following routine to preteach the Lesson Vocabulary:

1. Distribute copies of this week's Word Cards (*ELL Handbook,* p. 167).

2. Display ELL Poster 24 and reread the Poster Talk-Through.

3. Using visual and contextual support the poster illustrations, model how a word's meaning can be expressed with other similar words: My mom collects the items needed for her recipe, or *ingredients,* before she begins baking bread.

4. Use these sentences to reveal the meaning of the other words.

   - My mother and I made a *batch* of cookies. (a group of things made together)

   - The chef *boils* water in a pot on the stove. (heats a liquid until it bubbles and steams)

   - We need many *ingredients* for this cake. (items used to make something)

   - Jackie stirred the *mixture* until it was smooth. (something consisting of things mixed together)

   - Mom *braided* my hair for the show tonight. (wove together from three sections)

   - The *dough* needs to rise before we can bake it. (a thick mixture of flour and water)

   - My aunt makes bread at a *bakery.* (a place where bread, pies, cakes, and pastries are made or sold)

Objectives
- Use accessible language and learn new and essential language in the process.
- Expand and internalize initial English vocabulary by learning and using high-frequency English words necessary for identifying and describing people, places, and objects, by retelling simple stories and basic information represented or supported by pictures, and by learning and using routine language needed for classroom communication.

 ELL *English Language Learners*

■ **Reteach** Ask questions to check and reinforce students' understanding of the vocabulary.

- Which word is a sticky mixture of flour and water? (dough)

- What does liquid do when heated to a high temperature? (boils)

- Which word describes something woven together? (braided)

- Where would you buy fresh bread and cookies? (bakery)

- What are the things called that are used in recipes? (ingredients)

- Which word means the same thing as *group*? (batch)

- What is a combination of different things called? (mixture)

■ **Writing** Use the visual support of a Word Grid to develop vocabulary need to comprehend challenging language. Have students write the vocabulary words and their meanings. Give students a copy of the T-Chart. Place the Word Cards facedown and have each student draw two cards. Have students work with peers to write one of the words in each of the two sections at the top of the chart. In the column below each word, have them write the meaning for the word in their own words. As a class, discuss the meanings of the words.

Beginning Have students draw and label a picture of each word in the row below the word's meaning.

Intermediate/Advanced/Advanced High Have students write a short sentence using each word in the row below the word's meaning. Provide a sentence frame, if necessary, such as *The _____ was _____.* (The *dough* was *braided.*)

Language Objectives

- Produce drawings, phrases, or short sentences to show comprehension of Lesson Vocabulary and challenging language.

ELL Teacher Tip

Provide opportunities for English learners to learn new words by grouping words that are related to a specific theme, quality, or activity. For this week's vocabulary, you might record the words on a word wall and continue to add words related to cooking and baking.

Graphic Organizer

Word	Word
Meaning	Meaning

ELL Workshop

Provide opportunities for students to give directions using newly acquired high-frequency words, concrete vocabulary, and key words and expressions. Give Directions (*ELL Handbook,* pp. 396–397) supports students in this task.

Objectives

- Expand and internalize initial English vocabulary by learning and using high-frequency English words necessary for identifying and describing people, places, and objects, by retelling simple stories and basic information represented or supported by pictures, and by learning and using routine language needed for classroom communication.
- Write using a variety of grade-appropriate sentence lengths, patterns, and connecting words to combine phrases, clauses, and sentences in increasingly accurate ways as English is acquired.

Support for English Language Learners

Content Objectives

- Monitor and adjust oral comprehension.

Language Objectives

- Discuss oral passages with accessible language.
- Use a graphic organizer to take notes.

Graphic Organizer

What is it?	Where does it come from?

ELL Teacher Tip

Students may benefit from looking at a map of the world to see where the countries are that are mentioned in the story.

ELL Workshop

As you give directions for using the graphic organizer, you might use Follow Directions (*ELL Handbook,* pp. 398–399) to support students in comprehending increasingly complex spoken directions.

ELL — English Language Learners

Listening Comprehension

Read Aloud

What Is American Food?

Quentin came into the kitchen where his mother was making dinner. "What is for dinner?" Quentin asked. His mother told him they were having meatloaf, potatoes, and salad.

"How come we never have anything interesting to eat?" asked Quentin. His mother said that their meals were always delicious. Quentin complained that everything they ate was American. He wanted to eat food from other countries. His mother asked him to give an example of an American food.

"Potatoes," said Quentin. But his mother told him that the first potatoes came from South America. "Tomatoes," said Quentin. But his mother told him that the first tomatoes also came from South America. Quentin suggested noodles. But his mother told him that people ate noodles in Italy and China long ago. Finally Quentin said, "Chocolate." But his mother told him that chocolate came from Mexico and Central America.

Quentin had not known so many foods came from other countries!

Prepare for the Read Aloud The modified Read Aloud above prepares students for listening to the oral reading "Quentin's Complaint" on p. 289b.

- **First Listening: Listen to Understand** Write the title of the Read Aloud on the board. This is a story about a boy who wants to eat food from other cultures. Listen to find out what he learns about American food. Where does it come from? Afterward, ask the question again. In their answers, have students use the accessible language, such as familiar foods, to learn new vocabulary words.

- **Second Listening: Listen to Check Understanding** Using a T-chart (*ELL Handbook,* p. 493), work with students to write about the foods mentioned in the story and where they came from originally. Now listen again to check that the facts are correct. Afterward, add in any additional information to the chart.

Objectives

- Demonstrate listening comprehension of increasingly complex spoken English by following directions, retelling or summarizing spoken messages, responding to questions and requests, collaborating with peers, and taking notes commensurate with content and grade-level needs.

Phonics and Spelling

■ **Vowel Patterns** Have students turn to p. 290 in the Student Edition. Teach the sounds, pronunciations, and spellings of *ei* and *eigh*.

• Point to the picture of the ceiling. This is *ceiling*. What is the vowel sound in this word? Say it with me: /ē/. Point to the letters *ei*. The sound /ē/ can be spelled ei. Have students say /ē/ as you point to the letters *ei*. What is the sound of these letters together?

• Write *ceiling* on the board and model blending. First we'll say the sounds for the letters and then we'll read the whole word. Write *c* and say /s/. Add *ei* and say /ē/. Add *l* and say /l/. Add *i* and say /i/. Add *ng* and say /ng/. Then run your hand under *ceiling* as you blend the whole word: /s//ē//l//i//ng/, *ceiling*.

• Follow the routine above to teach *eigh* (card 65).

Have students practice pronouncing these sounds with a partner. Monitor students' pronunciation as they practice and correct as needed.

Vocabulary Skill: Unfamiliar Words

■ **Preteach and Model** Display the following sentence and read it aloud. *We watched the water boil and steam on the stove.* Tell students that the words and sentences around unfamiliar words give clues about the meaning and are called context clues. When I look at the words in the sentence I know what a stove is. I know that a stove heats things up and makes them hot. The word *steam* means that the water is very hot. If the water boiled it was probably heated up until it got very hot and steamed. Explain to students that they can check and confirm the meaning of unfamiliar words by using a dictionary.

 Leveled Support

• **Practice** Write the following sentences on the board. Have students use context clues to figure out the meaning of the words. To keep her long hair out of her face, her mother braided it, or wove three sections of her hair together. Donna remembered that eggs were one of the ingredients she needed to make the cake.

Beginning Have pairs of students read the sentences aloud together and determine the meaning of the underlined words by using context clues. Have them use a dictionary to check meaning.

Advanced/Advanced High After pairs of students determine the meaning of each underlined word, have each pair work together to write a sentence using each word. Have the say each sentence aloud.

Content Objectives

• Read words with vowel digraphs *ei, eigh.*

• Use contextual support to understand unfamiliar words.

Language Objectives

• Apply phonics and decoding skills to vocabulary.

• Write sentences with unfamiliar words.

Transfer Skills

Vowel Patterns Because vowels in Spanish are never silent, Spanish speakers may pronounce vowel digraphs in English with two vowel sounds. Have students practice saying and writing words with long vowel digraphs.

ELL Teaching Routine

For more practice with digraphs, use the Sound-by-Sound Blending Strategy Routine (*ELL Handbook,* p. 472).

Content Objectives

- Identify how to draw conclusions from a text.

Language Objectives

- Draw conclusions from a reading.
- Write by drawing conclusions.

ELL Workshop

Encourage students to ask questions to monitor their understanding of instruction of comprehension skills. Use Ask Clarifying Questions (*ELL Handbook,* pages 404–405) for practice.

English Opportunity

Have students turn to p. EI•6 in the Student Edition. Explain to students what is happening in the picture. Do you think the boy's legs are tired after riding his bicycle up the hill? Is that information shown in the picture? We drew the conclusion that his legs were tired. It is not implicit information.

ELL *English Language Learners*

Comprehension
Draw Conclusions

- **Preteach** A conclusion is an idea about a passage that is based on details. Details in a passage can help you draw a conclusion. Have students turn to *Envision It!* on page EI•6 in the Student Edition. Read the text aloud together. Have students discuss how the picture and the information in the "What I Know" list helped lead to the conclusion on the page.

- **Reteach** Give each student a copy of Picture It! (*ELL Handbook,* p. 168). Have students look at the illustrations and then read the text aloud. Remind students that they should combine what they already know with the new information on the page to draw conclusions. Guide students in answering the questions at their language proficiency level.

Beginning/Intermediate Reread the story as students read along. Guide them as they answer the questions.

Advanced/Advanced High Have students reread the text, looking at the pictures as they read. Have them identify details that help them support their conclusion. Then have them answer the questions.

MINI-LESSON

Social Language

Explain to students that people draw conclusions every day about things that happen or things that they see. For example: The boy down the street is waving to me. I think he must be someone I know. Write the following phrases on the board: *snowy day, kids dressed warmly, a hill, sleds.* Have students draw a conclusion about what is going to happen from these details. Provide the sentence frame: I think that _____.

Objectives

- Learn new language structures, expressions, and basic and academic vocabulary heard during classroom instruction and interactions.
- Understand the general meaning, main points, and important details of spoken language ranging from situations in which topics, language, and contexts are familiar to unfamiliar.

Reading Comprehension
Jalapeño Bagels

Student Edition pp. 296–309

■ **Frontloading** Read aloud the title and discuss what jalapeños and bagels are. Ask students if they would like to try a jalapeño bagel. I wonder if the boy makes jalapeño bagels. Let's look through the selection to find clues. Guide students on a picture walk through *Jalapeño Bagels.* Ask students to predict why the title of the story is *Jalapeño Bagels* and record their predictions. During the reading, pause and invite students to adjust their predictions. Provide students with a T-chart (*ELL Handbook,* p. 493) to fill out as they read the selection. Supply these headings: *What is it? How does it get there?*

Sheltered Reading Ask questions such as the following to guide students' comprehension:

- p. 298: What does Pablo need to bring to school for International Day? (something from his culture)

- p. 300: How does Pablo help make pumpkin turnovers? (He spoons in the pumpkin filling.)

- p. 306: How do Pablo's parents make jalapeño bagels together? (Papa kneads dough Mama chops the jalapeños and adds to dough.)

- p. 308: Why does Pablo decide to bring jalapeño bagels for International Day? (Because they are a mixture of his mother and father, just like him.)

- p. 309 Why are recipes written with the ingredient shown in a list? (to make it easier to read)

■ **Fluency: Read with Accuracy** Remind students that reading accurately means saying the words correctly. Read p. 299. Model accurate reading. Have pairs of students choose a paragraph from page 304. Have students read the paragraph to their partners. The partners should read along silently, monitoring accuracy, and give feedback for improvement. For more practice, use the Fluency: Paired Reading Routine (*ELL Handbook,* p. 474).

■ **After Reading** Have students turn to p. 310 in the Student Edition. Help students summarize the text with the Retelling Cards shown. Give one card to each student. Have one student retell the part of the story represented in the picture to the other student.

Objectives
- Demonstrate listening comprehension of increasingly complex spoken English by following directions, retelling or summarizing spoken messages, responding to questions and requests, collaborating with peers, and taking notes commensurate with content and grade-level needs.

Content Objectives
- Monitor and adjust comprehension.
- Make and adjust predictions.

Language Objectives
- Read grade-level text with accuracy.
- Summarize text using visual support.

Graphic Organizer

What is it?	How does it get there?

Audio Support
Students can prepare for reading *Jalapeño Bagels* by using the eSelection or the AudioText CD. See the AudioText CD Routine (*ELL Handbook,* p. 477) for suggestions on using these learning tools.

English Opportunity
Have students turn to p. 309 in the Student Edition. Tell them to read the recipe aloud. Then tell them to write two ingredients on a piece of paper and pass that paper to the right. The next student should write one ingredient to the list. Continue until the ingredient list is complete. How many of you followed directions? What will happen if you don't follow the directions of a recipe?

Support for English Language Learners

ELL Reader   ELD Reader

For additional leveled instruction, see the **ELL/ELD Reader Teaching Guide.**

Comprehension
The Story of Pizza

■ **Before Reading** Distribute copies of the ELL and ELD Readers, *The Story of Pizza,* to students at their reading level.

• **Preview** Read the title aloud with students: This is a nonfiction text that tells how pizza became a popular food. Have them look through the pictures and predict where pizza was first invented.

• **Set a Purpose for Reading** Let's read to figure out how pizza became so popular.

■ **During Reading** Follow the Reading Routine for both reading groups.

1. Read the entire Reader aloud slowly.

2. Reread pp. 1–4, pausing to build background or model comprehension. Have Beginning students

finger-point as you read. Use the questions in the chart to check students' comprehension.

3. Have students reread pp. 1–4 in pairs, taking turns reading alternate pages.

4. Repeat steps 2–3 above for pp. 5–9 of the Reader.

■ **After Reading** Use the exercises on the inside back cover of each Reader and invite students to share their writing. What did the girls buy at the market? What else did they get for their mother? Record their answers on the board and invite them to point to pictures in the book to support their answers.

ELD Reader Beginning/Intermediate

■ **p. 1** How could people who did not have much money buy pizzas? (They were not expensive to make.)

■ **p. 6** Where was the world's biggest pizza made? (South Africa)

■ **p. 9** What might someone from Japan want on their pizza? (fish)

Writing What was most interesting to you about pizza? Find the sentence in the book that tells about it. Copy the sentence. Then read it aloud to your partner.

ELL Reader Advanced/Advanced High

■ **p. 3** How was the pizza that Rafaelle Esposito made for the queen special? (It looked like the flag of Italy.)

■ **p. 5** How did pizza first come to the United States? (Gennaro Lombardi opened a pizzeria in New York City in 1905.)

Study Guide Distribute copies of the ELL Reader Study Guide (*ELL Handbook,* p. 172). Have students make a list of things they like to have on their pizza before they draw the picture and finish the sentence. Review their responses together. (See *ELL Handbook,* pp. 209–212.)

Objectives
• Express opinions, ideas, and feelings ranging from communicating single words and short phrases to participating in extended discussions on a variety of social and grade-appropriate academic topics.

 **eReaders**

Conventions
Comparative and Superlative Adverbs

■ **Preteach** Display these sentences:
He spoke <u>louder</u> than the TV. She pushed the swing <u>higher</u> than I did. How did he speak? (louder) How did she push the swing? (higher) The words *louder* and *higher* are adverbs. They modify, or tell how someone or something performed an action. Sometimes adverbs are used to compare two actions. Look for an *-er* or *-est* ending as clues to a comparative adverb.

■ **Practice** Write the following adverbs: *very, faster, slower, quieter.*

Beginning Have pairs pick one adverb and use it in a sentence. Support students as they create their sentences.
Intermediate/Advanced/Advanced High Have pairs pick two adverbs. Ask students to use the words in sentences. Have students share their sentences with the class.

■ **Reteach** Write the following on the board:
Juan runs <u>fast</u>. Maria runs <u>faster</u> than Juan. Ian runs the <u>fastest</u> of all three. Remind students that a comparative adverb compares two actions and has the suffix *er* or the word *more,* as in *more quickly.* A superlative adverb compares three or more actions and ends in *-est* or has the word *most,* as in *the most easily.*

■ **Practice** Have students brainstorm a list of comparative and superlative adverbs.

Beginning/Intermediate Have students repeat the sentences on the board. Then have them replace the adverbs with different comparative and superlative adverbs, using examples from the board, such as *Juan runs more quickly.*
Advanced/Advanced High Have students write new sentences using their own verbs along with adverbs from the list. Provide these sentence frames Juan _____ _____. Maria _____ _____ than Juan. Ian _____ _____ out of all of them.

Content Objectives
• Decode and use comparative and superlative adverbs.
• Correctly form comparative and superlative adverbs.

Language Objectives
• Speak using comparative and superlative adverbs.
• Write phrases and sentences with comparative and superlative adverbs.

 Transfer Skills
Comparative Adverbs
English phrases can be challenging for students whose home language uses different phrasing, and students may say or write: *running quickly more than you* or *studying more hard than you.* Model sentences with comparative adverbs.

Grammar Jammer
For more practice with adverbs, use the Grammar Jammer for this target skill. See the Grammar Jammer Routine (*ELL Handbook,* p. 478) for suggestions on using this learning tool.

Objectives
• Speak using a variety of grammatical structures, sentence lengths, sentence types, and connecting words with increasing accuracy and ease as more English is acquired.
• Spell familiar English words with increasing accuracy, and employ English spelling patterns and rules with increasing accuracy as more English is acquired.

Support for English Language Learners

Content Objectives

- Identify the author's purpose of a text.

Language Objectives

- Write and narrate paragraphs with a specific purpose.
- Share feedback for editing and revising.

ELL Teaching Routine

For practice spelling words related to food of different cultures use the Spelling Routine (*ELL Handbook*, p. 476).

ELL Workshop

Students may use classroom resources to respond to questions they have about their writing. Use Classroom Resources (*ELL Handbook*, pp. 406–407) provides extra support.

ELL English Language Learners

Author's Purpose

■ **Introduce** When you write about familiar topics, it is important to think about why you are writing, or your purpose for writing. Display the model and read it aloud. What is the purpose of this writing? (to invite people to International Day) What information does the invitation give you about International Day? (the date, the time, what to bring) Is the author's purpose of this invitation to inform, entertain, persuade, or express emotions? (inform)

Writing Model

You are invited to attend International Day on October 6 at 9:00 A.M. Please bring a cultural item to share. It can be food, clothes, or anything else that represents your culture.

■ **Practice** Write the following paragraph on the board. Ask students to determine the purpose of the writing, whether to inform, persuade, entertain, or express emotions. Have students underline words that help determine the author's purpose.

I think International Day is one of the most important and exciting events at our school. We all get to learn so much about different cultures. And the food is always delicious!

■ **Write** Have students write an invitation to dinner to a friend. The invitations should include the time, place, and what will be served. Point out that the purpose of an invitation is to inform. Have students decide if the invitation will be formal or more casual, informal.

Beginning Have students draw an invitation and have them dictate to you details about the dinner. Write out their sentences and have students copy them.

Intermediate Have partners work together on the invitation. Supply students with prompts, such as Time: _____, Place: _____, and Food: _____. Students can then turn the information into an invitation.

Advanced/Advanced High Have students write their invitation independently. Then have pairs exchange papers and provide feedback for revising and editing.

Objectives

- Write using a variety of grade-appropriate sentence lengths, patterns, and connecting words to combine phrases, clauses, and sentences in increasingly accurate ways as more English is acquired.
- Narrate, describe, and explain with increasing specificity and detail to fulfill content area writing needs as more English is acquired.

This Week's ELL Overview

ELL Handbook

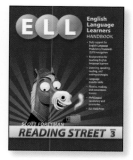

- Maximize Literacy and Cognitive Engagement
- Research Into Practice
- Full Weekly Support for Every Selection

Me and Uncle Romie
- Multi-Lingual Summaries in Five Languages
- Selection-Specific Vocabulary Word Cards
- Frontloading/Reteaching for Comprehension Skill Lessons
- ELD and ELL Reader Study Guides

- Transfer Activities
- Professional Development

Daily Leveled ELL Notes

ELL notes appear throughout this week's instruction and ELL Support is on the DI pages of your Teacher's Edition. The following is a sample of an ELL note from this week.

English Language Learners

Beginning After reading, have students find pairs of words that end with the same suffix.

Intermediate Have students work in pairs to chorally reread paragraphs from the Decodable Practice Reader.

Advanced After reading, have students choose words with different suffixes and use them orally in sentences.

Advanced High After reading the story, have students choose two or three words with the suffixes *-y, -ish, -hood,* or *-ment* and write a sentence for each word.

ELL by Strand

The ELL lessons on this week's Support for English Language Learners pages are organized by strand. They offer additional scaffolding for the core curriculum. Leveled support notes on these pages address the different proficiency levels in your class. See pages DI•116–DI•125.

ELL Guy
Dr. Jim Cummins

The Three Pillars of ELL Instruction

ELL Strands	Activate Prior Knowledge	Access Content	Extend Language
Vocabulary pp. DI•117–DI•118	Preteach	Reteach	Leveled Writing Activities
Reading Comprehension p. DI•122	Frontloading	Sheltered Reading	Fluency: Read with Appropriate Phrasing
Phonics, Spelling, and Word Analysis p. DI•120	Preteach/Model	Practice	Leveled Practice Activities
Listening Comprehension p. DI•119	Prepare for the Read Aloud	First Listening	Second Listening
Conventions and Writing pp. DI•124–DI•125	Preteach/Introduce	Practice	Leveled Practice Activities/ Leveled Writing Activities
Concept Development p. DI•116	Prior Knowledge	Discuss Concept	Daily Concept and Vocabulary Development

This Week's Practice Stations Overview

Six Weekly Practice Stations with Leveled Activities can be found at the beginning of each week of instruction. For this week's Practice Stations, see pp. 320h–320i.

Small Group
Teacher-led

Classroom Management Handbook for Differentiated Instruction Practice Stations

Practice Stations

Daily Leveled Center Activities

⬤ Below   ◻ Advanced

△ On-Level   🅔🅛🅛

Practice Stations Flip Charts

	Word Wise	Word Work	Words to Know	Let's Write	Read For Meaning	Get Fluent
Objectives	• Spell words with vowel patterns *ei, eigh*.	• Identify and pronounce words with vowel patterns *ei, eigh*.	• Identify the meaning of unfamiliar words.	• Write an invitation.	• Draw conclusions.	• Read aloud with accuracy.
Materials	• *Word Wise* Flip Chart Activity 25 • Teacher-made word cards • paper • pencils	• *Word Work* Flip Chart Activity 25 • Teacher-made word cards • paper • pencils	• *Words to Know* Flip Chart Activity 25 • magazines • dictionary • paper • pencils	• *Let's Write* Flip Chart Activity 25 • paper • pencils	• *Read for Meaning* Flip Chart Activity 25 • Leveled Readers • paper • pencils	• *Get Fluent* Flip Chart Activity 25 • Leveled Readers

This Week on Reading Street!

Question of the Week

How does city life compare to life in the country?

Cultures

Daily Plan

Don't Wait Until Friday

Whole Group
- ◉ Author's Purpose
- ◉ Homonyms
- • Fluency/Phrasing
- • Writing/Conventions
- • Research and Inquiry

MONITOR PROGRESS | **Success Predictor**

Day 1	Day 2	Day 3	Day 4	Day 5
Check Oral Vocabulary	Check Word Reading	Check Retelling	Check Fluency	Check Oral Vocabulary

Small Group

Teacher Led

- • Reading Support
- • Skill Support
- • Fluency Practice

Practice Stations

Independent Activities

Customize Literacy More support for a balanced literacy appoach, see pp. CL•1–CL•45

Customize Writing More support for a customized writing approach, see pp. CW•11–CW•20

Whole Group
- • Writing: Book Review
- • Conventions: Conjunctions
- • Spelling: Suffixes

Assessment
- • Weekly Tests
- • Day 5 Assessment
- • Fresh Reads

You Are Here! Unit 5 Week 5

This Week's Reading Selections

Main Selection Genre: Historical Fiction

Paired Selection 21st Century Skills

Decodable Readers

Leveled Readers

ELL and ELD Readers

Resources on Reading Street!

	Build Concepts	Phonics	Comprehension
Whole Group	 Let's Talk About pp. 320–321	 Phonics Skill Lesson pp. 322–323 Decodable Readers  Sound-Spelling Cards	 Envision It! Skills/ Strategies Comprehension Skill Lesson pp. 324–325
Go Digital	• Concept Talk Video	• Interactive Sound-Spelling Cards • Decodable eReaders	• Envision It! Animations • eSelections
Small Group and Independent Practice	 Me and Uncle Romie pp. 328–349 ELL and ELD Readers Leveled Readers Decodable Readers	Decodable Readers Practice Station Flip Chart	 Me and Uncle Romie pp. 328–349 ELL and ELD Readers Leveled Readers  Envision It! Skills/ Strategies Reader's and Writer's Notebook Practice Station Flip Chart
Go Digital	• eReaders • eSelections • Decodable eReaders	• Letter Tile Drag and Drop • Decodable eReaders	• Envision It! Animations • eSelections • eReaders
Customize Literacy	• Leveled Readers • Decodable Readers	• Decodable Readers	• Envision It! Skills/Strategies Handbook • Leveled Readers
Go Digital	• Concept Talk Video • Decodable eReaders • eReaders	• Decodable eReaders	• Envision It! Animations • eReaders • Decodable eReaders

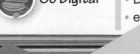

Question of the Week
How does city life compare to life in the country?

Vocabulary

Envision It!
Vocabulary
Cards

Vocabulary Skill Lesson
pp. 326–327

- Envision It! Vocabulary Cards
- Vocabulary Activities

Fluency

Let's Learn It!
pp. 358–359

Decodable and Leveled
Readers

- eSelection
- Decodable eReaders
- eReaders

Conventions and Writing

Let's Write It!
pp. 352–353

Decodable
Readers

- Grammar Jammer

Envision It!
Vocabulary
Cards

Me and Uncle Romie
pp. 328–349

Practice Station
Flip Chart

Words!

Reader's
and Writer's
Notebook

Me and Uncle Romie
pp. 328–349

Practice Station
Flip Chart

Leveled
Readers

ELL and ELD
Readers

Reader's
and Writer's
Notebook

Me and Uncle Romie
pp. 328–349

Practice Station
Flip Chart

- Envision It! Vocabulary Cards
- Vocabulary Activities
- eSelection

- eSelection
- eReaders

- Grammar Jammer

- Envision It! Vocabulary Cards

- Leveled Readers
- Decodable Readers

- Reader's and Writer's Notebook

- Vocabulary Activities

- eReaders
- Decodable eReaders

- Grammar Jammer

Week 5

You Are Here!
Unit 5
Week 5

Me and Uncle Romie **320c**

My 5-Day Planner for Reading Street!

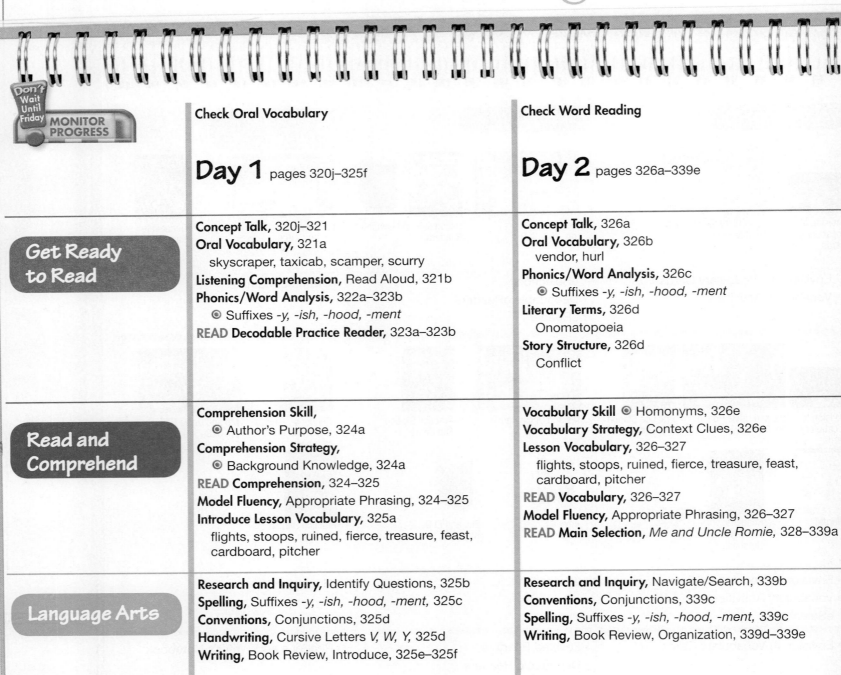

MONITOR PROGRESS
Don't Wait Until Friday

	Check Oral Vocabulary **Day 1** pages 320j–325f	**Check Word Reading** **Day 2** pages 326a–339e

Get Ready to Read	**Concept Talk,** 320j–321
	Oral Vocabulary, 321a
	  skyscraper, taxicab, scamper, scurry
	Listening Comprehension, Read Aloud, 321b
	Phonics/Word Analysis, 322a–323b
	  ◉ Suffixes -y, -ish, -hood, -ment
	READ Decodable Practice Reader, 323a–323b
		Concept Talk, 326a
		Oral Vocabulary, 326b
		  vendor, hurl
		Phonics/Word Analysis, 326c
		  ◉ Suffixes -y, -ish, -hood, -ment
		Literary Terms, 326d
		  Onomatopoeia
		Story Structure, 326d
		  Conflict

Read and Comprehend	**Comprehension Skill,**
	  ◉ Author's Purpose, 324a
	Comprehension Strategy,
	  ◉ Background Knowledge, 324a
	READ Comprehension, 324–325
	Model Fluency, Appropriate Phrasing, 324–325
	Introduce Lesson Vocabulary, 325a
	  flights, stoops, ruined, fierce, treasure, feast,
	  cardboard, pitcher
		Vocabulary Skill ◉ Homonyms, 326e
		Vocabulary Strategy, Context Clues, 326e
		Lesson Vocabulary, 326–327
		  flights, stoops, ruined, fierce, treasure, feast,
		  cardboard, pitcher
		READ Vocabulary, 326–327
		Model Fluency, Appropriate Phrasing, 326–327
		READ Main Selection, *Me and Uncle Romie,* 328–339a

Language Arts	**Research and Inquiry,** Identify Questions, 325b **Spelling,** Suffixes -y, -ish, -hood, -ment, 325c **Conventions,** Conjunctions, 325d **Handwriting,** Cursive Letters *V, W, Y,* 325d **Writing,** Book Review, Introduce, 325e–325f	**Research and Inquiry,** Navigate/Search, 339b **Conventions,** Conjunctions, 339c **Spelling,** Suffixes -y, -ish, -hood, -ment, 339c **Writing,** Book Review, Organization, 339d–339e

You Are Here!
Unit 5
Week 5

How does city life compare to life in the country?

Check Retelling	Check Fluency	Check Oral Vocabulary
Day 3 pages 340a–353c	**Day 4** pages 354a–359e	**Day 5** pages 359f–359q

Concept Talk, 340a
 Oral Vocabulary, 340b
  meager, gutter
 Phonics/Word Analysis, 340c–340d
  ◉ Suffixes *-y, -ish, -hood, -ment*
 Decodable Story, 340d
 Comprehension Check, 340e
 Check Retelling, 340f
	Concept Talk, 354a
	 Oral Vocabulary, 354b
	  bitter, ramble
	 Phonics/Word Analysis, 354c–354f
	  Review Vowel Patterns *ei, eigh*
	 Decodable Story, 354f
	 21st Century Skills: Online
	  Reference Sources, 354g
		Concept Wrap Up, 359f
		 Check Oral Vocabulary, 359g
		  skyscraper, taxicab, scamper,
		  scurry, vendor, hurl, meager, gutter,
		  bitter, ramble
		 Amazing Ideas, 359g
		  Review ◉ **Author's Purpose,** 359h
		  Review ◉ **Homonyms,** 359h
		  Review ◉ **Suffixes,** 359i
		  Review **Literary Terms,** 359i

READ Main Selection,
 Me and Uncle Romie, 340–349a
 Retelling, 350–351
 Think Critically, 351a
 Model Fluency, Appropriate Phrasing,
 351b
 Research and Study Skills, Electronic
 Text, 351c
	READ Paired Selection,
	 "Country to City," 354–357a
	 Let's Learn It! 358–359a
	  Fluency: Appropriate Phrasing
	  Vocabulary: ◉ Homonyms
	  Listening and Speaking:
	  Retelling
		Fluency Assessment,
		  WCPM, 359j–359k
		 Comprehension Assessment,
		  ◉ Author's Purpose, 359l–359m

Research and Inquiry, Analyze, 351d **Conventions,** Conjunctions, 351e **Spelling,** Suffixes *-y, -ish, -hood,* *-ment,* 351e **Let's Write It!** Book Review, 352–353 **Writing,** Book Review, Organizing Your Draft, 353a–353c	**Research and Inquiry,** Synthesize, 359b **Conventions,** Conjunctions, 359c **Spelling,** Suffixes *-y, -ish, -hood,* *-ment,* 359c **Writing,** Book Review, Revising, 359d–359e	**Research and Inquiry,** Communicate, 359n **Conventions,** Conjunctions, 359o **Spelling Test,** Suffixes *-y, -ish, -hood,* *-ment,* 359o **Writing,** Book Review, Conventions, 359p–359q **Quick Write for Fluency,** 359q

Week 5

Grouping Options for Differentiated Instruction
Turn the page for the small group time lesson plan.

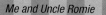

Planning Small Group Time on Reading Street!

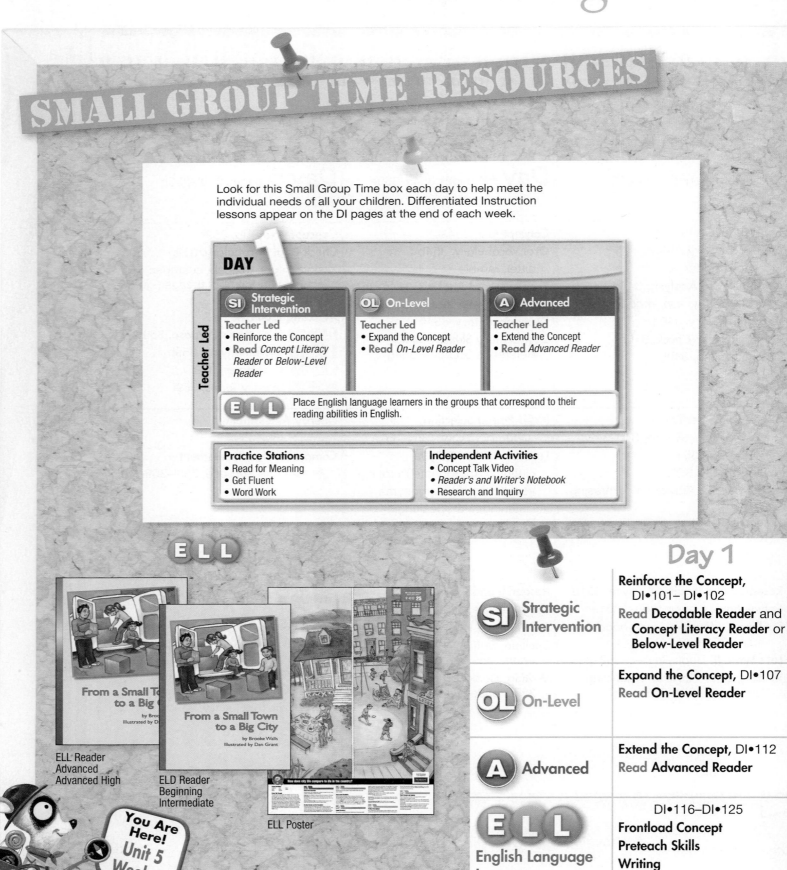

SMALL GROUP TIME RESOURCES

Look for this Small Group Time box each day to help meet the individual needs of all your children. Differentiated Instruction lessons appear on the DI pages at the end of each week.

DAY 1

Teacher Led

SI Strategic Intervention

Teacher Led
- Reinforce the Concept
- Read *Concept Literacy Reader* or *Below-Level Reader*

OL On-Level

Teacher Led
- Expand the Concept
- Read *On-Level Reader*

A Advanced

Teacher Led
- Extend the Concept
- Read *Advanced Reader*

ELL Place English language learners in the groups that correspond to their reading abilities in English.

Practice Stations
- Read for Meaning
- Get Fluent
- Word Work

Independent Activities
- Concept Talk Video
- *Reader's and Writer's Notebook*
- Research and Inquiry

ELL

From a Small Town to a Big City
by Brooke Walls
Illustrated by Dan Grant

ELL Reader
Advanced
Advanced High

From a Small Town to a Big City
by Brooke Walls
Illustrated by Dan Grant

ELD Reader
Beginning
Intermediate

How does city life compare to life in the country?

ELL Poster

You Are Here!
Unit 5
Week 5

Day 1

SI Strategic Intervention	**Reinforce the Concept,** DI•101– DI•102 **Read Decodable Reader** and **Concept Literacy Reader** or **Below-Level Reader**
OL On-Level	**Expand the Concept,** DI•107 **Read On-Level Reader**
A Advanced	**Extend the Concept,** DI•112 **Read Advanced Reader**
ELL English Language Learners	DI•116–DI•125 **Frontload Concept Preteach Skills Writing**

Reading Street
Response to
Intervention Kit

Reading Street
Practice Stations Kit

SI Strategic Intervention

OL On-Level

A Advanced

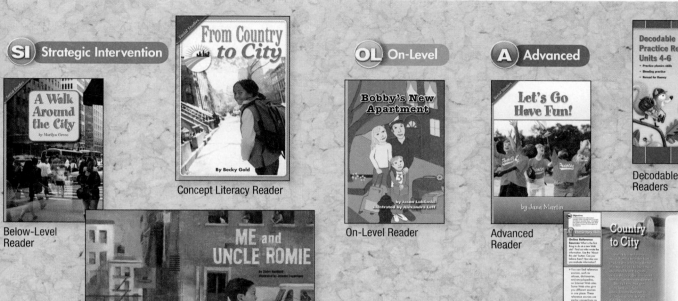

Below-Level
Reader

Concept Literacy Reader

On-Level Reader

Advanced
Reader

Decodable
Readers

Me and Uncle Romie pp. 328–349

Country to City pp. 354–357

Small Group Weekly Plan

Day 2	Day 3	Day 4	Day 5
Reinforce Comprehension, DI•103 **Revisit Main Selection**	**Reinforce Vocabulary,** DI•104 **Read/Revisit Main Selection**	**Reinforce Comprehension,** Practice Retelling, DI•105 Genre Focus **Read/Revisit Paired Selection**	**Practice Fluency,** DI•106 **Reread Concept Literacy Reader** or **Below-Level Reader**
Expand Comprehension, DI•100 **Revisit Main Selection**	**Expand Vocabulary,** DI•109 **Read/Revisit Main Selection**	**Expand Comprehension,** Practice Retelling, DI•110 Genre Focus **Read/Revisit Paired Selection**	**Practice Fluency,** DI•111 **Reread On-Level Reader**
Extend Comprehension, DI•113 **Revisit Main Selection**	**Extend Vocabulary,** DI•114 **Read/Revisit Main Selection**	**Extend Comprehension,** Genre Focus, DI•115 **Read/Revisit Paired Selection**	**Practice Fluency,** DI•115 **Reread Advanced Reader**
DI•116–DI•125 **Review Concept/Skills** **Frontload Main Selection** **Practice**	DI•116–DI•125 **Review Concept/Skills** **Reread Main Selection** **Practice**	DI•116–DI•125 **Review Concept** **Read ELL/ELD Readers** **Practice**	DI•116–DI•125 **Review Concept/Skills** **Reread ELL/ELD Reader** **Writing**

Week 5

Practice Stations for Everyone on Reading Street!

Word Wise
Vowel patterns *ei, eigh*

Objectives
• Spell words with vowel patterns *ei, eigh.*

Materials
• *Word Wise* Flip Chart Activity 25
• Teacher-made word cards
• paper • pencils

Differentiated Activities

● Choose five word cards. Write the words. Write sentences using each word. Think of other words you know with vowel patterns *ei,* and *eigh.* Add these words to the list.

▲ Choose seven word cards, and list the words. Write sentences using each word. Think of other words you know with vowel patterns *ei* and *eigh.* Add the words to the list.

■ Choose nine word cards, and list the words. Write sentences for each word. Think of other words you know with vowel patterns *ei* and *eigh,* and add the words to the list.

Technology
• Online Dictionary

Word Work
Vowel patterns *ei, eigh*

Objectives
• Identify and pronounce words with vowel patterns *ei, eigh.*

Materials
• *Word Work* Flip Chart Activity 25
• Teacher-made word cards
• paper • pencils

Differentiated Activities

● Choose eight word cards. Make a two-column chart with the headings *ei* and *eigh.* Write the words in the correct column. Say each word.

▲ Choose ten word cards. Make a two-column chart with the headings *ei* and *eigh.* Write the words in the correct column. Say each word.

■ Choose twelve word cards. Group the words by vowel patterns *ei* and *eigh,* and write each group in a list. Say each word. Write a rhyming word next to each word.

Technology
• Modeled Pronunciation Audio CD

Words to Know
Unfamiliar words

Objectives
• Identify the meaning of unfamiliar words.

Materials
• *Words to Know* Flip Chart Activity 25
• magazines • dictionary
• paper • pencils

Differentiated Activities

● Find three words you are unfamiliar with in a magazine. Write the words. Use a dictionary to look up each word's meaning. Write sentences using each of your words.

▲ Find four unfamiliar words in a magazine, and write the words. Use a dictionary to identify each word's meaning. Write sentences using each word. Use context to try to determine word meaning.

■ Use a magazine to find six unfamiliar words. Use context to try to determine word meaning. Check a dictionary for each word's definition

Technology
• Online Dictionary

You Are Here!
Unit 5
Week 5

Use this week's materials from the
Reading Street Leveled Practice Stations
Kit to organize this week's stations.

Key
● Below-Level Activities
▲ On-Level Activities
■ Advanced Activities

Practice Station
Flip Chart

Let's Write!
Invitation

Objectives
• Write an invitation.

Materials
• *Let's Write!* Flip Chart Activity 25
• paper   • pencils

Differentiated Activities

● Imagine you are having a party. Think of a friend you would like to invite. Write an invitation to your party. Tell the reason for the party. Include the time the party will start and end. Use colons.

▲ Imagine you are having a party. Write an invitation to a friend. Include the reason for your party, and tell when the party will start and end. Use colons in your start time and end time.

■ Write an invitation to an imaginary party you are hosting. Include information telling when the party will start and end. Use colons when writing times. Tell the reason you are celebrating.

Technology
• Online Dictionary

Read for Meaning
Draw conclusions

Objectives
• Draw conclusions.

Materials
• *Read for Meaning* Flip Chart Activity 25
• Leveled Readers
• paper   • pencils

Differentiated Activities

● Choose a book from those your teacher provided. Think about some of the details in the story. Draw a conclusion about one of the characters. Write one sentence that tells your conclusion.

▲ Read one of the books your teacher provided. Draw a conclusion about a character or event in your book. Write one sentence telling your conclusion. Write one sentence giving a story detail that supports your conclusion.

■ Choose and read a leveled reader. As you read your book, draw a conclusion about a character or story event. Write a short paragraph that tells your conclusion. Include details from the story that support your conclusion.

Technology
• Leveled Reader Database

Get Fluent
Practice fluent reading

Objectives
• Read aloud with accuracy.

Materials
• *Get Fluent* Flip Chart Activity 25
• Leveled Readers

Differentiated Activities

● Work with a partner. Choose a Concept Literacy Reader or Below-Level Reader. Take turns reading a page from the book. Use the readers to practice reading with accuracy. Provide feedback as needed.

▲ Work with a partner. Choose an On-Level Reader. Take turns reading a page from the book. Use the reader to practice reading with accuracy. Provide feedback as needed.

■ Work with a partner. Choose an Advanced Reader. Take turns reading a page from the book. Use the reader to practice reading with accuracy. Provide feedback as needed.

Technology
• Leveled Reader Database
• Reading Street Readers CD-ROM

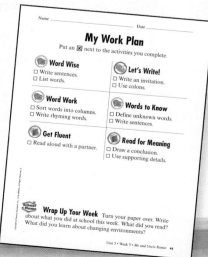

My Weekly Work Plan

week 5

Objectives
- Introduce the weekly concept.
- Develop oral vocabulary.

Today at a Glance

Oral Vocabulary
skyscraper, taxicab, scamper, scurry

Phonics/Word Analysis
◉ Suffixes *-y, -ish, -hood, -ment*

Comprehension
◉ Author's purpose
◉ Background knowledge

Reading
"New York City"

Fluency
Appropriate phrasing

Lesson Vocabulary
Tested Vocabulary

Research and Inquiry
Identify questions

Spelling
Suffixes *-y, -ish, -hood,* and *-ment*

Conventions
Conjunctions

Handwriting
Cursive letters *V, W, Y*

Writing
Book review

Concept Talk

Question of the Week

How does city life compare to life in the country?

Introduce the concept

To further explore the unit concept of Cultures, this week students will read, write, and talk about how city life compares to country life. Write the Question of the Week on the board.

> **ROUTINE** **Activate Prior Knowledge** **Team Talk**
>
> 1. **Think** Have students think about how life in a city is similar to life in the country.
> 2. **Pair** Have pairs of students discuss the Question of the Week.
> 3. **Share** Call on a few students to share their ideas with the group. Guide the discussion and encourage elaboration with prompts such as:
>   - What kinds of things do people like to do in a city?
>   - What kinds of things do people like to do in the country?

Routines Flip Chart

Anchored Talk

Develop oral vocabulary

Have students turn to pp. 320–321 in their Student Editions. Look at each of the photos. Then, use the prompts to guide discussion and create the *How does city life compare to life in the country?* concept map.

- What kind of animals might *scamper* or *scurry*? (**rabbits, deer**) Are those city or country animals? (**country**) Are there animals in both the country and the city? (**yes**) What kinds? (**horses, dogs, cats, cows**) Let's add *Animals* to our concept list.

- Do you see *skyscrapers* in the city or the country? (**city**) What kinds of buildings are in the country? (**houses, barns**) Both places have buildings. Let's add *Buildings* to our concept list.

Objectives
● Listen closely when someone speaks, ask questions about the topic he or she is talking about, and comment about the topic. ● Speak clearly and to the point while making eye contact, changing how fast, loud, and clearly you speak to communicate your ideas.

Oral Vocabulary

Let's Talk About

City and Country Life

● Ask relevant questions about urban and rural life.

● Express opinions about life in the city versus life in the country.

● Describe life in the city or the country.

READING STREET ONLINE
CONCEPT TALK VIDEO
www.ReadingStreet.com

● You've learned **2 3 6** Amazing Words ★ so far this year!

Student Edition pp. 320–321

Amazing Words

You've learned **2 3 6** words so far.

You'll learn **0 1 0** words this week!

skyscraper	hurl
taxicab	meager
scamper	gutter
scurry	bitter
vendor	ramble

 Writing on Demand

Writing Fluency
Ask students to respond to the photos on pp. 320–321 by writing as well as they can and as much as they can about how city life and country life are alike.

• How is it different to get around in the city and the country? (In the city, there is public transportation. In both places, people walk.) Let's add "Transportation" to the concept map.

• After discussing the photos, ask: How does city life compare to life in the country?

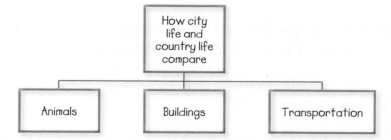

Connect to reading

Tell students that this week they will be reading about a boy who lives in the country and visits a city. Throughout the week, encourage students to add concept-related words to this week's concept map.

ELL **Preteach Concepts** Use the Day 1 instruction on ELL Poster 25 to assess and build background knowledge, develop concepts, and build oral vocabulary.

ELL

English Language Learners
ELL support Additional ELL support and modified instruction is provided in the *ELL Handbook* and in the ELL lessons on pp. DI•116–125.

Listening comprehension
English learners will benefit from additional visual support to understand the key terms in the concept map. Use the pictures on pp. 320–321 to scaffold understanding.

Frontload for read aloud Use the modified Read Aloud on p. DI•119 of the *ELL Handbook* to prepare students to listen to "Nature in the City" (p. 321b).

ELL Poster 25

Me and Uncle Romie **320–321**

Objectives
- Develop listening comprehension.
- Develop oral vocabulary.

— **Check Oral Vocabulary**
○ **SUCCESS PREDICTOR**

Oral Vocabulary
Amazing Words

Introduce Amazing Words

"Nature in the City" on p. 321b is about nature preserves in big cities. Tell students to listen for this week's Amazing Words—*skyscraper, taxicab, scamper,* and *scurry*—as you read.

Model fluency

As you read "Nature in the City," model appropriate phrasing by grouping words in a meaningful way and paying attention to punctuation cues.

Amazing Words **Oral Vocabulary Routine**

> skyscraper
> taxicab
> scamper
> scurry

Teach Amazing Words

1 **Introduce** Write the word *skyscraper* on the board. Have students say it aloud with you. In "Nature in the City," *skyscrapers* line busy streets. How does the context help you understand the meaning of *skyscraper*? Supply a student-friendly definition.

2 **Demonstrate** Have students answer questions to demonstrate understanding. How do you get to the top floors of a *skyscraper*? How can you tell a *skyscraper* from other buildings on a street?

3 **Apply** Have students who have seen a *skyscraper* describe it. Have them tell how they feel when they look at *skyscrapers* from the ground.

See p. OV•2 to teach *scamper, scurry,* and *taxicab.*

Routines Flip Chart

Apply Amazing Words

To build oral language, lead the class in a discussion about the Amazing Words' meanings. Remind students to answer questions with appropriate detail.

Don't Wait Until Friday

MONITOR PROGRESS **Check Oral Vocabulary**

During discussion, listen for students' use of the Amazing Words.

If… students are unable to use the Amazing Words to discuss the concept,

then… use Oral Vocabulary Routine in the Routines Flip Chart to demonstrate words in different contexts.

Day 1	Day 2	Day 3	Day 4	Day 5
Check Oral Vocabulary	Check Word Reading	Check Retelling	Check Fluency	Check Oral Vocabulary

Success Predictor

Read Aloud

Nature in the City

What kind of sounds do you hear in the city? You hear a car and a taxicab honking their horns at each other. You hear people talking and big machines roaring. Cities around the world are getting louder every day.

Not all the sounds in big cities are loud. Some of the biggest cities in Texas also have different, softer kinds of sounds. Sounds like birds singing in bushes and wind rushing through trees. Sounds like clear cool water flowing gently over rocks. Sounds that rabbits make when they scamper through woods and that squirrels make when they scurry through fields.

The area around Austin is called the Edwards Plateau. A long time ago, it belonged to the animals. Some very special animals still make their homes in Austin. Bats live under the bridges, and foxes live in the canyons. Salamanders swim in the springs, and birds nest in the trees. However as the city has gotten bigger, it is harder for animals to live there and for plants to survive.

Studies have been done to learn what makes people who live in cities happy. We've learned that many people feel happy when they spend time in city parks or nature preserves. Nature preserves are places people can visit to see plants and animals living in their natural habitats, or homes.

The people of Austin understand the importance of such places. They work hard to keep their city green. Green cities have clean air and clear streams with clean water.

In 2007, Austin became a Community Wildlife Habitat. This means that city planners work to keep the animals safe. They build nature preserves so there is plenty of food and shelter for the animals. People are taught to care for the animals and understand their needs.

Today Austin has over 200 parks and 12 nature preserves scattered around town. There are over 50 miles of trails for hiking. One of these trails winds up a hill. From there, you can see a skyscraper or two lining a busy city street.

Another city in Texas, Fort Worth, has done a spectacular job of preserving the beauty of nature. At the Fort Worth Botanical Gardens, you can see a variety of gardens and garden types, including a Japanese garden and a fragrance garden. If you take a walk on the Texas Native Forest Boardwalk, you can learn about native trees and efforts that are being made to conserve them.

As our cities grow larger, we need to protect these special places where plants can grow as they were meant to grow. We need to save land for the animals without changing the way they live. Then we can hear nature not far from our doorsteps. We can feel good about helping animals by giving them the space they need to live and grow.

Oral Vocabulary

Success Predictor

Objectives

◉ Use word analysis to recognize words with suffixes *-y, -ish, -hood, -ment*.

◉ Read and write words with suffixes *-y, -ish, -hood, -ment*.

Skills Trace

◉ **Suffixes** *-y, -ish, -hood, -ment*

Introduce U5W5D1

Practice U5W5D3, U5W5D4

Reteach/Review U5W5D5, U6W1D4

Assess/Test Weekly Test U5W5

Benchmark Test U5

Key: U = Unit, W = Week, D = Day

Word Analysis

↻ Suffixes *-y, -ish, -hood, -ment*

ROUTINE **Word Parts Strategy**

① **Connect** Connect today's lesson to previous learning. Write *leader* and *conductor*. Point out that students have already studied words with suffixes. Ask them to read each word and identify the suffix. Today you will learn how to spell and read words with other suffixes.

② **Model** Write *squeaky*. When I see a word with a suffix, I break it into parts. I read the base word first. Cover the *-y* and read the base word. Uncover the *-y*. Next I read the suffix. Then I put the parts together to read the word. Have students read the word with you. *Squeaky* is a two-syllable word formed from the base word *squeak* and the suffix *-y*. Adding *-y* changes the noun *squeak* to an adjective, *squeaky*.

③ **Guide Practice** Write the words below. Have the group read the words with you. Then have them identify each base word and the suffix that has been added. Discuss the meaning of each suffix.

yellowish	healthy	entertainment	thirsty	adulthood
payment	falsehood	stormy	frosty	brownish

④ **Review** What do you know about reading words with suffixes? When you see a word with a suffix, break it into parts. Read the base word first. Then read the suffix. Put the parts together to read the whole word.

Routines Flip Chart

Model Have students turn to p. 322 in their Student Editions. Each word on this page has a suffix. The first word, *bumpy,* has the suffix *-y.* The word *boyish* has the suffix *-ish. Childhood* has the suffix *-hood. Enjoyment* has the suffix *-ment,* and *funny* has the suffix *-y.*

Guide practice For each word in Words I Can Blend, ask students to segment the word by identifying the base word and the suffix. Then have them put the parts together to read the words.

Corrective feedback If... students have difficulty reading a word,

then... model reading the parts and then the whole word, and then ask students to read it with you.

Student Edition pp. 322–323

Differentiated Instruction

SI Strategic Intervention

Read words with suffixes If students have difficulty reading base words, then use the Blending Strategy Routine on the Routines Flip Chart to practice blending decodable words.

Vocabulary Support

You may wish to explain the meanings of these words.

falsehood a lie or an untruth

entertainment the act of entertaining; something done to interest or amuse others

Decode and Read

Read words independent of context

After students can successfully combine the word parts to read the words on p. 322 in their Student Editions, point to words in random order and ask students to read them naturally.

Read words in context

Have students read each of the sentences on p. 322. Have them identify words in the sentences that have the suffixes -y, -ish, -hood, and -ment.

Team Talk Pair students and have them take turns reading each of the sentences aloud.

Chorally read the I Can Read! passage on p. 323 with students. Then have them read the passage aloud to themselves.

On their own

For additional practice, use the *Reader's and Writer's Notebook* p. 360.

Reader's and Writer's Notebook, p. 360

E L L

English Language Learners

Language transfer Point out to Spanish speakers that the suffix -ment does not have the same meaning as the suffix -mente in Spanish. In English the suffix is often used to change a verb into a noun (enjoy/enjoyment). In Spanish -mente is used to change an adjective into an adverb (rápido, rápidamente).

Objectives

- Apply knowledge of base words and suffixes to decode unknown multisyllabic words when reading.
- ◉ Decode and read words with the suffixes -y, -ish, -hood, -ment.
- Practice fluency with oral rereading.

Decodable Practice Reader 25A
Suffixes -y, -ish, -hood, -ment

Read words independent of context

Have students turn to page 109 in *Decodable Practice Readers 3.2*. Have students read each word.

Read high-frequency words

Have students read the high-frequency words *was, a, what, wanted, very, the, of, everyone, to, they, could, any, said, warm, sure, friends, one, been, having* and *there* on the first page.

Preview Decodable Practice Reader

Have students read the title and preview the story. Tell them that they will read words with the suffixes -y, -ish, -hood, and -ment.

Read words in context

Pair students for reading and listen as they read. One student begins. Students read the entire story, switching readers after each page. Partners reread the story. This time the other student begins. Make sure students are monitoring their accuracy when they decode words.

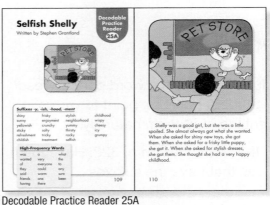

Decodable Practice Reader 25A

Corrective feedback

If... students have difficulty reading a word, **then...** refer them to the Sound-Spelling Cards to identify the word parts. Have them read the word parts individually and then together to say the word.

- What is the new word?
- Is the new word a word you know?
- Does it make sense in the story?

Check decoding and comprehension

Have students retell the story to include characters, setting, and events. Then have students find words in the story that have the suffixes *-y*, *-ish*, *-hood*, and *-ment*. Students should supply *shiny*, *childhood*, *neighborhood*, *crunchy*, *sticky*, *icy*, *rocky*, *treatment*, *frisky*, *sunny*, *wispy*, *yummy*, *salty*, *refreshment*, *grumpy*, *selfish*, *stylish*, *enjoyment*, *yellowish*, *cheesy*, *thirsty*, *tricky*, and *childish*.

Reread for Fluency

Have students reread Decodable Practice Reader 25A to develop automaticity decoding words with suffixes.

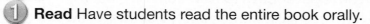

ROUTINE **Oral Rereading**

1. **Read** Have students read the entire book orally.

2. **Reread** To achieve optimal fluency, students should reread the text three or four times.

3. **Corrective Feedback** Listen as students read. Provide corrective feedback regarding their fluency and decoding.

Routines Flip Chart

English Language Learners

Suffixes

Beginning Write on the board words with the suffix *-ish* from the Decodable Practice Reader, such as *selfish*, *stylish*, and *childish*. Cover the suffix in each word and read the base word aloud. Then uncover the suffix and read that syllable. Have students put the word parts together to read the word with you. Repeat the procedure for the suffixes *-y*, *-hood*, and *-ment*.

Intermediate After reading, have students each choose a word with the suffix *-y*, *-ish*, *hood*, or *-ment*. Have them write sentences that use the words. Then have them each identify the base word and write a second sentence that uses that word. For example: *There is a park in my neighborhood./My neighbor and I like to play there.*

Advanced/Advanced High After reading the story, have students choose four or five words with the suffixes *-y*, *-ish*, *-hood*, and *-ment* and write a sentence for each word.

Objectives
◉ Identify author's purpose to aid comprehension.
◉ Use background knowledge to aid comprehension.
• Read grade-level text with appropriate phrasing.

Skills Trace
◉ **Author's purpose**
Introduce U1W5D1; U2W4D1; U5W5D1
Practice U1W5D2; U1W5D3; U2W4D2; U2W4D3; U3W1D2; U3W3D2; U5W5D2; U5W5D3; U6W1D2
Reteach/Review U1W5D5; U2W4D5; U5W5D5
Assess/Test Weekly Tests U1W5; U2W4; U5W5
Benchmark Tests U3
Key: U = Unit, W = Week, D = Day

Skill ↔ Strategy
🔄 Author's Purpose
🔄 Background Knowledge

Student Edition p. EI•2

Introduce author's purpose

The author's purpose is the reason the author has for writing. What are some purposes an author has for writing? (to inform, to persuade, to entertain, to express an opinion) Have students turn to p. EI•2 in the Student Edition to review author's purpose. Then read "New York City" with students.

Model the skill

Think Aloud Have students follow along as you read paragraph 2 of "New York City." This paragraph gives information about a famous building in New York. Is the author's purpose to inform, persuade, entertain, or express feelings? (The author's purpose is to persuade the reader that New York City has amazing buildings.)

Guide practice

Have students finish reading "New York City" on their own. After they read, have them use a graphic organizer like the one on p. 324 to figure out the author's purpose for writing the passage.

Strategy check

Background Knowledge Remind students that they can use what they already know to help understand what they read. They can think about their own lives or other things they have read. Model the strategy of using background knowledge to monitor understanding.

Model the strategy

Think Aloud I have never been to New York City, but I have seen it in movies and TV shows. I saw pictures of it in a book. I remember seeing skyscrapers. This helps me understand how tall the Empire State building is. Have students review the strategy of using background knowledge on p. EI•18 of the Student Edition.

Student Edition p. EI•18

On their own

Use p. 361 in the *Reader's and Writer's Notebook* for additional practice with author's purpose.

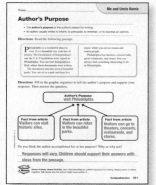
Reader's and Writer's Notebook p. 361

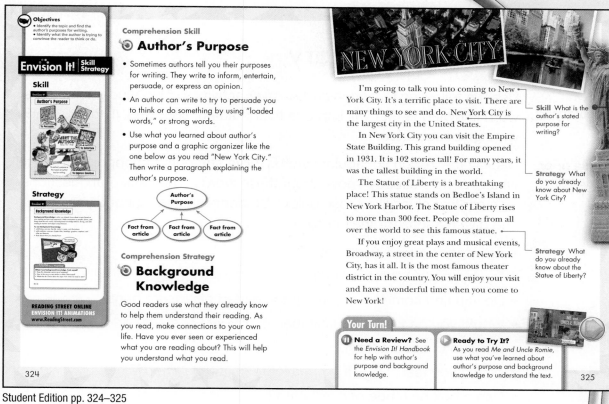

Student Edition pp. 324–325

Skill The author wants to persuade me to visit New York City.

Strategy I know that New York City has a large population and a lot of buildings.

Strategy I know that the Statue of Liberty is very tall.

Model Fluency
Appropriate Phrasing

Model fluent reading

Have students listen as you read paragraph 2 of "New York City" with appropriate phrasing. Explain that you use the punctuation to guide the way you phrase the sentences.

ROUTINE Paired Reading

1. **Select a passage** For "New York City," use the whole passage.

2. **Reading 1** Students read the entire passage, switching readers at the end of each paragraph.

3. **Reading 2** Partners reread the passage. This time the other student begins.

4. **Reread** For optimal fluency, have partners continue to read three or four times.

5. **Corrective Feedback** Listen as students read. Listen to make sure they pause when appropriate and provide feedback as needed.

Routines Flip Chart

ELL

English Language Learners
Author's purpose Have a student find sentences with dates in them. Have a volunteer find a sentence that tells how tall something is. Explain that these sentences tell facts and facts are used to inform.

Vocabulary
Tested Vocabulary

Lesson vocabulary

Use the following Question and Answer activity to help students acquire word knowledge that will improve their reading, speaking, listening, and writing vocabularies.

Activate prior knowledge

Display the lesson vocabulary words. Give students the opportunity to tell whatever they already know about these words. Then ask oral questions with context clues like those below. Students should respond *yes* or *no* and give reasons for their choices.

- Are *stoops* found in windows?
- Does a *pitcher* throw a ball?
- Do you find something good at the end of a *treasure* hunt?
- Would you be tired if you climbed five *flights* of stairs?
- Is a cup of soup a *feast*?
- Would you feel happy if your favorite coat got *ruined*?
- Can a box be made of *cardboard*?
- Does a friendly dog look *fierce*?

Word origins

Explain to students that the word *stoop* comes from the Dutch word *stoep*, meaning front porch. Ask students if they can understand how the word came to have its new pronunciation and spelling.

By the end of the week, students should know the lesson vocabulary words. Have them write *yes* and *no* questions for classmates to answer.

Preteach Academic Vocabulary

 Academic Vocabulary Write the following terms on the board:

conjunction	conflict
eye contact	historical fiction
interview	critique

Have students share what they know about this week's Academic Vocabulary. Use the students' responses to assess their prior knowledge. Preteach the Academic Vocabulary by providing a student-friendly description, explanation, or example that clarifies the meaning of each term. Then ask students to restate the meaning of the Academic Vocabulary term in their own words.

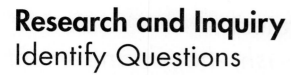 Vocabulary Activities

Research and Inquiry
Identify Questions

Teach
Discuss the Question of the Week: *How does city life compare to life in the country?* Tell students they will research how family life in cities and the country are alike and different. They will write articles to present to the class on Day 5.

Model
(*Think Aloud*) I'll start by brainstorming a list of questions about city life and country life. I know that people have families in both places. First, I wonder about how families are changed by the kind of place they live in. I am interested in sports. We play a lot of soccer where I live in the country, but I wonder if kids can play soccer in the city. Some possible questions could be *Are the sports you can play in the city the same as in the country*? *What kinds of sports leagues are there in different places*? and *What kind of sports do families do together*?

Guide practice
After students have brainstormed open-ended inquiry questions, explain that tomorrow they will conduct online research using their questions. Help students identify keywords that will guide their search.

On their own
Have students work individually, in pairs, or in small groups to write an inquiry question.

INTERNET GUY
Don Leu

21st Century Skills

Weekly Inquiry Project
Day 1 Identify Questions
Day 2 Navigate/Search
Day 3 Analyze
Day 4 Synthesize
Day 5 Communicate

Academic Vocabulary
interview a written conversation between two people, often a reporter and a person from whom information is sought

Small Group Time

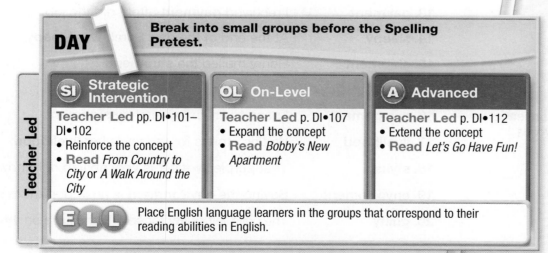

DAY 1

Break into small groups before the Spelling Pretest.

Teacher Led

SI **Strategic Intervention**
Teacher Led pp. DI•101–DI•102
• Reinforce the concept
• **Read** *From Country to City* or *A Walk Around the City*

OL **On-Level**
Teacher Led p. DI•107
• Expand the concept
• **Read** *Bobby's New Apartment*

A **Advanced**
Teacher Led p. DI•112
• Extend the concept
• **Read** *Let's Go Have Fun!*

ELL Place English language learners in the groups that correspond to their reading abilities in English.

Practice Stations
• Read for Meaning
• Get Fluent
• Word Work

Independent Activities
• Concept Talk Video
• *Reader's and Writer's Notebook*
• Vocabulary Activities

ELL

English Language Learners
Multilingual vocabulary
Students can apply knowledge of their home languages to acquire new English vocabulary by using the Multilingual Vocabulary Lists (*ELL Handbook*, pp. 443–444).

Objectives
- Spell words with suffixes *-y*, *-ish*, *-hood*, and *-ment*.
- Use and understand conjunctions.
- Write cursive uppercase *V*, *W*, and *Y* with correct letter spacing.

Spelling Pretest
Suffixes *-y*, *-ish*, *-hood*, and *-ment*

Introduce Tell students to think of words that end with the suffixes *-y (sleepy)*, *-ish (sheepish)*, *-hood (brotherhood)*, and *-ment (department)*. This week we will spell words that end with the suffixes *-y*, *-ish*, *-hood*, and *-ment*. As you spell these words, remember to divide the words with suffixes into base word and suffix to spell them.

Pretest Use these sentences to administer the spelling pretest. Say each word, read the sentence, and repeat the word.

1. **rocky**	This is a **rocky** beach.
2. **foolish**	Anthony regretted his **foolish** behavior.
3. **rainy**	**Rainy** days make me feel sad.
4. **childhood**	**Childhood** should be a time of learning.
5. **selfish**	Sometimes it is **selfish** not to share.
6. **treatment**	I went to the doctor for **treatment.**
7. **movement**	Cops tracked the robber's **movement.**
8. **neighborhood**	My **neighborhood** is friendly.
9. **childish**	They think his pouting is **childish.**
10. **parenthood**	**Parenthood** can be stressful.
11. **crunchy**	This **crunchy** cereal is delicious.
12. **bumpy**	The bus bounced on the **bumpy** road.
13. **payment**	I received **payment** after I did the job.
14. **sleepy**	At the end of the day, Sarah was **sleepy.**
15. **shipment**	Henry mailed the **shipment.**

Challenge words

16. **assignment**	I need to finish my math **assignment.**
17. **livelihood**	Writing stories for money is her **livelihood.**
18. **stylish**	That purple sweater is very **stylish** right now.
19. **environment**	Saving the **environment** is an important topic.
20. **guilty**	The child felt **guilty** for spilling the juice on the rug.

Self-correct After the pretest, you can either display the correctly spelled words or spell them orally. Have students self-correct their pretests by rewriting misspelled words correctly.

On their own For additional practice, use *Let's Practice It!* page 329 on the *Teacher Resources DVD-ROM.*

Let's Practice It!
TR DVD•329

Conventions
Conjunctions

Teach
Display Grammar Transparency 25, and read aloud the explanation and examples in the box. Point out the ways to use *and, but, or,* and *because.*

Model
Model writing the correct conjunction to complete numbers 1 and 2. Apply the rules for conjunctions to show how you determined the correct one to use.

Guide practice
Guide students to complete items 3–5. Remind them to think about whether they are adding information or showing a choice, difference, or reason. Record the correct responses on the transparency.

Daily Fix-It
Use Daily Fix-It numbers 1 and 2 in the right margin.

Connect to oral language
Have students read sentences 6–10 on the transparency and circle the correct word in the parentheses to complete each sentence.

Grammar Transparency 25, TR DVD

Handwriting
Cursive Letters *V, W, Y*

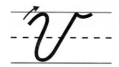  

Model letter formation
Display the uppercase cursive letters *V, W,* and *Y.* Follow the stroke instruction pictured to model letter formation.

Model letter spacing
Explain that writing legibly means that the space between letters is not too large or too small. Model writing this sentence with proper letter spacing: *Vicky asked Wayne if he knows Yvonne.* Make sure the letters aren't too light, dark, or jagged.

Guide practice
Have students write these sentences. *What is the capital of West Virginia? Young's Yo-Yo Shop sells games.* Circulate around the room, guiding students.

Academic Vocabulary
A **conjunction** is a word that connects words or groups of words.

Daily Fix-It
1. Jeffs uncle lives in a city neighborhod. *(Jeff's; neighborhood)*
2. His sister and him visits Uncle Jim every summer. *(he; visit)*

ELL

English Language Learners
Conjunctions Write two sentences that use two of the conjunctions. Provide support for students based on their proficiency levels:

Beginning Read the sentences aloud and have students echo. Then have them say the conjunction used in each sentence.

Intermediate Have students write the sentences and circle the conjunctions. Have them tell the purpose of each conjunction.

Advanced/Advanced High Remove the conjunctions from the sentences, and have students rewrite them with the missing information.

Handwriting: Proper names To provide practice in handwriting uppercase cursive letters *V, W,* and *Y,* and to extend language opportunities, have students write proper names that begin with these letters. (*Valentín, Wendy, Yi-Min*)

Objectives
• Understand and identify the features of a book review.

MINI-LESSON

5 Day Planner
Guide to Mini-Lessons

DAY 1	Read Like a Writer
DAY 2	Preparing to Review
DAY 3	Organizing Your Review
DAY 4	Revising Strategy: Adding
DAY 5	Proofread for Conjunctions

Writing—Book Review
Introduce

MINI-LESSON

Read Like a Writer

■ **Introduce** This week you will write a critique. A critique is a review of someone's work. There are many kinds of critiques, and one of them is a **book review.** A book review gives information and opinions about a book. People who have not read the book use the review to help them decide whether they want to read it.

Prompt	Think about this story or another story or book you have read recently. Write a book review of it, explaining to readers whether they should read it.
Trait	Conventions
Mode	Narrative

Reader's and Writer's Notebook p. 362

■ **Examine Model Text** Let's read an example of a book review for a book called *My Colors, My World/Mis colores, mi mundo.* Have students read the book review on p. 362 of their *Reader's and Writer's Notebook.*

■ **Key Features** Book reviews should include the title of the book being reviewed. The title of the book should be underlined in a review. **Have students circle the title of the book in the model.**

A book review also tells what the book is about. **Have students write a sentence summarizing the book.**

Book reviews either urge readers to read or to avoid the book. What is the writer of this book review trying to persuade the reader to do? **Have students list reasons the writer thinks others should read the book.**

A good book review demonstrates that the writer has a good understanding of what the book is about. **Discuss whether the writer demonstrates a good understanding of the text.**

Review key features Review the key features book review with students. You may want to post the key features in the classroom for students to reference as they work on their book reviews.

Key Features of a Book Review

- tells the name of the book and what the book is about
- gives an opinion about the story or subject
- often urges others to read, or avoid, the book
- demonstrates an understanding of the text

ROUTINE

Quick Write for Fluency **Team Talk**

1. **Talk** Pairs discuss the key features of a book review.
2. **Write** Each student writes two sentences about where a book review might appear.
3. **Share** Partners read aloud their writing to one another.

Routines Flip Chart

Wrap Up Your Day

✔ **Build Concepts** Have students discuss how city life compares to life in the country.

✔ **Oral Vocabulary** Have students use the Amazing Words sentences.

✔ Homework Send home this week's Family Times Newsletter, *Let's Practice It!* pages 330–331 on the *Teacher Resources DVD-ROM.*

Let's Practice It!
TR DVD•330–331

Write Guy
Jeff Anderson

Trait-by-Trait Organization

Organization is a trait of good writing, but let's not be so concerned with form that we forget about meaning. A student may develop a good way to communicate ideas that does not precisely follow the format we expect.

ELL

English Language Learners

Book review Read the writing model aloud and help students understand it. Remind students that book reviews tell about the book and then encourage their audience to read it or to avoid it. Ask students what qualities make a good book.

Academic Vocabulary

A **critique** is a review of a piece of writing, drama, music, or other works of art.

Preview DAY 2

Tell students that tomorrow they will read about a boy from North Carolina who went to visit New York City.

Objectives
- Expand the weekly concept.
- Develop oral vocabulary.

Today at a Glance

Oral Vocabulary
vendor, hurl

Phonics/Word Analysis
◉ Suffixes *-y, -ish, -hood, -ment*

Literary Terms
Onomatopoeia

Story Structure
Conflict

Lesson Vocabulary
◉ Homonyms

Reading
"A Different Treasure Hunt"

Me and Uncle Romie

Fluency
Appropriate phrasing

Research and Inquiry
Navigate/Search

Spelling
Suffixes *-y, -ish, -hood,* and *-ment*

Conventions
Conjunctions

Writing
Book review

Concept Talk

Question of the Week

How does city life compare to life in the country?

Expand the concept

Remind students of the weekly concept question. Tell students that today they will begin reading *Me and Uncle Romie.* As they read, encourage students to think about how city life compares to country life.

Anchored Talk

Develop oral vocabulary

Use the photos on pp. 320–321 and the Read Aloud, "Nature in the City," to talk about the Amazing Words: *taxicab, scamper, scurry,* and *skyscraper.* Add these and other concept-related words to the concept map to develop students' knowledge of the topic. Encourage detailed responses to the questions. Discuss the following questions.

- What would you see *scurry* down a country lane? down a city street?
- How do *skyscrapers* and *taxicabs* go together?
- What animals *scamper* in both the city and the country?

Oral Vocabulary
Amazing Words

Amazing Words

skyscraper	hurl
taxicab	meager
scamper	gutter
scurry	bitter
vendor	ramble

Teach Amazing Words

> **Amazing Words** Oral Vocabulary Routine
>
> ① **Introduce** Write the Amazing Word *vendor* on the board. Have students say it aloud with you. Relate *vendor* to "New York City." *What kinds of vendors might you see on the streets in New York?* (You might see vendors selling food, hats, or books.) Have students use context clues to determine the definition of the word. *A vendor is someone who sells things, usually outdoors.*
>
> ② **Demonstrate** Have students answer questions to demonstrate understanding. *What kinds of vendors have you seen at a fair? What might a vendor say to get your attention?*
>
> ③ **Apply** Have students apply their understanding. *Would you buy a house from a vendor? What is something you might buy from a vendor?*
>
> See p. OV•2 to teach *hurl.*

Routines Flip Chart

Apply Amazing Words

As students read "A Different Treasure Hunt" on p. 327, have them think about how a pitcher *hurls* a baseball and what a *vendor* sells at a baseball game.

Connect to reading

Explain that today students will read about James who leaves the country to go visit his aunt and uncle in New York City. As they read, remind students to think about the Question of the Week and how the Amazing Words *vendor* and *hurl* apply to James's experience.

ELL **Reinforce Vocabulary** Use the Day 2 instruction on ELL Poster 25 to teach lesson vocabulary and discuss the lesson concept.

ELL Poster 25

Objectives
◎ Apply knowledge of base words and suffixes to decode words in context and independent of context.
• Identify onomatopoeia.
• Understand conflict in stories.

Check Word Reading
SUCCESS PREDICTOR

Word Analysis
 Suffixes *-y, -ish, -hood, -ment*

Review

Review the suffixes *-y, -ish, -hood,* and *-ment,* pointing out that suffixes are added at the end of base words.

Read words independent of context

Display these words. Have the class decode the words. Then point to the words in random order and ask students to read them quickly.

knighthood	wooly	Scottish	girlhood
treatment	boyish	honesty	grayish

Corrective feedback

Model reading the base word and then the suffix, and then ask students to read the word with you.

Read words in context

Display these sentences. Have the class read the sentences.

Team Talk Have pairs take turns reading the sentences naturally.

> My **English** grandmother likes to tell stories about her **neighborhood.**
> **Bravery** was important in the **olden days.**
> The **measurement** of the wall was off by two inches.

Don't Wait Until Friday

MONITOR PROGRESS **Check Word Reading**

Write the following words and have the class read them. Notice which words students miss during the group reading. Call on individuals to read some of the words.

tasty	reddish	brotherhood	skinny
planner	pianist	hostess	editor
unlikely	unselfish	reworked	discontented

Spiral Review
Row 2 reviews words with suffixes *-er, -ist, -ess, -or.*

Row 3 contrasts words with prefixes and suffixes.

If... students cannot read words with suffixes at this point, **then...** use the Day 1 Word Parts Strategy routine on p. 322a to reteach suffixes. Use words from the Decodable Practice Passages (or Reader). Continue to monitor students' progress using other instructional opportunities during the week. See the Skills Trace on p. 322a.

Day 1	Day 2	Day 3	Day 4	Day 5
Check Oral Vocabulary	Check Word Reading	Check Retelling	Check Fluency	Check Oral Vocabulary

Success Predictor

Literary Terms
Onomatopoeia

Academic Vocabulary

conflict the struggle in a story between two people, between a person and a force of nature, or between two groups of people

Teach onomatopoeia

Tell students that words that sound like their meanings are called onomatopoeia. These sound words help reinforce meanings, dramatize events, and appeal to the senses.

Model onomatopoeia

Think Aloud Let's look at "New York City." When I think of the sounds of cities, I think of onomatopoeia. There's the *honk-honk* of car horns and the *screech* of cars hitting their brakes. Can you think of other words to describe city sounds? (Answers will vary. Students should identify onomatopoeic words.)

Guide practice

Point out an example of onomatopoeia on p. 332 of *Me and Uncle Romie.* Have students read the words *chug-a-chug-a-chug-a-chug* aloud and notice how they sound like the sound of a train.

On their own

Have students find other examples of onomatopoeia in other selections of their Student Edition.

Story Structure
Conflict

Teach conflict

Tell students that many fictional stories have a conflict or problem. It is usually introduced at the beginning of the story and may be between two people, a person and nature, between two groups of people, or within a person.

Model the strategy

Think Aloud Story structure can help us understand what happens when we read fiction. In "A Different Treasure Hunt," the narrator of the story has a conflict between living in the city and living in the country. Knowing that will help us predict what might happen.

Guide practice

Have students identify the conflict in *Me and Uncle Romie.* Point out that recognizing the conflict helps students predict what will happen in a story.

On their own

Have students look for conflicts in other selections of their Student Edition.

Word Reading

Success Predictor

Vocabulary Strategy for
🔁 Homonyms

Student Edition p. W•11

Teach homonyms

Envision It!

Read and discuss the first paragraph on p. 326. Explain how the strategy of context clues can help students determine the meaning of a homonym. Refer students to *Words!* on p. W•11 in the Student Edition for additional practice.

Model the strategy

Think Aloud

Write on the board: *I see pots of flowers on all the front stoops of the apartments. The boy stoops down to pick up a coin off the sidewalk.* *Stoops* is a homonym. I can figure out the meaning of each homonym by reading the words around it. In the first sentence, I read that the stoops are on the front of apartments. This homonym means "area by the front door." In the second sentence, the boy stoops down to the sidewalk. This homonym means "bends over." Context clues help me understand what each homonym means.

Guide practice

Write these sentences on the board: *I ran up three flights of stairs to get to the third floor. The family left their carry-on luggage behind after their flight.* Have students determine the meaning of *flight* using context clues. Let students use a dictionary to confirm their answers. For additional support, use *Envision It! Pictured Vocabulary Cards* or *Tested Vocabulary Cards.*

On their own

Read "A Different Treasure Hunt" on p. 327. Have students identify the context clues that help them define each lesson vocabulary word before they write their responses. For additional practice, use the *Reader's and Writer's Notebook* p. 363.

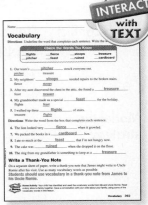

Reader's and Writer's Notebook p. 363

Objectives
• Use context clues to figure out words you don't know or words that have more than one meaning.
• Identify words that are opposites, similar, have more than one meaning, and that sound the same even though they mean different things.

Envision It! Words to Know

cardboard

feast

treasure

fierce
flights
pitcher
ruined
stoops

READING STREET ONLINE
VOCABULARY ACTIVITIES
www.ReadingStreet.com

326

Vocabulary Strategy for

Homonyms

Context Clues You may read a familiar word that doesn't make sense in the sentence. The word could be a homonym. Homonyms are words that are pronounced and spelled the same, but have different meanings. For example, *saw* means "looked at" and "a tool for cutting." Use the context—the words and sentences around the word—to figure out the correct meaning.

1. Reread the words and sentences around the word that doesn't make sense.

2. Draw a conclusion about another meaning for the word using context clues.

3. Try the meaning in the sentence. Does it make sense?

Read "A Different Treasure Hunt" on page 327. Use context clues to help you find the meanings of homonyms.

Words to Write Reread "A Different Treasure Hunt." Write your answer to the question at the end of the selection. Give reasons for your answer. Use homonyms and words from the Words to Know list in your answer.

A DIFFERENT TREASURE HUNT

The summer I turned eight, my family moved from New York City to North Carolina. In the city, we climbed four flights of stairs to our apartment. The building was ten stories high! People sat on their front stoops and listened to the noise. I was a pitcher on the neighborhood baseball team.

In North Carolina, we live in a house. All the houses have front porches and yards. At night it is very dark and quiet. At first, I thought my life was ruined.

My mother saw my fierce face. She suggested I have a treasure hunt, but instead of looking for gold, I should look for baseball players. She promised to help by preparing a feast with all my favorite food. I made signs on cardboard and posted them at the grocery store, the library, and the post office. The signs said:

I'm looking for
baseball players.
Come to 124 Willow Street
June 28 at 2:00 P.M.
FREE FOOD!
Do you think anyone
showed up?

Your Turn!

⏸ **Need a Review?** For additional help with homonyms, see *Words!*

▶ **Ready to Try It?** Read *Me and Uncle Romie* on pp. 328–349.

327

Student Edition pp. 326–327

Reread for Fluency
Appropriate Phrasing

Model fluent reading

Read paragraph 2 of "A Different Treasure Hunt," pausing for commas and periods to emphasize appropriate phrasing. Tell students to notice the punctuation as they follow along.

ROUTINE Paired Reading

1. **Select a passage** For "A Different Treasure Hunt," use the whole passage.

2. **Reading 1** Students read the entire passage, switching readers at the end of each paragraph.

3. **Reading 2** Partners reread the passage. This time the other student begins.

4. **Reread** For optimal fluency, have partners continue to read three or four times.

5. **Corrective Feedback** Listen as students read. Provide feedback about whether they pause when and where it makes sense to stop.

Routines Flip Chart

Lesson Vocabulary

cardboard thick, stiff paper
feast a meal with a lot of food
fierce frightening, scary
flights a set of stairs
pitcher a person who throws a baseball to a batter
ruined destroyed or damaged
stoops small porches with steps, usually at the front of a house
treasure valuables; prizes

Differentiated Instruction

SI Strategic Intervention
Have students use a dictionary to determine which of the following words are homonyms: *flight, stoop, bear, pound,* and *fair* (all of the words are homonyms).

ELL

English Language Learners
Build Academic Vocabulary
Use the lesson vocabulary pictured on p. 326 to teach the meanings of *cardboard, feast,* and *treasure.* Call on pairs to write the words on sticky notes and use them to label images of the words on the ELL Poster.

Objectives

- Understand the elements of historical fiction.
- Use title and illustrations to preview and predict.
- Set a purpose for reading.

Genre **Historical fiction** is set in the past. Some of the details are factual, but others are made up or loosely based on history. Look for the factual details as you read.

Question of the Week
How does city life compare to life in the country?

Student Edition pp. 328–329

Build Background

Discuss city life

Team Talk Have students turn to a partner and discuss the Question of the Week and these questions about city life. Remind students to ask and answer questions with appropriate detail and to build on each other's ideas.

- What modes of transportation do people use in a city?
- What kinds of buildings do you see in a city?
- What activities do people do for fun in a city?

Connect to selection

Have students discuss their answers with the class. Possible responses: People use different forms of public transportation in a city, such as subways, buses, and trains. Apartment buildings and tall buildings such as skyscrapers are found often in cities. Fun activities people do in cities include going to museums, parks, and sporting events. For additional opportunities to build background, use the Background Building Audio.

Prereading Strategies

Genre
Remind students that **historical fiction** tells a made-up story that takes place in the past. Setting is important in historical fiction as it demonstrates how the characters lived at that time.

Preview and predict
Have students read the title, the author, and the illustrator for *Me and Uncle Romie.* Have them use the title and illustrations to predict what they think the selection will be about. Let them use the illustrations to identify the story setting.

Set purpose
Prior to reading, have students set their own purposes for reading this selection. To help students set a purpose, ask them to think about how life in the country is similar to life in the city.

Strategy Response Log

 INTERACT with TEXT

Have students use p. 31 in the *Reader's and Writer's Notebook* to identify the characteristics of historical fiction.

Small Group Time

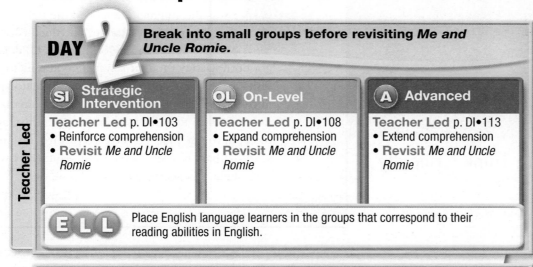

DAY 2

Break into small groups before revisiting *Me and Uncle Romie.*

Teacher Led

SI Strategic Intervention	**OL** On-Level	**A** Advanced
Teacher Led p. DI•103 • Reinforce comprehension • **Revisit** *Me and Uncle Romie*	**Teacher Led** p. DI•108 • Expand comprehension • **Revisit** *Me and Uncle Romie*	**Teacher Led** p. DI•113 • Extend comprehension • **Revisit** *Me and Uncle Romie*

ELL Place English language learners in the groups that correspond to their reading abilities in English.

Practice Stations	**Independent Activities**
• Words to Know • Get Fluent • Word Wise	• Background Building Audio • *Reader's and Writer's Notebook* • Research and Inquiry

Differentiated Instruction

 Strategic Intervention
Work with students to set a purpose for reading, or if time permits, have students work with partners to set purposes.

A Advanced
Have students trace on a United States map the route James most likely took from North Carolina to New York City.

 Multidraft Reading
For **Whole Group** instruction, choose one of the reading options below. For each reading, have students set the purpose indicated.

Option 1
Day 2 Read the selection. Use Guide Comprehension to monitor and clarify understanding.
Day 3 Reread the selection. Use Extend Thinking to develop higher-order thinking skills.

Option 2
Day 2 Read the first half of the selection, using both Guide Comprehension and Extend Thinking instruction.
Day 3 Read the second half of the selection, using both Guide Comprehension and Extend Thinking instruction.

 **ELL**

English Language Learners
Build background To build background, review the summary selection in English (*ELL Handbook*, p. 175). Use the Retelling Cards to provide visual support for the summary.

DAY 2 Read and Comprehend

Objectives

◎ Identify and analyze author's purpose to aid comprehension.

OPTION 1 Guide Comprehension Skills and Strategies

Teach Author's Purpose

Author's Purpose Ask students to explain why the author describes Uncle Romie before James meets him. (Possible response: She wants the reader to understand how James pictures Uncle Romie so the reader can understand why James is nervous, and be curious about the visit.)

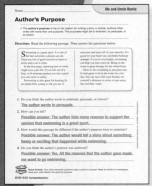

Let's Practice It!
TR DVD•332

Corrective Feedback

If... students are unable to explain the author's purpose,

then... use the model to help them infer the author's purpose.

Model the Skill

Think Aloud To figure out why the author describes Uncle Romie, I first think about how she describes him. She says he is "a bald-headed, fierce-eyed giant," and makes it clear that James finds him scary and is unsure about the upcoming visit.

Student Edition pp. 330–331

It was the summer Mama had the twins that I first met my uncle Romie. The doctor had told Mama she had to stay off her feet till the babies got born. Daddy thought it was a good time for me to visit Uncle Romie and his wife, Aunt Nanette, up north in New York City. But I wasn't so sure. Mama had told me that Uncle Romie was some kind of artist, and he didn't have any kids. I'd seen his picture too. He looked scary—a bald-headed, fierce-eyed giant. No, I wasn't sure about this visit at all.

330

OPTION 2 Extend Thinking Think Critically

Higher-Order Thinking Skills

Author's Purpose • Analysis How does the author use the last paragraph on page 331 to help you understand that James is nervous about the trip? Possible response: James says he is lucky to get to ride on the train, but then he thinks "maybe." The author wrote this to show that James is unsure about the trip.

Cause and Effect • Analysis Which sentence tells why James had to go north to New York City? The doctor had told Mama she had to stay off her feet till the babies got born.

I think the author wants the reader to wonder what Uncle Romie will be like in real life and if James will continue to be afraid of him.

On Their Own

Have students reread pp. 330–331 to find other reasons the writer wrote what she did. For additional practice with author's purpose, see *Let's Practice It!* page 332 on the *Teacher Resources DVD-ROM.*

Connect to Social Studies

Trains were very important to the expansion of the United States. Long before there were airplanes, people and freight traveled throughout the United States by train. Up until World War II, most Americans traveled long distances by train, and train service was available from coast to coast.

T he day before I left home was a regular North Carolina summer day. "A good train-watching day," my friend B. J. said.

We waited quietly in the grass beside the tracks. B. J. heard it first. "It's a'coming," he said. Then I heard it too—a low rumbling, building to a roar. *WHOOO—OOO!*

"The *Piedmont!*" we shouted as the train blasted past.

"I'm the greatest train-watcher ever," B. J. boasted.

"Yeah," I answered, "but tomorrow I'll be *riding* a train. I'm the lucky one."

Lucky, I thought as we headed home. *Maybe.*

331

Review **Draw Conclusions • Analysis** What conclusion can you draw about the relationship between James and B.J.? What evidence can you use to draw this conclusion? **Possible response:** They seem to be very good friends, probably because they share an interest in trains: when James spends a "regular North Carolina summer day," he spends it with B.J. watching trains, and the two boys boast playfully to each other about being great at identifying trains and getting to ride an actual train.

English Language Learners
Activate prior knowledge Create a web to record students' prior knowledge of trains. We're going to read about a boy who likes to watch trains and takes a trip on a train. What do you know about trains? Where have you seen them? How do trains move? On what do they travel?

Objectives
- Draw conclusions about characters.

OPTION 1

Skills and Strategies, continued

Teach Draw Conclusions

Review **Draw Conclusions** Ask students why they think James is telling his mother he will miss the way she makes his birthday special. (James will be celebrating his birthday in New York with Uncle Romie and Aunt Nanette instead of at home with his mother.)

Corrective Feedback

If... students are unable to draw a conclusion about James's birthday, **then...** model for students how to draw a conclusion.

Let's Practice It!
TR DVD•333

Model the Skill

Think Aloud To figure out why James will miss the way his mother makes his birthday special, I must figure out why this birthday will be different.

Student Edition pp. 332–333

> That evening I packed my suitcase. Voices drifted up from the porch below.
>
> "Romie's got that big art show coming up," Mama said quietly. "I hope he's not too busy for James, especially on his birthday."
>
> "Romie's a good man," Daddy replied. "And Nanette'll be there too."
>
> The light faded. Mama called me into her bedroom. "Where's my good-night kiss?" she said.
>
> I curled up next to her. "I'll miss the way you make my birthday special, Mama. Your lemon cake and the baseball game."
>
> "Well," Mama sighed, "it won't be those things. But Uncle Romie and Aunt Nanette are family, and they love you too. It'll still be a good birthday, honey."
>
> Mama pulled me close. Her voice sang soft and low. Later, in my own bed, I listened as crickets began their song and continued into the night.
>
> The next morning I hugged Mama good-bye, and Daddy and I headed for the train. He got me seated, then stood waving at me from the outside. I held tight to the jar of pepper jelly Mama had given me for Uncle Romie.
>
> "ALL A-BOARD!" The conductor's voice crackled over the loudspeaker.
>
> The train pulled away. *Chug-a-chug-a-chug-a-chug.* I watched my town move past my window—bright-colored houses, chickens strutting across the yards, flowers everywhere.
>
> 332

OPTION 2

Think Critically, continued

Higher-Order Thinking Skills

Review **Draw Conclusions • Analysis** How does Daddy probably think James's birthday will be? Daddy says Romie is a good man and notes that Nanette will be there too, so he probably feels Romie and Nanette will help James celebrate and have a nice birthday.

Review **Draw Conclusions • Evaluation** How do you think James feels about the trip? Explain your answer. Possible response: He is still nervous. He stays up late listening to crickets instead of getting a good night's sleep, and once on the train he holds tight to the jar of pepper jelly for Uncle Romie, which shows he is nervous about losing it.

His mother tells him that Uncle Romie and Aunt Nanette are family and that James will still have a good birthday. I can tell that James's birthday will happen during his visit, so his mother will not be with him for it.

333

Figurative Language • Analysis How does the onomatopoeia on page 332 help the reader experience what traveling by train is like? The *chug-a-chug-a-chug-a-chug* helps the reader understand the sound James hears the train making as it travels down the track.

On Their Own

Have students use the information on p. 332 to draw other conclusions about James's trip. For additional practice with drawing conclusions, see *Let's Practice It!* page 333 on the *Teacher Resources DVD-ROM.*

Differentiated Instruction

 Advanced

Connect text-to-text Help students locate other books illustrated by Jerome Lagarrigue. Ask them to compare the art in these books with the illustrations in *Me and Uncle Romie.*

ELL

English Language Learners

Extend language Point out the contractions *Nanette'll* and *It'll* on p. 332. Explain that this particular type of contraction or blending of subject and verb (*Nanette will* and *It will*) occurs only in informal dialogue and is not considered standard English.

OPTION 1 Skills and Strategies, continued

Teach Homonyms

◉ **Homonyms** Point out the word *kind* on p. 334. Tell students that it is a homonym. Have them identify the word's meaning as it is used in the sentence in the story.

Corrective Feedback

If... students are unable to determine the meaning of *kind*,

then... model replacing *kind* in the sentence with each definition to find the one that fits.

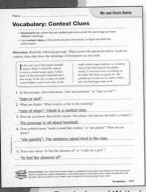

Reader's and Writer's
Notebook p. 367

Model the Skill

Think Aloud What do we call words that have the same pronunciation and the same spelling but different meanings? (homonyms) I found two entries for *kind* in the dictionary. Which meaning of *kind* is the author using? (nearly; almost; somewhat)

After a while I felt hungry. Daddy had packed me a lunch and a dinner to eat one at a time. I ate almost everything at once. Then my belly felt tight and I was kind of sleepy. I closed my eyes and dreamed about Mama and Daddy getting ready for those babies. Would they even miss me?

Later, when I woke up, I ate the last bit of my dinner and thought about my birthday. Would they make my lemon cake and take me to a baseball game in New York?

The sky turned from dark blue to black. I was getting sleepy all over again.

"We're almost there, son," the man next to me said.

Then I saw it . . . New York City. Buildings stretching up to the sky. So close together. Not like North Carolina at all.

334

Student Edition pp. 334–335

OPTION 2 Think Critically, continued

Higher-Order Thinking Skills

◉ **Homonyms • Analysis** Use context clues to tell the meaning of the homonym *close* in the first paragraph on page 335. Possible response: In the sentence before, it says that James got down to the platform. This sentence has "to the train" after the word *close*. The direction word *down* and "to the train" help me see that *close* is a direction word. In this sentence *close* means "near."

Monitor and Clarify • Synthesis How long do you think it takes James to get from North Carolina to New York? How do you know? Possible response: When I reread parts of the story, I notice that it doesn't say exactly how long the trip takes. It says that James leaves in the morning and that his father packs him a lunch and a dinner to eat on the train. Also, it says that the sky turns from blue to black which means by the time he gets there it is night. I think the train ride probably takes at least ten hours.

On Their Own

Have students use context clues to figure out the meaning of *last* as it is used in the second paragraph on p. 334. (the only part left) For additional practice with homonyms, see *Reader's and Writer's Notebook* p. 367.

Differentiated Instruction

SI Strategic Intervention

Homonyms Have students illustrate the different meanings for the homonyms *pack* and *close*.

"Penn Station! Watch your step," the conductor said, helping me down to the platform. I did like Daddy said and found a spot for myself close to the train. Swarms of people rushed by. Soon I heard a silvery voice call my name. This had to be Aunt Nanette. I turned and saw her big smile reaching out to welcome me.

She took my hand and guided me through the rushing crowds onto an underground train called the subway. "This will take us right home," she explained.

335

Background Knowledge • Evaluation •

Text to Self Do you think it is safe for a child to travel alone? Explain why or why not using details from the selection and your own experience. Possible response: I think it is safe because no one bothered James on the ride. The man next to him and the conductor were helpful to James. When I traveled alone on a plane, the flight attendant made sure I was safe.

E L L

English Language Learners

Verbs Review the irregular verbs used on pp. 334–335. Show how each verb changes and help students practice the verbs to memorize them.

feel	felt	felt
eat	ate	eaten
say	said	said
see	saw	seen
hear	heard	heard

Objectives

◎ Use background knowledge to confirm character's predictions.

Teach Background Knowledge

🔊 **Background Knowledge** Have students reread James's description of Uncle Romie on p. 330. Then ask if James's descriptions or ideas of Uncle Romie are accurate. (Possible response: Before he meets him, James describes Uncle Romie as "a bald-headed, fierce-looking giant." In New York, he describes him as a giant who has a deep and loud voice. However, when I look at the illustration of Uncle Romie on p. 337, he doesn't seem fierce-looking. James's ideas might not be accurate.)

Corrective Feedback

If... students have difficulty answering the question,
then... model how to use background knowledge to understand a story.

Model the Strategy

Think Aloud On page 330, how does James describe Uncle Romie's picture? (bald-headed, fierce-looking giant) On page 337, how is Uncle Romie described? (heavy footsteps, giant, deep and loud voice)

Home was like nothing I'd ever seen before. No regular houses anywhere. Just big buildings and stores of all kinds—in the windows I saw paints, fabrics, radios, and TVs.

We turned into the corner building and climbed the stairs to the apartment—five whole flights up. *Whew!* I tried to catch my breath while Aunt Nanette flicked on the lights.

"Uncle Romie's out talking to some people about his big art show that's coming up. He'll be home soon," Aunt Nanette said. She set some milk and a plate of cookies for me on the table. "Your uncle's working very hard, so we won't see much of him for a while. His workroom—we call it his studio—is in the front of our apartment. That's where he keeps all the things he needs to make his art."

336

🔊 **Homonyms • Analysis** Point out the word flights on p. 336. How can you confirm that the word *flight* is a homonym? I can look in a dictionary to see if there are different numbered entries for the word.

Student Edition pp. 336–337

Higher-Order Thinking Skills

🔊 **Background Knowledge • Synthesis • Text to Self**
What happens when you describe or judge someone before you know that person? Possible response: When I have an idea about someone before I meet that person, it can be difficult to get to know him or her because often my ideas about that person are wrong.

How does Uncle Romie look in the illustration? (friendly and nice) I think that James thought Uncle Romie was going to be fierce, but he is not.

"Doesn't he just paint?" I asked.

"Uncle Romie is a collage artist," Aunt Nanette explained. "He uses paints, yes. But also photographs, newspapers, cloth. He cuts and pastes them onto a board to make his paintings."

"That sounds kinda easy," I said.

Aunt Nanette laughed.

"Well, there's a little more to it than that, James. When you see the paintings, you'll understand. Come, let's get you to bed."

Lying in the dark, I heard heavy footsteps in the hall. A giant stared at me from the doorway. "Hello there, James." Uncle Romie's voice was deep and loud, like thunder. "Thanks for the pepper jelly," he boomed. "You have a good sleep, now." Then he disappeared down the hall.

337

⟲ Background Knowledge • Synthesis

Where would you look back to find a description of James's regular home to contrast with the description of his new home on p. 336? I would look back at the description of what he saw looking out of the moving train on p. 332.

On Their Own

Have students tell why using background knowledge can help them understand and enjoy a story.

Differentiated Instruction

SI Strategic Intervention

Monitor and clarify Have students work in pairs to reread pp. 336–337, identifying passages they don't understand and using rereading, reading ahead, or the illustrations to clarify.

ELL

English Language Learners

Background knowledge Discuss students' prior knowledge of types of housing. In this story, James goes to an apartment. How would you describe an apartment? What other kinds of houses are there? How are they like apartments? How are they different?

Objectives

◉ Use context clues and text features to identify author's purpose.

OPTION 1 Skills and Strategies, continued

Teach Author's Purpose

🎯 **Author's Purpose** After students have read p. 338, ask why they think the author describes the things James does on his first day in New York. (Possible response: She wants to show that, so far, he is having a good time and that his trip is turning out well.)

Corrective Feedback

If... students are unable to explain the author's purpose,
then... use the model to help them infer the author's purpose.

Model the Skill

Think Aloud What did James do on his first day in New York? (He went to a market, played stickball, and ate ice cream and barbecue.) How would you describe a day filled with these activities? (fun)

The next morning the door to Uncle Romie's studio was closed. But Aunt Nanette had plans for both of us. "Today we're going to a neighborhood called Harlem," she said. "It's where Uncle Romie lived as a boy."

Harlem was full of people walking, working, shopping, eating. Some were watching the goings-on from fire escapes. Others were sitting out on stoops greeting folks who passed by—just like the people back home calling out hellos from their front porches. Most everybody seemed to know Aunt Nanette. A lot of them asked after Uncle Romie too.

We bought peaches at the market, then stopped to visit awhile. I watched some kids playing stickball. "Go on, get in that game," Aunt Nanette said, gently pushing me over to join them. When I was all hot and sweaty, we cooled off with double chocolate scoops from the ice cream man. Later we shared some barbecue on a rooftop way up high. I felt like I was on top of the world.

As the days went by, Aunt Nanette took me all over the city—we rode a ferry boat to the Statue of Liberty . . . zoomed 102 floors up at the Empire State Building . . . window-shopped the fancy stores on Fifth Avenue . . . gobbled hot dogs in Central Park.

But it was Harlem that I liked best. I played stickball with the kids again . . . and on a really hot day a whole bunch of us ran through the icy cold water that sprayed out hard from the fire hydrant. In the evenings Aunt Nanette and I sat outside listening to the street musicians playing their saxophone songs.

338

Student Edition pp. 338–339

OPTION 2 Think Critically, continued

Higher-Order Thinking Skills

🎯 **Author's Purpose • Analysis** Why did the author use ellipsis between each of the activities in the fourth paragraph on page 338? She is showing that James and Aunt Nanette did not do all of the activities in one day and that this is just a sampling of some of the activities they did.

Genre • Evaluation Where do you find evidence that this story is historical fiction? Does the author do a good job of letting the reader know that this story is set in the past? Possible response: The illustrations show the story is set in the past. However, since this story could take place today, it is fine that there is not much evidence of exactly when the story takes place.

What is the author saying about James's first day? (He had fun.) James had fun on his first day so the author is showing that the trip is going well.

On Their Own

Have students reread p. 338 to find other reasons why the author wrote what she did.

Differentiated Instruction

SI Strategic Intervention

Visualize Working in small groups, have students make a collage that portrays what James and Aunt Nanette did while in New York. Let each group display and describe the collage.

A Advanced

Analyze Discuss why James might like Harlem best, comparing the things he does there with the things he does in other places around New York and noting the connection with Uncle Romie's childhood.

339

ELL

English Language Learners

Graphic organizer Help students make a web to record and organize details about all the different things that James does with Aunt Nanette in New York.

Background knowledge Help students find nonfiction books that include photographs of New York City. Have students describe what they see in the pictures. If possible, include pictures of places James visited. Have students match photos to the text descriptions.

Background Knowledge • Evaluation •

Text to Self How did using background knowledge help you understand the story? Possible response: I like watching trains when I am stopped at a crossing, so I could understand the fun James and B.J. were having. I have seen movies set in New York and could imagine people sitting on stoops and visiting the Statue of Liberty and Empire State Building.

Check Predictions Have students look back at the predictions they made earlier and discuss whether they were accurate. Then have students preview the rest of the selection and either adjust their predictions accordingly or make new predictions.

 If you want to teach this selection in two sessions, stop here.

Research and Inquiry
Navigate/Search

Teach

Have students generate a research plan for gathering relevant information. Discuss with students how they might search the Internet using their inquiry questions and keywords. Tell them to skim and scan each site for information that helps them answer their inquiry question or leads them to specific information that will be useful. Bolded or italicized words may be clues to what kind of information the Web site will provide. Have students look for other features, such as headings, illustrations, captions, or highlighting. Remind them to take notes as they gather information from multiple sources.

Model

Think Aloud When I started looking for soccer teams, I found professional ones and some in other parts of the country. When I added my local area to my keywords, I got more helpful information. When I went to the site, I looked for the boldfaced heads and read captions on pictures to help me get more information.

Guide practice

Have students continue their review of Web sites they identified. Remind students that some Web sites are more reliable than others. Explain that Web addresses ending in *.gov, .org,* or *.edu* are more likely to have reliable information than some sites ending in *.com.*

On their own

Have students identify valid and reliable sources and discuss the importance of citing valid and reliable sources.

Conventions
Conjuctions

Teach

Write this sentence: *Uncle Romie and Aunt Nanette are family, and they love you too.* Ask students to identify the coordinating conjunction in this sentence. (*and*) Remind students that a *conjunction* is a word that connects words or groups of words.

Guide practice

Write the following sentences on the board: *I wish I could go to the movies. I don't have any allowance left.* Ask students which coordinating conjunction could be used to join the sentences together. (*but*) Help students join the two sentences into one compound sentence.

Daily Fix-It

Use Daily Fix-It numbers 3 and 4 in the right margin.

Connect to oral language

Have students look for and read aloud conjunctions in *Me and Uncle Romie.* (*and*, p. 332; *but*, p. 331)

On their own

For more practice, use *Reader's and Writer's Notebook* p. 364.

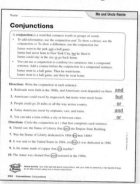

Reader's and Writer's Notebook p. 364

Spelling
Suffixes -y, -ish, -hood, and -ment

Teach

Remind students that their spelling words for this week include the suffixes *-y*, *-ish*, *-hood*, and *-ment*. Model again how to spell words with these suffixes. The parts in *foolish* are *fool* and *ish*. First I spell the base word. Write *fool*. Then I write the suffix. Write *ish*. Then I spell *foolish*. f-o-o-l-i-s-h.

Guide practice

Write the remaining spelling words on the board. Have students write them and underline each base word.

On their own

For more practice, use *Reader's and Writer's Notebook* p. 365.

Reader's and Writer's Notebook p. 365

E L L

English Language Learners

Conventions To provide students with practice on conjunctions, use the modified grammar lessons in the *ELL Handbook* and the Grammar Jammer online at: www.ReadingStreet.com

Conjunctions To help students differentiate between *and, but,* and *or,* ask students questions while using physical cues, such ask *Would you like to use a crayon or a marker?* (Hold out one and then the other.) or *Would you like to use a pencil and an eraser?* (Hold out both.)

Writing—Book Review
Writing Trait: Organization

Introduce the prompt

Review the key features of a book review and remind students to think about these features as they plan their writing. Explain that today they will begin the writing process for a book review that either encourages their audience to read the book or discourages them from reading the book. They are in effect, writing responses to texts. Read aloud the writing prompt.

Writing Prompt

Think about this story or another story or book you have read recently. Write a book review of it, explaining to readers whether they should read it

Select a topic

Think Aloud A book review is a piece of writing that discusses the good and bad qualities of a book. A negative review doesn't necessarily mean that the writer dislikes the book. Critiques can be positive, too. I want to write a book review about a book I really liked. Let's make a list of books we really enjoy and reasons why we like them. **Ask students to name titles to add to the list. Remind students that they will choose a book to generate a first draft of their book review.**

Books We Like	Reasons Why We Like These Books
How a Plant Grows	Interesting subject and pictures
Charlotte's Web	Interesting plot and creative characters
Amelia Earhart: Free in the Skies	Humorous and unlikely situations
How to Eat Fried Worms	Funny and gross story

Corrective feedback

Circulate around the room as students choose a book to write about. If students are having trouble choosing a book, provide a list of titles of popular books from the classroom or school library. Ask each struggling student to tell you which book they like best out of the last three books they have read.

MINI-LESSON

Preparing to Review

■ Display the book review graphic organizer. I want to write a book review about the book <u>How a Plant Grows</u>. I will write this title on the first line of the graphic organizer. This book does not have an illustrator listed, so I won't write anything on that line.

■ This book is about plants and how they grow. I will write this information on the *Plot/Topic* line. I really liked the subject, and pictures, so I will write this information on the *My Opinion* line. In the box, I will write additional information to demonstrate my understanding. Write *I learned a lot about how seeds travel.*

Have students begin their own book reviews using the form on p. 366 of their *Reader's and Writer's Notebook.* Explain that they will fill it in with information about the book they've chosen.

ROUTINE

Quick Write for Fluency   Team Talk

1. **Talk** Have pairs discuss the books they want to review.
2. **Write** Each student writes a few sentences about the book.
3. **Share** Partners read one another's writing and ask one question about each other's books.

Routines Flip Chart

Wrap Up Your Day

✔ **Build Concepts** What did you learn about life in North Carolina?

✔ **Author's Purpose** What do you think the author's purpose was in telling this story?

✔ **Background Knowledge** How can you use what you know about cities and the country to understand how James felt?

Differentiated Instruction

 Advanced

Create a graphic Challenge students to create a wordless booklet that shows the plot or nonfiction details of the book in a coherent and organized way.

Reader's and Writer's Notebook p. 366

Teacher Tip

Remind students that they can write a negative review if they prefer, but they will need to a give detailed, reasonable explanation of why they didn't like the book.

Preview DAY 3

Tell students that tomorrow they will read about what happens when James is left with Uncle Romie.

Objectives
- Expand the weekly concept.
- Develop oral vocabulary.

Today at a Glance

Oral Vocabulary
meager, gutter

Phonics/Word Analysis
◉ Suffixes *-y, -ish, -hood, -ment*

Comprehension Check/Retelling
Discuss Questions

Reading
Me and Uncle Romie

Think Critically
Retelling

Fluency
Appropriate phrasing

Research and Study Skills
Electronic text

Research and Inquiry
Analyze

Spelling
Suffixes *-y, -ish, -hood,* and *-ment*

Conventions
Conjunctions

Writing
Book review

Concept Talk

Question of the Week
How does city life compare to life in the country?

Expand the concept

Remind students of the weekly concept question. Discuss how the question relates to *Me and Uncle Romie*. Tell students that today they will read about what James will do with Uncle Romie when Aunt Nanette goes out of town. Encourage students to think about what vendors James sees at the baseball game.

Anchored Talk

Develop oral vocabulary

Use illustrations to review pp. 338–339 of *Me and Uncle Romie*. Discuss the Amazing Words *vendor* and *hurl*. Add these and other concept-related words to the concept map. Use the following questions to develop students' understanding of the concept.

- A pitcher *hurls* a baseball to the batter. Think about what the verb *hurl* means. Pantomime *hurling* a ball.

- What *vendors* did James see in the city? How are they like *vendors* in the country?

Oral Vocabulary
Amazing Words

Amazing Words

skyscraper	hurl
taxicab	meager
scamper	gutter
scurry	bitter
vendor	ramble

Teach Amazing Words

Amazing Words — Oral Vocabulary Routine

1 Introduce Write the word *meager* on the board. Have students say it with you. Yesterday, you read that James and Aunt Nanette shared barbecue. They each only ate a *meager* amount because they weren't very hungry. Have students determine a definition of *meager*. (*Meager* means a small or little amount.)

2 Demonstrate Have students answer questions to demonstrate understanding. Was the double chocolate scoop ice cream James ate a *meager* amount? Explain. (No, because that is a lot of ice cream.)

3 Apply Have students apply their understanding. What is the opposite of a *meager* meal? (a feast)

See p. OV•2 to teach *gutter*.

Routines Flip Chart

Apply Amazing Words

As students read pp. 340–349 of *Me and Uncle Romie,* have them consider how the Amazing Words *meager* and *gutter* apply to the rest of James's experiences.

Connect to reading

Explain that today students will read about how James spends his birthday in the city with his Uncle Romie. As they read, instruct students to think about how The Question of the Week and the Amazing Words *meager* and *gutter,* apply to what James sees and does.

ELL Expand Vocabulary Use the Day 3 instruction on ELL Poster 25 to help students expand vocabulary.

ELL Poster 25

Objectives
◎ Segment and read words with suffixes.
◎ Apply knowledge of base words and suffixes to decode unknown words when reading.
• Decode and read words independent of context.

Word Analysis
Sort Words

Model word sorting
Write -y, -ish, -hood, and -ment as heads in a four-column chart. Now we are going to sort words. We'll put words with the suffix -y in the first column. Words with the suffix -ish will go in the second column. Words with the suffix -hood will go in the third column. Words with the suffix -ment will go in the fourth column. I will start. Write statement and model how to read it, using the Word Parts Strategy Routine on p. 322a. Statement is made up of the base word state and the suffix -ment, so I will write it in the last column. Model reading shaky and excitement in the same way.

Guide practice
Use the practice words from the activities on p. 322a for the word sort. Point to a word. Have students read the word, identify its parts, and tell where it should be written on the chart.

Corrective feedback
For corrective feedback, model reading the base word and the suffix and then putting the word parts together to read the whole word.

-y	-ish	-hood	-ment
healthy	yellowish	adulthood	payment
stormy	brownish	falsehood	entertainment
thirsty			
frosty			

Fluent Word Reading

Model
Write basement. I see the base word base and the suffix -ment. When I put the parts together I can read the word basement. How does the suffix change the meaning of the base word? (The suffix changes the word to a place. A basement is the lowest part of a building.)

Guide practice
Write the words below. Look for word parts you know. When I point to a word, we'll read it together. Allow one second per word part previewing time for the first reading.

development	**contentment**	**environment**	**stylish**
guilty	**livelihood**	**assignment**	**knighthood**

On their own
Have students read the list above three or four times, until they can read one word per second.

Decode and Read

Read words independent of context

Have students turn to p. 117 in *Decodable Practice Readers 3.2* and find the first list of words. Each word in this list has a suffix. Be sure that students correctly pronounce the suffix in each word.

Next, have students read the high-frequency words.

Preview Decodable Practice Passage

Have students read the title and preview the story. Tell them that they will read words that include the suffixes *-y, -ish, -hood,* and *-ment.*

Read words in context

Chorally read the story along with students. Have students identify words in the story that include the suffixes *-y, -ish, -hood*, and *-ment.* Make sure that students are monitoring their accuracy when they decode words.

Team Talk Pair students and have them take turns reading the story aloud to each other. Monitor students as they read to check for proper pronunciation and appropriate pacing.

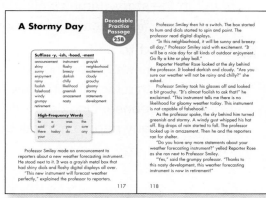
Decodable Practice Passage 25B

Differentiated Instruction

 Advanced

Build vocabulary Have students come up with lists of other words that have the suffixes *-y, -ish, -hood,* and *-ment.* Have them choose two or three words and write sentences that use the words.

Comprehension Check

Have students discuss each question with a partner. Ask several pairs to share their responses.

☑ **Genre • Synthesis**

How does the author make New York City come to life for the reader? Possible response: The author's descriptions of the people, places, and activities make it possible for the reader to imagine them. Her descriptions of the people greeting one another, the stickball games, and the hot-day activities are especially realistic.

☑ **Author's purpose • Analysis**

How can you tell the author's purpose in writing this story is to entertain? Possible response: The author is telling a fictional story about a boy having an adventure. It includes dialogue and descriptions of interesting places.

☑ **Background knowledge • Evaluation**

What about the places Aunt Nanette took James to would be fun for most children? Possible response: Most children like to play games and eat good food.

☑ **Homonyms • Analysis**

Which meaning of the homonym *flight* did James have an experience with? In the story, James walked up many *flights* in the apartment, so in this case *flight* means "a section of stairs."

☑ **Connect text to self**

How are James's experiences in New York City like an experience you have had with a big city or other place unlike where you usually live? Possible response: One time I visited a different big city—Houston—and I saw many people and tall buildings, just like James saw in New York.

Strategy Response Log

Have students revisit p. 3 in the *Reader's and Writer's Notebook* to add additional information about historical fiction.

Check Retelling

Have students retell *Me and Uncle Romie.*

Corrective feedback

If... the students leave out important details,
then... have students look back through the illustrations in the selection.

Small Group Time

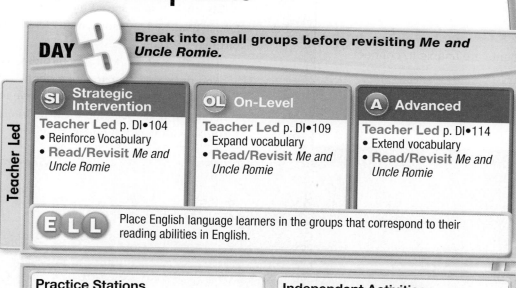

DAY 3 Break into small groups before revisiting *Me and Uncle Romie.*

Teacher Led

SI Strategic Intervention
Teacher Led p. DI•104
• Reinforce Vocabulary
• **Read/Revisit** *Me and Uncle Romie*

OL On-Level
Teacher Led p. DI•109
• Expand vocabulary
• **Read/Revisit** *Me and Uncle Romie*

A Advanced
Teacher Led p. DI•114
• Extend vocabulary
• **Read/Revisit** *Me and Uncle Romie*

ELL Place English language learners in the groups that correspond to their reading abilities in English.

Practice Stations
• Let's Write
• Get Fluent
• Word Work

Independent Activities
• AudioText: *Me and Uncle Romie*
• *Reader's and Writer's Notebook*
• Research and Inquiry

ELL

English Language Learners
Check Retelling To support retelling, review the multilingual summary for *Me and Uncle Romie* with appropriate Retelling Cards to scaffold understanding.

DAY 3 Read and Comprehend

45–50 min

OPTION 1 Skills and Strategies, continued

Teach Background Knowledge

◉ **Background Knowledge** After students read p. 340, have them think about their experiences with birthdays. How do you feel about birthdays? Do you think James feels his birthday is ruined? (I know how special birthdays can be to people. I can relate to James and his fear that his birthday is ruined. I imagine he is worried that spending his birthday with his uncle, whom he has hardly seen, won't be special.)

Corrective Feedback

If... students are unable to connect text-to-self,

then... model using background knowledge.

Multidraft Reading

If you chose . . .

Option 1 Return to the Extend Thinking instruction starting on p. 331a.

Option 2 Read pp. 340–349. Use the Guide Comprehension and Extend Thinking instruction.

Student Edition pp. 340–341

OPTION 2 Think Critically, continued

Higher-Order Thinking Skills

◉ **Background Knowledge • Synthesis • Text to Self**
Does James remind you of another character you have read about? In what way? Responses will vary.

Model the Strategy

Think Aloud What does James's experience remind you about experiences you have had with your own birthday? (Possible response: I have celebrated birthdays at school. Once, I thought the teacher forgot. I thought my birthday was not going to be celebrated.)

On rainy days I wrote postcards and helped out around the apartment. I told Aunt Nanette about the things I liked to do back home—about baseball games, train-watching, my birthday. She told me about the special Caribbean lemon and mango cake she was going to make.

My uncle Romie stayed hidden away in his studio. But I wasn't worried anymore. Aunt Nanette would make my birthday special.

4 . . . 3 . . . 2 . . . 1 . . . My birthday was almost here! And then Aunt Nanette got a phone call.

"An old aunt has died, James. I have to go away for her funeral. But don't you worry. Uncle Romie will spend your birthday with you. It'll be just fine."

340

Literary Elements: Plot • Synthesis What is the new event in the story that makes James think his birthday is ruined? Aunt Nanette has to leave because her aunt died and now James thinks his birthday is ruined because Uncle Romie doesn't know how to make his birthday special.

How is that like James's feelings? (We both wanted our birthday to be special.)

On Their Own

Have students reread the section to find other ways they can relate to James's experiences.

That night Aunt Nanette kissed me good-bye. I knew it would not be fine at all. Uncle Romie didn't know about cakes or baseball games or anything except his dumb old paintings. My birthday was ruined.

When the sky turned black, I tucked myself into bed. I missed Mama and Daddy so much. I listened to the birds on the rooftop—their songs continued into the night.

The next morning everything was quiet. I crept out of bed and into the hall. For the first time the door to Uncle Romie's studio stood wide open. What a glorious mess! There were paints and scraps all over the floor, and around the edges were huge paintings with all sorts of pieces pasted together.

341

Review **Draw Conclusions • Synthesis**

Why did Uncle Romie most likely stay inside his studio with the door closed while James is visiting? Uncle Romie was busy working in his studio.

Differentiated Instruction

 Strategic Intervention

Text structure Point out "4 ... 3 ... 2 ...1..." in the text and help students understand it indicates four days passing. Have students tell other ways the author could have conveyed this information to the reader.

Connect to Social Studies

As different groups came to the United States, they brought their birthday traditions with them. Chinese children pay their respects to their parents and receive money as a gift. Children from England find money mixed in with the birthday cake. Children from India wear colorful clothes and pass out candy to their classmates. No matter what culture you come from, everyone agrees that birthdays are special days.

English Language Learners
Background knowledge Before students read p. 341, help them complete a concept map about art supplies. Remind them that Uncle Romie is an artist but that James has never seen Uncle Romie's art studio. Let students add to the map as they read the page and look at the illustration.

Objectives

◎ Infer author's purpose to aid comprehension.

OPTION **1** Skills and Strategies, continued

Teach Author's Purpose

◉ **Author's Purpose** Have students reread the first paragraph on p. 342. What is the author trying to say about Harlem in this paragraph? (Possible response: The author is trying to say that Harlem is alive with activity.)

Corrective Feedback

If... students are unable to identify the author's purpose,

then... model how to determine author's purpose.

Model the Skill

Think Aloud I try to picture what James sees in Uncle Romie's paintings. The images communicate all of the activity on the streets of Harlem. I think the author is trying to help us appreciate Harlem the way she feels it.

I saw saxophones, birds, fire escapes, and brown faces. *It's Harlem,* I thought. *The people, the music, the rooftops, and the stoops.* Looking at Uncle Romie's paintings, I could *feel* Harlem—its beat and bounce.

Then there was one that was different. Smaller houses, flowers, and trains. "That's home!" I shouted.

"Yep," Uncle Romie said, smiling, from the doorway. "That's the Carolina I remember."

342

Student Edition pp. 342–343

OPTION **2** Think Critically, continued

Higher-Order Thinking Skills

◉ **Author's Purpose • Analysis** Why did the author have Uncle Romie paint paintings of Harlem and one of North Carolina? The author's purpose is to show that Uncle Romie knows both places.

Compare and Contrast • Analysis How is James discovering he is like his uncle? When they talk about North Carolina, they find they both have similar memories and a love of pepper jelly.

On Their Own
Have students explain why the author has Uncle Romie say *Mmm* on p. 343.

Differentiated Instruction

SI Strategic Intervention

Context clues Review with students how to use context clues in the words and sentences around unfamiliar words, like *feast,* to figure out the meanings. Have students use the definition in place of the word in the sentence to see if it makes sense.

"Mama says you visited your grandparents there most every summer when you were a kid," I said.

"I sure did, James. *Mmm.* Now that's the place for pepper jelly. Smeared thick on biscuits. And when Grandma wasn't looking . . . I'd sneak some on a spoon."

"Daddy and I do that too!" I told him.

We laughed together, then walked to the kitchen for a breakfast feast—eggs, bacon, grits, and biscuits.

"James, you've got me remembering the pepper jelly lady. People used to line up down the block to buy her preserves."

"Could you put someone like that in one of your paintings?" I asked.

343

Author's Purpose • Analysis Why did the author think pepper jelly was important enough to put in an illustration by itself? James and Uncle Romie find common ground when they begin talking about pepper jelly from North Carolina.

ELL

English Language Learners
Author's purpose Have partners read James and Uncle Romie's dialogue aloud with accuracy. Have them explain why informal dialogue shows that the author's purpose is to entertain.

Objectives

◎ Use background knowledge to aid comprehension.

OPTION 1 Skills and Strategies, continued

Teach Background Knowledge

◎ **Background Knowledge** Have students work in pairs to answer the question: What do I know about baseball that helps me understand this story?

Corrective Feedback

If... students have difficulty using background knowledge,
then... use the model to show how to use background knowledge to answer the question.

Student Edition pp. 344–345

OPTION 2 Think Critically, continued

Higher-Order Thinking Skills

◎ **Background Knowledge • Synthesis • Text to Self**
What do James and Uncle Romie have in common? How does having something in common with someone affect how you feel about that person? Uncle Romie lived in North Carolina and used to sneak pepper jelly and watch the trains like James does. He also knows about baseball. People who have something in common can understand each other, usually are friends, and can talk about their common experiences. Uncle Romie understands James and can make his birthday special.

Model the Strategy

Think Aloud I think about how the game of baseball is played. Pitchers throw the baseball for the batters to swing at and try to hit. Baseballs are sometimes hit into the stands, so that's why James and Uncle Romie brought their mitts.

"I guess I could." Uncle Romie nodded. "Yes, that's a memory just right for sharing. What a good idea, James. Now let's get this birthday going!"

He brought out two presents from home. I tore into the packages while he got down the pepper jelly and two huge spoons. Mama and Daddy had picked out just what I wanted—a special case for my baseball cards, and a model train for me to build.

"Pretty cool," said Uncle Romie. "I used to watch the trains down in North Carolina, you know."

How funny to picture big Uncle Romie lying on his belly!

"B. J. and me, we have contests to see who can hear the trains first."

"Hey, I did that too. You know, it's a funny thing, James. People live in all sorts of different places and families. But the things we care about are pretty much the same. Like favorite foods, special songs, games, stories . . . and like birthdays." Uncle Romie held up two tickets to a baseball game!

It turns out Uncle Romie knows all about baseball— he was even a star pitcher in college. We got our mitts and set off for the game.

Way up in the bleachers, we shared a bag of peanuts, cracking the shells with our teeth and keeping our mitts ready in case a home run ball came our way. That didn't happen—but we sure had fun.

344

Review **Draw Conclusions • Synthesis** Why did Uncle Romie get out two spoons with the jelly? Uncle Romie and James will eat the jelly with spoons like they talked about on p. 343.

I know that a home run is when the ball is hit and allows the batter to circle the bases and score a run.

345

Predict • Synthesis Compare James's New York birthday celebration with the one he would have had in North Carolina. Use the comparison to predict what kind of cake he will have.
Possible response: Since he got to go to a baseball game, he will probably have lemon cake.

On Their Own
Have students reread p. 344 and note other times they utilized background knowledge to understand what was going on.

Differentiated Instruction

Advanced
Compare and contrast: Venn diagram As students read the story, have them complete a Venn Diagram that compares and contrasts James and Uncle Romie. Let them use their diagrams to discuss how the two became friends.

English Language Learners
Sequence Have pairs of students draw a comic strip that depicts the story events on pp. 341–345. Help students differentiate between the character's memories and the events in the story.

Objectives

◎ Infer author's purpose to aid comprehension.

OPTION 1 Skills and Strategies, continued

Teach Author's Purpose

⦿ **Author's Purpose** After students have read pp. 346–347, have them explain why the author uses people's conversations to tell the reader about Uncle Romie's paintings. (Possible response: It is a way to explain what the paintings look like without showing pictures of them.)

Corrective Feedback

If... students are unable to identify the author's purpose,

then... model how to determine author's purpose.

Student Edition pp. 346–347

OPTION 2 Think Critically, continued

Higher-Order Thinking Skills

⦿ **Author's Purpose • Analysis** What did the author mean when she said that Aunt Nanette and Uncle Romie took James to the train station? She was telling that it was time for James to go home.

Model the Skill

Think Aloud What text tells you about Uncle Romie's paintings? ("Remember our first train ride from Chicago to New York" tells that the painting is of a train. "That guitar-playing man reminds me of my Uncle Joe" tells that the painting is of a man playing a guitar.)

Aunt Nanette came home that night. She lit the candles, and we all shared my Caribbean birthday cake.

After that, Uncle Romie had to work a lot again. But at the end of each day he let me sit with him in his studio and talk. Daddy was right. Uncle Romie is a good man.

The day of the big art show finally came. I watched the people laughing and talking, walking slowly around the room from painting to painting. I walked around myself, listening to their conversations.

346

Unknown Words • Analysis How can context clues help you figure out the meaning of the word *conversations* at the bottom of page 346? The text at the top of p. 347 tells what people are saying and paragraph 3 says "strangers talking." This helps me understand that *conversation* means "talking."

How else could the author have let readers know what the paintings look like? (She could have described them. She could have shown them in the art.)

"Remember our first train ride from Chicago to New York?" one lady asked her husband.

"That guitar-playing man reminds me of my Uncle Joe," said another.

All these strangers talking to each other about their families and friends and special times, and all because of how my uncle Romie's paintings reminded them of these things.

Later that night Daddy called. I had a brand-new brother and sister. Daddy said they were both bald and made a lot of noise. But he sounded happy and said how they all missed me.

This time Aunt Nanette and Uncle Romie took me to the train station.

347

Inferring • Evaluation Do you think Uncle Romie's art show was successful? Use facts from the text to support your answer. **Possible response:** I think it was successful because the text says people were laughing and talking as they slowly looked at the paintings. The comments people made about the paintings were all positive.

On Their Own

Have students explain why the author mentions that Uncle Romie's paintings remind people of special things in their lives.

Differentiated Instruction

SI Strategic Intervention

Sequence Have students use a graphic organizer to list events, in order, as they occur in the story. Let them use organizers to retell the story in their own words.

ELL

English Language Learners

Background knowledge Have students tell if they have ever seen art in a museum or art show. Encourage them to share what their experiences were like. Have them describe their favorite art piece that was on display.

DAY 3 Read and Comprehend

OPTION 1 Skills and Strategies, continued

Teach Homonyms

Homonyms Have students reread the last sentence on p. 348 and find the homonym *streak*. Encourage them to use context clues to determine the correct meaning for *streak*. Have them identify the meaning as it is used in the story. (move very fast)

Corrective Feedback

If... students are unable to determine the meaning of *streak*,

then... model replacing *streak* in the sentence with each definition to find the one that fits.

Model the Skill

Think Aloud I have heard the word *streak* used in different ways. A *streak* can be "a long, thin mark," or "a short period" such as a *streak* of bad luck. *Streak* can also mean, "to move very fast."

"Here's a late birthday present for you, James," Uncle Romie said, holding out a package. "Open it on the train, why don't you. It'll help pass the time on the long ride home."

I waved out the window to Uncle Romie and Aunt Nanette until I couldn't see them anymore. Then I ripped off the wrappings!

And there was my summer in New York. Bright sky in one corner, city lights at night in another. Tall buildings. Baseball ticket stubs. The label from the pepper-jelly jar. And trains. One going toward the skyscrapers. Another going away.

Back home, I lay in the soft North Carolina grass. It was the first of September, almost Uncle Romie's birthday. I watched the birds streak across the sky.

348

Student Edition pp. 348–349

OPTION 2 Think Critically, continued

Higher-Order Thinking Skills

Homonyms • Analysis Use context clues to tell the meaning of the homonym *like* in paragraph 1 on page 349. Possible response: I know that James is back from his summer in New York, and he is thinking that the birds are also back. This tells how James and the birds are similar. The meaning of *like* is "the same or similar."

Review **Draw Conclusions • Synthesis** What lesson did James learn from his trip? Possible response: Don't judge someone until you get to know him or her.

When I substitute these definitions in the sentence, "to move very fast" seems to be what the author intended.

On Their Own

Have students use a dictionary to look up other meanings of the word *streak*. Then have them write a sentence for each meaning.

Differentiated Instruction

SI Strategic Intervention

Text structure Have students find examples of italicized text throughout the story. Have them identify what the italics show. Have them copy the passages that show thought and punctuate them with quotation marks.

A Advanced

Predict Have students write an additional page to the story that shows what happens after Uncle Romie's birthday.

Rooftop birds, I thought. *Back home from their summer in New York, just like me.* Watching them, I could still feel the city's beat inside my head.

A feather drifted down from the sky. In the garden tiger lilies bent in the wind. *Uncle Romie's favorite flowers.* I yanked off a few blossoms. And then I was off on a treasure hunt, collecting things that reminded me of Uncle Romie.

I painted and pasted them together on a big piece of cardboard. Right in the middle I put the train schedule. And at the top I wrote:

349

Comprehension Check

Spiral Review

Literary Elements: Theme • Synthesis What is the theme, or author's message, of this story? Possible response: The theme of the story is that even though people come from different places and backgrounds, they care about the same things like favorite foods, birthdays, and special times.

Sequence • Analysis What clues in the text tell you this story is written as a flashback and happened a long time ago? The first sentence of the story tells that the author is looking back on some previous summer. The clothing in the art shows that it took place in the past.

Check Predictions Have students return to the predictions they made earlier and confirm whether they were accurate.

ELL

English Language Learners
Idioms Point out paragraph 1 on p. 348 and explain to students that "pass the time" means "to do something to keep busy when waiting." Ask students, If I look at a magazine in a doctor's waiting room, am I doing it to pass the time? What might you do to pass the time while waiting at a bus stop?

Objectives
◎ Locate the author's purpose.
◎ Use background knowledge to check understanding.

Check Retelling
SUCCESS PREDICTOR

Plan to Assess Retelling

☑ **Week 1** Assess Strategic Intervention students.

☑ **Week 2** Assess Advanced students.

☑ **Week 3** Assess Strategic Intervention students.

☑ **Week 4** Assess On-Level students.

☑ **This week assess any students you have not yet checked during this unit.**

Objectives
• Identify whether the speaker or person telling a story is a first- or third-person narrator. • Make connections between literary and informational texts with similar ideas and support your ideas with details from the texts.

Envision It! Retell

READING STREET ONLINE
STORY SORT
www.ReadingStreet.com

350

Think Critically

1. Compare and contrast North Carolina and New York City back in the 1920s. How are these places alike and different from where you live now? **Text to World**

2. Is this story written in first or third person? Why do you think the author wrote from this point of view? **Think Like an Author**

3. Read "Meet the Author" on page 351. Why did the author write this story? Why do you think the author chose to write this selection as historical fiction and not as a biography like *Rocks in His Head*? Explain your answer with evidence from the text. **Author's Purpose**

4. What did you know about New York City or Harlem before you read the story? How did your knowledge help you as you read? **Background Knowledge**

5. **Look Back and Write** Look back at the adventures James had in New York City. Now write about why you would or would not like to visit Uncle Romie in Harlem. Provide evidence to support your answer.

TEST PRACTICE Extended Response

Meet the Author and the Illustrator

Claire Hartfield and Jerome Lagarrigue

Claire Hartfield began taking dance lessons when she was five. Dance is her way of telling stories. In *Me and Uncle Romie*, she wanted to show how an artist can use art to tell stories. Although *Me and Uncle Romie* is fiction, it is based on the life of collage artist Romare Bearden.

Today, Ms. Hartfield is a lawyer in Chicago.

Jerome Lagarrigue grew up in Paris, France, in a family of artists. His art has appeared in magazines, and he has illustrated several picture books. Mr. Lagarrigue teaches drawing and painting in New York City. For *Me and Uncle Romie*, he used some elements of collage in his paintings—like Romare Bearden.

Read some books about great art projects.

Loo-Loo, Boo, and Art You Can Do by Denis Roche

Recycled Crafts Box by Laura C. Martin

Use the Reader's and Writer's Notebook to record your independent reading.

351

Student Edition pp. 350–351

Retelling

Envision It!

Have students work in pairs to retell the selection, using the Envision It! Retelling Cards as prompts. Remind students that they should accurately describe the main topic and important ideas and use key vocabulary in their retellings. Monitor students' retellings.

Scoring rubric

Top-Score Response A top-score response makes connections beyond the text, describes the main topic and important ideas using accurate information and draws conclusions from the text.

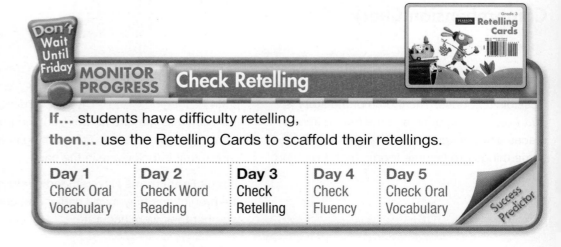

Don't Wait Until Friday

MONITOR PROGRESS Check Retelling

Grade 3 Retelling Cards

If... students have difficulty retelling,

then... use the Retelling Cards to scaffold their retellings.

Day 1	Day 2	Day 3	Day 4	Day 5
Check Oral Vocabulary	Check Word Reading	Check Retelling	Check Fluency	Check Oral Vocabulary

Success Predictor

Think Critically

Text to world

1. Possible response: In the 1920's, North Carolina was mostly rural and New York City was a big city with skyscrapers. People played baseball in both places. I live in a big city that is more like New York with skyscrapers, apartments, and many people.

Think like an author

2. Possible response: The story is written in the first person. The author chose to write this way because she wanted the reader to see the story from James's viewpoint, so we would understand what his life was like.

Author's purpose

3. Possible response: She wrote the story to show what life was like in New York. The genre of historical fiction allowed the author to include facts about New York and what life was like back then as seen through the eyes of a young boy.

Background knowledge

4. Possible response: Before I read, I knew that New York is a big city with many people. I did not know anything about Harlem. Knowing that New York is a big city helped me because I expected James to find it very different than North Carolina.

 Writing on Demand

5. **Look Back and Write** To build writing fluency, assign a 10–15 minute time limit.

Suggest that students use a prewriting strategy, such as brainstorming or using a graphic organizer, to organize their ideas. Remind them to establish a topic sentence and support it with facts, details, or explanations. As students finish, encourage them to reread their responses, revise for organization and support, and proofread for errors in grammar and conventions.

Scoring rubric

> **Top-Score Response** A top score response uses details to tell why the students would or would not like to visit Uncle Romie.
>
> **A top-score response should include:**
>
> - I would like to visit Uncle Romie. I could play stickball, run through fire hydrants, have ice cream, and barbecue, and go to a baseball game. I could also watch Uncle Romie create collages and see his exhibit.
>
> - I would not like to visit Uncle Romie. The city has too many big buildings, too many people, and a lot of noise and I would miss my family and friends. I also don't play baseball.

Differentiated Instruction

SI Strategic Intervention

Have students work in pairs to review the story and discuss the adventures James had in New York City. Encourage them to list the adventures in sequential order.

Meet the Author and Illustrator

Have students read about the author Claire Hartfield and illustrator Jerome Lagarrigue on p. 351. Ask them why they think Ms. Hartfield chose to base the story on Romare Bearden's life and why Mr. Lagarrigue used collage in some of his paintings.

Independent Reading

After students enter their independent reading information into their Reading Logs, have them paraphrase a portion of the text they have just read. Remind students that when we paraphrase, we express the meaning of a passage using other words and maintaining meaning and logical order.

ELL

English Language Learners

Retelling Use the retelling cards to discuss the selection with students. Place the cards in an incorrect order and have volunteers correct the mistake. Then have students explain where each card should go as they describe the sequence of the story.

Check Retelling

Success Predictor

Objectives
- Read grade-level text with appropriate phrasing.
- Understand how to use electronic text.

Model Fluency
Appropriate Phrasing

Model fluent reading
Have students turn to p. 336 of *Me and Uncle Romie.* Have students follow along as you read the page. Point out how dashes and other punctuation marks guide the way you phrase the sentences.

Guide practice
Have students follow along as you read the page again. Then have them reread the pages with partners until they can read them with appropriate phrasing and no mistakes. Continue in this way with p. 337.

Reread for Fluency

Corrective feedback
If... students are having difficulty reading with correct phrasing, **then...** prompt:

- Where can we break up this sentence? Which words are related?
- Read the sentence again. Pause after each group of words.
- Tell me the sentence. Now read it with pauses after each group of words.

ROUTINE Paired Reading

1. **Select a passage** For *Me and Uncle Romie,* use p. 343.
2. **Reading 1** Students read the entire page, switching readers at the end of each paragraph.
3. **Reading 2** Partners reread the page. This time the other student begins.
4. **Reread** For optimal fluency, have partners continue to read three or four times.
5. **Corrective Feedback** Listen as students read. Provide feedback and encourage students to pause briefly at the ends of phrases.

Routines Flip Chart

Research and Study Skills
Electronic Text

Teach

Ask students if they have ever used the Internet to find the answer to a question. If possible, display a search engine page on your classroom computer. Review these terms and concepts:

- Search engines can help you locate information on the Internet.
- A search engine links you to Web sites that may be related to your topic.
- At the top of the search engine is a box to type in keywords. Search engines locate these keywords on various Web sites and display those sites on the screen.

Have groups of students discuss keywords they might use to research a given topic.

Guide practice

Discuss these questions:

Why should you try different search engines? (Each search engine is linked to different Web sites, so different search engines give different results.)

How can you narrow your search? (Possible response: I could add more keywords.)

Have groups use different search engines to answer the same question. Have them compare the keywords they chose and see their different results.

On their own

Have students review and complete p. 368 of the *Reader's and Writer's Notebook*.

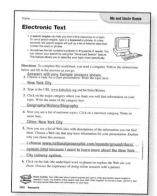

Reader's and Writer's Notebook
p. 368

English Language Learners

Professional Development: What ELL Experts Say

Paired reading "When students participate in shared reading and echo the spoken text or read the words aloud chorally, anxiety about pronunciation or decoding errors is reduced." —Dr. Georgia Earnest García

Objectives
- Analyze data for usefulness
- Identify and correctly use conjunctions.
- Spell frequently misspelled words.

Research and Inquiry
Analyze

Teach

Tell students that today they will analyze their research findings. Have students sort the information from their notes into an outline. This outline should include categories such as main ideas and supporting details. Remind students that an outline is a plan for writing. Then explain that students may have to improve the focus of their research by interviewing experts.

Model

Think Aloud
While scanning a Web site, I noticed that there are many sports and games played in both the city and the country. I talked to a youth soccer league coach, and she said that even though soccer is popular in cities, there are some sports that are more popular there. I decided to focus on if any sports are more popular in one place or the other. Now my inquiry question is *Which sports and games are most popular in the city and which are most popular in the country?*

Guide practice

Have students analyze their findings. They may need to refocus their inquiry question to better fit the information they found. Remind students that if they have difficulty improving their focus, they can ask a reference librarian or the local expert for guidance.

On their own

Have partners share their outlines and summarize the information they have gathered. Partners should discuss whether they need to collect additional information to answer the inquiry question.

Conventions
Conjunctions

Review Remind students that this week they learned about conjunctions. Introduce the conjunction *therefore* and review *and, or, but,* and *because.*

- Conjunctions are words that connect words or groups of words.
- To show a result of something, use the conjunction *therefore.*
- To add information, use the conjunction *and.*
- To show a choice, use the conjunction *or.*
- To show a difference, use the conjunction *but.*
- To show a reason, use the conjunction *because.*
- *Because* and *therefore* can also be used as transitions.

Daily Fix-It Use Daily Fix-It numbers 5 and 6 in the right margin.

Connect to oral language Have the class complete these sentence frames orally.

> After school, I _____ and _____.
>
> My mother said _____, therefore I will _____.

On their own For additional support, use *Let's Practice It!* page 334 on the *Teacher Resources DVD-ROM.*

Spelling
Suffixes -y, -ish, -hood, and -ment

Frequently misspelled words The words *different* and *very* are words that students often misspell. Think carefully before you write these words. Have students practice writing the words by writing sentences using each word.

1. I want to watch a _____ television show. (different)
2. This television show is _____ boring. (very)
3. I like birds _____ much. (very)

On their own For additional support, use *Reader's and Writer's Notebook* p. 369.

Differentiated Instruction

SI Strategic Intervention

Conjunction practice Create flashcards for *therefore, because, and, but,* and *or.* Write *result, reason, information, choice,* and *difference* on the back of the cards. Have partners practice identifying the purposes of the conjunctions by using the flashcards.

Daily Fix-It

5. My mom spent her child hood in New York city. (*childhood; City*)
6. She say it is busiest there than in North Carolina. (*says; busier*)

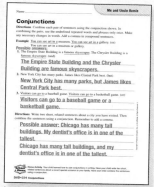

Let's Practice It!
TR DVD•334

Reader's and Writer's
Notebook p. 369

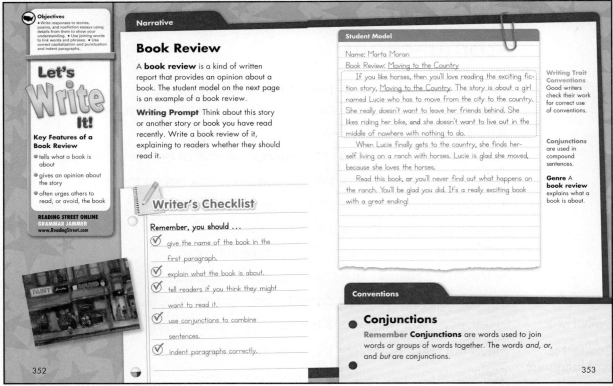

Student Edition pp. 352–353

Let's Write It!
Book Review

Teach

Use pp. 352–353 in the Student Edition. Direct students to read the key features of a book review, which appear on p. 352. Remind students that they can refer to the information in the Writer's Checklist as they write their own book reviews.

Read the student model on p. 353. Point out the underlined title in the model and the paragraphs that explain what the book is about.

Connect to conventions

Remind students that a conjunction is a word that connects words or groups of words. Point out the correct use of conjunctions in compound sentences in the model.

Writing—Book Review
Organizing Your Draft

Display rubric

Display Scoring Rubric 25 from the *Teacher Resources DVD-ROM* and go over the criteria for each trait under each score. Then, using the model in the Student Edition, choose students to explain why the model should score a 4 for one of the traits. If a student offers that the model should score below 4 for a particular trait, the student should offer support for that response. Remind students that this is the rubric that will be used to evaluate the book reviews they write.

Scoring Rubric: Book Review

	④	③	②	①
Focus/Ideas	Clear, focused review with many supporting details	Most ideas in review clear and supported	Some ideas in review unclear or off-topic	Review with no clarity or development
Organization	Organized logically, no gaps; clearly presented book topic	Organized logically, few gaps; book topic presented	Organizational pattern attempted but not clear; book topic unclear	No organizational pattern evident; book topic not presented clearly
Voice	Engaging; shows writer's feelings/ opinion about subject	Evident voice connecting with reader; shows writer's feelings	Weak voice; weak display of writer's feelings/opinion about subject	Flat writing with no voice; writer doesn't state his/her opinion
Word Choice	Vivid, precise word choice	Accurate word choice	Limited or repetitive word choice	Incorrect or very limited word choice
Sentences	Clear sentences of various lengths and types; correct punctuation	Sentences of a few lengths and types; mostly correct punctuation	Sentences of similar length and type; weak use of punctuation	No attempt at sentences of various lengths or types; incorrect or no punctuation
Conventions	Few, if any, errors; correct use of conjunctions	Several minor errors; mostly correct use of conjunctions	Many errors; weak use of conjunctions	Numerous errors; incorrect or no use of conjunctions

Book Review

Have students take out the review forms they worked on yesterday. If their forms are not complete, allow additional time to complete them.

Write

You will be using your review forms to help you write the paragraphs as you develop the first draft of your book reviews. When you are drafting, don't worry if your review doesn't sound exactly as you want it. You will have a chance to revise it tomorrow.

Me and Uncle Romie **353a**

Differentiated Instruction

 Advanced

Comparing Challenge students to create a book review that compares two different books. Have them describe both books and tell how they are alike and different. Then have them write an opinion about which book they think is better.

ELL

English Language Learners

Plot or topic Help students with organizing the plot or topic of the book they have chosen to review.

Beginning Have students orally describe the plot or topic of the book. Help them make notes to use while drafting.

Intermediate Help students create a beginning-middle-end chart for the plot or topic of the books they will review.

Advanced/Advanced High Have students create a main idea and details chart or a beginning-middle-end chart for the plot or topic of the book they plan to review.

Writing, continued
Organizing Your Draft

MINI-LESSON

Organizing Your Review

■ **Introduce** Explain to students that organizing a review means making sure to include all of the elements of a book review and demonstrating understanding of the book. Display the Drafting Tips for students. Remind them that the focus of drafting is to record their ideas using organized paragraphs. Then display Writing Transparency 25A and explain the process of drafting.

Writing Transparency 25A, TR DVD

Drafting Tips

✔ To get started, study your review form.

✔ Read aloud parts of your review. Ask yourself: *Is my information in the review organized so that the writing makes sense?*

✔ Don't worry about grammar or mechanics while drafting. You'll concentrate on them during the revising stage.

Think Aloud I'm going to write the first draft of a book review about <u>How Plants Grow</u>. When I draft, I develop my ideas. I don't worry about revising or proofreading because those tasks will come later. I will refer to my review form to make sure that I include all of the elements I need to generate a complete review.

Have students use the drafting tips as a guide as they draft their book reviews. Remind them to check their work carefully for presentation of ideas, organize their ideas into coherent paragraphs, and make sure to underline the book title.

ROUTINE Quick Write for Fluency — Team Talk

1. **Talk** Pairs talk about two details they want to include in their book reviews.
2. **Write** Each student writes two sentences about these details.
3. **Share** Partners read and check each other's writing for the correct use of conjunctions.

Routines Flip Chart

Wrap Up Your Day

✔ **Build Concepts** Have students discuss the differences between city and country life.

✔ **Author's Purpose** How can understanding the author's purpose help you understand the story?

✔ **Background Knowledge** How was your summer vacation the same as James's?

Differentiated Instruction

SI Strategic Intervention

Partner support Have groups of two or three students work together to confirm organization in their drafts. Each student in the group should ask the question: *Is the information in the review organized so that the writing makes sense?*

Preview DAY 4

Tell students that tomorrow they will read about using online references to find out about Romare Bearden.

Objectives
- Expand the weekly concept.
- Build oral vocabulary.

Today at a Glance

Oral Vocabulary
bitter, ramble

Phonics/Word Analysis
Vowel Patterns *ei, eigh*

21st Century Skills
Online reference sources

Reading
"Country to City"

Let's Learn It!
Fluency: Appropriate phrasing
Vocabulary: ⊙ Homonyms
Listening and Speaking: Retelling

Research and Inquiry
Synthesize

Conventions
Conjunctions

Spelling
Suffixes *-y, -ish, -hood,* and *-ment*

Writing
Book review

Concept Talk

Question of the Week
How does city life compare to life in the country?

Expand the concept

Remind students that this week they have read about several characters' experiences living in both the country and the city. Tell students that today they will read about a student who uses online sources to learn more about Romare Bearden's country life and city life.

Anchored Talk

Develop oral vocabulary

Use illustrations to review pp. 340–349 of *Me and Uncle Romie.* Discuss the Amazing Words *meager* and *gutter.* Add these and other concept-related words to the concept map. Use the following questions to develop students' understanding of the concept.

- *Gutters* catch and carry off rainwater. Where have you seen *gutters*?
- When do you eat *meager* amounts of food? Could this happen in the city or the country?

 Strategy Response Log

Have students rewrite the characteristics of historical fiction in their Strategy Response logs on p. 31 of the *Reader's and Writer's Notebook.* Then have them compare *Me and Uncle Romie* to another example of historical fiction that they have read or know about.

Oral Vocabulary
Amazing Words

Amazing Words

skyscraper	hurl
taxicab	meager
scamper	gutter
scurry	bitter
vendor	ramble

Teach Amazing Words

Amazing Words · Oral Vocabulary Routine

1 Introduce Write the word *bitter* on the board. Have students say it aloud with you. James felt *bitter* when Aunt Nanette left and he found out he was going to have to spend his birthday with Uncle Romie. Supply a student-friendly definition: *Bitter* describes something that causes sharp pain or grief.

2 Demonstrate Have students answer questions to demonstrate understanding. How do you know James felt *bitter*? (He says that his birthday is ruined.) How do *bitter* winds feel? (They cause sharp pain.) Are you happy when you feel *bitter*? (no)

3 Apply Have students apply their understanding. Have them name synonyms for *bitter.* (biting, sharp, unpleasant)

See p. OV•2 to teach *ramble.*

Routines Flip Chart

Apply Amazing Words

As students read "Country to City," on pp. 354–357, have them think of ways the Amazing Words *bitter* and *ramble* show how city and country life are alike.

Connect to reading

As students read about where Romare Bearden *rambled,* have them think about how he felt about life in the country and life in the city. Let them ask themselves if they think he ever felt *bitter* and why.

ELL Produce oral language Use the Day 4 instruction on ELL Poster 25 to extend and enrich language.

ELL Poster 25

Me and Uncle Romie **354b**

Objectives
- Identify and read words with /ā/, /ē/, and /ī/ spelled *ei* and *eigh*.
- Read words fluently independent of context.

Phonics Review
Vowel Patterns *ei, eigh*

Review sound-spellings

To review last week's phonics skill, write *veil* and *eight*. You studied words like these last week. What do you know about the vowel sounds in these words? (Both words have the long *a* sound.) What letters spell the sound /ā/ in *veil*? (*ei*) In *eight*? (*eigh*) Continue in the same way for /ē/ in *ceiling* and *receive* and /ī/ in *height*.

Corrective feedback

If students are unable to answer the questions about the vowel patterns, refer them to Sound-Spelling Cards 64, 65, and 66.

Guide practice

Draw a three-column chart. When I say a word, listen for the long vowel sound. Shake your head if the word has /ā/. Point to your knee if the word has /ē/. Point to your eye if the word has /ī/. Write each word in the appropriate column. Then have students read the words and ask volunteers to underline the letters that spell the long vowel sound in each word.

/ā/	/ē/	/ī/
neighbor	seize	height
weigh	deceive	eiderdown
neigh	receipt	sleight
reign	weird	
reindeer		
vein		

On their own

For additional practice, use *Let's Practice It!* p. 335 on the *Teacher Resources DVD-ROM.*

Let's Practice It!
TR DVD•335

Fluent Word Reading
Spiral Review

Read words independent of context

Display these words. Tell students that they can decode some words on this list. Explain that other words they should know because they appear often in reading.

Have students read the list three or four times until they can read at the rate of two to three seconds per word.

Word Reading

all	watch	aunt	saw	meat
saucer	would	taught	fawns	stalking
raw	deer	paused	thought	your
ant	should	meet	two	dear

Corrective feedback

If... students have difficulty reading whole words,
then... have them use sound-by-sound blending for decodable words or chunking for words that have word parts, or have them say and spell high-frequency words.

If... students cannot read fluently at a rate of two to three seconds per word,
then... have pairs practice the list until they can read it fluently.

Differentiated Instruction

 Strategic Intervention

Long vowel patterns To assist students having difficulty with the vowel patterns *ei* and *eigh*, focus on only one vowel sound at a time. Write words with /ā/ spelled *ei* and *eigh* on separate cards. Have students sort the words by long *a* spelling and then read all the words. Repeat with /ē/ words spelled *ei* and *eigh*.

Spiral Review

These activities review

- previously taught high-frequency words *watch, would, should, two, your.*
- vowel patterns for /ò/ spelled *a, au, aw, augh, ough*; homophones.

E L L

English Language Learners
Fluent word reading Have students listen to a more fluent reader say the words. Then have listening students repeat the words.

Objectives

- Read words fluently in context.
- Apply knowledge of sound-spellings to decode unknown words when reading.
- Practice fluency with oral rereading.

Read words in context

Display these sentences. Call on individuals to read a sentence. Then randomly point to review words and have students read them. To help you monitor word reading, high-frequency words are underlined and decodable words are italicized.

MONITOR PROGRESS | **Sentence Reading**

We *paused* to <u>watch</u> the <u>two</u> *fawns.*
You <u>should</u> not eat *raw meat.*
My *aunt* <u>would</u> like me to *meet* her *dear* friends.
Dad *taught* me *all* about *stalking deer.*
I *thought* I saw an *ant* on <u>your</u> *saucer.*

If... students are unable to read an underlined high-frequency word,
then... read the word for them and spell it, having them echo you.

If... students have difficulty reading an italicized decodable word,
then... guide them in using sound-by-sound blending or chunking.

Reread for Fluency

Have students reread the sentences to develop automaticity decoding words.

ROUTINE **Oral Rereading**

1. **Read** Have students read all the sentences orally.
2. **Reread** To achieve optimal fluency, students should reread the sentences three or four times.
3. **Corrective Feedback** Listen as students read. Provide corrective feedback regarding their fluency and decoding.

Routines Flip Chart

Decode and Read

Read words independent of context

Have students turn to p. 119 in *Decodable Practice Readers 3.2* and find the first list of words. Each word in this list has a suffix added to the base word. Be sure that students correctly pronounce the suffix in each word.

Next, have students read the high-frequency words.

Preview Decodable Practice Passage

Have students read the title and preview the story. Tell them that they will read words with the suffixes *-y, -ish, -hood,* and *-ment.*

Read words in context

Chorally read the story along with the students. Have students identify words in the story that include the suffixes *-y, -ish, -hood,* and *-ment.* Make sure that students are monitoring their accuracy when they decode words.

Team Talk Pair students and have them take turns reading the story aloud to each other. Monitor students as they read to check for proper pronunciation and appropriate pacing.

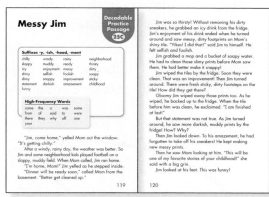

Decodable Practice Passage 25C

Differentiated Instruction

 Advanced

Decodable words Have students write their own sentences using some of the decodable words found in the sentences on p. 354e.

English Language Learners

Suffixes

Beginning After reading, have students find pairs of words that end with the same suffix.

Intermediate Have students work in pairs to chorally reread paragraphs from the Decodable Practice Reader.

Advanced/Advanced High After reading the story, have students choose two or three words with the suffixes *-y, -ish, -hood,* or *-ment* and write a sentence for each word.

Me and Uncle Romie **354f**

Objectives
• Introduce online reference sources.

21st Century Skills
Online Reference Sources

Introduce online reference sources

Explain to students that technology is all around us. Tell them that online reference sources are one type of technology we use today. Ask students to share what they already know about online reference sources, such as what they are and when to use them.

Discuss the skill

Discuss with students some of the reference sources they have used. What reference materials have you used to write informational articles? (encyclopedias, almanacs, and atlases) Explain: In the past, people had to go to libraries to find reference materials. They looked through the books and took notes. They could not take the reference materials home. Now, you can search on the Internet and easily find reference materials.

On the board, draw a Venn diagram like the one below. Label the sides *Books* and *Online.* Ask the following questions:

• How are reference books and online reference materials different? Possible responses: Reference books are on different shelves of the library and online references are found on a computer. Some Web sites even give you different reference sources in one place. Online reference materials may be updated often but only the newest books are up-to-date. Online materials have easy links to other sites.

• How are reference books and online reference materials alike? Possible responses: The information is organized in the same way. The sources look alike. They usually contain the same information.

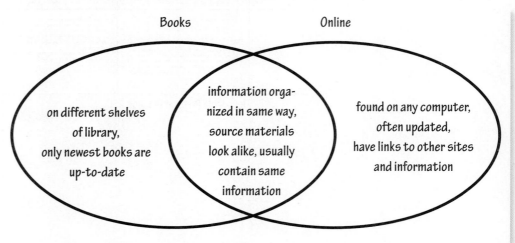

Books   Online

on different shelves of library, only newest books are up-to-date

information organized in same way, source materials look alike, usually contain same information

found on any computer, often updated, have links to other sites and information

Guide practice

Have students work in pairs to list the benefits of using online reference sources. Let them share their lists with the class.

Connect to reading

Tell students they will now read about a student who uses online reference sources to get information. Have the class think about times when using online reference sources for this purpose might be helpful and what conventions might be necessary.

Small Group Time

Teacher Led

 DAY 4 Break into small groups before reading or revisiting "Country to City."

 Strategic Intervention

Teacher Led p. DI•105
• Practice retelling
• Genre focus
• **Read/Revisit** "Country to City"

OL On-Level

Teacher Led p. DI•110
• Practice retelling
• Genre focus
• **Read/Revisit** "Country to City"

A Advanced

Teacher Led p. DI•115
• Genre focus
• **Read/Revisit** "Country to City"

ELL Place English language learners in the groups that correspond to their reading abilities in English.

Practice Stations
• Read for Meaning
• Get Fluent
• Words to Know

Independent Activities
• AudioText: "Country to City"
• *Reader's and Writer's Notebook*
• Research and Inquiry

ELL

English Language Learners

Cognates The French word *technologie,* the Italian word *tecnologia,* and the Spanish word *tecnologia* may be familiar to speakers of those languages as cognates for *technology.*

Objectives
• Use design features in online reference sources.

Student Edition pp. 354–355

Guide Comprehension

Teach online reference sources

21st Century Skills: Online Reference Sources Have students preview "Country to City" on pp. 354–355. Have students look at the information on p. 355 and ask: What text features helped Denise learn about Romare Bearden?

Corrective feedback

If... students are unable to identify text features on a Website, **then...** use the model to guide students through the page.

Model the skill

Think Aloud

I know that online reference sources organize information similar to printed reference sources. I see the heading *Encyclopedia* that tells me the kind of reference used and the name of the Web site. I see the heading *Romare Bearden* and a bulleted list of facts. Sometimes information will include links to other sources of information related to the topic.

On their own

Have students work in pairs to search other online reference sources for information on Romare Bearden. Discuss with them how the information is organized and how the same information could be presented in other formats.

Extend Thinking
Think Critically

Higher-order thinking skills

 Background Knowledge • Analysis • Text to Text
What do you learn about Romare Bearden in "Country to City" that connects to events in *Me and Uncle Romie*? What can you conclude from this? Possible response: Romare Bearden lived in North Carolina and in Harlem like Uncle Romie and James. Romare Bearden was a collage artist like Uncle Romie. I conclude that *Me and Uncle Romie* is a story based on the life of a real person.

Graphic Sources • Analysis Based on the types of online sources here, what kinds of information can you find about Romare Bearden? Possible response: I can find out where and when he was born, what his childhood was like, the types of collages he created.

Differentiated Instruction

 Strategic Intervention

Graphic organizer Have pairs of students make a two-column chart labeled *Romare Bearden* and *Uncle Romie.* In the first column, have them list where Romare Bearden was born, where he lived, and what he is best known for. Then, have them find the same facts about Uncle Romie and add to the chart. Help students conclude that Uncle Romie and Romare Bearden are the same person.

A **Advanced**

Search topics Have students brainstorm other search topics they could use when researching information on Romare Bearden's life such as, *collage artists* and *Harlem Renaissance.*

English Language Learners

Access content Have students preview the text by locating the words *North Carolina* and *New York* in the encyclopedia entry on Romare Bearden, and then finding the atlas and almanac entry for each state on the following pages.

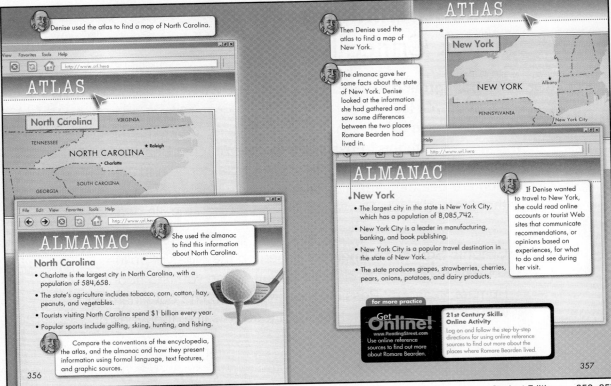

Student Edition pp. 356–357

Guide Comprehension

Teach online reference sources

21st Century Skills: Online Reference Sources Have students identify the two reference sources on pp. 356–357. Then ask: How is the information in an atlas different from that provided by an almanac?

Corrective feedback

If... students are unable to contrast the two reference sources,
then... use the model to guide students in how they are different.

Model the skill

Think Aloud

I see maps for each state in the atlases. I see a list of facts about each state in the almanacs. Atlases provide maps and almanacs provide facts.

On their own

Have students search an online atlas and almanac for information about their state.

Extend Thinking
Think Critically

Higher-order thinking skills

Graphic Sources • Analysis What types of graphic sources do the online materials on pages 356–357 include? Would you expect to find this kind of information in a story like *Me and Uncle Romie*? **Possible response:** The graphic sources are a map of each state and lists of what each state is known for. This kind of information is more common in reference material than in a story.

⟲ **Author's Purpose • Analysis** How do you know the author's purpose in writing "Country to City" is to inform? **Possible response:** The passage includes facts about Denise's online search that inform the reader about online reference sources and about Romare Bearden.

21st Century Skills

For more practice

Online Reference Sources Show students how to locate Web sites by clicking on the appropriate links. Be sure that they follow the step-by-step directions for finding articles about Harlem. Discuss with students how the information in an encyclopedia is different than that found in a dictionary.

Connect to Social Studies

Almanacs have been written for hundreds of years. Published annually and according to the calendar, they often show times of ocean tides, solar eclipses, and lunar eclipses. The name comes from a medieval Arabic word, but early almanacs have been traced back to the ancient Greeks. They used almanacs to list weather changes that they traced to astronomical computations.

ELL

English Language Learners
Graphic organizers Provide support to students as they create a T-chart to show the differences between an atlas and an almanac. Help them add details in each column.

Objectives
- Read with fluency and comprehension.
- Use context clues.
- Retell a story.

Fluency WCPM
SUCCESS PREDICTOR

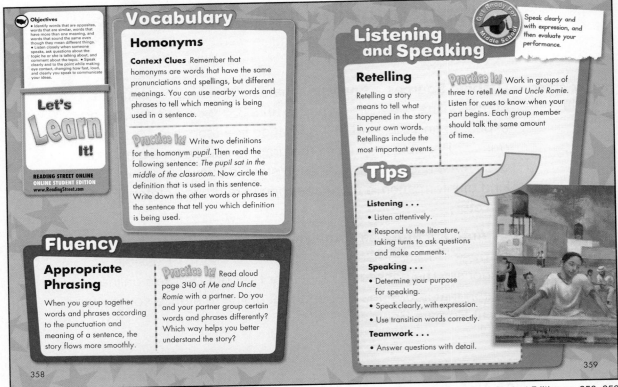

Student Edition pp. 358–359

Fluency
Appropriate Phrasing

Guide practice

Use the Student Edition activity as an assessment tool. Make sure the reading passage is at least 200 words in length. As students read aloud with partners, walk around to make sure their phrasing is correct and that they group words together to enhance the meaning of what they are reading.

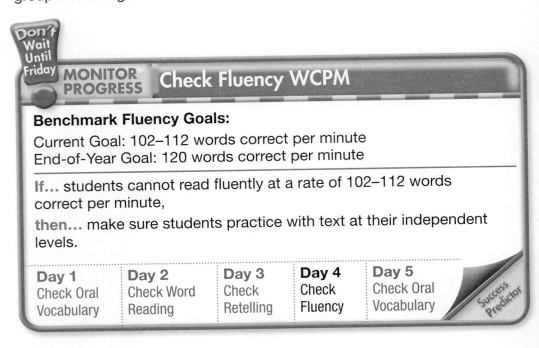

Don't Wait Until Friday

MONITOR PROGRESS Check Fluency WCPM

Benchmark Fluency Goals:

Current Goal: 102–112 words correct per minute
End-of-Year Goal: 120 words correct per minute

If... students cannot read fluently at a rate of 102–112 words correct per minute,

then... make sure students practice with text at their independent levels.

Day 1	**Day 2**	**Day 3**	**Day 4**	**Day 5**
Check Oral Vocabulary	Check Word Reading	Check Retelling	Check Fluency	Check Oral Vocabulary

Success Predictor

Vocabulary
 Homonyms

Teach homonyms

Context Clues Remind students that homonyms are words that have the same pronunciation but different meanings. Write the sentence *Uncle Romie's apartment was several stories tall.* Have students tell definitions for the word *stories.* Underline the context clues in the sentence that tell which meaning is used.

Guide practice

Have students write two sentences that illustrate different meanings for each of the following homonyms: *second, match, bowl.* Have them underline the context clues in each sentence.

On their own

As students work independently, make sure they also know the meaning of *pupil* as a part of the eye. Check to make sure they can identify the context clues in the sentence.

Listening and Speaking
Retelling

Teach retelling

Explain to students that when they retell a story, it is as important to be a good listener as it is to be a good speaker. Remind speakers to first determine their purpose for speaking: to inform, to persuade, or to entertain. Then when they retell the story, they should speak so everyone can understand them by using good pronunciation, looking at their audience, and using a good rate and volume. Remind the audience to listen attentively and to raise their hands before asking any relevant questions of the speaker or making pertinent comments.

Guide practice

Help students find appropriate places to break the story into three parts that are equal in length. You may want to let students practice their parts using a timer to keep them the same length. Ask them to think about the words they would choose for an audience of kindergarten children or one of parents and teachers.

On their own

Have groups take turns retelling *Me and Uncle Romie.* Allow time for a question and answer session for each group. Encourage students to ask and answer questions with appropriate detail and provide suggestions that build on the ideas of others.

Retelling

Remind students that the rate and pace at which they speak will help them effectively communicate the ideas and emotions in the story. Suggest that they vary the rate and pace for effect, emphasize key words, and use emotion in their voices when communicating a character's feelings.

DAY 4 Language Arts

30–35 min

Objectives
- Synthesize information from interviews and electronic sources into a graphic organizer.
- Review conjunctions
- Spell words with suffixes -*y*, -*ish*, -*hood*, and -*ment* correctly.

Research and Inquiry
Synthesize

Teach

Have students synthesize their research findings and results. Remind them that when they synthesize, they integrate important information and relevant details from various sources to create an answer to their inquiry questions. Explain that their outline will help them synthesize and organize the information for their article and presentation.

Guide practice

Meet with students and review their material. Have them use a word processing program for their articles. If students have not collected enough information to answer their inquiry questions, then guide them in revisiting online resources and doing further research, including interviewing experts.

On their own

Have students finish writing their informational articles, and then write a brief explanation of their research findings. Then have them organize and combine information and plan their presentations.

Conventions
Conjunctions

Test practice

Remind students that grammar skills, such as coordinating conjunctions, are often assessed on important tests. Remind students that conjunctions are words that connect words or groups of words. Review the conjunction *because.* To show a reason, use the conjunction *because.* I fell asleep early *because* I was tired. Then review *and, or, but,* and *therefore.*

Daily Fix-It

Use Daily Fix-It numbers 7 and 8 in the right margin.

On their own

For additional practice, use *Reader's and Writer's Notebook* p. 370.

Reader's and Writer's Notebook p. 370

Spelling
Suffixes *-y, -ish, -hood,* and *-ment*

Practice spelling strategy

Supply pairs of students with index cards on which the spelling words have been written. Have one student read a word while the other writes it. Then have students switch roles. Have them use the cards to check their spelling and correct any misspelled words.

On their own

For additional practice, use *Let's Practice It!* page 336 on the *Teacher Resources DVD-ROM.*

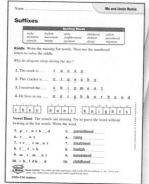

Let's Practice It! TR DVD•336

Daily Fix-It

7. Her and me lived with our familys in New York City. *(She and I; families)*

8. On Sundays, childrn feed the ducks and gooses in Central Park. *(children; geese)*

ELL

English Language Learners

Suffixes Write the spelling words on note cards with the suffixes separated from their base words. Provide support for students based on their proficiency levels:

Beginning Have students match the cards by referring to their spelling lists.

Intermediate Have students match the cards and then write the complete words.

Advanced/Advanced High Remove the suffixes. Have students write the complete spelling words by looking at the base words.

Objectives
- Revise draft of a book review.
- Apply revising strategy of adding.
- Include organized and coherent paragraphs that demonstrate understanding of text.

Writing—Book Review
Revising Strategy

MINI-LESSON

Revising Strategy: Adding

Writing Transparency 25B, TR DVD

■ Yesterday we wrote book reviews about books that we've read. Today we will revise our drafts. The goal is to make your writing clearer, more interesting, and more informative.

■ Display Writing Transparency 25B. Remind students that revising does not include corrections of grammar and mechanics. Tell them that this will be done during the lesson as they proofread their work. Then introduce the revising strategy of adding.

■ When you revise, ask yourself *How can I make my writing more informative and interesting*? The revising strategy adding is when you add more details to your sentences to better explain or describe what you are writing about. The second paragraph of my book review is very plain. I'll revise the first sentence by adding the text *how plants can be used to create food, clothing, and even furniture!* Then I'll revise the second sentence by replacing the word *neat* with *useful* and adding the words *that show the different parts of the plant* after the word *illustrations*. Finally, I'll add the text *showing why plants are important* to the end of the third sentence. Reread your review for places where you might want to add informative and interesting details.

Tell students that as they revise, not only should they look for places where they might add information to help make their reviews clearer, better organized, and more interesting, but they should also make sure they have organized their ideas into coherent paragraphs.

Revising Tips

✓ Check your work to make sure the writing is well-organized.

✓ Add specific information or details to make your writing more interesting and solidify your argument.

Peer conferencing

Peer Revision Have pairs of students exchange papers for peer revision. Students should write three questions about their partner's writing. Tell students that their questions should focus on where the partner could revise by adding information to make the writing clearer.

Have students revise their book reviews using the key features of a book review and questions or suggestions from their partners. Be sure students are using the revising strategy of adding.

Corrective feedback

Circulate around the room to monitor and confer with students as they revise. Remind students correcting errors that they will have time to edit tomorrow. They should be working on content and organization today.

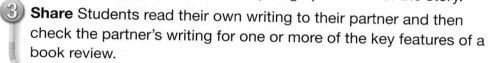

ROUTINE — Quick Write for Fluency — Team Talk

1. **Talk** Pairs discuss the selection, *Me and Uncle Romie.*
2. **Write** Each student writes a one-paragraph review of the story.
3. **Share** Students read their own writing to their partner and then check the partner's writing for one or more of the key features of a book review.

Routines Flip Chart

Wrap Up Your Day

✔ **Build Concepts** What did you learn about life in North Carolina and New York?

✔ **Oral Vocabulary** Monitor students' use of oral vocabulary as they respond: Do you think you will see animals scurry and scamper in skyscrapers in the city?

✔ **Text Features** Discuss how understanding the climax helps students understand text.

Write Guy
Jeff Anderson

Show Off—in a Good Way

Post student's successful sentences or short paragraphs. Celebrate them as writers. Select a sentence of the week, and write it large! Students learn from each others' successes.

Differentiated Instruction

 Strategic Intervention

Oral response If students have trouble writing their book reviews, then suggest that they respond orally to the prompt.

ELL

English Language Learners
Showing opinions Provide additional phrases for students to use to show their opinions, such as *the book does not; I enjoyed; I do not understand why; the illustrations are; the book could use more,* etc.

Preview DAY 5

Remind students to think about how city life compares to country life.

Objectives
- Review the weekly concept.
- Review oral vocabulary.

Today at a Glance

Oral Vocabulary

Comprehension
◉ Author's purpose

Lesson Vocabulary
◉ Homonyms

Phonics/Word Analysis
◉ Suffixes

Literary Terms
Onomatopoeia

Assessment
Fluency
Comprehension

Research and Inquiry
Communicate

Spelling
Suffixes -y, -ish, -hood, -ment

Conventions
Conjunctions

Writing
Book review

Check Oral Vocabulary
SUCCESS PREDICTOR

Concept Wrap Up

Question of the Week
? How does city life compare to life in the country?

Review the concept

Have students look back at the reading selections to find examples that best demonstrate comparing city life to country life.

Review Amazing Words

Display and review this week's concept map. Remind students that this week they have learned ten Amazing Words related to comparing city life and country life. Have students use the Amazing Words and the concept map to answer the question *How does city life compare to life in the country?*

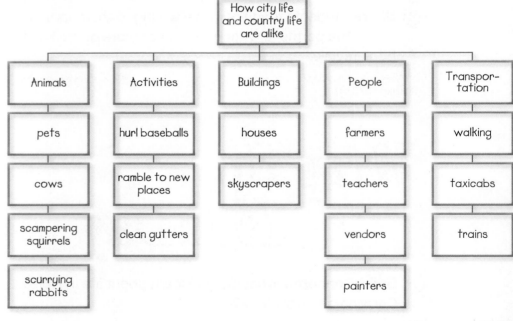

How city life and country life are alike

Animals	Activities	Buildings	People	Transportation
pets	hurl baseballs	houses	farmers	walking
cows	ramble to new places	skyscrapers	teachers	taxicabs
scampering squirrels	clean gutters		vendors	trains
scurrying rabbits			painters	

ELL Check Concepts and Language Use the Day 5 instruction on ELL Poster 25 to monitor students' understanding of the lesson concept.

ELL Poster 25

Amazing Ideas

Connect to the Big Question

Have pairs of students discuss how the Question of the Week connects to the Big Question: *What happens when two ways of life come together?* Tell students to use the concept map and what they have learned from this week's Anchored Talks and reading selections to form an Amazing Idea–a realization or "big idea" about Cultures. Remind partners to answer questions with appropriate detail. Then ask each pair to share its Amazing Idea with the class.

Amazing Ideas might include these key concepts:

• City life and country life are two different ways of life.

• People who live in the city often have the same interests as people who live in the country.

• Although people come from different ways of life, they can find common interests and form friendships.

Write about it

Have students write a few sentences about their Amazing Idea, beginning with "This week I learned..."

Amazing Words

skyscraper	hurl
taxicab	meager
scamper	gutter
scurry	bitter
vendor	ramble

It's Friday

MONITOR PROGRESS Check Oral Vocabulary

Have individuals use this week's Amazing Words to describe city life and country life. Monitor students' abilities to use the Amazing Words and note which words you need to reteach.

If... students have difficulty using the Amazing Words,

then... reteach using the Oral Vocabulary Routine, pages 321a, 326b, 340b, 354b, OV•2.

Day 1	Day 2	Day 3	Day 4	Day 5
Check Oral Vocabulary	Check Word Reading	Check Retelling	Check Fluency	Check Oral Vocabulary

Success Predictor

ELL

English Language Learners
Concept map Work with students to add new words and phrases to the concept map.

Me and Uncle Romie **359g**

Objectives
◎ Review author's purpose.
◎ Review homonyms.
◎ Review suffixes -y, -ish, -hood, -ment.
• Review onomatopoeia.

Comprehension Review
↻ Author's Purpose

Teach author's purpose

Envision It!

Review the definition of author's purpose on p. 324. Remind students that the author's purpose is the reason or reasons the author has for writing. Writers may write to inform, persuade, entertain, or express an opinion. For additional support have students review p. EI•2 on author's purpose.

Guide practice

Have students find an example that illustrates the author's purpose in *Me and Uncle Romie*. Remind them that using background knowledge can help them determine the author's purpose. Then have pairs tell what the author's purpose is.

On their own

For additional practice with author's purpose, use *Let's Practice It!* page 337 on the *Teacher Resources DVD-ROM*.

Student Edition p. EI•2

Let's Practice It!
TR DVD•337

Vocabulary Review
↻ Homonyms

Teach homonyms

Remind students to use context clues to help them understand the meanings of homonyms.

Guide practice

Write on the board: *I got tired after I walked down four <u>flights</u> of stairs.* Review with students how context clues can help them determine the meaning of the homonym *flights* in the sentence.

On their own

Have students write sentences to illustrate two meanings for the homonyms *flights* and *stoops.* Let them exchange papers with a partner and use context clues to identify the correct meaning of each homonym.

Word Analysis Review
 Suffixes

Teach suffixes

Write the following sentences on the board. Have students read each one, first quietly to themselves and then aloud as you track the print.

1. **My neighborhood was filled with excitement about the festival.**
2. **This juicy orange is a very healthy snack.**
3. **Our homework assignment is lengthy.**
4. **She says it's childish to get dirty playing in the mud.**
5. **What is Ted's punishment for his dishonesty?**

Team Talk Have students discuss with a partner which words are base words with the suffixes *-y, -ish, -hood,* and *-ment.* Ask them to identify the base word and the suffix in each word. Then call on individuals to share with the class.

Literary Terms Review
Onomatopoeia

Teach

Have students reread *Me and Uncle Romie* on p. 336. Remind them that onomatopoeia describes words that sound like their meaning.

Guide practice

Find an example of onomatopoeia on p. 336. Discuss why the author used *Whew!* Have students find another example of onomatopoeia on p. 343.

On their own

Have students reread p. 348. Have them identify onomatopoeic words the author could have used on James's train ride home.

Lesson Vocabulary

cardboard thick, stiff paper
feast a meal with a lot of food
fierce frightening, scary
flights a set of stairs
pitcher a person who throws a baseball to a batter
ruined destroyed or damaged
stoops a small porch with steps, usually at the front of a house
treasure valuables; prizes

E L L

English Language Learners
Suffixes Point out to Spanish speakers that the suffix *-ment* does not have the same meaning as the suffix *-mente* in Spanish. In English the suffix is often used to change a verb into a noun *(enjoy/enjoyment).* In Spanish, *-mente* is used to change an adjective into an adverb *(rápido, rápidmente).*

Using words with suffixes
Have students provide base words to orally complete sentences that use a base word plus a suffix. For example: *Someone who is **dirty** is covered with* (dirt). *A **foolish** man acts like a* (fool).

Objectives
- Read grade-level text with fluency.

Plan to Assess Fluency

☑ **Week 1** Assess Advanced students.

☑ **Week 2** Assess Strategic Intervention students.

☑ **Week 3** Assess On-Level students.

☑ **Week 4** Assess Strategic Intervention students.

☑ **This week assess any students you have not yet checked during this unit.**

Set individual goals for students to enable them to reach the year-end goal.
- Current Goal: 102–112 WCPM
- Year-End Goal: 120 WCPM

Assessment

Check words correct per minute

Fluency Make two copies of the fluency passage on page 359k. As the student reads the text aloud, mark mistakes on your copy. Also mark where the student is at the end of one minute. To check the student's comprehension of the passages have him or her retell what was read. To figure words correct per minute (WCPM), subtract the number of mistakes from the total number of words read in one minute.

Corrective feedback

WCPM

If... students cannot read fluently at a rate of 102–112 WCPM,
then... make sure they practice with text at their independent reading level. Provide additional fluency practice by pairing nonfluent readers with fluent readers.

If... students already read at 120 WCPM,
then... have them read a book of their choice independently.

Small Group Time

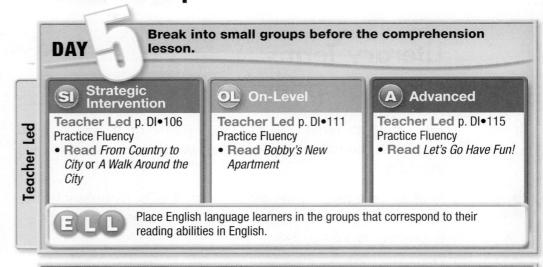

DAY 5 **Break into small groups before the comprehension lesson.**

Teacher Led

SI Strategic Intervention
Teacher Led p. DI•106
Practice Fluency
- **Read** *From Country to City* or *A Walk Around the City*

OL On-Level
Teacher Led p. DI•111
Practice Fluency
- **Read** *Bobby's New Apartment*

A Advanced
Teacher Led p. DI•115
Practice Fluency
- **Read** *Let's Go Have Fun!*

ELL Place English language learners in the groups that correspond to their reading abilities in English.

Practice Stations
- Words to know
- Get Fluent
- Read for Meaning

Independent Activities
- Grammar Jammer
- Concept Talk Video
- Vocabulary Activities

Name _____

Hunting Treasure

"What fine feast have you prepared for the crew's enjoyment?" the | 11

Captain asked as he opened the hatch and went down the short flight of | 25

steps to the kitchen. He had to bend down to enter the low doorway. | 39

"The usual, Sir," I said as cheerfully as possible. *Ruined soup, moldy* | 51

apples, and lumpy oatmeal is what I thought. I poured the captain a cup | 65

of goat's milk from my pitcher. | 71

I had left my childhood home in London to make my livelihood as a | 85

cook at sea. I would have been better off living in a garbage dump. I | 100

was sleepy and cold the entire voyage. But now it was spring, and our | 114

voyage was almost over. | 118

"Land ho!" a voice called from aloft. | 125

At last! I went up on deck. There was a fair green strip of land | 141

before us. The next morning, I set out with my shipmates to explore it. | 155

The captain came seeking furs and spices. I had more practical things | 166

in mind. | 168

I searched the creek sides for green sprouts that are good to eat. I | 182

filled my cap full of walnuts from the ground. Then, in an open meadow, | 196

I found what I had been dreaming of for months. Fresh strawberries, | 208

treasure enough for this ship's cook. | 214

Assessment

Check author's purpose

Author's Purpose Use "The Last Night" on p. 359m to check students' understanding of author's purpose.

1. What is Warren worried about? (Warren is moving from a farm to a city, and he wonders if he will be happy in a city.)

2. What is the author's purpose in writing paragraph 1? (The author is writing to give a description of Warren's farm.)

3. Why does the author describe the city in paragraph 2? (This shows all the good things Warren is looking forward to.)

Corrective feedback

If... students are unable to answer the comprehension questions, **then...** use the Reteach lesson in the *First Stop* book.

The Last Night

Warren gazed out the upstairs bedroom window into the night. The moon shone brightly and lit up the farmyard. Warren studied the old wooden barn, the towering silo, and the animal pens. He took a deep breath. Through the window screen he could smell the farm. He could smell animals and fields of hay. He loved the summertime smells of this farmland. Then Warren heard a distant train whistling as it rumbled through a rail crossing on its way to the city.

Warren took another deep breath and wondered what his new life would be like. Tomorrow, his family would move into that huge city. Warren was looking forward to it. The city was full of excitement. There were busy people rushing around. There were zoos and museums. There were baseball parks and football stadiums. There were interesting things to do and interesting people to meet. City living would be a great adventure.

Yet Warren felt sad tonight. He knew he would miss this old farm. He would miss the sounds of roosters in the morning, of cows waiting to be milked, of pigs snorting as the gobbled down their food.

Warren wondered if he would ever again ride on a tractor or climb in a hayloft. He wondered if his mom and dad would be happy working in the city. City work would have to be easier than farming!

Warren leaned closer to the window and to the farm outside of it. Would he be happy in the city?

MONITOR PROGRESS   • Author's purpose

Objectives
- Present inquiry results in a clear, coherent manner.
- Administer spelling test.
- Review conjunctions.

Research and Inquiry
Communicate

Present ideas   Have students share their inquiry results by presenting their information and giving a brief talk on their research.

Listening and speaking   Remind students how to be good speakers and how to communicate effectively with their audience.

- Respond to relevant questions with appropriate details.
- Speak clearly and loudly.
- Keep eye contact with audience members.

Remind students of these tips for being a good listener.
- Wait until the speaker has finished before raising your hand to ask a relevant question or make a comment.
- Be polite, even if you disagree.
- Sit up straight and listen attentively.

Spelling Test
Suffixes *-y, -ish, -hood, -ment*

Spelling test
To administer the spelling test, refer to the directions, words, and sentences on p. 325c.

Conventions
Extra Practice

Teach
Remind students that conjunctions are words that connect words or groups of words.

- To add information, use the conjunction *and*.
- To show a choice, use the conjunction *or*.
- To show a difference, use the conjunction *but*.
- To show a result, use the conjunction *therefore*.
- To show a reason, use *because*.

Guide practice
Have students work with a partner to list the conjunction that goes with each action.

> **show a difference** (but)   **show a reason** (because)

Daily Fix-It
Use Daily Fix-It numbers 9 and 10 in the right margin.

On their own
Write these sentences. Have students use the correct conjunctions to complete the sentences. Students should complete *Let's Practice It!* page 338 on the *Teacher Resources DVD-ROM*.

> 1. I like strawberries, _____ I like bananas more. (but)
>
> 2. The sunset is pink _____ orange. (and)
>
> 3. It is raining, _____ I will need an umbrella. (therefore)
>
> 4. I am unprepared _____ I forgot my gym bag. (because)
>
> 5. Do you want sausage _____ bacon for breakfast? (or)

Daily Fix-It

9. There is much trafic in the city, there is not much in the country. (*traffic; but*)

10. Arent the city sights interesting to James and she? (*Aren't; her*)

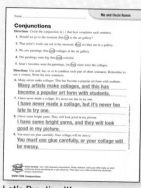

Let's Practice It!
TR DVD•338

Objectives
- Proofread revised drafts of a book review, including correct use of conjunctions.
- Create and present final draft.

Writing—Book Review
Writing Trait: Conventions

Review revising

Remind students that yesterday they revised their book reviews, paying particular attention to adding details that would make their writing more interesting and informative. Today they will proofread their book reviews.

MINI-LESSON

Proofread for Conjunctions

■ **Teach** When we proofread, we look closely at our work, searching for errors in mechanics such as spelling, capitalization, punctuation, and grammar. Today we will focus on making sure conjunctions are used correctly.

Writing Transparency 25C, TR DVD

■ **Model** Let's look at the last few paragraphs of my book review from yesterday. Display Writing Transparency 25C. Explain that you will look for errors in the use of conjunctions. In the second sentence, I used *but* instead of *and.* In the last sentence, I used *therefore* instead of *because.* Point out the title in the first line. I also need to underline <u>How Plants Grow</u> because it is the title of the book. Now I will reread the review several more times looking for errors. Explain to students that they should reread their reviews a number of times, each time looking for different types of errors: spelling, punctuation, capitalization, grammar, and any specific requirements of the writing product, such as underlining the book title.

Proofread

Display the Proofreading Tips. Ask students to proofread their reviews using the Proofreading Tips and paying particular attention to conjunctions. Circulate around the room answering students' questions. When students have finished editing their own work, have pairs proofread one another's book reviews.

Proofreading Tips

✔ Be sure that conjunctions are being used correctly.

✔ Do not rely solely on a word processing spell-checker; use a dictionary to find and double-check spelling.

Present

Have students incorporate revisions and proofreading edits into their book reviews to create a final draft.

Have small groups create book review magazines from their writing. Have students find or create art for the cover of their book reviews. Suggest that students draw their book covers or find images to accompany the story lines or topics of their book reviews. Remind students to create a table of contents for their magazines. When students have finished, have each student complete the Writing Self-Evaluation Guide.

ROUTINE **Quick Write for Fluency** **Team Talk**

1. **Talk** Pairs discuss what they learned about reviewing books this week.
2. **Write** Each person writes a few sentences about why someone might want to read book reviews.
3. **Share** Partners read their writing to their partner.

Routines Flip Chart

Teacher Note

Writing self-evaluation Make copies of the Writing Self-Evaluation Guide on p. 39 of the *Reader's and Writer's Notebook* and hand out to students.

Preview NEXT WEEK

Tell students that next week they will review this unit's skills and the Big Question: *What happens when two ways of life come together?*

UNIT 5 Reading Poetry

Objectives

- Identify characteristics of free verse.
- Understand alliteration and assonance.
- Read poetry fluently.

Student Edition pp. 360–361

Guide Comprehension
Literary Terms

Teach free verse poems

Free Verse Poems Review the definition of free verse on p. 360. Remind students that poems written in free verse do not have rhymes or regular rhythm, but are clearly not prose.

Guide practice

Have students discuss "My Friend in School." Point out that most lines begin with lowercase letters and there is little punctuation. Ask them to think about all the information the poet gives the reader or listener.

On their own

Have students read the poem aloud. Have them first read it as if it were prose. Then have them read it carefully, thinking about the best way to group the words. Encourage them to try different ways to read the poem and discuss which they like best.

Guide Comprehension
Literary Terms

Teach alliteration and assonance

Alliteration and Assonance Review the definitions of alliteration and assonance on p. 360. Explain that poets often use alliteration or assonance to create a musical effect. They also use these techniques to draw attention to important words in a poem.

Guide practice

Have students compare ways in which the narrator talks and ways in which they might really say the same thing. Have them notice the run-on quality to the speech.

On their own

Have students read the poem with expression. Remind them to pause slightly before beginning each verse so the listener can hear the repetition of the line.

Let's Think About...

1. I can find the assonance using the long e sound. It is in *Tse* many times and in the verse with *C, see, sea,* and *sí.* There is alliteration at the end of the poem in the phrases *wonder what* and *wonder why.*

2. Possible response: "My Friend in School" is free verse because there is no rhyme, regular rhythm, or cadence. Many of the words and rhythms are like regular speech. The poem creates a picture of two boys, one Chinese and one not, having fun together, laughing a lot about silly things.

Differentiated Instruction

 Strategic Intervention

Alliteration Have students make alliterative versions of their names. Have them illustrate the name (e.g., Silly Sam, Muddy Max).

 Advanced

Assonance Have students work together to write a short poem that emphasizes the long *a* sound.

ELL

English Language Learners

Assonance Explain to students that poets often use assonance to create musical effects. However, the spellings of the same sounds can be very different. Make a chart with students of all the words with different spellings of the long *e* sound in the poem. Have them add other words they know either in English or their own languages.

Objectives
- Identify the characteristics of narrative poems.
- Read poetry fluently.
- Write a poem.

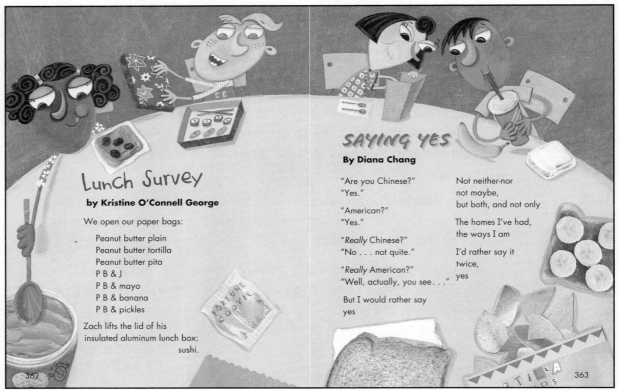

Lunch Survey
by Kristine O'Connell George

We open our paper bags:

Peanut butter plain
Peanut butter tortilla
Peanut butter pita
P B & J
P B & mayo
P B & banana
P B & pickles

Zach lifts the lid of his
insulated aluminum lunch box:
           sushi.

SAYING YES
By Diana Chang

"Are you Chinese?"
"Yes."

"American?"
"Yes."

"*Really* Chinese?"
"No . . . not quite."

"*Really* American?"
"Well, actually, you see . . ."

But I would rather say
yes

Not neither-nor
not maybe,
but both, and not only

The homes I've had,
the ways I am

I'd rather say it
twice,
yes

Student Edition pp. 362–363

Guide Comprehension
Literary Terms

Teach narrative poems

Narrative Poems Review the definition of narrative poems on p. 360. Remind students that narrative poems can be funny or sad, quiet or dramatic. The important thing is that they tell a story.

Guide practice

Have students discuss the story in "Lunch Survey" and identify why it is a narrative poem. (It tells a story.) Point out the similarity and difference between "We open our paper bags" and "Zach lifts the lid of his insulated aluminum lunch box." (Everyone is taking out lunch, but only Zach has a lunch box instead of a paper bag.)

On their own

Have students read the poem aloud, pausing before the last line to make it stand out.

Extend Thinking
Think Critically

Higher-order thinking skills

Poetry • Analysis What would be different if you told the story in "Saying Yes" in prose? **Possible response:** I would probably identify the speakers. I would also add punctuation and probably some more words to make the text more clear.

Author's Purpose • Evaluation Why do you think the author chose to write "Lunch Survey" as free verse? **Possible response:** The story works well when it lists all the lunches. The sameness might be lost in a rhyme.

Inferring • Analysis In the second half of "Saying Yes," what idea is the speaker trying to express? **Possible response:** She is a whole rather than a half. She is more rather than less. She is the sum of all of her experiences.

Practice Fluent Reading

Have partners read "Saying Yes" aloud, one student reading only lines 1, 3, 5, and 7, and the other reading all the other lines. (Students can then switch parts.) Encourage the student reading the main speaker's lines to use a clipped, conversational tone for the dialogue, and a slower, more reflective tone for the second half of the poem. When they are finished, have students listen to the AudioText of the poem and compare it to their own readings.

Writing Poetry

Have students write a poem about a kind of food, sports, or clothing that has become a part of American culture, but that originated elsewhere. (To get students started, you might write *egg roll, soccer,* and *poncho* on the board.) Invite students to read their works aloud, grouping poems by culture, if possible.

Weekly Assessment

Use pp. 176–182 of *Weekly Tests* to check:

✔ **Phonics** Suffixes *-y, -ish, -hood, -ment*

✔ ◉ **Comprehension Skill** Author's Purpose

✔ **Lesson Vocabulary**

✔ Review **Comprehension Skill** Draw Conclusions

cardboard	pitcher
feast	ruined
fierce	stoops
flights	treasure

Weekly Tests

A
Advanced

Differentiated Assessment

OL
On-Level

Use pp. 145–150 of *Fresh Reads for Fluency and Comprehension* to check:

✔ ◉ **Comprehension Skill** Author's Purpose

✔ Review **Comprehension Skill** Draw Conclusions

✔ **Fluency** Words Correct Per Minute

SI
Strategic Intervention

Fresh Reads for Fluency and Comprehension

Managing Assessment

Use *Assessment Handbook* for:

✔ **Weekly Assessment Blackline Masters for Monitoring Progress**

✔ **Observation Checklists**

✔ **Record-Keeping Forms**

✔ **Portfolio Assessment**

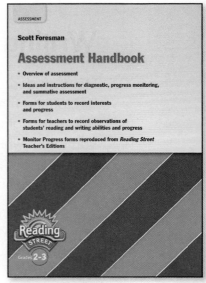

Assessment Handbook

Teacher Notes

Pacing Small Group Instruction

15–20 min

5-Day Plan

DAY 1	• Reinforce the concept • Read Leveled Readers Concept Literacy Below Level
DAY 2	• Author's Purpose • Background Knowledge • Revisit Student Edition pp. 328–339
DAY 3	• Homonyms • Revisit Student Edition pp. 340–349
DAY 4	• Practice Retelling • Read/Revisit Student Edition pp. 354–357
DAY 5	• Reread for fluency • Reread Leveled Readers

3- or 4-Day Plan

DAY 1	• Reinforce the concept • Read Leveled Readers
DAY 2	• Author's Purpose • Background Knowledge • Revisit Student Edition pp. 328–339
DAY 3	• Homonyms • Revisit Student Edition pp. 340–349
DAY 4	• Practice Retelling • Read/Revisit Student Edition pp. 354–357 • Reread for fluency • Reread Leveled Readers

3-Day Plan: Eliminate the shaded box.

SI *Strategic Intervention*

DAY 1

Build Background

■ **Reinforce the Concept** Discuss the weekly question *How does city life compare to life in the country?* What do you already know about country life and city life from your own experience? *(Accept all reasonable responses.)* What do books, movies, and TV shows tell you about city and country life? *(Students may say that these sources usually show country life as peaceful and city life as noisy and exciting.)* Depending on whether you live in a city, a suburb, or a country area, you might have different chores or hobbies. How would your life change if you moved to a different place? *(Students may say that they would make new friends or learn new skills.)* Discuss the words on the concept map. This week we're going to read about a boy who leaves his home in the country for a long visit with his aunt and uncle in the city. What would you like and dislike about visiting relatives in a faraway place? *(Students may say that they would enjoy seeing the sights but might become homesick.)*

Preview Decodable Practice Reader 25A

■ **Before Reading** Review the words on p. 109 of Decodable Practice Reader 25A. Then have students blend these words from the text: *shiny, frisky, neighborhood, sundress, wispy, fabric,* and *admitted.* Be sure students understand the meaning of such words as *frisky* and *wispy.* Guide students through the text by doing a picture walk.

Decodable Practice Readers Units 4–6
• Practice phonics skills
• Blending practice
• Reread for fluency

Objectives

• Participate in teacher-led discussions by answering questions with appropriate detail.

For a complete literacy instructional plan and additional practice with this week's target skills and strategies, see the **Leveled Reader Teaching Guide.**

Concept Literacy Reader

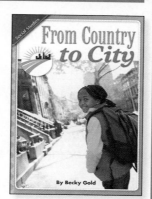

- **Read** *From Country to City*

- **Before Reading** Preview the book with students, focusing on key concepts and vocabulary. Then help students set a purpose for reading.

- **During Reading** Read the first two pages aloud while students track along with the print. Then have students finish reading the book with a partner.

- **After Reading** After students finish reading, ask: Why do you think some city apartment buildings are so tall? *(so more people can live in them)* What do the city and the country have in common? *(People live and can have fun and friends in both places.)*

Below-Level Reader

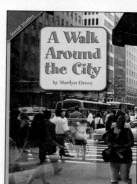

- **Read** *A Walk Around the City*

- **Before Reading** Have students use the photographs and captions to preview the book. Then help students set a purpose for reading.

- **During Reading** Read pp. 3–5 aloud. Then do a choral reading of pp. 6–9. If students are able, have them read and discuss the remainder of the book with a partner.

- **After Reading** Ask students to look at and discuss the concept map. Connect the Below-Level Reader to the weekly question. How different do you think city life and country life are? *(Even outside the city, people have jobs as teachers and police officers, and people buy and sell things or go to parks for fun.)*

MONITOR PROGRESS

If... students have difficulty reading the selection with a partner,
then... have them follow along as they listen to the Leveled Readers DVD-ROM.

If... students have trouble understanding the descriptions of city life,
then... look at the photographs in the book and discuss their relationship to the text.

Objectives
• Participate in teacher-led discussions by answering questions with appropriate detail.

Small Group Time

Student Edition p. EI•2

More Reading

Use additional Leveled Readers or other texts at students' instructional levels to reinforce this week's skills and strategies. For text suggestions, see the Leveled Reader Database or the Leveled Readers Skills Chart on pp. CL22–CL27.

Reinforce Comprehension

◉ **Skill Author's Purpose** Review with students *Envision It!* p. EI•2 on Author's Purpose. Then use p. 324 to review the definition of the skill. An author has a reason for choosing a certain subject and writing about it in that particular way. Some writers want to persuade you to think or act in a certain way. What are some other purposes that authors might have? *(to inform; to entertain; to express feelings, an opinion, or a mood)*

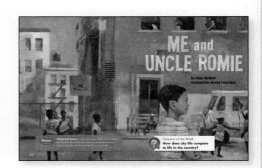

◉ **Strategy Background Knowledge** Review the definition of background knowledge. For additional support, refer students to *Envision It!* p. EI•18.

Revisit *Me and Uncle Romie* on pp. 328–339. As students read, have them apply the comprehension skill and strategy. The author's purpose could be to persuade readers that even people who live in different places have many things in common.

- Why do you think the author has James talk on p. 332 about how he will miss the way they always celebrate his birthday with cake and a baseball game? *(This tells you his idea of a perfect birthday, so you can watch for what happens later to see if it is as good.)*

- How does the scene on p. 338 where James plays stickball with the kids in Harlem help you see that the author may want to persuade? *(James has fun with the kids in the city, just as he had fun with his friend back home.)*

Use the During Reading Differentiated Instruction for additional support for struggling readers.

MONITOR PROGRESS

If... students have difficulty reading along with the group,

then... have them follow along as they listen to the AudioText.

Objectives
- Locate the author's stated purposes in writing the text.
- Monitor comprehension, making corrections when that understanding breaks down.

 **Strategic Intervention** DAY **3**

Reinforce Vocabulary

■ **Reread for Fluency** Use Decodable Practice Reader 25A.

■ **Decoding Multisyllabic Words** Write *underground* and model how to use meaningful parts to read it. First, I ask myself if I recognize parts of the word. I see *under* at the beginning and *ground* at the end, so this is a compound word. I put the words together and figure out that *underground* means "below the surface of the ground."

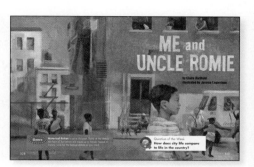

Use the Multisyllabic Word routine from *Routines Flip Chart* to help students read other words from the story, such as *rumbling* and *conversations*.

◉ **Homonyms/Context Clues** Write the word *stoop* on the board. I know the word *stoop* means "to hunch down," as in "He's so tall that he stoops to walk through doorways." Point out the use of *stoops* on p. 338. James talks about people "sitting out on stoops." The meaning I know doesn't make sense in context. If I check the dictionary, I see that a stoop is "the entrance stairway at the front door of a house." That makes sense, so the two *stoops* are homonyms—words with the same spelling and pronunciation, but different meanings.

■ **Revisit** *Me and Uncle Romie* on pp. 340–349. Then review *Words!* on pp. W•7 and W•11. Ask: Which definition of *block* makes more sense on p. 343: "a small area of a city or town with streets on each edge" or "an obstacle"? *(The passage is about people lining up in the street, so the first definition makes more sense.)*

Use the During Reading Differentiated Instruction for additional support for struggling readers.

MONITOR PROGRESS

If... students need more practice with the lesson vocabulary,
then... use *Envision It! Pictured Vocabulary Cards*.

Student Edition p. W•11

More Reading

Use additional Leveled Readers or other texts at students' instructional levels to reinforce this week's skills and strategies. For text suggestions, see the Leveled Reader Database or the Leveled Readers Skills Chart on pp. CL22–CL27.

Objectives
• Use context to determine meaning of homonyms.
• Use context to determine the relevant meaning of unfamiliar words.

Small Group Time

Practice Retelling

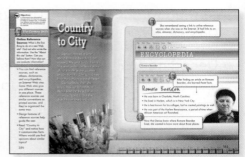

■ **Retell** Guide students in using the Retelling Cards to list events from *Me and Uncle Romie* in order. How do the narrator's uncle and aunt help him celebrate his birthday? *(His uncle takes him to a baseball game, and his aunt makes him a cake.)*

If students struggle, model a fluent retelling.

Genre Focus

■ **Before Reading or Revisiting** "Country to City" on pp. 354–359, read aloud the genre information about online reference sources on p. 354. Now that you know *Me and Uncle Romie* is based on a real-life artist, Romare Bearden, you might want to learn more about him. This selection shows how to use online references to do that. Then have students note the different online sources reprinted in the article.

■ **During Reading or Revisiting** Have students perform a choral reading of the selection. Stop to discuss concepts and terms such as the Harlem Renaissance. How could you learn more about the Harlem Renaissance if you were sitting at a computer? *(search for "Harlem Renaissance" in an online encyclopedia)*

■ **After Reading or Revisiting** Have students share their reactions to the selection. Then guide students through the Get Online! activity.

• What did you learn from the online almanac about North Carolina and New York? *(statistics like their populations and facts like sources of income)*

• What did you learn from *Me and Uncle Romie* about North Carolina and New York? *(an idea of what it is like to be in those places)*

MONITOR PROGRESS

If... students have difficulty retelling the selection,
then... have them review the story using the illustrations.

Objectives
• Make connections between literary and informational texts with similar ideas.

SI Strategic Intervention

DAY 5

For a complete literacy instructional plan and additional practice with this week's target skills and strategies, see the **Leveled Reader Teaching Guide.**

Concept Literacy Reader

■ **Model** Model the fluency skill of appropriate phrasing. Ask students to listen carefully as you read aloud the first two pages of *From Country to City.* Have students note the difference between grouping words in a way that makes sense and reading each word in a word-by-word staccato manner.

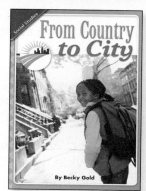

From Country to City

■ **Fluency Routine**

1. Have students reread passages from *From Country to City* with a partner.

2. For optimal fluency, students should reread three to four times.

3. As students read, monitor fluency and provide corrective feedback.

See *Routines Flip Chart* for more help with fluency.

■ **Retell** Have students retell *From Country to City.* Prompt as necessary.

Below-Level Reader

■ **Model** Ask students to listen carefully as you read aloud the first two pages of *A Walk Around the City,* emphasizing appropriate phrasing.

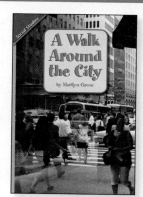

A Walk Around the City

■ **Fluency Routine**

1. Have students reread passages from *A Walk Around the City* with a partner or individually.

2. For optimal fluency, students should reread three to four times.

3. As students read, monitor fluency and provide corrective feedback.

See *Routines Flip Chart* for more help with fluency.

■ **Retell** For additional practice, have students retell *A Walk Around the City* section by section, using the photographs. Prompt as necessary.

• What is the section called "People Work in Cities" about? *(the jobs people have and the businesses they operate)*

• What did you learn about cities from reading this book? *(Cities are busy places with different kinds of people in them.)*

MONITOR PROGRESS

If... students have difficulty reading fluently,

then... provide additional fluency practice by pairing nonfluent readers with fluent ones.

Objectives

• Read aloud grade-level text with fluency.

Small Group Time

Pacing Small Group Instruction

15–20 min

5-Day Plan

DAY 1	• Expand the concept • Read On-Level Reader
DAY 2	• ◎ Author's Purpose • ◎ Background Knowledge • Revisit Student Edition pp. 328–339
DAY 3	• ◎ Homonyms • Revisit Student Edition pp. 340–349
DAY 4	• Practice Retelling • Read/Revisit Student Edition pp. 354–357
DAY 5	• Reread for fluency • Reread On-Level Reader

3- or 4-Day Plan

DAY 1	• Expand the concept • Read On-Level Reader
DAY 2	• ◎ Author's Purpose • ◎ Background Knowledge • Revisit Student Edition pp. 328–339
DAY 3	• ◎ Homonyms • Revisit Student Edition pp. 340–349
DAY 4	• Practice Retelling • Read/Revisit Student Edition pp. 354–357 • Reread for fluency • Reread On-Level Reader

3-Day Plan: Eliminate the shaded box.

OL On-Level · **DAY 1**

Build Background

■ **Expand the Concept** Discuss the weekly question *How does city life compare to life in the country?* Is our school in the city, the country, or someplace in between? What do the people who live around here do for work and for fun? Have students add new words to the concept map.

On-Level Reader

For a complete literacy instructional plan and additional practice with this week's target skills and strategies, see the **Leveled Reader Teaching Guide.**

■ **Before Reading** *Bobby's New Apartment,* have students create a blank time line and divide it into three sections labeled *Beginning, Middle,* and *End.* The book you are about to read tells the story of a family who moves from a house in the country to an apartment in a big city. As you read, keep track of the important events, and record them in the correct section of your time line.

Bobby's New Apartment

by Jason Lublinski
illustrated by Alexandra Leff

■ **During Reading** Read aloud the first three pages of *Bobby's New Apartment* as students follow along. Then have them finish reading the book on their own. Remind students to write events on their time lines as they go along. When do you think Bobby first begins to suspect he might like his new home? *(possible answer: when he invites Hazel to come see their apartment)*

■ **After Reading** Have partners compare their time lines.

• How did you decide to break up the story into a beginning, middle, and end? *(Possible answer: The beginning is when Bobby does not like the idea of the apartment, the middle is when he thinks he might like it, and the end is when he has decided he definitely likes it.)*

• How does the topic relate to the weekly question *How does city life compare to life in the country? (There is a lot to like about living in both the country and the city.)*

Objectives
• Participate in teacher-led discussions by answering questions with appropriate detail.

 OL On-Level DAY 2

Expand Comprehension

◉ Skill Author's Purpose Use p. 324 to review the definition of *author's purpose.* For additional review, see Author's Purpose in *Envision It!* p. EI•2. Authors almost never tell their reasons for writing something. Instead, you need to watch for clues in the text. Think about why the author includes certain details and not others. Is it to make *you* feel a certain way or to express feelings that the author has? It might also be to persuade you to do something or believe something, or to provide you with helpful information.

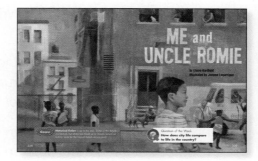

Student Edition p. EI•2

More Reading

Use additional Leveled Readers or other texts at students' instructional levels to reinforce this week's skills and strategies. For text suggestions, see the Leveled Reader Database or the Leveled Readers Skills Chart on pp. CL22–CL27.

◉ Strategy Background Knowledge Encourage students to apply what they already know to what they are reading. For additional support, use the Extend Thinking questions during reading or refer students to EI•18 of *Envision It!*

Revisit *Me and Uncle Romie* on pp. 328–339. As students read, have them apply the comprehension skill and strategy.

• Reread the description of the aunt and uncle's home at the top of p. 336. What purpose might this serve? *(to inform)*

• On that same page, the narrator tells how he feels after climbing stairs: *"Whew!"* Why? *(to inform by describing how high the apartment is; to express the narrator's feelings)*

• How does your background knowledge of country life and city life help you understand the story? *(Cities are noisy and crowded, so James will need time to get used to things.)*

OL On-Level — DAY 3

Expand Vocabulary

Student Edition p. W•11

More Reading

Use additional Leveled Readers or other texts at students' instructional levels to reinforce this week's skills and strategies. For text suggestions, see the Leveled Reader Database or the Leveled Readers Skills Chart on pp. CL22–CL27.

Homonyms/Context Clues Write the word *flight* as you say it aloud.

- What are some different meanings of *flight*? *("the act of flying," "the act of running away," "a group of stairs from one level to the next")*

- Where does this word appear in this story, and what does it mean? *(It is on p. 336 where James and his aunt climb the stairs, so it means "a group of stairs.")*

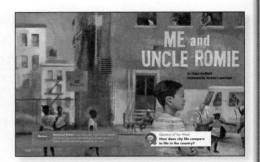

Revisit *Me and Uncle Romie* on pp. 340–349. Then have them review the entire selection for homonyms and context clues. Have students consult a dictionary as needed.

- The conductor says, "Penn Station! Watch your step." What is the meaning of *station* in this context? *(a place where trains let people on and off, not a channel on a TV or radio)*

- Aunt Nanette says, "Uncle Romie's out talking to some people about his big art show that's coming up." What is the meaning of *show* in this context? *(It means "display," not "point out" or "prove.")*

- Uncle Romie says, "Here's a late birthday present for you, James." What is the meaning of *present* in this context? *(It means "gift," not "the opposite of absent.")*

Objectives
- Use context to determine meaning of homonyms.
- Use context to determine the relevant meaning of unfamiliar words.

 On-Level

DAY **4**

Practice Retelling

■ **Retell** To assess students' comprehension, use the Retelling Cards. Monitor retelling and prompt students as needed.

Genre Focus

■ **Before Reading or Revisiting** "Country to City" on pp. 354–357, read aloud the genre information about online reference sources on p. 354. Explain that these sources can help students find information for research papers. Have students preview "Country to City" and set a purpose for reading. What is the purpose of the text boxes in the selection? *(They tell what Denise did as she explored the online sources.)*

■ **During Reading or Revisiting** Have students read with you.

• Why is this selection called "Country to City"? *(Romare Bearden was born in the country and later moved to the city.)*

• In what format do the article on Romare Bearden and the almanac entry present information? *(bulleted lists)*

• In what way is a bulleted list a helpful way to present information? *(The information is presented in small chunks. It is easy to review a page quickly and find exactly what you are seeking.)*

• On the maps, what does the star symbol mean? *(It indicates the state capital.)*

■ **After Reading or Revisiting** Have students share their reaction to "Country to City." Then have them research a state of their choice online and make a list of facts like those shown.

Objectives
• Make connections between literary and informational texts with similar ideas.

Me and Uncle Romie **DI•110**

Small Group Time

On-Level Reader

■ **Model** Read aloud the first page of the On-Level Reader *Bobby's New Apartment,* emphasizing appropriate phrasing.

■ **Fluency Routine**

1. Have students reread passages from *Bobby's New Apartment* with a partner.

2. For optimal fluency, students should reread passages three to four times.

3. As students read, monitor fluency and provide corrective feedback. Have students note how you read natural-sounding groupings of words instead of pronouncing words one by one.

See *Routines Flip Chart* if students require more help with fluency.

■ **Retell** For additional practice, have students use the illustrations as a guide to retell the story. Prompt as necessary.

• What is the problem in this story? *(Bobby is nervous about moving from a house into a large apartment building.)*

• What does Bobby do? *(He moves into a new building, finds his way around, makes a friend, and learns that a large apartment building is something like a small town—everyone has to work together.)*

• Why do you think the author wrote this story? *(to explain what it is like to move to a new place; to persuade readers that moving to a new apartment and taking on new challenges can be fun)*

Objectives
• Read aloud grade-level appropriate text with fluency.

A Advanced **DAY 1**

Build Background

■ **Extend the Concept** Lead a discussion about the weekly question *How does city life compare to life in the country?* Then extend the concept. Think about the different places you have visited or read about. How would you like to live in one of those places? Or, would you rather stay here?

Advanced Reader

For a complete literacy instructional plan and additional practice with this week's target skills and strategies, see the **Leveled Reader Teaching Guide.**

■ **Before Reading** *Let's Go Have Fun!,* have students look at the illustrations in the book and use them to predict what will happen in the text. Today you will read about fun in the city and fun in the country. Based on what you know now, which do you think you would like better? Have students set a purpose for reading.

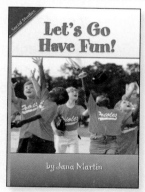
Let's Go Have Fun!

■ **During Reading** Have students read the Advanced Reader independently, and encourage them to think critically and creatively.

• How does the author make you want to visit each place or participate in each activity?

• Which place or activity sounds most interesting to you? Why?

• What place or activity would you add to this book? Why?

■ **After Reading** Have students choose at least five new or interesting words from the Advanced Reader and determine their meanings with context clues or the dictionary. Have students write a paragraph about the place in the Advanced Reader that they would most like to visit or about a place that they would like to add to the book. Ask them to use each of their selected words in a context that conveys its meaning to someone who did not already know it.

■ **Now Try This** Assign "Now Try This" at the end of the Advanced Reader.

Pacing Small Group Instruction

15–20 min

5-Day Plan

DAY 1	• Extend the concept • Read Advanced Reader
DAY 2	• Author's Purpose • Background Knowledge • Revisit Student Edition pp. 328–339
DAY 3	• Homonyms • Revisit Student Edition pp. 340–349
DAY 4	• Online Reference Sources • Read/Revisit Student Edition pp. 354–357
DAY 5	• Reread for fluency • Reread Advanced Reader

3- or 4-Day Plan

DAY 1	• Extend the concept • Read Advanced Reader
DAY 2	• Author's Purpose • Background Knowledge • Revisit Student Edition pp. 328–339
DAY 3	• Homonyms • Revisit Student Edition pp. 340–349
DAY 4	• Online Reference Sources • Read/Revisit Student Edition pp. 354–357 • Reread for fluency • Reread Advanced Reader

3-Day Plan: Eliminate the shaded box.

Objectives
• Participate in teacher-led discussions by answering questions with appropriate detail.

More Reading

Use additional Leveled Readers or other texts at students' instructional levels to reinforce this week's skills and strategies. For text suggestions, see the Leveled Reader Database or the Leveled Readers Skills Chart on pp. CL22–CL27.

Extend Comprehension

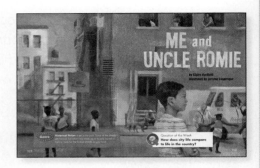

Skill Author's Purpose Discuss the idea that authors may have more than one purpose for writing a particular book, article, or other work. Then have students begin reading *Me and Uncle Romie,* keeping in mind the idea of author's purpose as they read. Have students pause at the last paragraph on p. 337. Ask: In your opinion, what is the purpose of making Uncle Romie such a mysterious character here? *(It could be to entertain by making the situation more suspenseful.)*

Strategy Background Knowledge Review the definition of the strategy of using background knowledge. Then remind students that applying their own knowledge and experience will deepen their understanding of the story.

Revisit *Me and Uncle Romie* on pp. 328–339. Remind students to use the comprehension skill and strategy as they read.

- What do you already know about country life? How does that help you understand what James's life in North Carolina is like? *(Students should be able to cite information from books, television programs, movies, Web sites, or their own experience and explain how that information improves their understanding of the story.)*

- The author spends a whole page describing James and B. J. watching trains. Why do you think she did this? *(Some students may say that the author did this to show that the pace of the boys' life in North Carolina is slow but pleasant. Others may say that it shows how James and B. J. can have fun together just hanging out, without making complicated plans or spending lots of money.)*

During reading, use the Extend Thinking questions and the During Reading Differentiated Instruction for additional support.

Objectives

- Locate the author's stated purposes in writing the text.
- Monitor comprehension, making corrections when that understanding breaks down.

Advanced

DAY 3

Extend Vocabulary

◉ **Homonyms/Context Clues** Read a sentence from the story containing a homonym, such as "Mama and Daddy had picked out just what I wanted—a special case for my baseball cards."

- What are some meanings of the word *case*? *("occurrence or situation; "container"; "legal argument", as in "The lawyer argued the case.")*

- What clues surrounding the word help you figure out which meaning is correct? *(A case for baseball cards must be a container.)*

Revisit *Me and Uncle Romie* on pp. 340–349. Challenge students to list as many homonyms as they can find in the story. Which homonyms can you spot in this sentence: "Can you watch the trains down in North Carolina"? *(can, watch, trains, down)* Have small groups check a dictionary to find the multiple meanings of these words.

■ **Creative Thinking/Critical Thinking** Challenge students to think creatively and critically about the selection.

- How would the story be different if James lived in New York City and went to North Carolina for a visit? *(Students may say that he would have to get used to how quiet things are. He would probably make friends and play sports, as he did in Harlem.)*

- What did you think of the decision by James's parents to send him away? *(Some students may not like it and may say that James should have been allowed to stay home to welcome his new brother and sister. Others may like the decision and may say that he got to see lots of sights in New York City, make new friends, and learn more about his aunt and uncle.)*

More Reading

Use additional Leveled Readers or other texts at students' instructional levels to reinforce this week's skills and strategies. For text suggestions, see the Leveled Reader Database or the Leveled Readers Skills Chart on pp. CL22–CL27.

Objectives
- Use context to determine meaning of homonyms.
- Use context to determine the relevant meaning of unfamiliar words.

Small Group Time

A Advanced — DAY 4

Genre Focus

■ **Before Reading or Revisiting** "Country to City" on pp. 354–357, read the panel information on online reference sources. Have students use the text features to set a purpose for reading, and then have students read "Country to City" on their own.

■ **During Reading or Revisiting** Ask students to consider how this selection differs from most other readings in the book.

  • How is the information in these Web pages presented differently from information in a story? *(It is organized in bulleted lists rather than paragraphs.)*

  • How does this format make the text easier to read? *(It's easy to find the specific facts or details you need.)*

■ **After Reading or Revisiting** Have students complete the Get Online! activity.

"Country to City"

Objectives
• Make connections between literary and informational texts with similar ideas.

A Advanced — DAY 5

■ **Reread for Fluency** Have students silently reread passages from the Advanced Reader *Let's Go Have Fun!* Then have them reread aloud with a partner or individually. As students read, monitor fluency and provide corrective feedback. If students read fluently on the first reading, they do not need to reread three to four times. Assess the fluency of students in this group, using p. 359j.

■ **Retell** Have students summarize the main idea and key details from the Advanced Reader *Let's Go Have Fun!*

■ **Now Try This** Have students complete their travel posters. You may wish to meet with them to see if they need help brainstorming additional ideas. Have students share and discuss their finished posters with the class.

Objectives
• Read aloud grade-level text with fluency.

English Language Learners

The ELL lessons are organized by strands. Use them to scaffold the weekly curriculum of lessons or during small group time instruction.

Academic Language

Students will hear or read the following academic language in this week's core instruction. As students encounter the vocabulary, provide a simple definition or concrete example. Then ask students to suggest an example or synonym of the word and identify available cognates.

Skill Words	purpose suffix *(sufijo)* homonym fiction *(ficción)*	conjunction *(conjuncion)* historical fiction
Concept Words	city *(ciudad)* country	apartment *(apartamento)* subway

*Spanish cognates in parentheses

Concept Development

How does city life compare to life in the country?

■ **Preteach Concept**

• **Prior Knowledge** Have students turn to pp. 320–321 in the Student Edition. Call attention to the pictures of the country and city and tap into students' knowledge of city and country life. Which picture shows the city? Which pictures show things in the country? What are some other things you might find in the city? What are some other things you might find in the country?

• **Discuss Concept** Elicit students' knowledge and experience of the difference between city and country life. What are the differences between the city and the country? What is in the city that is not in the country? Supply background information and teach basic vocabulary in the pictures.

• **Poster Talk-Through** Read aloud the Poster Talk-Through on ELL Poster 25 and work through the Day 1 activities.

■ **Daily Concept and Vocabulary Development** Use the daily activities on ELL Poster 25 to build concept and vocabulary knowledge.

Objectives
• Use prior knowledge and experiences to understand meanings in English.

Content Objectives
• Use basic concept vocabulary related to how city life and country life compare.

Language Objectives
• Express ideas in response to art and discussion.

Daily Planner	
DAY 1	• **Frontload Concept** • **Preteach** Comprehension Skill, Vocabulary, Phonics/Spelling, Conventions • **Writing**
DAY 2	• **Review** Concept, Vocabulary, Comprehension Skill • **Frontload Main Selection** • **Practice** Phonics/Spelling, Conventions/Writing
DAY 3	• **Review** Concept, Comprehension Skill, Vocabulary, Conventions/Writing • **Reread Main Selection** • **Practice** Phonics/Spelling
DAY 4	• **Review Concept** • **Read ELL/ELD Readers** • **Practice** Phonics/Spelling, Conventions/Writing
DAY 5	• **Review** Concept, Vocabulary, Comprehension Skill, Phonics/Spelling, Conventions • **Reread ELL/ELD Readers** • **Writing**

See the ELL Handbook for ELL Workshops with targeted instruction.

Concept Talk Video

Use Concept Talk Video Routine (*ELL Handbook,* p. 477) to build background knowledge about city and country life. For listening practice, see Use Classroom Resources (*ELL Handbook,* pp. 406–407).

Support for English Language Learners

Language Objectives

- Understand and use basic vocabulary.
- Learn meanings of grade-level vocabulary.

Basic Vocabulary

■ **High-Frequency Words** Use the ELL Vocabulary Routine on p. 471 of the *ELL Handbook* to systematically teach newcomers the first 300 sight words in English. Students who began learning ten words per week at the beginning of the year are now learning words 241–250 (*ELL Handbook,* p. 455). P. 446 of the handbook contains a bank of strategies that you can use to ensure students' mastery of high-frequency words.

Lesson Vocabulary

■ **Preteach** Use the following routine to introduce the Lesson Vocabulary:

1. Distribute copies of this week's Word Cards (*ELL Handbook,* p. 173).

2. Display ELL Poster 25 and reread the Poster Talk-Through.

3. Using the poster illustrations, model how a word's meaning can be expressed with other similar words: Here is a picnic table with a *feast,* or big meal, on it.

4. Use these sentences to reveal the meaning of the other words.

   - The *pitcher* is throwing the baseball. (the player who throws the ball to the batter)

   - There are *stoops* on all of the buildings. (front steps)

   - The box contains *treasures* that her grandmother gave her. (special things)

   - Her family's apartment is on the first floor, up one *flight* of stairs. (set)

   - My book was *ruined* after it was left out in the rain. (destroyed)

   - The stray dog looked *fierce* and unfriendly. (mean)

   - The computer came in a large *cardboard* box. (a stiff material used to make packaging)

Objectives

- Use accessible language and learn new and essential language in the process.
- Expand and internalize initial English vocabulary by learning and using high-frequency English words necessary for identifying and describing people, places, and objects, by retelling simple stories and basic information represented or supported by pictures, and by learning and using routine language needed for classroom communication.

ELL English Language Learners

■ **Reteach** Have students work in pairs to pantomime clues corresponding to the Lesson Vocabulary words. Help students practice their clues for one another. Provide an example. Demonstrate *pitcher* by pretending to throw a ball. As students rehearse, watch for clues that will challenge the class to guess the words.

Divide the class into teams. Have students perform their clues for the class. If the opposing team can guess each student's clue, that team will get a point. If they cannot guess the word, the performing student's team will get the point.

■ **Writing** Place students into mixed proficiency groups. Have students work in pairs and select a Word Card. Ask each pair to draw a picture illustrating the selected word. Circulate and help each pair write a caption that includes the selected word and describes the picture. Have each pair share their picture and sentence with the class. Before students begin, model the activity by drawing a picture of a person sitting on a stoop. Write the sentence: *I sit on the stoop.*

Beginning Have students dictate their sentence to you. Then have both students copy the sentence.

Intermediate Have partners write the sentences together.

Advanced/Advanced High Have students select two Word Cards and draw a picture using both words. Have students write one or two sentences using both words.

Language Objectives

• Produce drawings, phrases, or short sentences to show understanding of Lesson Vocabulary.

ELL Teacher Tip

Role-playing is a great way to motivate students to use oral language in a creative context. Have pairs of students take on the roles of the characters in *Me and Uncle Romie,* using Lesson Vocabulary whenever possible.

ELL Workshop

Provide opportunities for students to give directions using newly acquired abstract and content-based vocabulary. Give Directions (*ELL Handbook,* pp. 396–397) supports students in this task.

Objectives

• Expand and internalize initial English vocabulary by learning and using high-frequency English words necessary for identifying and describing people, places, and objects, by retelling simple stories and basic information represented or supported by pictures, and by learning and using routine language needed for classroom communication.

Support for English Language Learners

Content Objectives
- Understand information and adjust oral comprehension.

Language Objectives
- Discuss oral passages.
- Use a graphic organizer to take notes.

Graphic Organizer

I Know	I Want to Know	I Learned

ELL Teacher Tip
Students may benefit from a third listening to confirm their answers.

Listening Comprehension

Keeping Nature in the City

There are many loud sounds in the city. You may hear car horns honking, people talking, and machines roaring. Some cities also have quiet sounds. These are the sounds of nature. Many people in cities visit parks and nature preserves to hear and see nature.

The area around Austin, Texas, is called the Edwards Plateau. Many animals live there. The city of Austin is growing bigger. It is harder for the animals and plants to survive. In 2007 the city of Austin became a Community Wildlife Habitat. City planners have built nature preserves to keep the animals safe. Today there are 200 parks in Austin. There are also 12 nature preserves with 50 miles of trails.

The city of Fort Worth also protects its plants and animals. The Fort Worth Botanical Gardens has many types of gardens. The Texas Native Boardwalk teaches people how to protect trees.

It is important to protect the plants and animals in our cities so they will always be there.

Prepare for the Read Aloud The modified Read Aloud above prepares students for listening to the oral reading "Nature in the City" on p. 321b. Have students turn to p. El•2 in the Student Edition and tell students a writer, or author, always has a reason for writing. Have them listen to hear what the author's purpose is in this passage.

■ **First Listening: Listen to Understand** Write the title of the Read Aloud on the board. This is about how two cities in Texas protect the plants and animals there. Listen to find out which cities do this. What do they do? Afterward, ask the question again and have students share their answers.

■ **Second Listening: Listen to Check Understanding** Using a KWL chart (*ELL Handbook,* p. 480), work with students to ask each other what they know about nature preserves and help them with language to inform their questions. Record their ideas in the K and W columns. Now listen again to check your facts and get answers for your questions.

Objectives
- Demonstrate listening comprehension of increasingly complex spoken English by following directions, retelling or summarizing spoken messages, responding to questions and requests, collaborating with peers, and taking notes commensurate with content and grade-level needs.

English Language Learners

Phonics and Spelling

- **Suffixes** Use Sound-Spelling Cards 170, 174, and 177 to teach the sounds, pronunciations, and spellings patterns of suffixes *-y, -ish,* and *-ment.*

- **Preteach/Model** Display Sound-Spelling Cards *sandy, greenish,* and *equipment.* Each of these words is made up of a base word and a suffix. A suffix is a word part that is added to the end of a word to change its meaning. Write the word *sandy* and circle the *-y.* This word part *-y* is a suffix. The base word in *sandy* is *sand.* Ask students to find base words in the other three words. Have them tell what each base word means. Discuss the meanings of each of the four suffixes: *-y* = having the quality of; *-ish* = describing nationality or language; somewhat; *-ment* = a state, action, or quality.

- **Practice** Write the following suffixes and base words on index cards: *-y, -ish, -ment, smell, excite, self, wind, brown, ship.* Have students use the cards in different combinations to make words that have suffixes.

For more practice with these suffixes, use the *ELL Handbook* (pp. 290, 297).

Vocabulary Skill: Homonyms

- **Preteach and Model** Have students turn to p. W•11 in the Student Edition. Read the information on the page. A seal is an animal. I seal the envelope before mailing it. A homonym is a word that is spelled and sometimes pronounced the same way as another word but has a different meaning.

- **Practice** Write the following homonyms on the board: *change, fair, bear, stalk.*

Leveled Support

Beginning/Intermediate Have students use dictionaries to find definitions for one or two of the words. Then have them use the words in a phrase.

Advanced/Advanced High Have students use their dictionaries to find definitions for each homonym. Then have them write a sentence for at least two of the words, using each definition.

Content Objectives
- Identify homonyms.
- Identify the spelling pattern in suffixes *-y, -ish,* and *-ment* in words.

Language Objectives
- Apply phonics and decoding skills to vocabulary.
- Read comprehend and write homonyms.

Transfer Skills

Suffixes Some English suffixes have equivalent forms in the Romance languages. Students who are literate in these languages may be able to transfer their understanding of suffixes by using parallel examples in their home language and in English.

ELL Teaching Routine

For more practice with word endings, use the Multisyllabic Word Strategy Routine (*ELL Handbook,* p. 473).

Objectives
- Practice producing sounds of newly acquired vocabulary such as long and short vowels, silent letters, and consonant clusters to pronounce English words in a manner that is increasingly comprehensible.

Support for English Language Learners

Content Objectives

- Identify the various purposes an author may have for writing.

Language Objectives

- Discuss the various different kinds of purposes authors have for writing.
- Identify the author's purpose from a reading.
- Express feelings and seek clarification about the author's purpose.

ELL Workshops

Encourage students to ask questions to monitor their understanding of instruction of comprehension skills. Use Ask Clarifying Questions (*ELL Handbook,* pp. 404–405) for practice.

Discuss that authors often express feelings in writing. Give students the opportunity to express feelings about the selection. Express Feelings (*ELL Handbook,* pp. 416–417) provides extra support.

ELL *English Language Learners*

Comprehension
Author's Purpose

■ **Preteach** Writers have a reason, or a purpose, for writing. They might want to convince the reader to do something, to inform the reader about a particular topic, to entertain the reader, or to express a mood or feeling. Understanding an author's purpose can help us better understand what we read. **Have students turn to** *Envision It!* **on p. EI•2 in the Student Edition. Read aloud the text together. Have students express their feelings about how the cover and title of each book.** What do you think the author's feelings are?

■ **Reteach** Give each student a copy of Picture It! (*ELL Handbook,* p. 174). Have students look at the illustrations. Then read the text aloud. Explain that students should write the author's purpose as well as details from the paragraph that reveal the author's purpose in the graphic organizer. Guide students in completing the graphic organizer at their language proficiency level.

Beginning/Intermediate Reread the story as students read along. Ask students if the writer thinks New York is a good place or not a good place.

Advanced/Advanced High Ask students what they think the author wants them to do after reading the story. Have them explain what details tell them this.

MINI-LESSON

Social Language

Tell students that they will often have to determine an author's purpose for writing in everyday life. Have students discuss the author's purpose in the following statements: Use a hammer to nail the board in place. The new vampire movie is frighteningly good. Help keep our park clean! Have students use the following sentence frames: I think the author wants to _____. Or seek clarification by asking Why would the author want to _____? Remind students to seek further clarification of any sentence they don't understand.

Objectives

- Learn new language structures, expressions, and basic and academic vocabulary heard during classroom instruction and interactions.
- Express opinions, ideas, and feelings ranging from communicating single words and short phrases to participating in extended discussions on a variety of social and grade-appropriate academic topics.

ELL English Language Learners

Reading Comprehension
Me and Uncle Romie

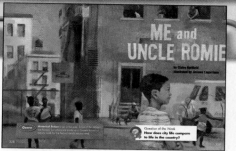

Student Edition pp. 328–329

■ **Frontloading** Read aloud the title and explain that in the story a boy comes from the country to stay with his aunt and uncle in the city for the first time. Why does the boy use formal language like Uncle Romie? I wonder what James does in the city. Let's look through the selection to find clues. Guide students on a picture walk through *Me and Uncle Romie.* Ask students to predict what the boy does during his stay with his aunt and uncle. During the reading, pause and invite students to adjust their predictions. Provide students with a two-column chart to fill out as they read the selection. Supply these headings: Where is James? What is he doing?

Sheltered Reading Ask questions such as the following to guide students' comprehension:

• p. 330: Why does James go to stay with his aunt and uncle in New York City? (because his mother is pregnant with twins and needs some rest)

• p. 334: What does James want for his birthday? (lemon cake; baseball game)

• p. 337: What kind of work does Uncle Romie do? (He is a collage artist.)

• p. 338: What does James like to do in Harlem? (play stickball, run through the fire hydrant water, listen to street musicians)

• pp. 344–346: What happens on James' birthday? (He gets presents from home, he goes to a baseball game, and his aunt makes him a cake.)

• p. 348: What is Uncle Romie's present to James? (a collage about their time in New York)

■ **Fluency: Read with Appropriate Phrasing** Remind students that reading with appropriate phrasing means pausing at commas, stopping when you come to the end of a sentence, and not running sentences together. Read p. 331 and model appropriate phrasing. Have students read a paragraph from p. 334 to a partner. The partners should monitor appropriate phrasing, and give feedback for improvement. For more practice, use the Fluency: Paired Reading Routine (*ELL Handbook,* p. 474).

Have students show that they understand the story by analyzing how James would have felt after visiting his aunt and uncle in the city. Would James have had a different experience if he had visited them when he was older?

Objectives
• Understand the general meaning, main points, and important details of spoken language ranging from situations in which topics, language, and context are familiar to unfamiliar.

Content Objectives
• Monitor and adjust comprehension.
• Make and adjust predictions.

Language Objectives
• Read grade-level text with appropriate phrasing.
• Summarize text using visual support.

Graphic Organizer

Where is James?	What is he doing?

Audio Support
Students can prepare for reading *Me and Uncle Romie* by using the eSelection or the AudioText CD. See the AudioText CD Routine (*ELL Handbook,* p. 477) for suggestions on using these learning tools.

ELL Workshops
Students can work cooperatively to share information about the selection. Support students with Discuss with Classmates (*ELL Handbook,* pp. 419–420).

Students can use the illustrations to retell the story. Support students with Retell or Summarize (*ELL Handbook,* pp. 408–409).

Support for English Language Learners

ELD Reader 3.5.5   ELL Reader 3.5.5

For additional leveled instruction, see the **ELL/ELD Reader Teaching Guide.**

Comprehension
From a Small Town to a Big City

- **Before Reading** Distribute copies of the ELL and ELD Readers, *From a Small Town to a Big City,* to students at their reading level.

  - **Preview** Read the title aloud with students. This is a story about a boy who moves from a small town to a big city. Have them predict what will be different for the boy when he moves.

  - **Set a Purpose for Reading** Let's read to figure out how the big city is different from the small town.

- **During Reading** Follow the Reading Routine for both reading groups.

  1. Read the entire Reader aloud slowly.

2. Reread pp. 2–5, pausing to build background or model comprehension. Have Beginning students finger-point as you read. Use the questions in the chart to check students' comprehension.

3. Have students reread pp. 2–5 silently and independently for increased comprehension.

4. Repeat steps 2–3 above for pp. 6–10.

- **After Reading** Use the exercises on the inside back cover of each Reader and invite students to share their writing. How was the big city different from the small town? Record their answers on the board and invite them to point to pictures in the book to support their answers.

ELD Reader Beginning/Intermediate

- **p. 2** Where is Josh and his family moving? (to a big city) Read aloud the sentence that gives you the answer. (Today they are moving to a big city)

- **p. 6** What kind of home did Josh and his family move to? (an apartment building)

Writing What is one thing that was different about the city as compared to the small town? Find a sentence in the book that tells about it. Copy the sentence. Then read it aloud to your partner.

ELL Reader Advanced/Advanced High

- **p. 3** What did Josh's house look like? (It had a big yard, lots of trees, and a flower garden.)

- **pp. 7–8** What does the city have more of than Josh's old town? (It has more schools, cars, and noise.)

Study Guide Distribute copies of the ELL Reader Study Guide (*ELL Handbook,* p. 178). Have students look through the Reader for ideas before they draw the picture and finish the sentence. Review their responses together. (See *ELL Handbook,* pp. 209–212.)

Objectives
- Express opinions, ideas, and feelings ranging from communicating single words and short phrases to participating in extended discussions on a variety of social and grade-appropriate academic topics.

 ELL English Language Learners

Conventions
Conjunctions

■ **Preteach** Display the following sentences:

John went to the store. Rosa stayed home.

These sentences can be combined into one sentence that is much easier to read. Words or phrases can be joined together in a sentence with a conjunction. Display the conjunctions *and, but,* and *or.* Ask which one is needed to combine the sentences above. Display the following sentence: *John went to the store, but Rosa stayed home.*

■ **Practice** Have students write sentences that tell things that people in the city and in the country both do. Remind them to join the sentences with a conjunction.

 Leveled LS Support

Beginning/Intermediate Have students complete the following sentence frames: *City people _____. Country people _____.*

Advanced/Advanced High Have students write at least three sentences with conjunctions.

■ **Reteach** Remind students that conjunctions are used to join sentences together. Write the following on the board:

Small towns have lots of open space. Large cities only have small parks.

Explain that these two sentences are related because they are making a comparison. Two sentences that make a comparison can be linked by using the conjunction *but.* Display the following sentence: *Small towns have lots of open space, but large cities only have small parks.* Point out that a comma comes before the conjunction when two sentences are combined.

■ **Practice** Write the following sentences on the board:

Tom is wearing green. Tim is wearing blue.

Sylvie is from a small town. Sylvie moved to a big city.

Leveled LS Support

Beginning/Intermediate Have students answer questions aloud with accuracy and ease about the sentences using conjunctions, such as: *What color are the boys wearing? Where is Sylvie from?*

Advanced/Advanced High Have students rewrite the two pairs of sentences using the conjunctions *and, but,* or *or.* Have students read the new sentences aloud with accuracy and ease.

Objectives

- Speak using a variety of grammatical structures, sentence lengths, sentence types, and connecting words with increasing accuracy and ease as more English is acquired.
- Spell familiar English words with increasing accuracy, and employ English spelling patterns and rules with increasing accuracy as more English is acquired.

Content Objectives
- Decode and use conjunctions.
- Correctly write sentences with conjunctions.

Language Objectives
- Speak using conjunctions.
- Write sentences with conjunctions with accuracy and ease.

 Transfer Skills

Conjunctions An equivalent of the conjunction *and* is common in most of the world's languages. Ask students to share a word in their language that is used to join words or phrases together.

Grammar Jammer

For more practice with conjunctions use the Grammar Jammer for this target skill. See the Grammar Jammer Routine (*ELL Handbook,* p. 478) for suggestions on using this learning tool.

Support for English Language Learners

Content Objectives

- Identify how to check writing.

Language Objectives

- Write paragraphs with correct spelling, grammar, and punctuation.
- Share feedback for editing and revising.
- Monitor written language production and employ self-corrective techniques.

ELL Teaching Routine

For practice spelling words related to the city and the country use the Spelling Routine (*ELL Handbook,* p. 476).

ELL Workshop

Students can collaborate with peers to discuss their writing. Discuss with Classmates (*ELL Handbook,* pp. 419–420) provides assistance with discussion.

Check Your Work

■ **Introduce** Display the model and read it aloud. Explain that it is important to check your work every time you write something. You need to make sure that your spelling and grammar are correct, that you used the correct punctuation, and that the verb tense is consistent throughout. Underline the second sentence. What is wrong with this sentence? (wrong verb tense) How can we fix it? (Change *is* to *was.*) Underline the fourth sentence. What is wrong with this sentence? (wrong end punctuation) How can we fix it? (change *?* to *.*)

> **Writing Model**
> The boy went to stay with his Uncle Romie one summer. He is missing his parents. But Uncle Romie made his birthday special. The boy was very happy?

■ **Practice** Write the following paragraph on the board. Work with students to identify and correct errors in the text. Point out that sometimes it helps to read your work aloud so you can hear if something sounds wrong.

(Possible answer: I like the city. It was a very exciting place. There are tall buildings and lots of people on the street. All the cars make lots of noise, but I do not mind.)

> I like the city. It was a really exciting place. There are buildings tall and lots of people on the street. All the cars makes lots of noise. But I do not mind?

■ **Write** Have students write a paragraph about things they like about the city or the country. For ideas, they can use *Me and Uncle Romie* or *From a Small Town to a Big City.* Have them check their work for correct spelling, punctuation, and grammar and correct mistakes. Track their work for increasing accuracy.

Beginning Have students dictate to you three sentences about the country or the city. Write out their sentences and have students copy them. Have them check their work to make sure the sentences make sense.

Intermediate Have students write one or two sentences about the city or country. Have them check their work to make sure the sentences make sense.

Advanced/Advanced High Have students write their paragraph independently. Then have pairs exchange papers and provide feedback for revising and editing.

Objectives

- Internalize new basic and academic language by using and reusing it in meaningful ways in speaking and writing activities that build concept and language attainment.
- Write using a variety of grade-appropriate sentence lengths, patterns, and connecting words to combine phrases, clauses, and sentences in increasingly accurate ways as more English is acquired.

Interactive
Review Week

☑ Choose skills and strategies to **review** based on progress-monitoring.

☑ Focus on **target skills** or use the **flexible plan** to adjust instruction.

☑ Provide opportunities for interacting with texts—underlining, highlighting, and circling **model text** in the *Reader's and Writer's Notebook*.

☑ Develop students' understanding of genre and text structure using the **Strategy Response Log** in the *Reader's and Writer's Notebook*.

Reader's & Writer's Notebook

This Unit's Interactive Writing Review

Daily Quick Writes for Fluency

	Talk	Write	Share
Day 1	Have pairs discuss how clothing from different cultures has influenced modern American fashion.	Each student writes a paragraph describing clothing from different cultures, using adjectives and articles.	Partners read their paragraphs to one another.
Day 2	Have pairs discuss the traditions and celebrations they have learned about.	Students each write a few sentences about traditions or celebrations, using adjectives to compare and contrast them.	Students read each other's writing and check for comparative and superlative adjectives.
Day 3	Have pairs discuss ways of life in different cultures.	Each student writes a paragraph about life in different cultures, using adverbs to describe actions.	Partners read each other's writing and check for adverbs.
Day 4	Have pairs discuss combining foods from different cultures.	Each student writes a few sentences about a favorite food from a different culture using comparative adverbs.	Partners read their own writing to each other and check for correct usage of comparative adverbs.
Day 5	Have pairs talk about how life in the country and life in the city are different.	Each student writes a paragraph about the differences between country and city life, using conjunctions.	Students read their own writing to their partners, who then check for proper use of conjunctions.

Resources for Interactive Writing Review

Reader's and Writer's Notebook

Writing Rubrics and Anchor Papers

Digital Resources
- Grammar Jammer
- Online Journal
Teacher Resources
DVD-ROM

For 21st Century Writing practice, see the **E-Newsletter** Project in Unit 5, Volume 1.

For Process Writing practice, see the **Persuasive Essay** Lesson in Unit 5, Volume 2.

Review on Reading Street!

Cultures

Big Question

What happens when two ways of life come together?

Daily Plan

Review

- Concept Talk
- Oral Vocabulary
- Comprehension
- Vocabulary
- Fluency
- Phonics
- Conventions
- Spelling

Day 1	Day 2	Day 3	Day 4	Day 5
How does culture influence the clothes we wear?	How are cultures alike and different?	Why is it hard to adapt to a new culture?	How can different cultures contribute to the foods we eat?	How does city life compare to life in the country?

Customize Literacy
More support for a balanced literacy approach, see pp. CL•1– CL•45

Customize Writing
More support for a customized writing approach, see pp. CW•11– CW•20

Assessment
- Unit 5 Benchmark Test
- Assessment Handbook

Review this Unit's Reading Selections

Suki's Kimono
Genre: **Realistic Fiction**

I Love Saturdays y domingos
Genre: **Realistic Fiction**

Good-Bye, 382 Shin Dang Dong
Genre: **Realistic Fiction**

Jalapeno Bagels
Genre: **Realistic Fiction**

Me and Uncle Romie
Genre: **Historical Fiction**

You Are Here!
Unit 5
Week 6

Resources on Reading Street!

	Build Concepts		Phonics		Comprehension
Day 1 **Review Week 1** ❓ How does culture influence the clothes we wear?	 Retelling Cards	Routine Cards Flip Charts	Reader's and Writer's Notebook	Sound-Spelling Cards	 Student Edition pp. 198–211
Day 2 **Review Week 2** ❓ How are cultures alike and different?	 Retelling Cards	Routine Cards Flip Charts	Reader's and Writer's Notebook	Sound-Spelling Cards	 Student Edition pp. 230–245
Day 3 **Review Week 3** ❓ Why is it hard to adapt to a new culture?	 Retelling Cards	Routine Cards Flip Charts	Reader's and Writer's Notebook	Sound-Spelling Cards	 Student Edition pp. 262–279
Day 4 **Review Week 4** ❓ How can different cultures contribute to the foods we eat?	Retelling Cards	Routine Cards Flip Charts	Reader's and Writer's Notebook	Sound-Spelling Cards	 Student Edition pp. 296–309
Day 5 **Review Week 5** ❓ How does city life compare to life in the country?	 Retelling Cards	Routine Cards Flip Charts	Reader's and Writer's Notebook	Sound-Spelling Cards	 Student Edition pp. 328–349

 Go Digital

- Big Question Video
- Concept Talk Video

- Interactive Sound-Spelling Cards

- eSelection
- Envision It! Animations

Big Question
What happens when two ways of life come together?

Vocabulary	Fluency	Conventions and Writing
 Student Edition pp. 198–211	Reader's and Writer's Notebook	Reader's and Writer's Notebook
 Student Edition pp. 230–245	Reader's and Writer's Notebook	Reader's and Writer's Notebook
 Student Edition pp. 262–279	Reader's and Writer's Notebook	Reader's and Writer's Notebook
 Student Edition pp. 296–309	Reader's and Writer's Notebook	Reader's and Writer's Notebook
 Student Edition pp. 328–349	Reader's and Writer's Notebook	Reader's and Writer's Notebook

- eSelection
- Vocabulary Activities

- eSelection
- Let's Practice It! DVD-ROM
- eReaders

- Grammar Jammer

You Are Here! Unit 5 Week 6

My 5-Day Planner for Reading Street!

	Review Week 1 **Day 1** pages IR8–IR17	**Review Week 2** **Day 2** pages IR18–IR27
Get Ready to Read	**Concept Talk,** IR8 How does culture influence the clothes we wear? **Oral Vocabulary,** IR9 *traditional, fret, scarves, fabric, acceptable, inspire, robe, drape, elegant, stylish*	**Concept Talk,** IR18 How are cultures alike and different? **Oral Vocabulary,** IR19 *clan, dwelling, shield, headdress, concentrate, barbecue, belief, chant, procession, settler*
Read and Comprehend	**Comprehension,** IR10–IR15 Skill: Compare and Contrast Strategy: Visualize **Vocabulary Skill,** IR12–IR15 Synonyms **Fluency,** IR15 Read with Appropriate Rate	**Comprehension,** IR20–IR25 Skill: Main Idea and Details Strategy: Inferring **Vocabulary Skill,** IR22–IR25 Homophones **Fluency,** IR25 Read with Accuracy
Language Arts	**Phonics/Word Analysis and Spelling,** IR16 Syllable Pattern CV/VC **Conventions,** IR17 Adjectives and Articles **Quick Write for Fluency,** IR17 **Wrap Up Your Day,** IR17	**Phonics/Word Analysis and Spelling,** IR26 Homophones **Conventions,** IR27 Comparative and Superlative Adjectives **Quick Write for Fluency,** IR27 **Wrap Up Your Day,** IR27

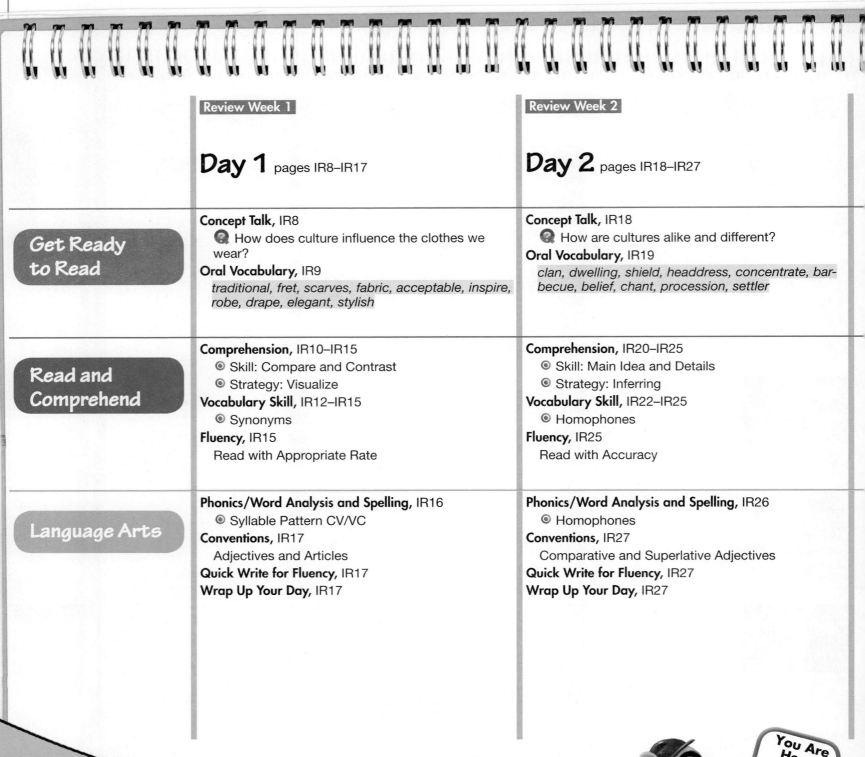

You Are Here!
Unit 5
Week 6

Big Question
What happens when two ways of life come together?

Review Week 3 **Day 3** pages IR28–IR37	**Review Week 4** **Day 4** pages IR38–IR47	**Review Week 5** **Day 5** pages IR48–IR57
Concept Talk, IR28 ❓ Why is it hard to adapt to a new culture? **Oral Vocabulary,** IR29 *native, homeland, aspect, advantage, sponsor, habit, impolite, manner, conscious, insult*	**Concept Talk,** IR38 ❓ How can different cultures contribute to the foods we eat? **Oral Vocabulary,** IR39 *nutrition, calorie, flavor, spice, nutmeg, grumble, allergic wholesome, grate, agent*	**Concept Talk,** IR48 ❓ How does city life compare to life in the country? **Oral Vocabulary,** IR49 *skyscraper, taxicab, scamper, scurry, vendor, hurl, meager, gutter, bitter, ramble*
Comprehension, IR30–IR35 ◉ Skill: Sequence ◉ Strategy: Monitor and Clarify **Vocabulary Skill,** IR32–IR35 ◉ Compound Words **Fluency,** IR35 Read with Expression	**Comprehension,** IR40–IR45 ◉ Skill: Draw Conclusions ◉ Strategy: Summarize **Vocabulary Skill,** IR42–IR45 ◉ Unfamiliar Words **Fluency,** IR45 Read with Accuracy	**Comprehension,** IR50–IR55 ◉ Skill: Author's Purpose ◉ Strategy: Background Knowledge **Vocabulary Skill,** IR52–IR53 ◉ Homonyms **Fluency,** IR55 Read with Appropriate Phrasing
Phonics/Word Analysis and Spelling, IR36 ◉ Vowel Patterns *a, au, aw, al, augh, ough* **Conventions,** IR37 Adverbs **Quick Write for Fluency,** IR37 **Wrap Up Your Day,** IR37	**Phonics/Word Analysis and Spelling,** IR46 ◉ Vowel Patterns *ei, eigh* **Conventions,** IR47 Comparative and Superlative Adverbs **Quick Write for Fluency,** IR47 **Wrap Up Your Day,** IR47	**Phonics/Word Analysis and Spelling,** IR56 ◉ Suffixes *-y, -ish, -hood, -ment* **Conventions,** IR57 Conjunctions **Quick Write for Fluency,** IR57 **Wrap Up Your Day,** IR57

Week 6

Turn the page for grouping suggestions to differentiate instruction.

Differentiate Instruction on Reading Street!

		Review Week 1 **Day 1** pages IR8–IR17	**Review Week 2** **Day 2** pages IR18–IR27
SI	**Strategic Intervention**	**Reteach and Review** • Concept Talk • Oral Vocabulary • Writing on Demand • Syllable Pattern CV/VC • Compare and Contrast • Synonyms • Read with Appropriate Rate • Spelling • Adjectives and Articles • Quick Write for Fluency	**Reteach and Review** • Concept Talk • Oral Vocabulary • Writing on Demand • Homophones • Main Idea and Details • Homophones • Read with Accuracy • Spelling • Comparative and Superlative Adjectives • Quick Write for Fluency
OL	**On-Level**	**Review** • Writing on Demand • Compare and Contrast • Synonyms • Read with Appropriate • Quick Write for Fluency	**Review** • Writing on Demand • Main Idea and Details • Homophones • Read with Accuracy • Quick Write for Fluency
A	**Advanced**	**Extend** • Compare and Contrast • Synonyms • Quick Write for Fluency	**Extend** • Main Idea and Details • Homophones • Quick Write for Fluency
ELL	**English Language Learners**	**Reteach and Review** • Concept Talk • Oral Vocabulary • ELL Poster • Syllable Pattern CV/VC • Compare and Contrast • Synonyms • Read with Appropriate Rate • Spelling • Adjectives and Articles • Quick Write for Fluency	**Reteach and Review** • Concept Talk • Oral Vocabulary • ELL Poster • Homophones • Main Idea and Details • Homophones • Read with Accuracy • Spelling • Comparative and Superlative Adjectives • Quick Write for Fluency

You Are Here!
Unit 5
Week 6

Reading Street Response
to Intervention Kit

Big Question

What happens when two ways of life come together?

Review Week 3	Review Week 4	Review Week 5
Day 3 pages IR28–IR37	**Day 4** pages IR38–IR47	**Day 5** pages IR48–IR57

Day 3 — Review Week 3

Reteach and Review
- Concept Talk
- Oral Vocabulary
- Writing on Demand
- Vowel Patterns for /ò/ (a, au, aw, al, augh, ough)
- Sequence
- Compound Words
- Read with Expression
- Spelling
- Adverbs
- Quick Write for Fluency

Review
- Writing on Demand
- Sequence
- Compound Words
- Read with Expression
- Quick Write for Fluency

Extend
- Sequence
- Compound Words
- Quick Write for Fluency

Reteach and Review
- Concept Talk
- Oral Vocabulary
- ELL Poster
- Vowel Patterns au, augh, ou, ough
- Sequence
- Compound Words
- Read with Expression
- Spelling
- Adverbs
- Quick Write for Fluency

Day 4 — Review Week 4

Reteach and Review
- Concept Talk
- Oral Vocabulary
- Writing on Demand
- Vowel Patterns ei, eigh
- Draw Conclusions
- Unfamiliar Words
- Read with Accuracy
- Spelling
- Comparative and Superlative Adverbs
- Quick Write for Fluency

Review
- Writing on Demand
- Draw Conclusions
- Unfamiliar Words
- Read with Accuracy
- Quick Write for Fluency

Extend
- Draw Conclusions
- Unfamiliar Words
- Quick Write for Fluency

Reteach and Review
- Concept Talk
- Oral Vocabulary
- ELL Poster
- Vowel Patterns ei, eigh
- Draw Conclusions
- Unfamiliar Words
- Read with Accuracy
- Spelling
- Comparative and Superlative Adverbs
- Quick Write for Fluency

Day 5 — Review Week 5

Reteach and Review
- Concept Talk
- Oral Vocabulary
- Writing on Demand
- Suffixes -y, -ish, -hood, -ment
- Author's Purpose
- Homonyms
- Read with Appropriate Phrasing
- Spelling
- Conjunctions
- Quick Write for Fluency

Review
- Writing on Demand
- Author's Purpose
- Homonyms
- Read with Appropriate
- Quick Write for Fluency

Extend
- Author's Purpose
- Homonyms
- Quick Write for Fluency

Reteach and Review
- Concept Talk
- Oral Vocabulary
- ELL Poster
- Suffixes -y, -ish, -hood, -ment
- Author's Purpose
- Homonyms
- Read with Appropriate Phrasing
- Spelling
- Conjunctions
- Quick Write for Fluency

Week 6

Objectives
- Review the weekly concept.
- Connect the weekly selection to the Big Question.

Today at a Glance

Oral Vocabulary
fabric, traditional, fret, scarves, acceptable, inspire, robe, drape, stylish, elegant

Comprehension
◉ Compare and contrast

Vocabulary
◉ Synonyms

Fluency
Rate

Phonics/Word Analysis
◉ Syllable pattern CV/VC

Spelling
Syllable pattern CV/VC

Conventions
Adjectives and articles

Writing
Quick write for fluency

Concept Talk

 Question of the Week
How does culture influence the clothes we wear?

Revisit the concept

Today students will explore how the Unit 5 Big Question connects to *Suki's Kimono*. Remind students of the Question of the Week for *Suki's Kimono*.

> **ROUTINE** **Activate Prior Knowledge** **Team Talk**
>
> **Think** Have students think about how culture influences the clothes we wear.
>
> **Pair** Have pairs of students discuss how the Question of the Week applies to the characters in *Suki's Kimono*.
>
> **③ Share** Call on a few students to share their ideas with the group. Guide the discussion and encourage elaboration with prompts such as:
> - How does Japanese culture influence what Suki wears to school?
> - How does American culture influence what Suki's sisters wear to school?

Routines Flip Chart

Anchored Talk

Connect to the Big Question

Remind students of the Unit 5 Big Question, *What happens when two ways of life come together?* Use the prompts below to discuss how cultures can influence the clothes we wear.

- Why do some people wear their traditional clothing in their new culture?
- Why do some people wear only what is acceptable in their new culture?
- How much do the clothes people wear say about who they are?

Oral Vocabulary
Amazing Words

Review Amazing Words

Display the Amazing Words from *Suki's Kimono*. Remind students that the words are related to the week's concept, how culture influences the clothes we wear.

Amazing Words

fabric	inspire
traditional	robe
fret	drape
scarves	stylish
acceptable	elegant

Amazing Words — Oral Vocabulary Routine

1. **Review** Ask students for definitions of the words, starting at the top of the list. Listen for accurate definitions. Prompt students to connect the words to the unit concept of cultures whenever possible.

2. **Demonstrate** Have students use two or more Amazing Words in the same sentence. Guide the discussion by providing an example that shows the meaning of each word. Clothing that is *stylish* in one culture may not be *acceptable* in another. Follow this pattern to the end of the list, covering as many of the ten words as possible.

3. **Apply** Assign the words in random order and have students come up with more new sentences for them. To show that you are becoming more comfortable using these Amazing Words, think up more new sentences for them.

Routines Flip Chart

Writing on Demand

Writing Fluency

Ask students to write as well as they can and as much as they can about how cultures influence what we wear.

Apply Amazing Words

Have students use the Retelling Cards for *Suki's Kimono* to talk about the Amazing Words.

Connect to reading

Tell students that today they will be reading about a boy's first day in a new school and rereading passages from *Suki's Kimono*. As they read, ask students to think about how culture influences what we wear.

ELL Build Background Use ELL Poster 21 to review the week 1 lesson concept and to practice oral language. Point out and read a question: How does culture influence the clothes we wear?

ELL Poster 21

Objectives
- Review compare and contrast.
- Make text connections.

Once in a while, Suki would lift her arms and let the butterfly sleeves flutter in the breeze. It made her feel like she'd grown her own set of wings.

Let's Think About...
How do you feel when others tease you? How might Suki feel?
Background Knowledge

When they reached the school, Mari and Yumi hurried across the yard to a group of their friends. Suki stopped and looked around. Some of the children turned and stared at her, and others giggled and pointed at her kimono.

But Suki ignored them.

204   **5**

She took a seat on a swing to wait for the bell. A girl dressed in overalls just like a pair Suki had at home sat on the swing beside her.

"Hi, Suki," said the girl.

"Hi, Penny," said Suki.

"How come you're dressed so funny?" Penny asked. "Where did you get those shoes?"

Suki lifted her feet off the sand and wiggled her toes. "I'm not dressed funny," she said. "My grandma gave me these shoes."

Suki started pumping her legs. After a moment, Penny did the same, and soon they were both swinging as fast and as high as they could. *Swoosh, swoosh,* up and up.

Let's Think About...
What do you think might happen next for Suki and Penny?
Predict

205   **6**

Student Edition pp. 204–205

Guide Comprehension
Skills and Strategies

Review
Compare and contrast

Compare and Contrast Review the definitions of compare and contrast on p. 194. Remind students that when they compare and contrast two or more things, they tell how the things are alike and different. Tell students that clue words are sometimes used to signal that things are being compared or contrasted.

Guide practice

Point out the clue words *same* and *both* in the last paragraph on p. 205. Have students explain how Suki and Penny are alike in this paragraph. Have them look at the illustrations to explain how the two girls are different.

On their own

Have students look at the illustrations again and reread the text on p. 205 to find something else that is being compared and contrasted.

Extend Thinking
Think Critically

Higher-order thinking skills

 Compare and Contrast • Analysis Reread the bottom of page 204. Compare and contrast how Suki and her sisters interact with the other students at school. **Possible response:** Suki's sisters immediately join a group of their friends. Suki stays by herself.

Text to World • Synthesis When the other children laugh and point at Suki's kimono, Suki ignores them and sits on a swing by herself. Why do you think she does this? **Possible response:** She thinks the other students are being dumb for judging her because she's wearing unusual clothing.

Text to Self • Evaluation Penny recognizes that Suki is dressed differently, but she swings with her anyway. Do you think Penny's loyalty helps Suki get through her first day of school? Have your close friends supported you when others didn't? Explain. **Possible response:** Suki probably feels more comfortable knowing that her friend Penny accepts her for who she is. My friends supported me when others criticized me for playing chess. This helped me understand that I need to do what is important to me and not worry about pleasing others.

Differentiated Instruction

 Strategic Intervention

Compare and contrast Have students make a T-Chart with "Compare" in the left column and "Contrast" in the right column. Tell students to list similarities and differences between characters as they read.

A Advanced

Author's purpose Have students write a few sentences about the role Penny plays in the story. Ask volunteers to read their compositions aloud.

On the first day of school, Suki wanted to wear her kimono. Her sisters did not approve.

"You can't wear that," said Mari. "People will think you're weird."

"You can't wear that," said Yumi. "Everyone will laugh, and no one will play with you."

"You need something new, Suki."

"You need something cool."

But Suki shook her head. She didn't care for new. She didn't care for cool. She wanted to wear her favorite thing. And her favorite thing was her kimono.

Suki's obāchan had given her the kimono. The first time Suki wore it, her obāchan took her to a street festival where they slurped bowls of slippery, cold sōmen noodles and shared a cone of crunchy, shaved ice topped with a sweet red bean sauce.

Under strings of paper lanterns, Suki joined her obāchan in a circle dance. She followed her and copied her movements, trying to be as light and as graceful. She watched the other women and children who danced, especially those who were dressed in cotton kimonos like her.

Let's Think About...
How does the art help you form a picture in your mind of Suki in her kimono?
🔊 Visualize
①

Let's Think About...
The words in this description are meant to help you visualize. What can you do if you don't understand them?
🔊 Monitor and Clarify
②

200   201

Student Edition pp. 200–201

Guide Comprehension
Skills and Strategies

Review Synonyms

🔊 **Synonyms** Review the definition of synonyms on p. 196. Remind students that a synonym is a word that has the same or almost the same meaning as another word. Explain that an author can use a synonym of a word as a clue to the meaning of the word, as well as the context in which the word appears.

Guide practice

Point out the word *graceful* on p. 201. Have students look for a synonym for *graceful* in the same sentence. (*light*) Ask a volunteer to demonstrate light movements and explain that when movements are graceful, they are also light.

On their own

Use *Let's Practice It!* page 342 on the *Teacher Resources DVD-ROM* for additional practice.

Let's Practice It!
TR DVD•342

Extend Thinking
Think Critically

Higher-order thinking skills

 Synonyms • Analysis What synonym does the author use to help you figure out the meaning of the word *followed* on page 201? The synonym used for *followed* is *copied.*

Compare and Contrast • Analysis Compare and contrast Suki's personality with her sisters' personalities. Possible response: Suki is an independent thinker who is not afraid to be herself. Her sisters follow the crowd; they seek approval from others.

Text to Self • Synthesis Suki's sisters are willing to dress as others want them to in order to feel accepted. How do you think this makes them feel? Have you ever changed your dreams or wishes in order to earn the approval of others? Explain and tell how you felt. Possible response: Suki's sisters probably feel sad and hurt that they can't express themselves freely. Yes, I stopped playing the violin because my friends thought it was dumb. I felt angry and cheated because I gave in to their wishes instead of honoring my own.

Text to World • Evaluation Suki and her grandmother enjoy a traditional Japanese street festival. Do you think it's important for people to stay connected to their traditional culture after they've moved to a new culture? Why or why not? Possible response: Staying connected to their traditional culture gives people a sense of who they are and where they came from. But if the connection to the traditional culture is too strong, it can prevent people from feeling like part of their new culture.

Differentiated Instruction

SI Strategic Intervention
Synonyms Have students work in pairs to write one sentence using the synonyms *followed* and *copied* and one sentence using the synonyms *light* and *graceful.*

A Advanced
Synonyms Have students work in pairs to write sentences using a synonym as a context clue for a more difficult word. Then have students share their sentences with the class.

Objectives
- Review synonyms.
- Review compare and contrast.
- Review visualize.
- Read aloud fluently using an appropriate rate.

Name _____

Read the story. **Answer** the questions.

Aaron's First Day

"I don't get it, Mom," Aaron said. Since we moved, I can't wear what I want anymore. Why do I have to look like everyone else?"

"Now, Aaron," said Mom, "that's hardly what a school uniform means. Rules are rules, and uniforms are the rule in your new school. I don't hear your sister complaining."

"She *wants* to look like everyone else," Aaron replied.

"Uniforms aren't all bad," Mom continued. "With a uniform, you don't even have to think about dressing for school. You can just get out a pair of pants and a shirt, and you're ready to go."

Aaron thought about when his favorite baseball team, the Arrows, would be in town. He always wore one of their orange and purple jerseys to school. Now, he'd have to wear his school uniform instead.

The next morning, Aaron came into the kitchen in his brand new uniform.

"Your uniform looks sharp," said Dad. Then he looked at Aaron's shoes. "Wait a minute. Are those orange and purple shoelaces part of the school uniform?"

"The rules don't mention shoelaces," Aaron pointed out.

His parents decided to let Aaron wear the orange and purple laces, but he brought along some plain white ones, just in case.

When he got to school, Aaron walked into his classroom and found a seat. No one seemed to notice his shoelaces. They didn't seem to notice him at all, as a matter of fact. The other kids were talking and laughing as if they'd known each other their whole lives.

Comprehension DVD•343

Name _____

When recess time came, Aaron noticed a girl looking at him. *Oh no, she is coming over to talk*, Aaron thought, nervously.

"Are you an Arrows fan like I am?" she asked shyly.

"How'd you know?" Aaron asked, surprised.

"Your shoelaces!" she said, giggling and pointing.

Aaron looked down. He'd forgotten all about the shoelaces.

"Yeah, my favorite team is the Arrows," Aaron told her. "I used to live close enough to the ballpark that I could go to some of their games."

The girl said, "My name is Ashley. My brother just started pitching for the Arrows this summer! We're going to see him pitch in the playoffs this weekend. Maybe you'd like to go with us."

"You bet I would," said Aaron, excitedly. "I'll even wear my shoelaces!"

1. How is Aaron's new school different from his old one?

   He has to wear a uniform at his new school.

2. How are Aaron and his sister different?

   Possible response: His sister wants to look like everyone else in her class; he does not.

3. What is the same about Aaron and the girl at school who talks to him?

   They both like a baseball team named the Arrows.

School + Home **Home Activity** Your child compared and contrasted characters and places in a story. Have your child choose two people in your family or neighborhood and tell how they are alike and how they are different.

DVD•344 Comprehension

Let's Practice It! TR DVD•343–344

Guide Comprehension
Skills and Strategies

Review **compare and contrast**

What is the same about Aaron and the girl at school who talks to him? Possible response: They both like a baseball team named the Arrows.

Review with students that a clue word often signals when things are being compared or contrasted. In the sentence, *Are you an Arrows fan like I am?* the word *like* shows sameness. It signals that the two students have something in common.

Review **visualize**

What words help you visualize what Aaron experiences when he walks into his classroom? Possible response: The other kids were talking and laughing as if they'd known each other their whole lives.

Review
Synonyms

What is a synonym for the word *jersey* in paragraph 5? *(shirt)*. How do you know this? Possible response: Aaron remembers when he could choose which shirt he wanted to wear at his old school. If his favorite baseball team was in town, he always wore one of their jerseys.

Review with students that they can determine the meaning of an unfamiliar word by looking at nearby words and sentences for a synonym of the word. Ask students to use context clues to find a meaning for *uniform* in paragraph 2.

Review
Compare and contrast

How are Aaron and his sister different? Possible response: His sister wants to look like everyone else in her class; he does not.

Sometimes there are no clue words signaling a comparison or contrast. The reader may need to read several paragraphs to determine whether or not a person, place, or thing is being compared to or contrasted with another. Ask students to find another example of compare and contrast in the story.

Reread for Fluency

Model fluent reading

Read aloud the first four paragraphs of "Aaron's First Day" on p. 343, keeping your rate comfortable. Explain to students that you are reading the passage neither too slowly nor too quickly because you want your readers to understand what you are saying. Explain that you are pausing when you see a comma or period.

> **ROUTINE** **Oral Rereading**
>
> 1. **Select a passage** Read the first four paragraphs of "Aaron's First Day."
> 2. **Model** Have students listen as you read at an appropriate rate.
> 3. **Guide practice** Have students read along with you.
> 4. **On their own** For optimal fluency, students should reread three or four times at an appropriate rate.

Routines Flip Chart

Objectives

- Read words using the syllable pattern CV/VC.
- Spell words using the syllable pattern CV/VC.
- Identify and write adjectives and articles.
- Write about clothing from different cultures.

Word Analysis
Syllable Pattern CV/VC

Review

Read words independent of context

Review the syllable pattern CV/VC using Sound-Spelling Card 116.

Use *Let's Practice It!* p. 341 on the *Teacher Resources DVD-ROM.* Point out that students know how to read these words. Then tell students they will all read the words in each row together. Allow several seconds previewing time for the first reading.

Corrective feedback

If... students cannot read all the words in a row consecutively without an error,

then... return to the first word in the row, and have students reread all the words in the row. Repeat until students can read the words fluently.

Read words in context

Read the sentences. Point out that there are many words in the sentences that students already know how to read. Have students read the sentences together.

Corrective feedback

If... students have difficulty reading the syllable pattern CV/VC,

then... guide them in using the word parts strategy. Have students read each sentence. Repeat until students can read the sentences fluently.

Let's Practice It!
TR DVD•341

Spelling
Syllable Pattern CV/VC

Review
Spelling list

Write *create, medium,* and *pioneer.* Point out that these words have the CV/VC syllable pattern. Remind students that they have learned how to spell words with the CV/VC syllable pattern.

Use the following spelling strategy for words that are hard for you to spell.

Spelling strategy

We spell some words incorrectly because we say them wrong.

Step 1: Say the word correctly. Listen to the sound of each letter.

Step 2: Say the word again as you write it.

Reader's and Writer's
Notebook, p. 371

On their own

Use p. 371 in the *Reader's and Writer's Notebook* for additional practice with the syllable pattern CV/VC.

Conventions
Adjectives and Articles

- An **adjective** describes a noun. It tells us about the noun.
- An **article** comes before a noun. It introduces the noun.

Read the following sentences. Have students identify the adjectives and articles in each sentence.

> 1. I have a blue jacket.
> 2. The book is funny.
> 3. An elephant has a gray trunk.

On their own

For additional practice, use *Reader's and Writer's Notebook* p. 372.

Reader's and Writer's Notebook, p. 372

ROUTINE **Quick Write for Fluency** **Team Talk**

1. **Talk** Have pairs discuss how clothing from different cultures has influenced modern American fashion.

2. **Write** Each student writes a paragraph describing clothing from different cultures, using adjectives and articles.

3. **Share** Partners read their paragraphs to one another.

Routines Flip Chart

Wrap Up Your Day

✔ **Build Concepts** What cultures influence our clothes?

✔ **Compare and Contrast** Compare the cultures and clothing discussed in this week's selections.

✔ **Synonyms** How can learning synonyms help you learn new words?

✔ **Homework** Send home this week's Family Times newsletter, *Let's Practice It!* pages 339–340 on the *Teacher Resources DVD-ROM*.

Let's Practice It!
TR DVD•399–340

Preview DAY 2

Tell students that tomorrow they will review *I Love Saturdays y domingos.*

Objectives
- Review the weekly concept.
- Connect the weekly selection to the Big Question.

Today at a Glance

Oral Vocabulary
clan, dwelling, shield, headdress, concentrate, barbeque, belief, chant, procession, settler

Comprehension
◎ Main idea and details

Vocabulary
◎ Homophones

Fluency
Accuracy

Phonics/Word Analysis
◎ Homophones

Spelling
Homophones

Conventions
Comparative and superlative adjectives

Writing
Quick write for fluency

Concept Talk

Question of the Week
How are cultures alike and different?

Revisit the concept

Today students will explore how the Unit 5 Big Question connects to *I Love Saturdays y domingos.* Remind students of the Question of the Week for *I Love Saturdays y domingos.*

> **ROUTINE** **Activate Prior Knowledge** **Team Talk**
>
> **Think** Have students think about how cultures are alike and different.
>
> **Pair** Have pairs of students discuss how the Question of the Week applies to the story *I Love Saturdays y domingos.*
>
> **Share** Call on a few students to share their ideas with the group. Guide the discussion and encourage elaboration with prompts such as:
>
> - How are the grandparents in the story alike? How are they different?
> - How are your culture and your friend's culture alike? How are they different?

Routines Flip Chart

Anchored Talk

Connect to the Big Question

Remind students of the Unit 5 Big Question, *What happens when two ways of life come together?* Use the prompts below to discuss positive things that can happen when two cultures come together. Remind students to ask and answer pertinent questions with appropriate detail, building on the ideas of others.

- How can we appreciate more than one culture?
- How can the beliefs of one culture be similar to beliefs of another culture?
- What can we learn from people from different cultures?

Oral Vocabulary
Amazing Words

Review Amazing Words

Display the Amazing Words. Remind students that the words are related to the week's concept, how cultures are alike and different.

Amazing Words **Oral Vocabulary Routine**

1. **Review** Ask students for definitions of the words, starting at the top of the list. Listen for accurate definitions. Prompt students to connect the words to the unit concept of Cultures whenever possible.

2. **Demonstrate** Have students use two or more Amazing Words in the same sentence. Guide the discussion by providing an example that shows the meaning of each word. *The Bear clan of the Hopi tribe stood in front of the dwelling.* Follow this pattern to the end of the list, covering as many of the ten words as possible.

3. **Apply** Assign the words in random order and have students come up with more new sentences for them. *To show that you are becoming more comfortable using these Amazing Words, think up more new sentences for them.*

Routines Flip Chart

 Writing on Demand

Writing Fluency

Ask students to write as well as they can and as much as they can about how different cultures can come together.

Apply Amazing Words

Have students use the Retelling Cards for *I Love Saturdays y domingos* to talk about the Amazing Words.

Connect to reading

Tell students that today they will be reading about a child's first visit to his grandfather's house and rereading passages from *I Love Saturdays y domingos.* As they read, ask students to think of how cultures come together to create new traditions.

ELL **Build background** Use ELL Poster 22 to review the week 2 lesson concept and to practice oral language. Point out and read the question: *How are cultures alike and different?*

ELL Poster 22

Objectives
- Review main idea and details.
- Make text connections.

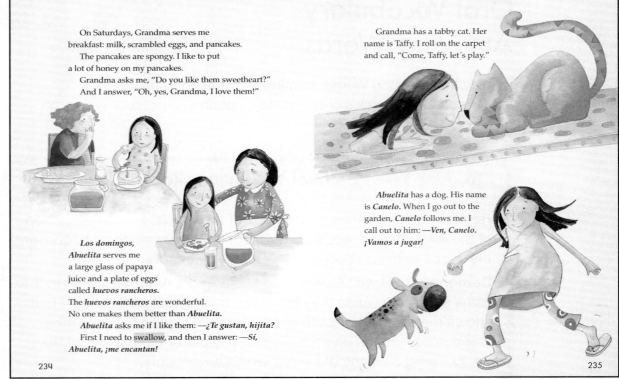

On Saturdays, Grandma serves me breakfast: milk, scrambled eggs, and pancakes.

The pancakes are spongy. I like to put a lot of honey on my pancakes.

Grandma asks me, "Do you like them sweetheart?" And I answer, "Oh, yes, Grandma, I love them!"

Los domingos, Abuelita serves me a large glass of papaya juice and a plate of eggs called *huevos rancheros.* The *huevos rancheros* are wonderful. No one makes them better than *Abuelita.*

Abuelita asks me if I like them: —*¿Te gustan, hijita?* First I need to swallow, and then I answer: —*Sí, Abuelita, ¡me encantan!*

234

Grandma has a tabby cat. Her name is Taffy. I roll on the carpet and call, "Come, Taffy, let´s play."

Abuelita has a dog. His name is *Canelo.* When I go out to the garden, *Canelo* follows me. I call out to him: —*Ven, Canelo. ¡Vamos a jugar!*

235

Student Edition pp. 234–235

Guide Comprehension
Skills and Strategies

Review Main idea and details	**Main Idea and Details** Review the definitions of main idea and details on p. 226. Remind students that the main idea is the most important idea about the topic. Details tell more about the main idea.
Guide practice	Have students read p. 234 and discuss what the first four paragraphs have in common with the last three. Help them to see that the main idea is that the girl's grandmothers make her breakfast.
On their own	Have students work in pairs to list details from p. 234 that support the main idea.

Extend Thinking
Think Critically

Higher-order thinking skills

 Main Idea and Details • Analysis How is the main idea in the first paragraph on page 235 like the main idea in the second paragraph? What are some details that are alike? Possible response: The main idea in each paragraph is that the grandmother has a pet. Details that are alike is that each animal has a name and that the girl likes to play with each pet.

Text to World • Analysis The girl's grandmothers have a cat and a dog. What other animals do people have as pets? Possible response: hamsters, fish, turtles

Text to Self • Synthesize The girl's grandmothers make her special breakfasts. What does your grandparent or other adult make you for a special breakfast? Possible response: My grandma makes me eggs, bacon, fresh fruit, and her special muffins for breakfast.

Differentiated Instruction

SI Strategic Intervention

Main idea Write the following two sentences on the board: *Dogs are fun to play with. Dogs are loving animals. Dogs are easy to take care of.* Ask students to identify the main idea for those sentences.

A Advanced

Main idea and details Have students write two sentences that can be details to support the main idea *My grandmothers make breakfast for me.*

Student Edition pp. 238–239

Guide Comprehension
Skills and Strategies

Review Homophones

Homophones Review the definition of homophones on p. 228. Remind students that they can often use context clues to figure out the meanings of homophones.

Guide practice

Point out the word *nose* on p. 238. Have students find a homophone for *nose* on p. 239. (*knows*) Ask students to explain the two meanings of the words. (*Nose* is "the part of the face, sticking above the mouth, used for breathing and smelling." *Knows* means "to be completely certain about some fact or facts.") Have them use context clues to know which word is correct on each page. Have them use each word in a sentence that shows understanding of the meaning.

On their own

Use *Let's Practice It!* page 346 on the *Teacher Resources DVD-ROM* for additional practice with lesson vocabulary.

Let's Practice It!
TR DVD•346

Extend Thinking
Think Critically

Higher-order thinking skills

 Homophones • Analysis On page 239, it says the kite "soars high in the air." How can you tell which homophone (*soars* or *sores*) is correct? Possible responses: I know that when something *soars,* it flies high in the air. *Sores* are things that hurt. A kite would *soar,* not *sore.*

Main Idea and Details • Evaluation Look at page 239. How are the details about each grandfather similar? Possible response: Both grandfathers bring the girl a present. Both presents are colorful.

Text to Text • Analysis Dialogue is important in stories because it allows the reader to hear the different characters' voices. On page 238, we hear Grandpa's and *Abuelito's* voices and know that *Abuelito* speaks Spanish. Think of another selection where dialogue is important. How did the dialogue help you understand the story? Possible response: The dialogue in *Tops & Bottoms* told me what kind of characters Hare and Bear are.

Text to Self • Synthesis *Abuelito* and the girl go to the pier and look at the water. They see some fish. Have you ever been to the ocean or a lake? Describe what you saw there. Possible response: I've been to the ocean, I saw a pier with restaurants and little shops on it. I saw many waves and people swimming and surfing in the water.

 **Differentiated Instruction**

SI Strategic Intervention

Homophones Write the following words on the board: *two, know, son,* and *hear.* Have students write a homophone for each word.

A Advanced

Homophones Have students think of a pair of homophones and use both words in one sentence. Have them write the sentence with blanks for the homophones. Have partners fill in the blanks.

Name _____   Unit 5 Week 2 Interactive Review

Read the story. **Answer** the questions.

Nana and Poppi

My name is Anthony, and I'm Italian. Last summer, my dad took me to Brooklyn, New York to meet his grandparents. They had come from Italy to the United States for a long visit. I was a little nervous about meeting these strangers who had come thousands of miles. "Will Nana and Poppi speak English?" I asked.

"Not very well," my dad said. "They know a few words, but they speak mostly Italian. The important thing is that they want to meet you. I've told them so much about you."

We went through the door of a big apartment building. "Nana and Poppi are staying with my cousin on the sixth floor," explained Dad, "so we have to take the elevator."

We got off on the sixth floor and rang the buzzer of apartment 612. An older man answered. "Poppi!" Dad cried as he hugged him. "Anthony, this is your great-grandfather Alfredo, but you may call him Poppi." I shook hands politely with Poppi and said, "Hello." He said, "Buongiorno," and motioned for me to come inside. Then he walked slowly to a couch and sat down.

Inside the apartment, Dad walked over to kiss and hug an older woman sitting in an armchair. *She was wearing a long, black dress. She must be my great-grandmother,* I thought. When I said hello, she smiled and said something in Italian to my dad. They both laughed, and then I didn't know what to do.

Comprehension DVD•347

Name _____   Unit 5 Week 2 Interactive Review

"Come with me, Anthony," Dad whispered.

"Where are we going?" I whispered back.

"Come see what Nana made today." Dad pointed to a kitchen counter and said, "Nana said she made these just for you. I told her how much you love cannolis. This is her own secret cannoli recipe. See what you think." As I bit into one of the light, gooey pastries, I could taste the love that Nana had baked right into it.

"These are the best cannolis I've ever tasted!" I said, my mouth full. "Nana makes the best cannolis ever!"

1. What is this story mostly about?

   A boy named Anthony meets his great-grandparents from Italy.

2. What are some details that tell you about Poppi? Underline them. **Suggested answers are given.**

3. What are two details that tell you about Nana?

   Possible responses: She wears a long, black dress, she is a
   good baker, and she doesn't speak much English.

4. Underline the sentence below that tells the main idea of this story.

   Cannolis are a kind of Italian dessert.

   Family members can show love in many ways.

   Families can live in apartments or houses.

 Home Activity Your child identified main ideas and details in a story. Have your child recall something that happened to him or her recently and tell a story about it. Remind your child to add interesting details.

DVD•348 Comprehension

Let's Practice It! TR DVD•347–348

Guide Comprehension
Skills and Strategies

Review
Main idea and details

What is this story mostly about? (A boy named Anthony meets his great-grandparents from Italy.)

Tell students when they are trying to determine what the main idea is, they should ask themselves *What is the story all about?* Remind them to look for details to support the main idea.

Review
Inferring

In the first paragraph on page 348, the great-grandfather says *"Buongiorno"* to Anthony. Reread the first paragraph. What can you infer that the great-grandfather said? (Since the great-grandfather is from Italy, I know he is speaking Italian. Since Anthony had said "Hello" and the great-grandfather responded with *"Buongiorno,"* I can infer that *buongiorno* is a greeting in Italian.)

**Review
Homophones**

What is a homophone for the word *made* on page 348? (*maid*) What is the meaning of each word? Use each in a sentence. (Possible response: *Made* is the past tense of *make*. *Maid* means "a person whose job is to do housework." *Nana made delicious cannolis. The maid cleaned up the kitchen.*)

Review with students that homophones are words that are pronounced the same but have different meanings and spellings. They can use context clues as they read to figure out which word and meaning is correct. Have students use the homophones *blue* and *blew* in a sentence. (Possible response: *The boy blew his blue horn.*)

**Review
Main idea
and details**

What are some details that tell about Poppi? (very old man, walked slowly)

Remind students that details are information that tell more about the main idea. Ask students to find details that tell about Nana. (She wears a long, black dress. She is a good baker. She doesn't speak much English.)

Reread for Fluency

Model fluent reading

Remind students that when we read, it is important to read with accuracy to help them understand what they are reading. Model reading the first paragraph of "Nana and Poppi" on p. 347 with accuracy and have students track the print as you read.

Pair students and have them read "Nana and Poppi."

ROUTINE Paired Rereading

1. **Reading 1 Begins** Students read the story, switching readers at the end of each page.
2. **Reading 2 Begins** Partners reread the story. This time the other partner begins.
3. **Reread** for optimal fluency, have partners continue to read three or four times.
4. **Corrective Feedback** Listen to students read and provide corrective feedback regarding their accuracy.

Routines Flip Chart

Objectives

- Identify homophones.
- Spell homophones.
- Use descriptive adjectives to compare and contrast two or more things.
- Write about traditions.

Word Analysis
Homophones

Review

Review homophones using Sound-Spelling Card 137.

Read words independent of context

Use *Let's Practice It!* page 345 on the *Teacher Resources DVD-ROM.* Point out that students know how to read these words. Then tell students they will all read the sentences together. Allow several seconds previewing time for the first reading.

Corrective feedback

If... students cannot read all the words in a sentence consecutively without an error,

then... return to the first word in the sentence, and have students reread all the words in the sentence. Repeat until students can read the words fluently.

Read words in context

Use *Let's Practice It!* page 345 on the *Teacher Resources DVD-ROM.* Point out that there are many words that students already know how to read. Have students determine which homophone fits the definition together.

Corrective feedback

If... students have difficulty reading homophones,

then... guide them in using the word parts strategy. Have students read each word. Repeat until students can read the homophones fluently.

Let's Practice It!
TR DVD•345

Spelling
Homophones

Review
Spelling list

Write *to, too,* and *two.* Point out that these words are homophones. Remind students that they have learned how to spell homophones.

Spelling strategy

Use the following spelling strategy for words that are hard for you to spell.

> **Step 1: Ask yourself: Which part of the word gives me a problem?**
>
> **Step 2: Underline your problem part.**
>
> **Step 3: Picture the word. Focus on the problem part.**

On their own

Use p. 373 in the *Reader's and Writer's Notebook* for additional practice with spelling homophones.

Reader's and Writer's
Notebook p. 373

Conventions
Comparative and Superlative Adjectives

- **Adjectives** describe things.
- To compare or contrast two or more things, we add *-er* to an adjective. This is called a **comparative adjective.**
- To compare and contrast three or more things, we add *-est* to an adjective. This is called a **superlative adjective.**

Guide practice

Read the following sentences. Have students identify the comparative and superlative adjectives.

1. A grown dog is **bigger** than a puppy.
2. This is the **longest** book I've ever read.
3. Justine is **faster** than Toni, but Kima is our **fastest** runner.

On their own

For additional practice, use *Reader's and Writer's Notebook* p. 374.

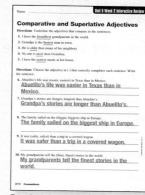

Reader's and Writer's
Notebook p. 374

ROUTINE **Quick Write for Fluency** **Team Talk**

1. **Talk** Have pairs discuss the traditions and celebrations they have learned about.

2. **Write** Students each write a few sentences about traditions or celebrations, using adjectives to compare and contrast them.

3. **Share** Students read each other's writing and check for comparative and superlative adjectives.

Routines Flip Chart

Wrap Up
Your Day

✔ **Build Concepts** How are cultures alike and different?

✔ **Main Idea and Details** What are the main ideas and details in this week's selections?

✔ **Homophones** How can learning homophones help you learn new words?

Preview DAY 3

Tell students that tomorrow they will review *Good-Bye, 382 Shin Dang Dong.*

Objectives
- Review the weekly concept.
- Connect the weekly selection to the Big Question.

Today at a Glance

Oral Vocabulary
native, homeland, aspect, advantage, sponsor, habit, impolite, manner, conscious, insult

Comprehension
◉ Sequence

Vocabulary
◉ Compound words

Fluency
Expression and punctuation cues

Phonics/Word Analysis
◉ Vowel patterns for /ò/ (*a, au, aw, al, augh, ough*)

Spelling
Vowel patterns *au, augh, ou, ough*

Conventions
Adverbs

Writing
Quick write for fluency

Concept Talk

 Question of the Week

Why is it hard to adapt to a new culture?

Revisit the concept

Today students will explore how the Unit 5 Big Question connects to *Good-Bye, 382 Shin Dang Dong.* Remind students of the Question of the Week for *Good-Bye, 382 Shin Dang Dong.*

> **ROUTINE** **Activate Prior Knowledge** **Team Talk**
>
> **1 Think** Have students think about difficulties people might have when they move to a new place.
>
> **2 Pair** Have pairs of students discuss how the Question of the Week applies to the characters in *Good-Bye, 382 Shin Dang Dong.*
>
> **3 Share** Call on a few students to share their ideas with the group. Guide the discussion and encourage elaboration with prompts such as:
>
> - Why was moving to America difficult for Jangmi?
> - What could you do to help someone who is new to this country?

Routines Flip Chart

Anchored Talk

Connect to the Big Question

Remind students of the Unit 5 Big Question, *What happens when two ways of life come together?* Use the prompts below to discuss how bringing together cultures can be difficult. Remind students to ask and answer questions with appropriate detail and provide suggestions that build upon the ideas of others.

- What things might people bring from their homeland to a new country?
- Why is it an advantage to have a sponsor in a new country?
- Why might people have to change their habits when they move to a new place?

Oral Vocabulary
Amazing Words

Review Amazing Words

Display the Amazing Words from *Good-Bye, 382 Shin Dang Dong.* Remind students that the words are related to the week's concept, adapting to a new culture.

native	habit
homeland	impolite
aspect	manner
advantage	conscious
sponsor	insult

Amazing Words Oral Vocabulary Routine

1. **Review** Ask students for definitions of the words, starting at the top of the list. Listen for accurate definitions. Prompt students to connect the words to the unit concept of smart solutions whenever possible.

2. **Demonstrate** Have students use two or more Amazing Words in the same sentence. Guide discussion by providing an example that shows the meaning of each word. Learning a new language is one *aspect* of leaving your *homeland* and moving to a new country. Follow this pattern to the end of the list, covering as many of the words as possible.

3. **Apply** Assign the words in random order and have students come up with more new sentences for them. To show that you are becoming more comfortable with these Amazing Words, think up more new sentences for them.

Routines Flip Chart

 **Writing on Demand**

Writing Fluency
Ask students to write as well as they can and as much as they can about the difficulties of adapting to a new culture.

Apply Amazing Words

Have students use the Retelling Cards for *Good-Bye, 382 Shin Dang Dong* to talk about the Amazing Words.

Connect to reading

Tell students that today they will be reading about a family's move to Florida. Note: and rereading passages from *Good-Bye, 382 Shin Dang Dong.* As they read, ask students to think about how cultures have both similarities and differences.

ELL **Build Background** Use ELL Poster 23 to review the week 3 lesson concept and to practice oral language. Point out and read a question: *Why is it hard to adapt to a new culture?*

ELL Poster 23

Objectives
• Review sequence.
• Make text connections.

Soon after we returned, family and friends began to arrive, carrying pots and plates of food. One by one they took off their shoes, then entered the house. Grandmother was dressed in her most special occasion *hanbok.* She set up the long *bap sang* and before I could even blink, on it were a big pot of dumpling soup and the prettiest pastel rice cakes I had ever seen. Kisuni and I peeled and sliced our chummy and carefully arranged the pieces on a plate.

Then everybody ate and sang traditional Korean songs and celebrated in a sad way. Love and laughter and tears rippled through our house. How I wanted to pack these moments into a big brown box and bring them with me to America.

Kisuni and I sneaked outside and sat beneath the willow tree. We watched the rain with glum faces.

"Kisuni, I wish we never had to move from this spot," I said.

"Me, too," she sighed. "Jangmi, how far away is America?"

"My mom says that it's halfway around the world. And my dad told me that when the moon is shining here, the sun is shining there. That's how far apart we'll be," I moaned.

"That's really far," Kisuni moaned back.

We watched the rain and grew more glum than ever. Then Kisuni perked up.

"So when you're awake, I'll be asleep. And when I'm awake, you'll be asleep," she declared. "At least we'll always know what the other one is doing."

268   269

Student Edition pp. 268–269

Guide Comprehension
Skills and Strategies

Review
Sequence of events

Sequence Review the definition of sequence on p. 258. Remind students that the sequence is the order in which events happen in a story. Tell students that they can look for transition words that signal a sequence, such as *first, next,* and *then.*

Guide practice

Ask students to look for transition words as they read p. 269. Have them identify the sequence.

On their own

Have partners use transition words to summarize the sequence on p. 269.

Extend Thinking
Think Critically

Higher-order thinking skills

 Sequence • Analysis What transition words and phrases does the author use on page 269? Possible responses: *Soon after, Then* Identify another place on this page where the author could use a transition word or phrase to signal the sequence. Possible response: The author could add the word *Next* at the beginning of the third paragraph.

Text to Self • Synthesis Jangmi's family celebrates their last day in Korea with a special meal. What special occasions do you celebrate with your family? Possible responses: My family celebrates birthdays, weddings, and new babies. We celebrate when a girl turns 15.

Text to World • Analysis Jangmi and Kisuni care about each other and they have a strong friendship. Why is it important for people to have friends? Possible responses: It is important to have friends because they are people you can play with and talk with. Friends help you when you have a problem or cheer you up when you are sad.

Differentiated Instruction

SI Strategic Intervention
List transition words and phrases on the board. Model using them to summarize the sequence of events in the first paragraph on p. 269. Then ask students to use these words and phrases in their summaries of the entire page.

A Advanced
Have students summarize the sequence of events in a favorite fiction selection.

Objectives

- Review using word structure to determine the meaning of compound words.

That moment our faces brightened. But a moment later we had to say good-bye.

Kisuni held back her tears. "Promise you'll write to me, Jangmi."

"I promise, Kisuni."

It was time to go to the airport.

"Kimpo Airport," Dad instructed the taxi driver.

The taxi slowly pulled away. I looked at our beautiful home one last time. Like rain on the window, tears streaked down my face.

"Good-bye, 382 Shin Dang Dong!" I cried.

270

On the long ride to the airport, Dad asked me, "Do you want to know what your new home looks like?"

"Okay," I shrugged.

"Let's see," Dad began, "it's a row house."

"A house that's attached to other houses," Mom explained.

"And inside the house are wooden floors," Dad added.

"No *ondal* floors?" I asked him. "How will we keep warm in the winter without ondal floors?"

"There are radiators in every room!" Mom said with an enthusiastic clap. "And a fireplace in the living room! Imagine!"

No, I could not imagine that. In our home we had a fire in the cellar called the *ondal*. It stayed lit all the time. The heat from the ondal traveled through underground pipes and kept our wax-covered floors warm and cozy. A fireplace in the living room sounded peculiar to me.

"And the rooms are separated by wooden doors," Mom added.

"No rice-paper doors?" I wondered.

My parents shook their heads. "No, Jangmi."

My eyes closed with disappointment. I had a hard time picturing this house. Would it ever feel like home?

271

Student Edition pp. 270–271

Guide Comprehension
Skills and Strategies

Review
Compound words

Compound Words Review how to identify a compound word on p. 260. Remind students that they can look for two small words in a long word. They may be able to use the meaning of the two small words to determine the meaning of the compound word.

Guide practice

Point out the word *airport* on p. 270. Have students identify the two small words in the compound word. Ask them to use the meaning of these words to determine the meaning of the compound word.

On their own

Use *Let's Practice It!* page 350 on the *Teacher Resources DVD-ROM* for additional practice.

Let's Practice It!
TR DVD•350

Extend Thinking
Think Critically

Higher-order thinking skills

 Compound Words • Analysis What are the two small words in the compound word *fireplace* on page 271? *fire, place* Use the meaning of these words to determine the meaning of the compound word. Possible response: A fire is a collection of wood that is burning. A place is a location. A fireplace is a location inside a home where a fire burns.

Sequence • Evaluation Summarize the sequence on page 270. Possible response: Jangmi says good-bye to Kisuni, gets in a taxi, and says good-bye to her home. Why do you think Jangmi says good-bye to her home as well as her friend? Possible response: Jangmi says good-bye to her home because, like her friend, it is something she loves and she will miss it once she is gone.

Text to Self • Synthesis Jangmi cries when she says good-bye to her best friend and to her home in Korea. Tell about a time when you said good-bye to a person, place, or thing that was very special to you. How did you feel? Possible response: I was five when my family moved here from California. I cried when I had to say good-bye to my best friend, but I was excited to come to a new home.

Differentiated Instruction

SI **Strategic Intervention**
Write *airport* and *fireplace* on the board. Draw a line to divide each compound word into two small words. Have students repeat this process with the word *underground*. Have partners use word structure to define each word.

A **Advanced**
Have students identify compound words in another selection and use word structure to determine each word's meaning.

Objectives
- Review sequence.
- Review monitor and clarify.
- Review compound words.
- Read aloud fluently with expression.

Name _____   **Unit 5 Week 3 Interactive Review**

Read the story. **Answer** the questions.

The Big Move

Moving from Colorado to Florida is like moving to another country, Will thought. He looked around his new neighborhood and tried to figure out what was so different. There were palm trees instead of pine trees. The air felt wet and sticky against his skin, instead of fresh and dry. He was sure there was something else, though. Suddenly, he knew. The mountains were missing! Almost everywhere he looked in Colorado, he could see the Rocky Mountains, often with snow on them. Florida was as flat as a pancake. There would be no more sled rides and no more snowball fights. Will felt sad and bored.

With nothing better to do, he reviewed what had brought them to Florida. <u>First</u>, there was the day his mom came home crying. She had lost her job as a chef in Denver. <u>Then</u>, for weeks, his mom tried to find a new job in Colorado. Nothing seemed as interesting as her old job, and nothing paid very well, either. <u>Finally</u>, his mom broke the news to him.

"Will, I can't find a job here in Colorado, so we'll have to move. We can't afford to live here without work for me."

Once Will's mom decided they should move, she learned about a few jobs she thought she would enjoy. The best one was in Miami, Florida. It sounded like a long way from Colorado, and it was. They packed all their belongings in a rental van. They said goodbye to all their friends, and then they were on the road.

Comprehension DVD•351

Name _____   **Unit 5 Week 3 Interactive Review**

Will enjoyed seeing new places on the trip to Florida. The first night away from home, they spent at Will's cousin's house. Will and his cousin stayed up late playing games and talking. The second night, his mom treated them to a stay in a motel with a swimming pool. The next morning, they crossed the state line. They were finally in Florida!

That far south, Will started to notice that the nights don't cool off as they do in Colorado. It is hot and humid all day in Florida and can be hot and humid all night, too. The heat made Will and his mom grumpy. So far, the move didn't feel very good to Will. Then they stopped for lunch in a beach town. Will had never seen the ocean or tasted its salty water. After an afternoon of playing in the waves, he decided that maybe Florida wasn't so bad after all!

1. Reread paragraph 2. Underline the time-order words that give clues about the order of events *before* the move.
   Suggested answers are given.
2. What did Will and his mom do with all their belongings?

   They packed them in a van.
3. What happened first, next, and last during the trip to Florida?

   1. They stopped at Will's cousin's house. 2. They stayed in a
   motel. 3. They crossed the state line.

4. What did Will do after lunch in the beach town?

   He played in the waves.

School + Home **Home Activity** Your child identified the sequence of events in a realistic story. Do an activity with your child. Then help him or her recall the sequence of events that you followed together.

DVD•352 Comprehension

Let's Practice It! TR DVD•351–352

Guide Comprehension
Skills and Strategies

Review Sequence

Reread paragraph 2. Identify the time-order words that give clues about the order of events *before* the move. *(First, Then, Finally)*

Tell students that the sequence is the order in which events in a story happen. They can look for words and phrases that show what happens first, next, and last.

Review Monitor and clarify

What could you do if you read the first two paragraphs and you did not understand why Will and his mother are moving to Florida? **Possible responses: reread the text; read on to find more information.**

Review Compound words

What are the two small words in the compound word *snowball* on page 351? *(snow, ball)* Use the word structure strategy to determine the meaning of the word *snowball*. Possible response: I break the word into its two parts. I know that *snow* is frozen water. I know that a *ball* is a round object you throw. I put the two word parts together and understand that a *snowball* is a round object you throw that is made of snow.

Review with students that a compound word is made up of two small words. They can use the meanings of the small words to help them figure out the meaning of the compound word. Have students find other examples of compound words in the story and use the word structure strategy to determine their meaning.

Review Sequence

What happened first, next, and last during the trip to Florida? 1. They stopped at Will's cousin's house. 2. They stayed in a motel. 3. They crossed the state line.

Have students use time-order words to summarize these events with a partner.

Reread for Fluency

Model fluent reading

Read p. 351 of "The Big Move" aloud using appropriate expression. Explain to students that you adjust your voice level to show excitement or sadness, and use punctuation cues to decide how to read and where to pause or stop.

ROUTINE Paired Reading

1. **Select a passage** Use the entire text of "The Big Move." Divide students into pairs.

2. **Reading 1** Students read the entire story, switching readers at the end of each paragraph.

3. **Reading 2** Partners reread the story. This time the other student begins.

4. **Reread** For optimal fluency, have partners continue to read three or four times.

5. **Corrective Feedback** Listen as students read. Provide feedback about their expression. Encourage them to adjust their voice levels to stress important words and phrases.

Objectives

- Use vowel patterns *a*, *au*, *aw*, *al*, *augh*, and *ough* to decode words.
- Spell words with abstract vowel patterns *au*, *augh*, *ou*, and *ough*.
- Use and understand adverbs.
- Write about different cultures.

Phonics
🔄 Vowel Patterns for /ȯ/ (*a, au, aw, al, augh, ough*)

Review
Read words independent of context

Review vowel patterns *a*, *au*, *aw*, *al*, *augh*, and *ough* using Sound-Spelling Cards 56, 57, 58, 97, 105, and 106.

Use *Let's Practice It!* page 349 on the *Teacher Resources DVD-ROM.* Point out that students know how to blend these words. Then tell students they will all read the words in each row together. Allow several seconds previewing time for the first reading.

Corrective feedback

If... students cannot blend all the words in a row consecutively without an error,

then... return to the first word in the row, and have students reread all the words in the row. Repeat until students can read the words fluently.

Read words in context

Use the sentences on *Let's Practice It!* page 349 on the *Teacher Resources DVD-ROM.* Point out that there are many words in the sentences that students already know how to read. Have students read the sentences together.

Corrective feedback

If... students have difficulty reading the vowel patterns *a*, *au*, *aw*, *al*, *augh*, and *ough*,

then... guide them in using sound-by-sound blending. Have students read each sentence. Repeat until students can read the sentences fluently.

Let's Practice It!
TR DVD•349

Reader's and Writer's
Notebook p. 375

Spelling
Vowel Patterns *au, augh, ou, ough*

Review
Spelling list

The vowel sound in *ball* can be spelled *au*, *augh*, and *ough*: **because, taught, bought.** The vowel pattern *ou* can spell short *u*: **touch,** and the vowel sound in **could.**

Spelling strategy

Use the following spelling strategy for words that are hard for you to spell.

> **Step 1: Ask yourself: Which part of the word gives me a problem?**
>
> **Step 2: Underline your problem part.**
>
> **Step 3: Picture the word. Focus on the problem part.**

On their own

Use p. 375 in the *Reader's and Writer's Notebook* for additional practice with spelling words with the vowel patterns *au*, *augh*, *ou*, and *ough.*

Conventions
Adverbs

Review
Adverbs

Guide practice

- An **adverb** describes an action. It can tell how, when, or where something happens. Adverbs often end in *-ly*.

Read the following sentences. Have students identify the adverbs in each sentence.

1. Chin Sen **recently** came to the United States.
2. We can **easily** paint this room.
3. My uncle lives **nearby**.
4. Daniel set the vase down **carefully**.
5. That store is **always** closed on Sundays.

On their own

For additional practice, use *Reader's and Writer's Notebook* p. 376.

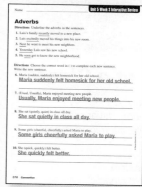

Reader's and Writer's Notebook p. 376

ROUTINE **Quick Write for Fluency** **Team Talk**

1. **Talk** Have pairs discuss ways of life in different cultures.
2. **Write** Each student writes a paragraph about life in different cultures, using adverbs to describe actions.
3. **Share** Partners read each other's writing and check for adverbs.

Routines Flip Chart

Wrap Up Your Day

✔ **Build Concepts** How do you think you would adapt to a new culture or way of life?

✔ **Sequence** What is the sequence of events in the selection?

✔ **Compound Words** How can learning compound words help you learn new words?

Preview DAY 4

Tell students that tomorrow they will review *Jalapeño Bagels*.

Objectives
• Review the weekly concept.
• Connect the weekly selection to the Big Question.

Today at a Glance

Oral Vocabulary
nutrition, calorie, flavor, spice, nutmeg, grumble, allergic, wholesome, grate, agent

Comprehension
◉ Draw conclusions

Vocabulary
◉ Unfamiliar words

Fluency
Accuracy

Phonics/Word Analysis
◉ Vowel patterns *ei, eigh*

Spelling
Vowel patterns *ei, eigh*

Conventions
Comparative and superlative adverbs

Writing
Quick write for fluency

Concept Talk

 Question of the Week

How can different cultures contribute to the foods we eat?

Revisit the concept

Today students will explore how the Unit 5 Big Question connects to *Jalapeño Bagels.* Remind students of the Question of the Week for *Jalapeño Bagels.*

ROUTINE **Activate Prior Knowledge** **Team Talk**

1) **Think** Have students think about how different cultures contribute to the foods we eat.

2) **Pair** Have pairs of students discuss how the Question of the Week applies to the foods in *Jalapeño Bagels.*

3) **Share** Call on a few students to share their ideas with the group. Guide the discussion and encourage elaboration with prompts such as:

• How did different cultures contribute to the foods that Pablo and his parents bake?

• What cultures contribute to the foods you eat?

Routines Flip Chart

Anchored Talk

Connect to the Big Question

Remind students of the Unit 5 Big Question, *What happens when two ways of life come together?* Use the prompts below to discuss how two or more cultures can come together to shape the foods we eat. Remind students to listen attentively and ask and answer questions with appropriate detail.

• What are some ingredients that come from other cultures?

• What are examples of flavors that usually go with a certain culture?

• What foods do you like that come from a culture other than your own?

Oral Vocabulary
Amazing Words

Review Amazing Words

Display the Amazing Words. Remind students that the words are related to the week's concept, how different cultures contribute to the foods we eat.

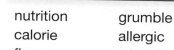

Amazing Words

nutrition	grumble
calorie	allergic
flavor	wholesome
spice	grate
nutmeg	agent

Amazing Words — Oral Vocabulary Routine

1 Review Ask students for definitions of the words, starting at the top of the list. Listen for accurate definitions. Prompt students to connect the words to the unit concept of Cultures whenever possible.

2 Demonstrate Have students use two or more Amazing Words in the same sentence. Guide the discussion by providing an example that shows the meaning of each word. *Nutmeg is a spice used to flavor desserts.* Follow this pattern to the end of the list, covering as many of the ten words as possible.

3 Apply Assign the words in random order and have students come up with more new sentences for them. *To show that you are becoming more comfortable using these Amazing Words, think up more new sentences for them.*

Routines Flip Chart

 **Writing on Demand**

Writing Fluency

Ask students to write as well as they can and as much as they can about how different cultures contribute to the foods we eat.

Apply Amazing Words

Have students use the Retelling Cards for *Jalapeño Bagels* to talk about the Amazing Words.

Connect to reading

Tell students that today they will be reading about a boy's bad day and rereading passages from *Jalapeño Bagels.* As they read, ask students to think about what cultures our favorite foods are from.

ELL Build Background Use ELL Poster 24 to review the week 4 lesson concept and to practice oral language. Point out and read that question: *How can different cultures contribute to the foods we eat?*

ELL Poster 24

Interactive Review **IR39**

Objectives
- Review draw conclusions.
- Make text connections.

Mama lets me pour in the chocolate chips and nuts. When she's not looking, I pour in more chocolate chips.
"I could bring chango bars. They're my favorite dessert."
"Mine, too," says Mama. "This batch should be especially good. I put in extra chips."

My father calls from the back room. "Pablo! Come help me with the bagels!" Papa speaks English and Yiddish. He learned Yiddish from his family in New York City. I know some words too. *Bubbe* means "grandmother." He uses my bubbe's recipe to make the bagels.

First he makes the dough in a big metal bowl. Then he rolls it out into a long rope shape. He cuts off pieces and shows me how to connect the ends in a circle. We put the circles on trays where they sit and rise.

302

303

Student Edition pp. 302–303

Guide Comprehension
Skills and Strategies

Review
Draw conclusions

Draw Conclusions Review the explanation of draw conclusions on p. 292. Remind students that you draw conclusions when you use facts and details presented in the text to make decisions about characters or events. You can also use what you already know to help you draw conclusions.

Guide practice

Have students reread p. 302 of *Jalapeño Bagels* and draw conclusions about how Pablo and his mother feel about chocolate chips. Encourage students to use facts and details presented in the text to draw conclusions. Provide prompts, such as: Does Pablo like chocolate chips? How do you know? How can you tell how Pablo's mother feels about chocolate chips?

On their own

Have students reread p. 302 of *Jalapeño Bagels* and draw conclusions about whether or not Pablo told his mother that he added extra chocolate chips to the *chango* bars.

Extend Thinking
Think Critically

Higher-order thinking skills

 Draw Conclusions • Synthesis Reread the first paragraph on page 303 of *Jalapeño Bagels.* Why do you think that Pablo's father uses the family recipe to make bagels? Possible response: Pablo's father probably uses the family recipe because he knows it well and he knows his customers enjoy the bagels.

Text to Self • Analysis Pablo and his mother both added extra chips to the batch of *chango* bars. Do you think it is possible to add too much of something when you cook, even if it is something you like? Explain. Possible responses: Yes, I like pepper flakes on my pizza but one time I added a lot and it was way too spicy.

Text to World • Evaluation Think of a bakery or restaurant in your community that reminds you of Pablo's family's bakery. What do you think makes the business succeed? Possible response: My favorite place to eat is the deli in the town center. I think that the business succeeds because the owners use fresh ingredients and always have new, delicious dishes and sandwiches for their customers to try.

Differentiated Instruction

 SI Strategic Intervention
Draw conclusions Review pp. 302–303 of *Jalapeño Bagels* with students and guide them to use facts from the story and what they know to draw conclusions about Pablo's relationship with his parents.

A Advanced
Draw conclusions Have students use facts from the text and background knowledge to discuss whether this batch of *chango* bars will be really good or not.

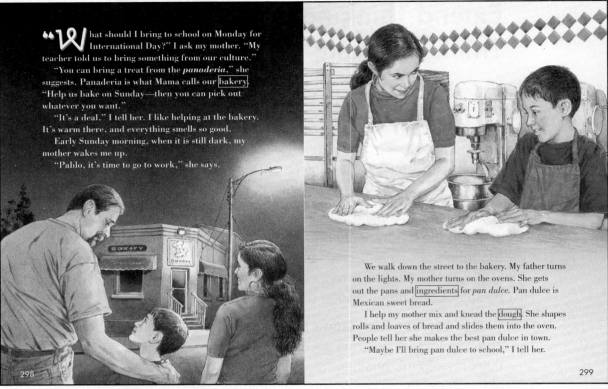

Student Edition pp. 298–299

Guide Comprehension
Skills and Strategies

Review Unfamiliar Words

Unfamiliar Words Review the definitions of unfamiliar words and context clues on p. 294. Remind students that when you come across an unfamiliar word, you read the words and sentences around the word, looking for context clues that can help you determine the meaning of the word.

Guide practice

Point out the word *panaderia* on p. 298. Explain that the word *panaderia* may be unfamiliar because it comes from another language. Do you know what language the word is from? Have students use context clues to determine the meaning of the unfamiliar word *panaderia*. Ask volunteers to share their meanings and the context clues they found with the class.

On their own

Use *Let's Practice It!* page 354 on the *Teacher Resources DVD-ROM* for additional practice with unfamiliar words and context clues.

Let's Practice It!
TR DVD•354

Extend Thinking
Think Critically

Higher-order thinking skills

◉ **Unfamiliar Words • Analysis** What context clues could you use to figure out the meaning of *ingredients* on page 299? Possible response: The text says Pablo's mother turns on the oven and gets out pans and ingredients for *pan dulce*. It also says *pan dulce* is a sweet bread. I know she is going to bake something. I know when you bake something, you need flour and sugar and other things to mix together before you put them in a pan. I think *ingredients* must be the things she needs to make *pan dulce.*

◉ **Draw Conclusions • Evaluation** What do you think Pablo's mother's *pan dulce* tastes like? Why do you think so? Possible response: I think that Pablo's mother's *pan dulce* tastes sweet and delicious. I think it's sweet because its name means "sweet bread." I think her *pan dulce* is probably delicious because people say it is the best *pan dulce* in town.

Text to Self • Evaluation Do you think you would like to work in bakery? Why or why not? Possible response: I don't think I'd like to work in a bakery. Although it smells good and you probably get to taste a lot of good stuff, it is very hot and probably hard work.

Text to World • Synthesis What are some of the things you could do to celebrate an International Day at your school? Think about how you could include foods, music, and entertainment from different cultures. Possible response: We could celebrate an International Day by having each student bring food, music, or games from their culture to school. We could play the music while we played the cultural games. Then we might enjoy a buffet of foods from different cultures.

Differentiated Instruction

SI Strategic Intervention
Unfamiliar words Guide students to identify the context clues that surround the words. Discuss how each clue helps them figure out the meaning of the word.

A Advanced
Unfamiliar words Have students pick one word from the selection and look it up in a dictionary or glossary. Then have them write one or two sentences using the word with context clues. Have other students read the sentences, find the context clues, and tell the meaning of the word.

Objectives

- Review draw conclusions.
- Review summarizing.
- Review unfamiliar words.
- Read aloud grade-level appropriate text with fluency and accuracy.

Unit 5 Week 4 Interactive Review

Name _____

Read the story. Then follow the directions and answer the questions.

A Very Bad Day

Kiran walked home glumly. It had been a very bad day and he was not in a good mood. He pushed open the front door and started up the stairs.

"Kiran, is that you?" his mom called from the kitchen.

Kiran didn't answer her. He went into his room and shut the door. He decided he might as well start on his homework. He didn't have anything better to do. Normally, he would go over to Pedro's house to play, but not today. Today he wasn't going anywhere near Pedro.

Kiran got out his math homework and stared at it. His bad day had all started with math. He had gotten a math test back. Now he pulled the test out of his folder and looked at it.

"Kiran, I'm disappointed in you," Mr. Murch had said as he handed Kiran back the test. "I know you can do better."

Kiran knew he could do better, too. That's why he was so mad at himself. Plus, everything had just gone downhill from there. It happened like that sometimes. One bad thing would just lead to another, until the whole day was ruined.

Kiran crumpled up the math test and threw it into the wastebasket. That was one test that wasn't going on the fridge. He lay back on his bed and put his arms under his head, staring at the ceiling.

Comprehension DVD•355

Unit 5 Week 4 Interactive Review

Name _____

Then he heard his mom calling. "Kiran, why don't you come down for a snack?" she yelled.

Kiran was feeling hungry. He got off his bed and trudged down the stairs. His mom had put samosas out on the table. Samosas were Kiran's favorite snack. He loved the crispy dough pieces filled with spicy potatoes and peas.

"Wow, thanks Mom," he said as he bit into one. Somehow, she could always make him feel better.

1. Why caused Kiran's bad day?

He got a bad grade on his math test.

2. Underline two sentences in the story that help you draw that conclusion. Possible answers are given.

3. Why do you think Kiran's mom made him his favorite snack?

Possible answer: She figured out that Kiran had a bad day in school and she wanted to help him feel better.

School + Home **Home Activity** Your child drew conclusions by connecting prior knowledge or experiences with information he or she read in the story. Have your child tell you why Kiran said he wasn't going anywhere near Pedro today and explain his or her reasoning.

DVD•356 Comprehension

Let's Practice It! TR DVD•355–356

Guide Comprehension
Skills and Strategies

Review Draw conclusions

What caused Kiran's bad day? Possible response: He got a bad grade on his math test.

Remind students that they can draw conclusions about characters and story events based on facts and details in a story. Point out that the story includes many details that help you draw a conclusion about what caused Kiran's bad day: he got a math test back that morning; his teacher was disappointed in him; he was mad at himself; he threw the test in the wastebasket.

Review Summarize

Summarize the main events that happen when Kiran gets home from a bad day at school. Possible response: When Kiran gets home, he goes to his room to do homework. In his room, he thinks about the events of his bad day. He recalls getting a bad grade on his math test, and thinks about the other bad events that followed from there. His mother calls him downstairs for a snack. Finally, he feels better.

Review Unfamiliar words

What context clues help you figure out the meaning of the unfamiliar word *samosa*? What is the meaning of the word? Possible response: The words and sentences around the unfamiliar word *samosa* tell me that it is a snack with crispy dough, spicy potatoes, and peas. A *samosa* is a pastry stuffed with spicy potatoes and peas.

Remind students that they can use the words and sentences around an unfamiliar word to predict a meaning for the word. Then they can try their meaning in the sentence to see if it makes sense.

Review Draw conclusions

Why do you think Kiran's mom made him his favorite snack? Possible response: She figured out that Kiran had a bad day in school and she wanted to make him feel better.

Remind students that they can use what they already know help them draw conclusions about characters and story events. Have students discuss how family members cheer them up when they are sad or have had a bad day. Discuss how their prior experience helps them draw a conclusion about why Kiran's mom made him his favorite snack.

Reread for Fluency

Model fluent reading

Read aloud the first three paragraphs of "A Very Bad Day" on p. 355 to model reading carefully and without skipping words. Remind students that to read accurately, you read carefully so you don't skip words or say the wrong word.

ROUTINE Oral Rereading

 Read Have students read "A Very Bad Day" orally.

 Reread To achieve optimal fluency, students should reread the text three or four times.

 Corrective Feedback Have students read aloud without you. Provide feedback about their accuracy and encourage them to take their time to read each word correctly.

Routines Flip Chart

Objectives

- Use the vowel patterns *ei* and *eigh* to decode words.
- Spell words with the vowel patterns *ei* and *eigh*.
- Use and understand adverbs about time.
- Write about foods from different cultures.

Phonics
Vowel Patterns *ei* and *eigh*

Review

Review the vowel patterns *ei* and *eigh* using Sound-Spelling Cards 64, 65, and 66.

Read words independent of context

Use *Let's Practice It!* page 353 on the *Teacher Resources DVD-ROM*. Point out that students know how to blend these words. Then tell students they will all read the words in the row together. Allow several seconds previewing time for the first reading.

Corrective feedback

If... students cannot blend all the words in the row consecutively without an error,
then... return to the first word in the row, and have students reread all the words in the row. Repeat until students can read the words fluently.

Read words in context

Point out that there are many words in the sentences that students already know how to read. Have students read the sentences together.

Corrective feedback

If... students have difficulty reading the vowel sounds *ei* and *eigh*,
then... guide them in using sound-by-sound blending. Have students read each sentence. Repeat until students can read the sentences fluently.

Let's Practice It!
TR DVD•353

Spelling
Vowel Patterns *ei* and *eigh*

Review Spelling list

The vowel pattern *ei* often spells long *e*: **ceiling**. The vowel pattern *eigh* can spell long *a* and long *i*: **neighbor, weight, height**.

Spelling strategy

Use the following spelling strategy for words that are hard for you to spell.

> **Step 1: Ask yourself: Which part of the word gives me a problem?**
>
> **Step 2: Underline your problem part.**
>
> **Step 3: Picture the word. Focus on the problem part.**

On their own

Use p. 377 in the *Reader's and Writer's Notebook* for additional practice with spelling words with the vowel patterns *ei* and *eigh*.

Reader's and Writer's
Notebook p. 377

Conventions
Comparative and Superlative Adverbs

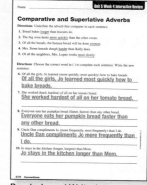

Reader's and Writer's Notebook p. 378

Review
Adverbs that compare

- **Adverbs** describe actions and tell how, when, or where.
- To compare or contrast two actions, we add *-er* to an adverb. This is a **comparative adverb.** To compare or contrast three or more actions, we add *-est.* This is a **superlative adverb.**

Guide practice

Read the following sentences. Have students identify the comparative and superlative adjectives in each sentence.

1. Helen finished her homework **sooner** than Kelley.
2. After the play, we clapped **loudest** in the whole audience.
3. I was up until 10 o'clock, so I slept **later** than Bill.
4. My cake tasted **better** than Mike's, but Ken's cake tasted **best.**

On their own

For additional practice, use the *Reader's and Writer's Notebook* p. 378.

ROUTINE **Quick Write for Fluency** **Team Talk**

1. **Talk** Have pairs discuss combining foods from different cultures.
2. **Write** Each student writes a few sentences about a favorite food from a different culture using comparative adverbs.
3. **Share** Partners read their own writing to each other and check for correct usage of comparative adverbs.

Routines Flip Chart

Wrap Up Your Day

✔ **Build Concepts** What cultures contribute to the foods we eat?

✔ **Draw Conclusions** What conclusions can you draw from the selection?

✔ **Unfamiliar Words** How can you use context clues to help you find the meanings of unfamiliar words?

Preview DAY 5

Tell students that tomorrow they will review *Me and Uncle Romie.*

Objectives

- Review the weekly concept.
- Connect the weekly selection to the Big Question.

Today at a Glance

Oral Vocabulary
skyscraper, taxicab, scamper, scurry, vendor, hurl, meager, gutter, bitter, ramble

Comprehension
◉ Author's purpose

Vocabulary
◉ Homonyms

Fluency
Appropriate phrasing

Phonics/Word Analysis
◉ Suffixes *-y, -ish, -hood, -ment*

Spelling
Suffixes *-y, -ish, -hood, -ment*

Conventions
Conjunctions

Writing
Quick write for fluency

Concept Talk

Question of the Week

How does city life compare to life in the country?

Revisit the concept

Today students will explore how the Unit 5 Big Question connects to *Me and Uncle Romie.* Remind students of the Question of the Week for *Me and Uncle Romie.*

> ## ROUTINE Activate Prior Knowledge Team Talk
>
> 1. **Think** Have students think about how city life compares to life in the country.
> 2. **Pair** Have pairs of students discuss how the Question of the Week applies to the characters in *Me and Uncle Romie.*
> 3. **Share** Call on a few students to share their ideas with the group. Guide the discussion and encourage elaboration with prompts such as:
>   - What did James and Uncle Romie miss about life in North Carolina?
>   - Do you live in the city or in the country? How does your community compare to the New York City James experiences?

Routines Flip Chart

Anchored Talk

Connect to the Big Question

Remind students of the Unit 5 Big Question, *What happens when two ways of life come together?* Use the prompts below to discuss what happens when two ways of life come together. Remind students to listen attentively, ask relevant questions, and make pertinent comments.

- What might happen if a vendor from the country moved her business to a city?
- How would country life change if a skyscraper were built on a farm?
- What might a taxicab driver do for work in the country?

Oral Vocabulary
Amazing Words

Review Amazing Words

Display the Amazing Words. Remind students that the words are related to the week's concept, comparing city and country life.

Amazing Words

skyscraper	hurl
taxicab	meager
scamper	gutter
scurry	bitter
vendor	ramble

Amazing Words **Oral Vocabulary Routine**

1 **Review** Ask students for definitions of the words, starting at the top of the list. Listen for accurate definitions. Prompt students to connect the words to the unit concept of Cultures whenever possible.

2 **Demonstrate** Have students use two or more Amazing Words in the same sentence. Guide the discussion by providing an example that shows the meaning of each word. I was late and had to *scurry* across the street to catch a *taxicab* to get a ride to my office in the *skyscraper.* Follow this pattern to the end of the list, covering as many of the ten words as possible.

3 **Apply** Assign the words in random order and have students come up with more new sentences for them. To show that you are becoming more comfortable using these Amazing Words, think up more new sentences for them.

Routines Flip Chart

 Writing on Demand

Writing fluency

Ask students to write as well as they can and as much as they can about what happens when two ways of life come together.

Apply Amazing Words

Have students use the Retelling Cards for *Me and Uncle Romie* to talk about the Amazing Words.

Connect to reading

Tell students that today they will be reading about birthday celebrations and rereading passages from *Me and Uncle Romie.* As they read, ask students to think about how city life compares to country life.

ELL **Build background** Use ELL Poster 25 to review the week 5 lesson concept and to practice oral language. Point out and read the question: *How does city life compare to life in the country?*

ELL Poster 25

Objectives
• Review author's purpose.

Home was like nothing I'd ever seen before. No regular houses anywhere. Just big buildings and stores of all kinds—in the windows I saw paints, fabrics, radios, and TVs.

We turned into the corner building and climbed the stairs to the apartment—five whole flights up. *Whew!* I tried to catch my breath while Aunt Nanette flicked on the lights.

"Uncle Romie's out talking to some people about his big art show that's coming up. He'll be home soon," Aunt Nanette said. She set some milk and a plate of cookies for me on the table. "Your uncle's working very hard, so we won't see much of him for a while. His workroom—we call it his studio—is in the front of our apartment. That's where he keeps all the things he needs to make his art."

336

"Doesn't he just paint?" I asked.

"Uncle Romie is a collage artist," Aunt Nanette explained. "He uses paints, yes. But also photographs, newspapers, cloth. He cuts and pastes them onto a board to make his paintings."

"That sounds kinda easy," I said.

Aunt Nanette laughed.

"Well, there's a little more to it than that, James. When you see the paintings, you'll understand. Come, let's get you to bed."

Lying in the dark, I heard heavy footsteps in the hall. A giant stared at me from the doorway. "Hello there, James." Uncle Romie's voice was deep and loud, like thunder. "Thanks for the pepper jelly," he boomed. "You have a good sleep, now." Then he disappeared down the hall.

337

Student Edition pp. 336–337

Guide Comprehension
Skills and Strategies

Review Author's purpose

◎ **Author's Purpose** Review the definition of author's purpose on p. 324. Remind students that authors write to inform, entertain, persuade, or express an opinion.

Guide practice

Have students read the first two paragraphs on p. 336. Have students identify the author's purpose in writing this passage. Have them identify facts that show the author's purpose is to inform the reader what the city looks like to James.

On their own

Have students read p. 337. In pairs, have students discuss and identify the author's purpose in writing this passage.

Extend Thinking
Think Critically

Higher-order thinking skills

 Author's Purpose • Analysis On page 336, the author had James think "Whew!" Does an author use words like this to inform, entertain, persuade, or express an opinion? Explain. Possible response: Words like *whew* are expressions that give the reader a feeling about someone. They are usually meant to entertain.

Text to Self • Synthesis James says that Aunt Nanette's home is like nothing he had ever seen before. How did James feel as he looked around? What would you have said to Aunt Nanette as you walked down the street? Possible response: James feels surprised at how different everything is. I would have said, "I have never seen anything like this before. Can we walk slowly so I can look in all the windows?"

Text to Text • Synthesis James describes Uncle Romie as having heavy footsteps, a deep and loud voice that booms, and that he was a giant in the doorway. What other character in literature do you know of who could be described this way? Possible response: the giant in *Jack and the Beanstalk*

Differentiated Instruction

SI Strategic Intervention

Author's purpose Have students make a web graphic organizer with facts from the story in the outer circles. Have them use the facts to determine the author's purpose and write that in the center.

A Advanced

Have students make a T-chart labeled *Same* and *Different* to compare their homes to Aunt Nanette's as described on pp. 336–337.

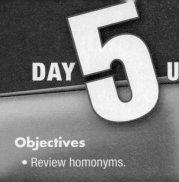

I saw saxophones, birds, fire escapes, and brown faces. *It's Harlem*, I thought. *The people, the music, the rooftops, and the stoops.* Looking at Uncle Romie's paintings, I could *feel* Harlem—its beat and bounce.

Then there was one that was different. Smaller houses, flowers, and trains. "That's home!" I shouted.

"Yep," Uncle Romie said, smiling, from the doorway. "That's the Carolina I remember."

"Mama says you visited your grandparents there most every summer when you were a kid," I said.

"I sure did, James. *Mmm.* Now that's the place for pepper jelly. Smeared thick on biscuits. And when Grandma wasn't looking . . . I'd sneak some on a spoon."

"Daddy and I do that too!" I told him.

We laughed together, then walked to the kitchen for a breakfast feast—eggs, bacon, grits, and biscuits.

"James, you've got me remembering the pepper jelly lady. People used to line up down the block to buy her preserves."

"Could you put someone like that in one of your paintings?" I asked.

342   343

Student Edition pp. 342–343

Guide Comprehension
Skills and Strategies

Review Homonyms

🔊 **Homonyms** Review the definition of homonyms on p. 326. Remind students that they should use context clues to figure out the meaning of a homonym.

Guide practice

Point out the word *trains* on p. 342. Have students discuss possible meanings of *train* ("a line of railroad cars hooked together and pulled by a locomotive along a track," "to make or become fit by exercise or diet"). Point out that context clues show *trains* is a noun, so the first meaning makes sense.

On their own

Use *Let's Practice It!* page 358 on the *Teacher Resources DVD-ROM* for additional practice.

Let's Practice It!
TR DVD•358

Extend Thinking
Think Critically

Higher-order thinking skills

 Homonyms • Analysis Look at the word *beat* on page 342. What part of speech is it? How can context clues help you determine its meaning? **Possible response:** *Beat* is a noun. I can look at the words around *beat* to figure out its meaning. Since the sentence talks about "beat and bounce," it must mean something like "rhythm."

 Author's Purpose • Analysis Read the first paragraph on page 342. What is the author trying to persuade the reader to think about Harlem? **Possible response:** The author is trying to persuade the reader that Harlem is lively. It has "beat and bounce."

Text to Text • Analysis Dialogue is important on page 343 because it is how Uncle Romie and James find out how alike they are. What is another selection where an author uses dialogue for characters to get to know each other? **Possible response:** Bear and Hare in *Tops & Bottoms;* Penny and Suki in *Suki's Kimono*

Differentiated Instruction

 SI Strategic Intervention

Homonyms Have students look up the homonyms *train* and *beat* in a dictionary to find how many different meanings each homonym has.

A Advanced

Homonyms Have students determine the meaning for the homonym *block* in paragraph 5 on p. 343. Have them write sentences that illustrate the different meanings for *block*.

Objectives
- Review author's purpose.
- Review background knowledge.
- Review homonyms.
- Read aloud fluently using appropriate phrasing.

Read the story. Then follow the directions and answer the questions.

Meet Me in St. Louis

I've always loved art. The only thing I love more than art is my grandma, because she's really special. She's a writer who writes books about all sorts of things. She says that when I get older, I can illustrate her books for her.

My dad and I live in St. Louis, but my grandma lives far away from us, in California. Every winter, she comes here to St. Louis to visit me and during the summer, I go to California and stay with her.

I love staying at Grandma's house because her sheets smell like sunshine and there's always something baking in her kitchen. Best of all, she doesn't worry about what I'm doing. I can draw all day if I want to. It's not like here at home, where my dad is always telling me to stop drawing and go out to play.

I never get to see Grandma on her birthday because her birthday is in the spring and she doesn't visit then. But I always make her a nice card. This year I worked especially hard on it. The card took me a whole week to make. It was a picture of Grandma and me swimming near her house in California.

School + Home **Home Activity** Your child read a story and identified the author's purpose and point of view. Ask your child to retell the story from the point of view of Janelle's dad or grandma.

Comprehension DVD•359

When I finished the card, I put it in the mail for her. Then, the morning of her birthday, I called her from my room as soon as I woke up. I called her on her cell phone and she answered after the first ring. "Happy Birthday, Grandma!" I shouted into the phone. "Did you get my card?"

"No, Janelle" she replied. "I didn't get it, but I will soon, I'm sure."

"What do you mean?" I asked, confused.

Grandma started to laugh. "I didn't get it because I'm not home. I flew into St. Louis late last night when you were already asleep. I'm downstairs in your kitchen. Surprise!"

1. Reread the beginning of the story. Why do you think the author explained how far away Grandma lived?

   to make Grandma's visit even more of a surprise for Janelle

2. Some stories tell facts about a topic. Others try to get you to agree with something. Many stories are written to entertain a reader. Which kind of story is this? How do you know?

   This story is written to entertain a reader. It has characters, setting, and a plot.

3. What do you think is the author's purpose for writing this story?

   to tell an interesting story about a Grandma and a girl who are very close

DVD•360 Comprehension

Let's Practice It!
TR DVD•359–360

Guide Comprehension
Skills and Strategies

Review
Author's purpose

Some stories tell facts about a topic. Others try to get you to agree with something. Many stories are written to entertain a reader. Which kind of story is this? How do you know? **Possible response: This story is written to entertain a reader. It has characters, setting, and a plot.**

Review
Background knowledge

Think about birthday celebrations. Do you like to celebrate with people you love? How do you think Janelle feels about celebrating her grandmother's birthday with her? **Possible response: I like celebrations. We always have a good dinner with special foods. It's fun to have a lot of family around. I think Janelle is happy to celebrate her grandmother's birthday with her.**

Review
Homonyms

Use context clues to tell the meaning of the homonym *sheets* in paragraph 3 on page 359.
Possible response: I know there can be sheets of paper, sheets of glass, sheets of ice, and sheets that you sleep on. It says Grandma's "sheets smell like sunshine." I know that sometimes the sheets on my bed smell really good. They could smell like sunshine. The other kinds of sheets wouldn't smell like that. *Sheets* must mean "cloth on a bed to sleep on or under."

Review
Author's purpose

What do you think is the author's purpose for writing this story?
Possible response: to tell an interesting story about a Grandma and a girl who are very close

Reread for Fluency

Model fluent reading

Remind students that when they read, it is important to read with appropriate phrasing. This will help them understand what they are reading. Model reading the first paragraph of "Meet Me in St. Louis" on p. 359 with the appropriate phrasing. Have students track the print as you read.

ROUTINE   Paired Reading

1. **Select a passage** For "Meet Me in St. Louis," use the whole passage.

2. **Reading 1 Begins** Students read the entire story, switching readers at the end of each page.

3. **Reading 2 Begins** Partners reread the story. This time the other student begins.

4. **Reread** For optimal fluency, have partners continue to read three or four times.

5. **Corrective Feedback** Listen to students read and provide corrective feedback regarding their phrasing.

Routines Flip Chart

Objectives
- Read words with suffixes -y, -ish, -hood, and -ment.
- Spell words with suffixes -y, -ish, -hood, and -ment.
- Use and understand coordinating conjunctions.
- Write about country and city life.

Word Analysis
Suffixes -y, -ish, -hood, and -ment

Review

Review the suffixes -y, -ish, -hood, and -ment using Sound-Spelling Cards 168, 170, 174, and 177.

Read words independent of context

Use *Let's Practice It!* page 357 on the *Teacher Resources DVD-ROM.* Point out that students know how to read these words. Then tell students they will combine the base word with the suffix and read the new word together. Allow several seconds previewing time for the first reading.

Corrective feedback

If... students cannot read all the words without an error,
then... return to the first word, and have students reread all the words. Repeat until students can read the words fluently.

Use the words on *Let's Practice It!* page 357 on the *Teacher Resources DVD-ROM.* Have students match the words with the definitions.

Corrective feedback

If... students have difficulty reading the suffixes -y, -ish, -hood, and -ment,
then... guide them in using the word parts strategy.

Spelling
Suffixes -y, -ish, -hood, and -ment

Review
Spelling list

Write *rocky, foolish, childhood,* and *movement.* Point out that these words have the suffixes -y, -ish, -hood, or -ment. Remind students that they have learned how to spell words with these suffixes.

Spelling strategy

Use the following spelling strategy for words that are hard for you to spell.

> **Step 1: Identify the base word.**
>
> **Step 2: Draw a line between the base word and the suffix.**
>
> **Step 3: Study each word part to remember the spelling.**

On their own

Use p. 379 in the *Reader's and Writer's Notebook* for additional practice spelling words with the suffixes -y, -ish, -hood, and -ment.

Let's Practice It!
TR DVD•357

Reader's and Writer's
Notebook p. 379

Conventions
Conjunctions

Review
Conjunctions

A **conjunction** connects words or groups of words. The conjunction *and* adds information. The conjunction *or* shows a choice. The conjunction *but* shows a difference.

Guide practice

Have students identify the conjunctions in each sentence.

1. Yesterday I ate an apple **and** a pear.

2. Will Carl **and** Angie be at the game, **or** will they miss it?

3. You can come with me **and** Jan, **but** we might meet Pete **or** Lou.

On their own

For additional practice with conjunctions, use the *Reader's and Writer's Notebook* p. 380.

Reader's and Writer's Notebook p. 380

ROUTINE **Quick Write for Fluency** **Team Talk**

1. **Talk** Have pairs talk about how life in the country and life in the city are different.

2. **Write** Each student writes a paragraph about the differences between country and city life, using conjunctions.

3. **Share** Students read their own writing to their partners, who then check for proper use of conjunctions.

Routines Flip Chart

Wrap Up Your Day

✔ **Build Concepts** Where would you like to live—in the city or in the country?

✔ **Author's Purpose** Is the author's purpose for writing the selection to persuade, to inform, to entertain, or to express feelings?

✔ **Homonyms** How can you use context clues to help you understand homonyms?

Unit Wrap-Up

 The Big Question

What happens when two ways of life come together?

 Question of the Week
How does culture influence the clothes we wear?

Concept Knowledge

Students will understand that people:

- wear special clothes for holidays

- wear traditional clothing

- react to clothing

 Question of the Week
How are cultures alike and different?

Concept Knowledge

Students will understand that cultures:

- have similarities and differences

- usually value family

- can be tied to countries

Understanding By Design

Grant Wiggins, Ed. D.
Reading Street Author

" . . . An understanding refers to transferable, big ideas having enduring value beyond a specific topic. Enduring understandings use discrete facts or skills to focus on larger concepts, principles, or processes. They derive from and enable transfer: They are applicable to new situations within or beyond the subject. "

Discuss the Big Question

Help students relate the Big Question for this unit to the selections and their own experiences. Write the question and prompt discussion with questions such as the following.

Think of a time you experienced something from another culture. Describe what it was like. Possible responses:

- I went to a celebration of Chinese New Year. There were dragon floats and fireworks.

- For *Cinco de Mayo,* I went to my friend's house. We had *mole poblano* and listened to mariachi music.

 Question of the Week
Why is it hard to adapt to a new culture?

Concept Knowledge

Students will understand that a new culture means:

• a new home and neighborhood

• a new language

• new traditions

 Question of the Week
How can different cultures contribute to the foods we eat?

Concept Knowledge

Students will understand that food:

• comes from different cultures

• is shared

• can be a mix from different cultures

 Question of the Week
How does city life compare to life in the country?

Concept Knowledge

Students will understand that:

• city life is busy

• cities have tall buildings

• the country has farms

How do two ways of life come together in each of the selections you read? Possible responses:

• *Suki's Kimono* Suki wears her Japanese kimono to her American school and teaches others about her two cultures.

• *I Love Saturdays y domingos* The girl has different experiences with her grandparents from two different ways of life.

• *Good-Bye, 382 Shin Dang Dong* Jangmi moves from Korea to America.

• *Jalapeño Bagels* Pablo's parents are from two different cultures, and he experiences foods from each of their cultures.

• *Me and Uncle Romie* James experiences life in the country at home and life in the city when he goes to visit his uncle.

Unit Assessment

Use Unit 5 *Benchmark Tests* to check:

✔ **Passage Comprehension**

✔ **Phonics**

✔ **Vocabulary Skills**

✔ **Writing Conventions**

✔ **Writing**

✔ **Fluency**

Benchmark Tests

Managing Assessment

Use Assessment Handbook for:

✔ **Weekly Assessment Blackline Masters for Monitoring Progress**

✔ **Observation Checklists**

✔ **Record-Keeping Forms**

✔ **Portfolio Assessment**

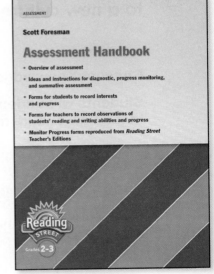

Assessment Handbook

Customize Your Writing

Writing Forms and Patterns

- Instruction focuses on a different **product** each week.
- Mini-lessons and models help students learn key features and **organizational patterns**.

Grade 3 Products fable, friendly letter, news article, autobiography, summary, realistic fiction, and so on

Grade 3 Organization Patterns poetic forms, compare and contrast, main idea and details, narrative, letter, and so on

Quick Writes for Fluency

- **Writing on Demand** Use the Quick Write routine for **writing on demand**.
- The Quick Write **prompt and routine** extend skills and strategies from daily writing lessons.

Writing Process ①②③④⑤

- Six **writing process** lessons provide structure to move students through the steps of the writing process.
- One-week and two-week pacing allows lessons to be used in **Writing Workshop**.

Steps of the Writing Process Plan and Prewrite, Draft, Revise, Edit, Publish and Present

Grade 3 Writing Process Products personal narrative, how-to report, cause-and-effect essay, problem-solution essay, persuasive essay, research report

Writing on Reading STREET

MINI-LESSON

- Daily 10-minute mini-lessons focus instruction on the **traits** and **craft** of good writing.
- Instruction focuses on one writing trait and one writer's craft skill every week.

Traits focus/ideas, organization, voice, word choice, sentences, conventions

Craft drafting strategies, revising strategies, editing strategies

Read Like a Writer

- Use **mentor text** every week as a model to exemplify the traits of good writing.
- **Interact with text** every week to learn the key features of good writing.

Mentor Text Examine literature in the Student Edition.

 Underline, circle, and highlight model text in the *Reader's and Writer's Notebook.*

Write Guy
Jeff Anderson

Need Writing Advice?

Writing instruction is all about creating effective writers. We don't want to crush the inner writer in a child by over-correcting and over-editing. What makes effective writing instruction? Children need to write, write, write! But is that enough? Probably not. All kinds of instruction and guidance go into making an effective writer.

The Write Guy offers advice on teacher and peer conferencing, focusing on writing traits, revising strategies, editing strategies, and much, much more.

Customize Your Writing

Sometimes you want to spend more time on writing—perhaps you do a **Writing Workshop**. This one- or two-week plan for the unit level writing projects can help.

1 Week Plan	Day 1	Day 2	Day 3	Day 4	Day 5
1 Plan and Prewrite	███	███			
2 Draft			███		
3 Revise				███	
4 Edit					███
5 Publish					███

2 Week Plan	Day 1	Day 2	Day 3	Day 4	Day 5	Day 6	Day 7	Day 8	Day 9	Day 10
1 Plan and Prewrite	███	███	███	███						
2 Draft					███	███	███			
3 Revise								███		
4 Edit									███	
5 Publish										███

Grade 3 Unit Writing Projects

Internet Guy
Don Leu

Unit Writing Project 1–21st Century Project

Unit 1 E-Pen Pals

Unit 2 Story Exchange

Unit 3 Photo Writing

Unit 4 Classroom Profile

Unit 5 E-Newsletter

Unit 6 Discussion Forum

Unit Writing Project 2–Writing Process

Unit 1 Personal Narrative

Unit 2 How-to Report

Unit 3 Cause-and-Effect Essay

Unit 4 Problem-Solution Essay

Unit 5 Persuasive Essay

Unit 6 Research Report

Persuasive Essay

Writing prompt

Write to persuade your parents to let you travel to another country, dress in a special way, or eat a particular food.

Purpose Convince parents to accept an idea.

Audience parents

Introduce genre and prompt

In this writing process lesson, you will study a persuasive essay and select an appropriate genre for writing a response to the prompt. In a persuasive essay, a writer tries to convince a reader to act or believe in a certain way.

Introduce key features

Key Features of a Persuasive Essay

- establishes a clear position on an issue or question
- supports the position with details, reasons, facts, and examples
- tries to convince readers to think or act in a certain way
- uses persuasive words to make reasons more convincing
- often organizes ideas and facts in order of importance

Academic Vocabulary

Persuasive Essay In a persuasive essay, a writer establishes a position and uses details to support that position and to convince readers to agree with it.

English Language Learners

Introduce Genre Write *persuasive* on the board. Explain to students that this word describes anything that tries to convince people to think or act in a certain way. Write *essay* on the board. Explain that this word names a short piece of writing. Therefore, a persuasive essay is a short piece of writing that tries to convince people to think or act in a certain way. Discuss with students the key features of a persuasive essay that appear on this page.

Objectives

- Understand and identify the features of a persuasive essay.
- Use strategies such as brainstorming, journals, and graphic organizers to generate ideas for writing.
- Select a topic from a list.

1 Plan and Prewrite
PREWRITE

MINI-LESSON

Reading Like a Writer

■ **Examine Model Text** Let's look at an example of a persuasive essay in which a student tries to convince a parent to let him make a particular food. Display and read aloud to students "Pizza Proposal" on Writing Transparency WP29. Ask them to identify key features of a persuasive essay in the student model.

Writing Transparency WP29, TR DVD

■ **Evaluate Model Text** Display and read aloud "Traits of a Good Persuasive Essay" on Writing Transparency WP30. Discuss each trait as it is shown in the model. For Focus/Ideas, ask students to explain what the writer's position is. Point out that the writing is focused because it discusses that position and only that position. For Organization, tell students that the writer gives several reasons to support his position. Ask students to name the reasons. Proceed in the same way for the remaining traits, defining them when necessary and helping students identify examples of the traits in the model.

Writing Transparency WP30, TR DVD

Generate ideas for writing

The writing prompt tells you the general topic of your writing assignment: persuading your parents to let you travel to another country, dress in a special way, or eat a particular food. Now you need to think of a specific topic: the particular country, type of dress, or food you will present and support in your essay. First, generate a list of as many possible topics as you can.

Use range of strategies

Encourage students to try a range of strategies for generating ideas, including these:

☑ Review foods, clothing, and places described in the selections in the unit. Write lists and add additional items to each list.

☑ Write a brief journal entry about a trip they would like to take.

☑ In small groups, brainstorm reasons that have proven effective in persuading parents or others to take a particular action.

Narrow topic

Once you have generated a list of topics, you need to narrow your choices to one topic. Have students look more closely at each of their topics and think about why it is or is not the most suitable topic for the assignment. They might ask: *Would I have to persuade my parents to let me do this? Can I think of good reasons that would convince my parents?*

Topics	Evaluate
wear my Indian sari to school	I can do this on International Day.
eat food from Thailand	I wouldn't have to persuade my parents to let me do this.
visit France on the school trip in fifth grade ★	I would really like to do this; it would take some persuading.

Corrective feedback

If... students have trouble thinking of possible reasons, then... suggest that they imagine a similar situation in which they tried to persuade their parents to allow them to do something and write brief notes on the kinds of reasons they used.

Choose a genre

Once you have chose a topic, you will need to choose a genre in which to write. I'll show you the process for writing a persuasive essay.

Write Guy
Jeff Anderson

Use Mentor Texts

Although it is not a persuasive essay, a main selection in this unit has persuasive elements. *Good-Bye, 382 Shin Dang Dong*, gives reasons why Jangmi will like living in America. Invite students to examine the text to find these reasons. Tell them they will likely include reasons to support their position in the persuasive essay they will write.

Differentiated Instruction

 Strategic Intervention

Alternative Writing Prompt
Think about going to a friend's house after school. Write a paragraph about why you want to visit your friend. Use persuasive words that will help convince your parent to let you go.

Write the list of persuasive words on the board. Have students write about one of the problems and describe a possible solution.

Ⓐ Advanced

Alternative Writing Prompt
Write a persuasive essay about studying in a different country. Find facts about the country that will help you persuade a parent to let you go there. Use the facts as well as examples and other supporting details as reasons in your essay.

Objectives
- Categorize and organize ideas to prepare to write a first draft.
- Understand the criteria for an effective problem-solution essay.

1 PREWRITE Plan and Prewrite

MINI-LESSON

Planning a First Draft

■ **Use a Persuasion Chart** Display Writing Transparency WP31 and read it aloud to students.

> **Think Aloud** This student wants to persuade her parents to allow her to go on the fifth-grade class trip to France. The writer has categorized her ideas by writing them in the Introduction, Reasons, and Conclusion boxes on this graphic organizer. Now that she has organized her ideas, she can start writing beginning, middle, and ending paragraphs for the first draft of her essay.

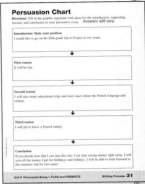

Writing Transparency WP31, TR DVD

■ Have students use *Reader's and Writer's Notebook* page 381 to help them plan their first draft. Before you begin writing, use this graphic organizer to categorize and organize your ideas about your position, reasons, and conclusion and to plan the paragraphs for your essay.

INTERACT with TEXT

Reader's and Writer's Notebook, p. 381

2 Draft

Display rubric

Display the Scoring Rubric WP5 from the *Teacher Resources DVD-ROM.* Review with students the criteria for each trait under each score. Explain that they need to keep these criteria in mind as they develop drafts of their persuasive essays. Remind them that this is the rubric that will be used to evaluate their persuasive essays when they are finished.

Scoring Rubric: *Persuasive Essay*

	④	③	②	①
Focus/Ideas	Well-focused essay; clear position	Generally focused essay; clear position	Essay lacking focus; unclear position	Essay without focus; no clear position
Organization	Supporting details given in order of importance	Supporting details given in fairly clear order	Supporting details given in confused order	No order; no supporting details
Voice	Sincere, persuasive voice	Voice somewhat sincere, persuasive	No clear, persuasive voice	Uninvolved or indifferent
Word Choice	Uses strong persuasive words to make reasons convincing	Uses some persuasive words	Uses few persuasive words	No attempt to use persuasive words
Sentences	Variety of strong, clear sentences	Mostly clear sentences; some variety	Little or no variety; some unclear sentences	Incoherent sentences or short, choppy sentences
Conventions	Few, if any, errors	Some minor errors	Many errors	Numerous serious errors

Prepare to draft

Have students review the persuasion charts they worked on earlier. Ask them to make sure that their persuasion charts are complete. If they are not, have students finish them now. You will be using your persuasion chart as you write the draft of your persuasive essay. Don't worry if your draft doesn't sound exactly the way you want your essay to sound. You will have a chance to revise your draft later.

Corrective feedback

If... students do not grasp the connection between the Scoring Rubric and their persuasive essays,
then... have them help you use the Scoring Rubric to evaluate and score one or more traits of the model persuasive essay on Writing Transparency WP29.

2 Draft

MINI-LESSON

Writing Trait: Word Choice

■ **Use Persuasive Words** Display and read aloud Writing Transparency WP32. Discuss the different kinds of persuasive words. Ask students to identify the persuasive words in each sentence and tell into which category the persuasive words fit.

Think Aloud Suppose I want to convince you to see a movie I've seen. I might say, "You should see this movie. It's the best movie I've ever seen." I used the persuasive words *should* and *best.* When I write a persuasive essay, I do the same thing: I use words that try to convince readers to take an action. I use words that make the action sound appealing.

■ Have students use *Reader's and Writer's Notebook* page 382 to practice writing sentences with persuasive words.

Writing Transparency WP32, TR DVD

Reader's and Writer's Notebook, p. 382

Tips for Including: Strong Adjectives

✔ Use adjectives that suggest traits readers value.

✔ Choose sensory words to help readers see, hear, touch, taste, and smell what is described.

✔ Use the comparative forms of adjectives to be more persuasive.

Develop draft Remind students that the focus of drafting paragraphs is to get their ideas down in an organized way. Display the Tips for Including Strong Adjectives for students. Direct them to use what they learned about persuasive words and strong adjectives as they write their drafts.

Objectives

- Add persuasive words and strong adjectives to supporting details.
- Write a first draft of a persuasive essay.
- Revise by adding adverbs.
- Revise a draft of a persuasive essay.

③ Revise

MINI-LESSON

Writer's Craft: Add Adverbs

■ One way to revise writing is to use adverbs that give specific details. Adding adverbs will help make writing clearer and more coherent. This in turn will make writing easier for the audience to understand and appreciate. Discuss this example with students.

General	A trip to Paris will help me learn to speak French.
More Specific	A trip to Paris will help me learn to speak French <u>easily</u> and <u>naturally</u>.

■ Have students practice using adverbs to add specific details on *Reader's and Writer's Notebook* page 383.

Reader's and Writer's Notebook, p. 383

Revise Model   Display Writing Transparency WP33 and use it to model revising. Point out the revising marks, which students should use when they revise their work. This is part of a persuasive essay about a future trip to France. In the fourth sentence, the writer added the adverb *maturely* to add a specific detail about the students' behavior. The writer also added the persuasive words *educational* and *the perfect* to make her reasons more persuasive.

Ask students to point out and explain other revisions the writer made. (The writer made the phrase *a good learning experience* even more persuasive by changing it to *the best learning experience in the world*.)

Writing Transparency WP33, TR DVD

Differentiated Instruction

Ⓐ Advanced

Apply Revising Skills As they revise their work, have students consider ways to improve it.

- Use one strong adjective or adverb with each reason.
- Try to include a question and an exclamation.
- Make sure the supporting details specifically appeal to the audience.

Revising Tip

Avoid Double Negatives
Explain to students that a sentence should not have more than one negative word *(no, not, never, nothing,* or a contraction with *not,* such as *can't, don't, and won't).* Discuss how to correct this sentence: *I <u>won't never</u> forget this.* (I <u>won't</u> forget this. I <u>won't ever</u> forget this.)

English Language Learners
Support Writing Use the following strategies to help students complete Writing Transparency WP32:

- Discuss words that communicate that action should be taken, such as *should, must,* and *ought,* and model them in sentences.
- Explain that some words describe traits most people admire, such as *educational, healthful,* and *safe,* so they are especially persuasive. Have students use these words in sentences.

Objectives
- Revise a draft of a persuasive essay.
- Edit a revised draft of a persuasive essay to correct errors in grammar, mechanics, and spelling.

 Revise

Revise draft

Earlier we wrote drafts of persuasive essays about persuading parents to let us do a particular action. Now we will revise our drafts. When we revise, we try to make our writing clearer and more interesting.

Peer conferencing

Peer Revision Write the Revising Checklist on the board or make copies to distribute. Have pairs of students exchange drafts for peer revision. Students can use the checklist to help them as they read their partner's paper. In addition to listing at least one genuine compliment about the essay, ask them to write at least three revision suggestions for their partner. These might include where to add persuasive words and adverbs to make the writing more coherent and convincing for the audience.

Have students revise their persuasive essays using the suggestions their partner wrote as well as the Revising Checklist and the list of key features of a persuasive essay (page CW•11) to guide them.

Corrective feedback

If... students are making spelling, mechanics, and grammar corrections, **then...** remind them that they will make those kinds of corrections later when they edit. When they revise, they should be working on the content and organization of their draft.

Revising Checklist

Focus/Ideas

☑ Is the persuasive essay focused on a position to convince a parent?

☑ Are there supporting details to strengthen the position?

Organization

☑ Are the reasons explained in order from the least important to the most important?

Voice

☑ Is the writer's voice persuasive and sincere?

☑ Does the writer's voice speak to the audience?

Word Choice

☑ Are persuasive words used to convince readers to take an action or agree with the position?

Sentences

☑ Have adverbs been used to add specific details that make the writing clearer and more coherent?

☑ Are sentences different lengths and kinds?

④ Edit

MINI-LESSON

Editing Strategy: Sentence by Sentence

■ Suggest that students use this editing strategy as they check their work: Read sentence by sentence. As you read each sentence, check for correct spelling, grammar, punctuation, and capitalization.

■ Display Writing Transparency WP34 and use it to model the sentence-by-sentence editing strategy. Point out the proofreading marks, which students should use when they edit their work. As I check sentence by sentence, I see that *France,* a proper noun, should be capitalized. In the next sentence, instead of the word *week*, its homophone *weak* has been used.

Writing Transparency WP34, TR DVD

■ Ask students to point out and explain the other edits the writer made. (In the last sentence, the possessive pronoun *your* should be used, not the contraction *you're*. Also, the adverb *soonest* should be changed to *sooner* since two things are being compared: now and two years from now.)

Have students edit the paragraph on *Reader's and Writer's Notebook* page 384 using proofreading marks.

You can create your own rubric using items from the rubric on p. CW15 and your own additions and changes, and have students use it to edit their own drafts for spelling, grammar, punctuation, and capitalization. Tell them to use proofreading marks to indicate needed corrections.

Technology Tips

Students who write their persuasive essays on computers should keep these tips in mind as they edit:

✔ Determine margins, line lengths, borders, shading, paragraph indents, and other features using the Format menu.

✔ See whether their word processor has templates, such as those for different writing formats. Sometimes these will be in a menu item called Templates or Project Gallery.

Write Guy
Jeff Anderson

What Do You Notice?

When students are editing one another's writing, ask, "What do you notice?" Giving students the responsibility of commenting on what they find effective in peer writing helps them build self-confidence, and they often begin to notice features of the writing they might not have otherwise.

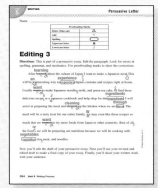

Reader's and Writer's Notebook, p. 384

English Language Learners
Support Editing When reviewing a student's draft, emphasize ideas rather than errors. Observe whether there are consistent grammatical errors. If so, they may reflect the writing conventions of the home language. Choose one or two skills, and use the appropriate lessons in the *ELL Handbook* to explicitly teach the English conventions.

Objectives
- Write and present a final draft of a persuasive essay.
- Evaluate one's own writing.

Present

 Publish

Point out that, as students read on *Reader's and Writer's Notebook* page 384, publishing their writing is the last step in the writing process. Have them incorporate peer suggestions and their own revisions and proofreading edits into their persuasive essay to create a final draft. Offer them two options for presenting their work:

Give their persuasive essays to the parent or parents they wrote to.	Make a class book containing their persuasive essays.

MINI-LESSON

Evaluating Writing

■ Display and read aloud Writing Transparency WP35. Model how to evaluate a persuasive essay using the Scoring Rubric on page CW15.

> **Think Aloud** I would give this persuasive essay a 4. It is focused on one topic: persuading parents to let the writer travel to another country. The reasons are developed and in order from least important to most important. The writer is sincere and convincing. She uses persuasive words and phrases effectively. Short and long sentences as well as questions and exclamations are included. Grammar, mechanics, and spelling are excellent.

■ Have students use the Scoring Rubric to evaluate their persuasive essays. Encourage them to use the evaluation process to help them identify areas for improvement in their future writing.

A Trip to Remember

As you know, each year some of the fifth graders at our school take a trip to France. They stay with French families for a week. I will be able to go on this trip in two years. I want to ask your permission for the trip sooner.

First of all, the trip is so much fun. Can you imagine traveling to Europe with your good friends? Many adults, both teachers and parents, go on the trip. They say that past groups have behaved maturely. Second, we will go on many educational outings. I will learn so much about French history and art! This trip will be the perfect introduction for studying French in high school and college. Third, we will stay in the home of a French family. Getting to know people with a different language and culture from our own is the best learning experience in the world.

I think you should give me permission for this trip so I can start saving money now. Then I can look forward to fun, educational outings, and meeting a French family for two years!

Unit 5 Persuasive Essay • PUBLISH and PRESENT   Writing Process **35**

Writing Transparency WP35, TR DVD

Customize Literacy in Your Classroom

Table of Contents
for Customize Literacy

Customize Literacy is organized into different sections, each one designed to help you organize and carry out an effective literacy program. Each section contains strategies and support for teaching comprehension skills and strategies. *Customize Literacy* also shows how to use weekly text sets of readers in your literacy program.

Weekly Text Sets
to Customize Literacy

The following readers can be used to enhance your literacy instruction.

	Decodable Readers	Concept Literacy Reader	Below-Level Reader	On-Level Reader	Advanced Reader	ELD Reader	ELL Reader
Unit 5 WEEK 4	Heidi and Her Mom; Sleigh Rides; Miranda Turns Eight	Bread!	The World of Bread!	Kapuapua's Magic Shell	Mixing, Kneading, and Baking: The Baker's Art	The Story of Pizza	The Story of Pizza
Unit 5 WEEK 5	Selfish Shelly; A Stormy Day; Messy Jim	From Country to City	A Walk Around the City	Bobby's New Apartment	Let's Go Have Fun!	From a Small Town to a Big City	From a Small Town to a Big City

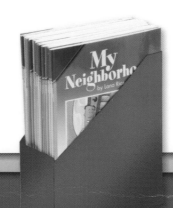

Customize Literacy

Customize Literacy in Your Classroom

Instruction in comprehension skills and strategies provides readers with avenues to understanding a text. Through teacher modeling and guided, collaborative, and independent practice, students become independent thinkers who employ a variety of skills and strategies to help them make meaning as they read.

Mini-Lessons for Comprehension Skills and Strategies

Envision It!
A Comprehension Handbook

Unit 1	Literary Elements, Sequence, Compare and Contrast, Author's Purpose, Background Knowledge, Summarize, Story Structure
Unit 2	Main Ideas and Details, Compare and Contrast, Draw Conclusions, Author's Purpose, Monitor and Clarify, Predict and Set Purpose
Unit 3	Draw Conclusions, Literary Elements, Graphic Sources, Generalize, Cause and Effect, Important Ideas, Text Structure
Unit 4	Generalize, Graphic Sources, Fact and Opinion, Cause and Effect, Inferring, Questioning
Unit 5	Draw Conclusions, Main Ideas and Details, Sequence, Compare and Contrast, Author's Purpose, Visualize, Summarize
Unit 6	Fact and Opinion, Cause and Effect, Graphic Sources, Literary Elements, Generalize, Questioning, Inferring

Envision It! Visual Skills Handbook

Author's Purpose
Categorize and Classify
Cause and Effect
Compare and Contrast
Draw Conclusions
Fact and Opinion
Generalize
Graphic Sources
Literary Elements
Main Idea and Details
Sequence

Envision It! Visual Strategies Handbook

Background Knowledge
Important Ideas
Inferring
Monitor and Clarify
Predict and Set Purpose
Questioning
Story Structure
Summarize
Text Structure
Visualize

Anchor Chart Anchor charts are provided with each strategy lesson. These charts incorporate the language of strategic thinkers. They help students make their thinking visible and permanent and provide students with a means to clarify their thinking about how and when to use each strategy. As students gain more experience with a strategy, the chart may undergo revision.

See pages 107–134 in the *First Stop on Reading Street* Teacher's Edition for additional support as you customize literacy in your classroom.

Good Readers DRA2 users will find additional resources in the *First Stop on Reading Street* Teacher's Edition on pages 110–112.

Contents

Pacing Guide

This chart shows the instructional sequence from *Scott Foresman Reading Street* for Grade 3. You can use this pacing guide as is to ensure you are following a comprehensive scope and sequence. Or, you can adjust the sequence to match your calendar, curriculum map, or testing schedule.

Grade 3

REVIEW WEEK

READING	UNIT 1					UNIT 2	
	Week 1	Week 2	Week 3	Week 4	Week 5	Week 1	Week 2
Comprehension Skill	Character, Setting, and Theme	Sequence	Sequence	Compare and Contrast	Author's Purpose	Main Idea and Details	Compare and Contrast
Comprehension Strategy	Background Knowledge	Summarize	Visualize	Background Knowledge	Story Structure	Monitor and Clarify	Visualize
Vocabulary Strategy/Skill	Context Clues/ Homonyms	Word Structure/ Compound Words	Dictionary/ Glossary/ Unknown Words	Context Clues/ Multiple-Meaning Words	Word Structure/ Prefixes and Suffixes	Context Clues/ Synonyms	Context Clues/ Unfamiliar Words
Fluency	Accuracy	Rate	Expression	Accuracy	Appropriate Phrasing	Accuracy	Expression
Phonics and Spelling	Short Vowels; Syllables VC/CV	Plurals -s, -es, -ies	Base Words and Endings	Vowel Digraphs	Vowel Diphthongs	Syllable Patterns V/CV, VC/V	Final Syllable -le

REVIEW WEEK

	UNIT 4					UNIT 5	
	Week 1	Week 2	Week 3	Week 4	Week 5	Week 1	Week 2
Comprehension Skill	Generalize	Graphic Sources	Fact and Opinion	Fact and Opinion	Cause and Effect	Compare and Contrast	Main Idea and Details
Comprehension Strategy	Summarize	Important Ideas	Inferring	Questioning	Monitor and Clarify	Visualize	Inferring
Vocabulary Strategy/Skill	Context Clues/ Unfamiliar Words	Dictionary/ Glossary/ Unknown Words	Context Clues/ Multiple-Meaning Words	Context Clues/ Multiple-Meaning Words	Dictionary/ Glossary/ Unknown Words	Context Clues/ Synonyms	Context Clues/ Homophones
Fluency	Accuracy	Appropriate Phrasing	Expression	Appropriate Phrasing	Rate	Rate	Accuracy
Phonics and Spelling	Irregular Plurals	Vowels: r-Controlled	Prefixes pre-, mid-, over-, out-, bi-, de-	Suffixes -er, -or, -ess, -ist	Syllable Pattern VCCCV	Syllable Pattern CV/VC	Homophones

Are you the adventurous type? Want to use some of your own ideas and materials in your teaching? But you worry you might be leaving out some critical instruction kids need? Customize Literacy can help.

REVIEW WEEK

UNIT 3

REVIEW WEEK

Week 3	Week 4	Week 5	Week 1	Week 2	Week 3	Week 4	Week 5
Draw Conclusions	Author's Purpose	Main Idea and Details	Draw Conclusions	Character, Setting, Plot	Graphic Sources	Generalize	Cause and Effect
Questioning	Predict and Set Purpose	Text Structure	Important Ideas	Inferring	Text Structure	Story Structure	Predict and Set Purpose
Word Structure/ Compound Words	Context Clues/ Antonyms	Context Clues/ Unfamiliar Words	Context Clues/ Homophones	Dictionary/ Glossary/ Unknown Words	Dictionary/ Glossary/ Unknown Words	Context Clues/ Unfamiliar Words	Word Structure/ Prefixes and Suffixes
Rate	Appropriate Phrasing	Rate	Expression	Accuracy	Appropriate Phrasing	Rate	Expression
Compound Words	Consonant Blends with *spl, thr, squ, str, scr*	Consonant Digraphs	Contractions	Prefixes	Consonant Sounds /j/, /s/ and /k/	Suffixes *-ly, -ful, -ness, -less, -able, -ible*	Consonant Patterns *wr, kn, mb, gn, st*

REVIEW WEEK

UNIT 6

REVIEW WEEK

Week 3	Week 4	Week 5	Week 1	Week 2	Week 3	Week 4	Week 5
Sequence	Draw Conclusions	Author's Purpose	Fact and Opinion	Cause and Effect	Graphic Sources	Plot and Theme	Generalize
Monitor and Clarify	Summarize	Background Knowledge	Questioning	Inferring	Important Ideas	Story Structure	Inferring
Word Structure/ Compound Words	Context Clues/ Unfamiliar Words	Context Clues/ Homonyms	Word Structure/ Prefix *un-*	Context Clues/ Antonyms	Dictionary/ Glossary/ Unknown Words	Word Structure/ Prefixes and Suffixes	Context Clues/ Homographs
Expression and Punctuation Cues	Accuracy	Appropriate Phrasing	Rate	Appropriate Phrasing	Accuracy	Rate	Expression
Vowel Patterns for /ò/	Vowel patterns *ei, eigh*	Suffixes *-y, -ish, -hood, -ment*	Vowel Sounds /ü/ and /ù/	Schwa	Final Syllables	Prefixes; Prefixes, Suffixes, Endings	Related Words

Pacing Guide

Grade 3

UNIT 1

LANGUAGE ARTS	Week 1	Week 2	Week 3	Week 4	Week 5
Speaking and Listening	News Report	Description	Tell a Story	Panel Discussion	Book Report
Grammar	Sentences	Subjects and Predicates	Types of Sentences	Types of Sentences	Compound Sentences
Weekly Writing	Narrative Poem	Fable	Thank-You Note	Description	Realistic Fiction
Trait of the Week	Word Choice	Conventions	Organization	Voice	Sentences
Writing	E-Pen Pals/Personal Narrative				

REVIEW WEEK

UNIT 2

	Week 1	Week 2
Speaking and Listening	Speech	Persuasive Speech
Grammar	Common and Proper Nouns	Singular and Plural Nouns
Weekly Writing	Poem	Fairy Tale
Trait of the Week	Word Choice	Word Choice

UNIT 4

	Week 1	Week 2	Week 3	Week 4	Week 5
Speaking and Listening	Presentation	Weather Forecast	Interview	Sportscast	Book Review
Grammar	Singular and Plural Pronouns	Subject and Object Pronouns	Possessive Pronouns	Contractions	Prepositions
Weekly Writing	Persuasive Text	Story	Biography	Autobiography	Summary
Trait of the Week	Conventions	Conventions	Sentences	Organization	Word Choice
Writing	Classroom Profile/Problem-Solution Essay				

REVIEW WEEK

UNIT 5

	Week 1	Week 2
Speaking and Listening	Introduction	Drama
Grammar	Adjectives and Articles	Adjectives That Compare
Weekly Writing	Letter to the Editor	Personal Narrative
Trait of the Week	Organization	Conventions

REVIEW WEEK

REVIEW WEEK

Week 3	Week 4	Week 5
Presentation	Interview	Description
Irregular Plural Nouns	Singular Possessive Nouns	Plural Possessive Nouns
Persuasive Ad	Friendly Letter	Directions
Focus/Ideas	Conventions	Organization

Story Exchange/How-to Report

UNIT 3

Week 1	Week 2	Week 3	Week 4	Week 5
Commercial	Drama	Voicemail	Description	Oral Report
Action and Linking Verbs	Main and Helping Verbs	Subject-Verb Agreement	Past, Present, and Future Tense	Irregular Verbs
Fiction	Drama: Play	Formal Letter	News Article	Compare/Contrast Composition
Voice	Sentences	Conventions	Sentences	Focus/Ideas

Photo Writing/Cause-and-Effect Essay

REVIEW WEEK

REVIEW WEEK

Week 3	Week 4	Week 5
Song or Poem	Radio Ad	Retelling
Adverbs	Adverbs That Compare	Conjunctions
Poem	Invitation	Book Review
Word Choice	Focus/Ideas	Conventions

E-Newsletter/Persuasive Essay

UNIT 6

Week 1	Week 2	Week 3	Week 4	Week 5
Announcement	Express an Opinion	Talk Show	Description	Song
Capital Letters	Abbreviations	Combining Sentences	Commas	Quotations and Parentheses
Notes	Poem	Description	Comic Book	Historical Fiction
Focus/Ideas	Organization	Word Choice	Conventions	Word Choice

Discussion Forum/Research Report

Teaching Record Chart

This chart shows the critical comprehension skills and strategies you need to cover. Check off each one as you provide instruction.

Reading/Comprehension	DATES OF INSTRUCTION		
Use ideas (e.g., illustrations, titles, topic sentences, key words, and foreshadowing clues) to make and confirm predictions.			
Ask relevant questions, seek clarification, and locate facts and details about stories and other text and support answers with evidence from text.			
Establish purpose for reading selected texts and monitor comprehension, making corrections and adjustments when that understanding breaks down (e.g., identifying clues, using background knowledge, generating questions, re-reading a portion aloud).			
Paraphrase the themes and supporting details of fables, legends, myths, or stories.			
Compare and contrast the settings in myths and traditional folktales.			
Describe the characteristics of various forms of poetry and how they create imagery (e.g., narrative poetry, lyrical poetry, humorous poetry, free verse).			
Explain the elements of plot and character as presented through dialogue in scripts that are read, viewed, written, or performed.			
Sequence and summarize the plot's main events and explain their influence on future events.			
Describe the interactions of characters including their relationships and the changes they undergo.			
Identify whether the narrator or speaker of a story is first or third person.			

Tired of using slips of paper or stickies to make sure you teach everything you need to? Need an easier way to keep track of what you have taught, and what you still need to cover? **Customize Literacy** *can help.* "

Reading/Comprehension	DATES OF INSTRUCTION		
Explain the difference in point of view between a biography and an autobiography.			
Identify language that creates a graphic visual experience and appeals to the senses.			
Read independently for a sustained period of time and paraphrase what the reading was about, maintaining meaning and logical order (e.g., generate a reading log or journal; participate in book talks).			
Identify the topic and locate the author's stated purposes in writing the text.			
Identify the details or facts that support the main idea.			
Draw conclusions from the facts presented in text and support those assertions with textual evidence.			
Identify explicit cause and effect relationships among ideas in texts.			
Use text features (e.g., bold print, captions, key words, italics) to locate information and make and verify predictions about contents of text.			
Identify what the author is trying to persuade the reader to think or do.			
Follow and explain a set of written multi-step directions.			
Locate and use specific information in graphic features of text.			
Establish purposes for reading selected texts based upon own or others' desired outcome to enhance comprehension.			
Ask literal, interpretive, and evaluative questions of a text.			
Monitor and adjust comprehension using a variety of strategies.			
Make inferences about a text and use evidence from the text to support understanding.			
Summarize information in a text, maintaining meaning and logical order.			
Make connections between literary and informational texts with similar ideas and provide evidence from the text.			

Draw Conclusions

Envision It! Visual Skills Handbook

Draw Conclusions

Combine what you already know with new information to draw conclusions.

What I know:
Riding uphill can make you tired. Sometimes your face scrunches up when you work hard. Exercise can make you feel warm.

→ **Conclusion:**
The girl is becoming hot and tired.

EI•6

Student Edition p. EI•6

Objectives:
- Students draw conclusions about characters, events, or information in their reading.
- Students use their prior knowledge and evidence from text to support conclusions.

What is it? A **conclusion** is a decision a person makes after thinking about some facts and details. Drawing conclusions means figuring out something by thinking about it. Drawing conclusions allows readers to go beyond the literal meaning of a text and put information together in order to make decisions about what they are reading. At Grade 3, students are drawing conclusions about fiction and nonfiction texts. They are using evidence and prior knowledge to support their conclusions.

How Good Readers Use the Skill Drawing conclusions, also called making inferences, is fundamental in reading and listening comprehension. When readers draw conclusions they synthesize and evaluate information from stories and informational articles as they bring their own life experiences and prior knowledge to the text. The result is a deeper understanding of what they are reading.

Texts for Teaching

Student Edition
- *Prudy's Problem and How She Solved It,* 3.1, pages 274–289
- *How Do You Raise a Raisin?* 3.1, pages 378–393
- *Jalapeño Bagels,* 3.2, pages 296–309

Leveled Readers
- See pages 24–29 for a list of Leveled Readers.

Mini-Lesson 1

Teach the Skill
Use the **Envision It!** lesson on page EI•6 to visually review draw conclusions.

Remind students that:
- a **conclusion** is a decision you reach that makes sense after you think about details or facts in what you read.
- to **draw a conclusion** think about what you know and make a decision about details in the text.

Practice
Tell students that when they use what they know to draw conclusions as they read, they will better understand what they read. Show the following graphic organizer and model using it with a piece of familiar text (see sample chart). Then have partners use the graphic together. Encourage them to always think about what they already know.

Detail in Text	What I Already Know	My Conclusion
Jan saw a rainbow.	Rainbows are caused by sunlight.	It had rained earlier, but had stopped.

If... students have difficulty drawing conclusions,
then... think aloud as you draw a conclusion.

Apply
As students read on their own, have them think about what they already know and add it to details in text.

Writing
Have students reread a familiar passage and record details and conclusions on a graphic organizer.

Teach the Skill

Use the Envision It! lesson on page EI•6 to visually review draw conclusions.

Remind students that:

- a **conclusion** is a decision you reach that makes sense after you think about details or facts in what you read.
- to **draw a conclusion** think about what you know and make a decision about details in the text.

Practice

Read a passage aloud and have students draw conclusions about characters, events, or information. Remind them to use text details and what they know to figure things out. Tell them to ask questions: *What happens in the story? What did the characters do that shows they are nice? mean? strong? smart? What details support my ideas?* Model the process of drawing conclusions about a character by thinking aloud. For example, Justin looked at the sky and then covered all the firewood at the campsite with a tarp. I think he is smart about weather and is forward-thinking about needing dry wood to make a fire.

If... students have difficulty drawing conclusions about a character,

then... review specific details about the character and ask: *What kind of person does this?*

Apply

As students read on their own, have them use what they already know to draw conclusions.

Writing

Students can draw pictures of characters and label them with details that show what the character is like.

Teach the Skill

Use the Envision It! lesson on page EI•6 to visually review draw conclusions.

Remind students that:

- a **conclusion** is a decision you reach that makes sense after you think about details or facts in what you read.
- to **draw a conclusion** think about what you know and make a decision about details in the text.

Practice

Talk about the kinds of questions students can ask when they draw conclusions. Explain that they might ask different questions depending on what they are reading. Remind students to always think about what they already know and match that with details in the text. Think aloud to demonstrate: Before I read, I preview to see what it will be about. Do I know anything about the topic? Have I read anything by this author before? As I read, I try to think what it means. Can I use the details to visualize what's happening? Can I draw conclusions about what the character is like or what his or her actions might lead to?

Talk with students about questions they ask.

If... students have difficulty drawing conclusions,

then... review specific details and ask: *What could this mean?*

Apply

As students read on their own, have them use what they already know to draw conclusions.

Writing

Students can write questions they ask themselves as they read.

Instruction

Section 2 Instruction

Student Edition p. EI•2

Author's Purpose

Objectives:

- Students understand that an author writes for one or more purposes.
- Students identify purposes for writing: to persuade, to inform, to entertain, to express a mood or feeling.
- Students infer an author's purpose from text features and specific language used.

What is it? An author may write to persuade, to inform, to entertain, or to express a mood or feeling. Readers can infer an **author's purpose** from text features and from specific language the author uses. At Grade 3, students are using the term *author's purpose* and are identifying persuasive language. Students are also becoming aware that an author may have more than one purpose for writing.

How Good Readers Use the Skill Students know that they read different kinds of selections for different reasons. Build on these experiences by introducing specific purposes for writing and helping readers classify things they read. At first, students learn that authors write to inform or entertain. More sophisticated readers learn other purposes; they learn that an author may have several purposes. Eventually we want readers to preview a selection for hints to author's purpose, and to think critically about whether an author met his or her purpose.

Texts for Teaching

Student Edition
- *My Rows and Piles of Coins,* 3.1, pages 168–183
- *Tops & Bottoms,* 3.1, pages 308–325
- *Me and Uncle Romie,* 3.2, pages 328–349

Leveled Readers
- See pages 22–27 for a list of Leveled Readers.

Mini-Lesson 1

Teach the Skill
Use the **Envision It!** lesson on page EI•2 to visually review author's purpose.

Remind students that:
- an author may write to **persuade**, to **inform**, to **entertain**, or to **express** a mood or feeling.
- readers can infer an **author's purpose** from text features and language.

Practice
Ask students to name movies, books, and TV shows. Add your experiences. Together, classify the list according to purpose. Have students ask: *Was this created to teach me something? entertain me? persuade me to think or act in a certain way?* Talk briefly about what parts of the movie, book, or TV show students used to decide on its purpose. For example, a diagram or a map may signal the author wants to inform. Lots of dialogue and cute subheads may signal the author wants to entertain. Make a chart for your responses.

If... students have difficulty identifying the author's purpose, **then...** provide two choices for a item and have students select from the choices.

Apply
As students read the assigned text, have them look at the classification chart you made and think about what purpose the author might have had.

Writing
Have students write their own definitions for *persuade, inform,* and *entertain* to use when classifying selections.

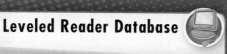

Mini-Lesson 2

Teach the Skill
Use the **Envision It!** lesson on page EI•2 to visually review author's purpose.

Remind students that:
- an author may write to **persuade**, to **inform**, to **entertain**, or to **express** a mood or feeling.
- readers can infer an **author's purpose** from text features and from specific language the author uses.
- an author may have more than one purpose for writing.

Practice
Provide examples of different reading materials. Include nonfiction informational articles, fictional stories, a poem or two, and at least one advertisement. Have small groups first decide on the purpose behind the piece and then point out language or text features to support their opinions. Bring the groups together and have them explain. Record the language they cite for each kind of writing. Ask: Could an author have more than one purpose? What makes you think that?

If... students have difficulty determining purpose from text features and language,

then... have them look at one kind of writing at a time and list some text features and language that help them make an inference about author's purpose.

Apply
As students read the assigned text, have them complete a graphic organizer to record details that help them figure out what the author's purpose may be.

Writing
Students can write a few sentences with one purpose in mind and have a classmate say what the purpose is.

Mini-Lesson 3

Teach the Skill
Use the **Envision It!** lesson on page EI•2 to visually review author's purpose.

Remind students that:
- an author may write to **persuade**, to **inform**, to **entertain**, or to **express** a mood or feeling.
- readers can infer an **author's purpose** from text features and from specific language the author uses.
- an author may have more than one purpose for writing.

Practice
Read aloud an advertisement to get students to think about how an author might use certain words to persuade readers to think or do something. Discuss what purpose the author of the ad had. Help identify language that is often used to persuade: *the very best, last offer, the stars use it,* and so on. Have students work together to write their own persuasive ad to share.

If... students have difficulty identifying persuasive language in an ad,

then... have them first separate factual information about the product.

Apply
As students read the assigned text, have them look for language that helps figure out the author's purpose for writing.

Writing
Students can write their own ads using persuasive language.

Instruction

Summarize

Mini-Lesson

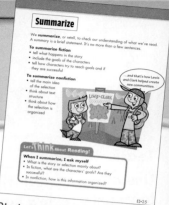

Student Edition p. EI•25

Student Edition p. EI•25

Objectives:

- Students identify a summary as the important ideas of an article or story.
- Students use the strategy of summarizing as they read.
- Students ask questions to help them summarize.

Texts for Teaching

Student Edition

- *What About Me?* 3.1, pages 64–77
- *The Man Who Invented Basketball,* 3.2, pages 28–41
- *Jalapeño Bagels,* 3.2, pages 296–309

Leveled Readers

- See pages 22–27 for a list of Leveled Readers.

Understand the Strategy

Summarizing means picking out the important ideas in a story or an article and restating them in your own words. Summarizing enables readers to organize information and evaluate the importance of what they read.

Teach

Use the **Envision It!** lesson on page EI•25 to visually review summarizing with students.

Remind students that summarizing what they read can help them organize and understand what they read and that this can be a helpful study tool. Using a piece of familiar text, model asking questions to identify important information that should be a part of a summary as well as the unimportant ideas. Then, write a summary in your own words.

Questions for Nonfiction	Questions for Fiction
What is this selection about?	What is this story about?
What are the main ideas?	What do the characters want to do?
Which information is important?	What problems do they face doing it?
Which information is interesting, but not that important? Why?	How do they solve the problem in the end? Or do they?

Practice

Supply students with a text and a good summary of that selection. Have them talk about what parts of the text were important to include and what parts were not important to include and why they thought so. Then provide a new text and have students read the text and write a summary. Using student ideas, work together to write a summary all agree on.

If... students have difficulty summarizing,

then... chunk the text for them and have them determine important points and summarize a small portion of the text. Later they can put their summaries together.

Apply

Ask students to write a summary of a text on their own. Students can use a graphic organizer, such as a web or a story structure chart, to help them organize information for a summary.

Anchor Chart

Anchor charts help students make their thinking visible and permanent. With an anchor chart, the group can clarify their thinking about how to use a strategy. Display anchor charts so readers can use them as they read. They may wish or need to review and edit the charts as they gain more experience with strategies. Here is a sample chart for writing a summary.

Writing a Summary

1. Be sure you understand the selection! Reread it if you don't get it.

2. Ask questions to help you understand what you read.

3. Write down the main points.

4. Write down the important details—try to distinguish the important details from the really interesting ones. Sometimes the details you remember aren't the most important ones!

5. If you are summarizing fiction, think about the characters, setting, plot, and theme.

6. If you are summarizing nonfiction, think about how the text is arranged.

7. Try writing a few sentences that tell the main points in your own words.

8. Reread your summary to see how it sounds.

Anchor Chart

Instruction

Using Multiple Strategies

Good readers use multiple strategies as they read. You can encourage students to read strategically through good classroom questioning. Use questions such as these to help students apply strategies during reading.

Answer Questions

- Who or what is this question about?
- Where can you look to find the answer to this question?

Ask Questions

- What do you want to know about _____?
- What questions to do you have about the _____ in this selection? Use the words *who, what, when, where, why,* and *how* to ask your questions.
- Do you have any questions after reading?

Graphic Organizers

- What kind of graphic organizer could you use to help you keep track of the information in this selection?

Monitor and Clarify

- Does the story or article make sense?
- What don't you understand about what you read?
- Do you need to reread, review, read on, or check a reference source?
- Do you need to read more slowly or more quickly?
- What is a _____? Where could you look to find out?

Predict/Confirm Predictions

- What do you think this story or article will be about? Why do you think as you do?
- What do you think you will learn from this selection?
- Do the text features help you predict what will happen?
- Based on what has happened so far, what do you think will happen next?
- Is this what you thought would happen?
- How does _____ change what you thought would happen?

Preview

- What do the photographs, illustrations, or graphic sources tell about the selection?
- What do you want to find out? What do you want to learn?

Background Knowledge

- What do you already know about _____?

- Have you read stories or articles by this author before?

- How is this selection like others that you have read?

- What does this remind you of?

- How does your background knowledge help you understand _____?

- Did the text match what you already knew? What new information did you learn?

Story Structure

- Who are the characters in this story? the setting?

- What is the problem in this story? How does the problem get solved?

- What is the point of this story?

Summarize

- What two or three important ideas have you read so far?

- How do the text features relate to the important ideas?

- Is there a graphic organizer that can help you organize the information before you summarize?

Text Structure

- How has the author organized the writing?

- What clues tell you that the text is structured _____?

Visualize

- When you read this, what do you picture in your mind?

- What do you hear, see, or smell?

- What do you think _____ looks like? Why do you think as you do?

> 66 **You know explicit strategy instruction is a must! But you also want students to use strategies every time they read. Customize Literacy shows you how to help them do this.** 99

Glossary of Literacy Terms

This glossary lists academic language terms that are related to literacy.
They are provided for your information and professional use.

A

alliteration	the repetition of a consonant sound in a group of words, especially in poetry
allusion	a word or phrase that refers to something else the reader already knows from history, experience, or reading
animal fantasy	a story about animals that talk and act like people
answer questions	a reading strategy in which readers use the text and prior knowledge to answer questions about what they are reading
antonym	a word that means the opposite of another word
ask questions	a reading strategy in which readers ask themselves questions about the text to help make sense of what they read
author's point of view	the author's opinion on the subject he or she is writing about
author's purpose	the reason the author wrote the text
autobiography	the story of a real person's life written by that person

B

background knowledge	the information and experience that a reader brings to a text
biography	the story of a real person's life written by another person

C

cause	why something happens
character	a person, an animal, or a personified object in a story
chronological order	events in a selection, presented in the order in which they occurred
classify and categorize	put things, such as pictures or words, into groups
climax	the point in a story at which conflict is confronted
compare	tell how things are the same
comprehension	understanding of text being read—the ultimate goal of reading
comprehension strategy	a conscious plan used by a reader to gain understanding of text. Comprehension strategies may be used before, during, or after reading.
conclusion	a decision or opinion arrived at after thinking about facts and details and using prior knowledge
conflict	the problem or struggle in a story
context clue	the words, phrases, or sentences near an unfamiliar word that give the reader clues to the word's meaning
contrast	tell how things are different

details small pieces of information

dialect form of a language spoken in a certain region or by a certain group of people that differs from the standard form of that language

dialogue written conversation

diary a day-to-day record of one's activities and thoughts

draw conclusions arrive at decisions or opinions after thinking about facts and details and using prior knowledge

D

effect what happens as the result of a cause

etymology an explanation of the origin and history of a word and its meaning

exaggeration a statement that makes something seem larger or greater than it actually is

expository text text that contains facts and information. Also called *informational text.*

E

fable a story, usually with animal characters, that is written to teach a moral, or lesson

fact piece of information that can be proved to be true

fairy tale a folk story with magical characters and events

fantasy a story that could not really happen

fiction writing that tells about imaginary people, things, and events

figurative language the use of language that gives words a meaning beyond their usual definitions in order to add beauty or force

flashback an interruption in the sequence of events of a narrative to include an event that happened earlier

folk tale a story that has been passed down by word of mouth

foreshadowing the use of hints or clues about what will happen later in a story

F

generalize make a broad statement or rule after examining particular facts

graphic organizer a drawing, chart, or web that illustrates concepts or shows how ideas relate to each other. Readers use graphic organizers to help them keep track of and understand important information and ideas as they read. Story maps, word webs, Venn diagrams, and KWL charts are graphic organizers.

graphic source a chart, diagram, or map within a text that adds to readers' understanding of the text

G

Instruction

H	**historical fiction**	realistic fiction that takes place in the past. It is an imaginary story based on historical events and characters.
	humor	writing or speech that has a funny or amusing quality
	hyperbole	an exaggerated statement not meant to be taken literally, such as *I'm so hungry I could eat a horse.*

I	**idiom**	a phrase whose meaning differs from the ordinary meaning of the words. *A stone's throw* is an idiom meaning "a short distance."
	imagery	the use of language to create beautiful or forceful pictures in the reader's mind
	inference	conclusion reached on the basis of evidence and reasoning
	inform	give knowledge, facts, or news to someone
	informational text	writing that contains facts and information. Also called *expository text.*
	interview	a face-to-face conversation in which someone responds to questions
	irony	a way of speaking or writing in which the ordinary meaning of the words is the opposite of what the speaker or writer is thinking; a contrast between what is expected and what actually happens

J	**jargon**	the language of a special group or profession

L	**legend**	a story coming down from the past about the great deeds of a hero. Although a legend may be based on historical people and events, it is not regarded as historically true.
	literary elements	the characters, setting, plot, and theme of a narrative text

M	**main idea**	the big idea that tells what a paragraph or a selection is mainly about; the most important idea of a text
	metacognition	an awareness of one's own thinking processes and the ability to monitor and direct them to a desired goal. Good readers use metacognition to monitor their reading and adjust their reading strategies.
	metaphor	a comparison that does not use *like* or *as*, such as *a heart of stone*
	meter	the pattern of beats or accents in poetry

monitor and clarify	a comprehension strategy by which readers actively think about understanding their reading and know when they understand and when they do not. Readers use appropriate strategies to make sense of difficult words, ideas, or passages.
mood	the atmosphere or feeling of a written work
moral	the lesson or teaching of a fable or story
motive	the reason a character in a narrative does or says something
mystery	a story about mysterious events that are not explained until the end, so as to keep the reader in suspense
myth	a story that attempts to explain something in nature

M

narrative	a story, made up or true, that someone tells or narrates
narrator	the character in a selection who tells the story
nonfiction	writing that tells about real things, real people, and real events

N

onomatopoeia	the use of words that sound like their meanings, such as *buzz* and *hum*
opinion	someone's judgment, belief, or way of thinking
oral vocabulary	the words needed for speaking and listening
outcome	the resolution of the conflict in a story

O

paraphrase	retell the meaning of a passage in one's own words
personification	a figure of speech in which human traits or actions are given to animals or inanimate objects, as in *The sunbeam danced on the waves.*
persuade	convince someone to do or to believe something
photo essay	a collection of photographs on one theme, accompanied by text
play	a story that is written to be acted out for an audience
plot	a series of related events at the beginning, middle, and end of a story; the action of a story
poem	an expressive, imaginative piece of writing often arranged in lines having rhythm and rhyme. In a poem, the patterns made by the sounds of the words have special importance.
pourquoi tale	a type of folk story that explains why things in nature came to be. *Pourquoi* is a French word meaning "why."

P

Instruction

P

predict   tell what a selection might be about or what might happen in a text. Readers use text features and information to predict. They confirm or revise their predictions as they read.

preview   look over a text before reading it

prior knowledge   the information and experience that a reader brings to a text. Readers use prior knowledge to help them understand what they read.

prop   an item, such as an object, picture, or chart, used in a performance or presentation

R

reading vocabulary   the words we recognize or use in print

realistic fiction   a story about imaginary people and events that could happen in real life

repetition   the repeated use of some aspect of language

resolution   the point in a story where the conflict is resolved

rhyme   to end in the same sound(s)

rhythm   a pattern of strong beats in speech or writing, especially poetry

rising action   the buildup of conflicts and complications in a story

S

science fiction   a story based on science that often tells what life in the future might be like

semantic map   a graphic organizer, often a web, used to display words or concepts that are meaningfully related

sensory language   the use of words that help the reader understand how things look, sound, smell, taste, or feel

sequence   the order of events in a selection or the order of the steps in which something is completed

sequence words   clue words such as *first*, *next*, *then*, and *finally* that signal the order of events in a selection

setting   where and when a story takes place

simile   a comparison that uses *like* or *as*, as in *as busy as a bee*

speech   a public talk to a group of people made for a specific purpose

stanza   a group of lines in a poem

steps in a process   the order of the steps in which something is completed

story map   a graphic organizer used to record the literary elements and the sequence of events in a narrative text

story structure	how the characters, setting, and events of a story are organized into a plot
summarize	give the most important ideas of what was read. Readers summarize important information in the selection to keep track of what they are reading.
supporting detail	piece of information that tells about the main idea
symbolism	the use of one thing to suggest something else; often the use of something concrete to stand for an abstract idea

S

tall tale	a humorous story that uses exaggeration to describe impossible happenings
text structure	the organization of a piece of nonfiction writing. Text structures of informational text include cause-effect, chronological, compare/contrast, description, problem/solution, proposition/support, and ask/answer questions.
theme	the big idea or author's message in a story
think aloud	an instructional strategy in which a teacher verbalizes his or her thinking to model the process of comprehension or the application of a skill
tone	author's attitude toward the subject or toward the reader
topic	the subject of a discussion, conversation, or piece of text

T

visualize	picture in one's mind what is happening in the text. Visualizing helps readers imagine the things they read about.

V

Instruction

Section 3 Matching Books and Readers

Leveled Readers Skills Chart

Scott Foresman Reading Street provides more than six hundred leveled readers.
Each one is designed to:

- Practice critical skills and strategies
- Build fluency
- Build vocabulary and concepts
- Develop a lifelong love of reading

Grade 3

Title	Level*	DRA Level	Genre	Comprehension Strategy
The Opposite Cousins	F	10	Realistic Fiction	Background Knowledge
It's a Fair Swap!	F	10	Expository Nonfiction	Summarize
Life in the Arctic	F	10	Nonfiction	Visualize
Let's Surprise Mom	F	10	Realistic Fiction	Background Knowledge
E-mail Friends	F	10	Realistic Fiction	Story Structure
The Frozen Continent: Antarctica	F	10	Expository Nonfiction	Monitor and Clarify
Buddy Goes to School	G	12	Realistic Fiction	Visualize
The Metal Detective	G	12	Realistic Fiction	Questioning
Growing Vegetables	G	12	Narrative Nonfiction	Predict and Set Purpose
All About Birds	G	12	Nonfiction	Text Structure
Raisins	G	12	Nonfiction	Important Ideas
The Hunters and the Elk	G	12	Fiction	Inferring
Pictures in the Sky	H	14	Expository Nonfiction	Text Structure
Rescuing Whales	H	14	Expository Nonfiction	Story Structure
The Field Trip	H	14	Expository Nonfiction	Predict and Set Purpose
The Winning Point	H	14	Realistic Fiction	Summarize
How to Measure the Weather	H	14	Expository Nonfiction	Important Ideas
Grandpa's Rock Kit	H	14	Narrative Nonfiction	Inferring
Across the English Channel	H	14	Expository Nonfiction	Questioning
Swimming Like Buck	I	16	Animal Fantasy	Monitor and Clarify
A Tea Party with Obâchan	I	16	Realistic Fiction	Visualize
Independence Day/El Día de la Independencia	I	16	Nonfiction	Inferring
A Child's Life in Korea	I	16	Expository Nonfiction	Monitor and Clarify
The World of Bread!	I	16	Expository Nonfiction	Summarize
A Walk Around the City	I	16	Expository Nonfiction	Background Knowledge
The Statue of Liberty: A Gift From France	I	16	Expository Nonfiction	Questioning
Camping with Aunt Julie	J	18	Realistic Fiction	Background Knowledge
Let's Make a Trade!	J	18	Expository Nonfiction	Summarize
Ice Fishing in the Arctic	J	18	Nonfiction	Visualize
The Shopping Trip	J	18	Fiction	Background Knowledge

* Suggested Guided Reading Level. Use your knowledge of students' abilities to adjust levels as needed.

The chart here and on the next few pages lists titles of leveled readers appropriate for students in Grade 3. Use the chart to find titles that meet your students' interest and instructional needs. The books in this list were leveled using the criteria suggested in *Matching Books to Readers* and *Leveled Books for Readers, Grades 3–6* by Irene C. Fountas and Gay Su Pinnell. For more on leveling, see the *Reading Street Leveled Readers Leveling Guide.*

Target Comprehension Skill	Additional Comprehension Instruction	Vocabulary
Character, Setting, and Theme	Draw Conclusions	Context Clues/Homonyms
Sequence	Fact and Opinion	Word Structure/Compound Words
Sequence	Generalize	Dictionary/Glossary/Unfamiliar Words
Compare and Contrast	Main Idea	Context Clues/Multiple Meanings
Author's Purpose	Compare and Contrast	Word Structure/Prefixes and Suffixes
Main Idea and Details	Generalize	Context Clues/Synonyms
Compare and Contrast	Sequence	Context Clues/Unfamiliar Words
Draw Conclusions	Realism and Fantasy	Compound Words/Word Structure
Author's Purpose	Generalize	Context Clues/Antonyms
Main Idea and Details	Compare and Contrast	Context Clues/Unfamiliar Words
Draw Conclusions	Generalize	Homophones/Context Clues
Character, Setting, and Plot	Theme	Unknown Words/Dictionary/Glossary
Graphic Sources	Author's Purpose	Unknown Words/Dictionary/Glossary
Generalize	Sequence	Context Clues/Unfamiliar Words
Cause and Effect	Draw Conclusions	Prefixes/Suffixes/Word Structure
Generalize	Plot	Unfamiliar Words/Context Clues
Graphic Sources	Main Idea	Unknown Words/Dictionary/Glossary
Fact and Opinion	Fact and Opinion	Context Clues/Multiple Meanings
Fact and Opinion	Generalize	Context Clues/Multiple Meanings
Cause and Effect	Character	Unknown Words/Dictionary/Glossary
Compare and Contrast	Generalize	Context Clues/Synonyms
Main Idea and Details	Draw Conclusions	Context Clues/Antonyms
Sequence	Author's Purpose	Word Structure/Compound Words
Draw Conclusions	Main Idea	Context Clues/Unfamiliar Words
Author's Purpose	Generalize	Context Clues/Homonyms
Fact and Opinion	Fact and Opinion	Word Structure/Prefixes
Character and Setting	Theme	Context Clues/Homonyms
Sequence	Draw Conclusions	Word Structure/Compound Words
Sequence	Author's Purpose	Dictionary/Glossary/Unfamiliar Words
Compare and Contrast	Character	Context Clues/Multiple Meanings

Section 3 Matching Books and Readers

Leveled Readers Skills Chart *Continued*

Grade 3

Title	Level*	DRA Level	Genre	Comprehension Strategy
New York's Chinatown	J	18	Expository Nonfiction	Inferring
One Forest, Different Trees	J	18	Realistic Fiction	Important Ideas
Swimming in a School	J	18	Animal Fantasy	Story Structure
Greek Myths	J	18	Nonfiction	Inferring
The Market Adventure	K	20	Realistic Fiction	Story Structure
These Birds Can't Fly!	K	20	Expository Nonfiction	Monitor and Clarify
Iguana Takes a Ride	K	20	Animal Fantasy	Visualize
The Last Minute	K	20	Realistic Fiction	Questioning
Our Garden	K	20	Realistic Fiction	Predict and Set Purpose
Bills and Beaks	L	24	Historical Fiction	Text Structure
In the Fields	L	24	Historical Fiction	Important Ideas
The Thunder and Lightning Men	L	24	Folktale	Inferring
Meet the Stars	L	24	Realistic Fiction	Text Structure
What a Day!	L	24	Realistic Fiction	Story Structure
Desert Life	L	24	Expository Nonfiction	Predict and Set Purpose
A Trip	M	28	Realistic Fiction	Summarize
Measuring the Earth	M	28	Expository Nonfiction	Important Ideas
Fun with Hobbies and Science!	M	28	Expository Nonfiction	Inferring
Great Women in U.S. History	M	28	Biography	Questioning
Buddy Ran Away	M	28	Realistic Fiction	Monitor and Clarify
Cowboy Slim's Dude Ranch	M	28	Realistic Fiction	Visualize
Celebrate Around the World	N	30	Nonfiction	Inferring
Joanie's House Becomes a Home	N	30	Realistic Fiction	Monitor and Clarify
Kapuapua's Magic Shell	N	30	Folktale	Summarize
Bobby's New Apartment	N	30	Realistic Fiction	Background Knowledge
Symbols, Signs, and Songs of America	N	30	Narrative Nonfiction	Text Structure
A Pet Bird	O	34	Expository Nonfiction	Inferring
Lily's Adventure Around the World	O	34	Realistic Fiction	Important Ideas
The Three Bears and Goldilocks	O	34	Animal Fantasy	Story Structure
Sweet Freedom!	O	34	Nonfiction	Inferring

* Suggested Guided Reading Level. Use your knowledge of students' abilities to adjust levels as needed.

You know the theory behind leveled books: they let you match books with the interest and instructional levels of your students. You can find the right reader for every student with this chart. 99

Target Comprehension Skill	Additional Comprehension Instruction	Vocabulary
Cause and Effect	Generalize	Context Clues/Antonyms
Graphic Sources	Generalize	Dictionary/Glossary/Unknown Words
Plot and Theme	Realism and Fantasy	Word Structure/Prefixes and Suffixes
Generalize	Compare and Contrast	Homographs/Context Clues
Author's Purpose	Generalize	Word Structure/Prefixes and Suffixes
Main Idea and Details	Compare and Contrast	Context Clues/Synonyms
Compare and Contrast	Draw Conclusions	Context Clues/Unfamiliar Words
Draw Conclusions	Sequence	Compound Words/Word Structure
Author's Purpose	Plot	Context Clues/Antonyms
Main Idea and Details	Setting	Context Clues/Unfamiliar Words
Draw Conclusions	Author's Purpose	Homophones/Context Clues
Character, Setting, and Plot	Main Idea	Unknown Words/Dictionary/Glossary
Graphic Sources	Plot	Unknown Words/Dictionary/Glossary
Generalize	Character	Context Clues/Unfamiliar Words
Cause and Effect	Generalize	Dictionary/Glossary/Unfamiliar Words
Generalize	Author's Purpose	Unfamiliar Words/Context Clues
Graphic Sources	Fact and Opinion	Unknown Words/Dictionary/Glossary
Fact and Opinion	Draw Conclusions	Context Clues/Multiple Meanings
Fact and Opinion	Main Idea and Details	Context Clues/Multiple Meanings
Cause and Effect	Sequence	Unknown Words/Dictionary/Glossary
Compare and Contrast	Main Idea	Context Clues/Synonyms
Main Idea and Details	Compare and Contrast	Homophones/Context Clues
Sequence	Draw Conclusions	Word Structure/Compound Words
Draw Conclusions	Theme	Context Clues/Unfamiliar Words
Author's Purpose	Realism and Fantasy	Context Clues/Homonyms
Main Idea	Fact and Opinion	Word Structure/Prefixes
Cause and Effect	Main Idea	Context Clues/Antonyms
Graphic Sources	Compare and Contrast	Unknown Words/Dictionary/Glossary
Plot and Theme	Character	Word Structure/Prefixes and Suffixes
Generalize	Author's Purpose	Homographs/Context Clues

Matching Books & Readers

Leveled Readers Skills Chart *Continued*

Grade 3 Title	Level*	DRA Level	Genre	Comprehension Strategy
Mr. Post's Project	P	38	Realistic Fiction	Background Knowledge
What's Money All About?	P	38	Expository Nonfiction	Summarize
Journey Across the Arctic	P	38	Fiction	Visualize
The Road to New York	P	38	Realistic Fiction	Background Knowledge
With a Twist	P	38	Fantasy	Story Structure
All About Penguins	P	38	Expository Nonfiction	Monitor and Clarify
Puppy Problems	Q	40	Realistic Fiction	Visualize
A Family of Collectors	Q	40	Realistic Fiction	Important Ideas
The Magic of Coyote	Q	40	Realistic Fiction	Predict and Set Purpose
Animals of the Concrete Jungle	Q	40	Expository Nonfiction	Text Structure
Grape Season	Q	40	Realistic Fiction	Important Ideas
Grandmother Spider Steals the Sun	Q	40	Folktale	Inferring
Animal Tracking: Learn More About Animals	Q	40	Expository Nonfiction	Text Structure
Whales and Other Amazing Animals	R	40	Expository Nonfiction	Story Structure
Coral Reefs	R	40	Expository Nonfiction	Predict and Set Purpose
Extraordinary Athletes	R	40	Biography	Summarize
Largest, Fastest, Lightest, Longest	R	40	Expository Nonfiction	Questioning
Gemstones Around the World	R	40	Expository Nonfiction	Inferring
Changing Times	R	40	Expository Nonfiction	Questioning
Toby the Smart Dog	R	40	Humorous Fiction	Monitor and Clarify
His Favorite Sweatshirt	S	40	Realistic Nonfiction	Visualize
Life Overseas	S	40	Expository Nonfiction	Inferring
It's a World of Time Zones	S	40	Expository Nonfiction	Monitor and Clarify
Mixing, Kneading, and Baking: The Baker's Art	S	40	Narrative Nonfiction	Summarize
Let's Go Have Fun!	S	40	Expository Nonfiction	Background Knowledge
The French Connection	S	40	Narrative Nonfiction	Questioning
China's Special Gifts to the World	T	50	Expository Nonfiction	Graphic Organizers
Thomas Hart Benton: Painter of Murals	T	50	Biography	Important Ideas
The Best Field Trip Ever!	T	50	Expository Fiction	Story Structure
Free in the Sea	T	50	Expository Nonfiction	Predict and Set Purpose

* Suggested Guided Reading Level. Use your knowledge of students' abilities to adjust levels as needed.

You know the theory behind leveled books: they let you match books with the interest and instructional levels of your students. You can find the right reader for every student with this chart. 99

Target Comprehension Skill	Additional Comprehension Instruction	Vocabulary
Character and Setting	Theme	Context Clues/Homonyms
Sequence	Draw Conclusions	Word Structure/Compound Words
Sequence	Setting	Dictionary/Glossary/Unfamiliar Words
Compare and Contrast	Character	Context Clues/Multiple Meanings
Author's Purpose	Sequence	Word Structure/Prefixes and Suffixes
Main Idea and Details	Compare and Contrast	Context Clues/Synonyms
Compare and Contrast	Cause and Effect	Context Clues/Unfamiliar Words
Graphic Sources	Realism and Fantasy	Compound Words/Word Structure
Author's Purpose	Sequence	Context Clues/Antonyms
Main Idea and Details	Fact and Opinion	Context Clues/Unfamiliar Words
Draw Conclusions	Main Idea	Homophones/Context Clues
Character, Setting, and Plot	Fact and Opinion	Dictionary/Glossary/Unfamiliar Words
Graphic Sources	Compare and Contrast	Unknown Words/Dictionary/Glossary
Generalize	Author's Purpose	Context Clues/Unfamiliar Words
Cause and Effect	Draw Conclusions	Prefixes and Suffixes/Word Structure
Generalize	Draw Conclusions	Unfamiliar Words/Context Clues
Compare and Contrast	Author's Purpose	Word Structure/Compound Words
Fact and Opinion	Cause and Effect	Context Clues/Multiple Meanings
Fact and Opinion	Generalize	Context Clues/Multiple Meanings
Cause and Effect	Character and Setting	Unknown Words/Dictionary/Glossary
Compare and Contrast	Draw Conclusions	Context Clues/Synonyms
Main Idea and Details	Cause and Effect	Homophones/Context Clues
Sequence	Draw Conclusions	Word Structure/Compound Words
Draw Conclusions	Main Idea	Context Clues/Unfamiliar Words
Author's Purpose	Compare and Contrast	Context Clues/Homonyms
Fact and Opinion	Generalize	Word Structure/Prefixes
Cause and Effect	Generalize	Context Clues/Antonyms
Graphic Sources	Author's Purpose	Unknown Words/Dictionary/Glossary
Plot and Theme	Realism and Fantasy	Word Structure/Prefixes and Suffixes
Generalize	Compare and Contrast	Context Clues/Synonyms

Matching Books & Readers

Section 3 Matching Books and Readers

What Good Readers Do

You can use the characteristics and behaviors of good readers to help all your students read better. But what are these characteristics and behaviors? And how can you use them to foster good reading behaviors for all your students? Here are some helpful tips.

Good Readers enjoy reading! They have favorite books, authors, and genres. Good readers often have a preference about where and when they read. They talk about books and recommend their favorites.

Develop this behavior by giving students opportunities to respond in different ways to what they read. Get them talking about what they read, and why they like or dislike it.

This behavior is important because book sharing alerts you to students who are somewhat passive about reading or have limited literacy experiences. Book sharing also helps you when you select books for the class.

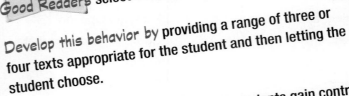

Good Readers select books they can read.

Develop this behavior by providing a range of three or four texts appropriate for the student and then letting the student choose.

This behavior is important because students gain control over reading when they can choose from books they can read. This helps them become more independent in the classroom.

Good Readers read independently for longer periods of time.

Develop this behavior by taking note of the level of support students need during guided reading. Use this information to gauge independent reading time accordingly.

This behavior is important because students become better readers when they spend time reading many texts at their independent level.

Customize Literacy

Good Readers use text features to help them preview and set purposes.

Develop this behavior by having students use the title and illustrations in fiction texts or the title, contents, headings, and other graphic features in nonfiction texts to make predictions about what they will be reading.

This behavior is important because previewing actually makes reading easier! Looking at features and sampling the text enables readers to predict and set expectations for reading.

 Want to improve student performance by fostering good reading behaviors? Customize Literacy can help.

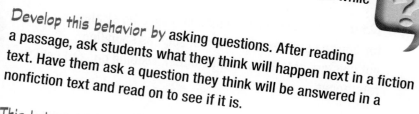

Good Readers predict and ask questions before and while they read.

Develop this behavior by asking questions. After reading a passage, ask students what they think will happen next in a fiction text. Have them ask a question they think will be answered in a nonfiction text and read on to see if it is.

This behavior is important because when students predict and ask questions as they read, they are engaged. They have a purpose for reading and a basis for monitoring their comprehension.

Good Readers read meaningful phrases aloud with appropriate expression.

Develop this behavior by giving students lots of opportunities to read orally. As they read, note students' phrasing, intonation, and attention to punctuation and give help as needed.

This behavior is important because reading fluently in longer, meaningful phrases supports comprehension and ease in reading longer, more complex texts.

Good Readers read aloud at an appropriate reading rate with a high percent of accuracy.

Develop this behavior by timing students' oral reading to calculate their reading rates. You can also record students' miscues to determine a percent of accuracy. This will help identify problems.

This behavior is important because when students read fluently texts that are "just right," they find reading more enjoyable. A fluent reader is able to focus more on constructing meaning and is more likely to develop a positive attitude toward reading.

Matching Books & Readers

Section 3 Matching Books and Readers

Good Readers use effective strategies and sources of information to figure out unknown words.

Develop this behavior by teaching specific strategies for figuring out unknown words, such as sounding out clusters of letters, using context, reading on, and using references.

This behavior is important because when readers have a variety of strategies to use, they are more able to decode and self-correct quickly. Readers who do these things view themselves as good readers.

CH-
QU-
ST-

Good Readers construct meaning as they read and then share or demonstrate their understanding.

Develop this behavior by having students retell what they read or write a summary of what they read in their own words.

This behavior is important because the ability to retell or write a summary is essential for success in reading. It shows how well a student has constructed meaning.

Good Readers locate and use what is explicitly stated in a text.

Develop this behavior by asking questions that require students to go back into the text to find explicitly stated information.

This behavior is important because the ability to recall, locate, and use specific information stated in a text enables readers to respond to literal questions as well as to support opinions and justify their responses.

Good Readers make connections.

Develop this behavior by asking questions to help students make connections: *What does this remind you of? Have you ever read or experienced anything like this?*

This behavior is important because making connections helps readers understand and appreciate a text. Making connections to self, the world, and other texts supports higher-level thinking.

Good Readers interpret what they read by making inferences.

Develop this behavior by asking questions to help students tell or write about what they think was implied in the text: *Why do you think that happened? What helped you come to that conclusion?*

This behavior is important because the ability to go beyond the literal meaning of a text enables readers to gain a deeper understanding. When students make inferences, they use background knowledge, their personal knowledge, and the text to grasp the meaning of what is implied by the author.

Good Readers determine importance and evaluate what they read.

Develop this behavior by always having students identify what they think is the most important message, event, or information in a text.

This behavior is important because readers must be able to sort out important from interesting information. The ability to establish and/or use criteria and provide support when making judgments is an important critical-thinking skill.

Good Readers support their responses using information from a text and/or their own background knowledge.

Develop this behavior by always asking students to give the reason(s) they identified an event, message, or idea as most important.

This behavior is important because the ability to justify one's response is important for all learners. It enables others to know the basis for a decision and provides an opening for further discussion.

Matching Books & Readers

Conversation Starters

Asking Good Questions When students read interesting and thought-provoking books, they want to share! You can encourage students to think critically about what they read. Use questions such as the following to assess comprehension as well as evoke good class/group discussions.

Author's Purpose

- Why did the author write this piece?

- How does figuring out the author's purpose help you decide how to read the text?

Cause and Effect

- Why did these events happen? How might they have been different if the causes had been different?

- Are there several causes that result in a single effect?

- Is there a single cause that has several effects?

Compare and Contrast

- What clue words show the author is comparing and/or contrasting in this article?

- How are the fictional characters and events in this story like and/or different from real people and events you know of?

Draw Conclusions

- Based on what you have read, seen, or experienced, what can you conclude about this event in the selection?

- This story seems to be a fantasy. Why might you conclude this?

- What words help you draw conclusions about the relationship between the characters?

Fact and Opinion

- What clue word or words signal that this is a statement of opinion?

- How could this statement of fact be proved true or false?

Generalize

- What generalization can you make about the story or the characters in it? What examples lead to that generalization?

- What details, facts, and logic does the author use to support this generalization?

Graphic Sources

- How does the author use graphic sources (chart, maps, illustrations, time lines, and so on) to support ideas and opinions?

- This selection has many graphic sources. Which one or ones best help you understand the events or ideas in the selection? Why?

Literary Elements: Character, Setting, Plot, Theme

- Describe the main character at the beginning of the story and at the end of the story. How and why does he or she change?

- How is the setting important to the story? How might the story be different if its time or its place were different?

- What does the main character want at the beginning of the story? How does the main character go about trying to achieve this?

- In a few sentences, what is the plot of the story?

- What is the theme of the story? Use details from the story to support your statement.

Main Idea and Details

- What is the main idea of this paragraph or article? What are some details?

- The author makes this particular statement in the article. What details does the author provide to support that statement?

Sequence

- How is the sequence of events important in the text?

- Is the order of events important in this story? Why or why not?

- Based on what has already happened, what will most likely happen next?

Matching Books & Readers

Connecting Science and Social Studies

Scott Foresman Reading Street Leveled Readers are perfect for covering, supporting, or enriching science and social studies content. Using these books ensures that all students can access important concepts.

Grade 3 Leveled Readers

Science

Earth and Space Science

Nonfiction Books
- *The Frozen Continent: Antarctica*
- *Fun with Hobbies and Science!*
- *Gemstones Around the World*
- *Grandpa's Rock Kit*
- *How to Measure the Weather*
- *Measuring the Earth*
- *Meet the Stars*
- *Pictures in the Sky*

Fiction Books
- *What a Day!*
- *Journey Across the Arctic*

Life Science

Nonfiction Books
- *A Pet Bird*
- *All About Birds*
- *All About Penguins*
- *Animal Tracking: Learn More About It*
- *Animals of the Concrete Jungle*
- *Coral Reefs*
- *Desert Life*
- *The Field Trip*
- *Free in the Sea*
- *Growing Vegetables*
- *Ice Fishing in the Arctic*
- *Largest, Fastest, Lightest, Longest*
- *Life in the Arctic*
- *Raisins*
- *Rescuing Whales*
- *These Birds Can't Fly!*
- *Whales and Other Amazing Animals*

Life Science

Fiction Books
- *The Best Field Trip Ever!*
- *Bills and Beaks*
- *Buddy Ran Away*
- *Grape Season*
- *The Hunters and the Elk*
- *In the Fields*
- *Swimming in a School*
- *Swimming Like Buck*
- *Toby the Smart Dog*

Grade 3 Leveled Readers

Social Studies

Citizenship

Nonfiction Books
- Sweet Freedom!
- Symbols, Signs, and Songs of America

Fiction Books
- Buddy Goes to School
- Camping with Aunt Julie
- The Opposite Cousins
- Our Garden
- Puppy Problems

Culture

Nonfiction Books
- A Child's Life in Korea
- A Walk Around the City
- Celebrate Around the World
- China's Special Gifts to the World
- His Favorite Sweatshirt
- Let's Go Have Fun!
- Life Overseas
- Mixing, Kneading, and Baking
- New York's Chinatown
- The French Connection
- The World of Bread!

Fiction Books
- A Tea Party with Obâchan
- Bobby's New Apartment
- Cowboy Slim's Dude Ranch
- E-mail Friends

Culture

- Grandmother Spider Steals the Sun
- Iguana Takes a Ride
- Kapuapua's Magic Shell
- The Last Minute
- Lily's Adventure Around the World
- The Magic of Coyote
- One Forest, Different Trees
- The Road to New York
- The Three Bears and Goldilocks
- The Thunder and Lightning Men

Economics

Nonfiction Books
- It's a Fair Swap!
- It's a World of Time Zones
- Let's Make a Trade
- What's Money All About?

Fiction Books
- A Family of Collectors
- Joanie's House Becomes a Home
- Let's Surprise Mom
- The Market Adventure
- The Metal Detective
- Mr. Post's Project
- The Shopping Trip

History

Nonfiction Books
- Across the English Channel
- Celebrate Independence Day/Celebra El Día de la Independencia
- Changing Times: Women in the Early Twentieth Century
- Greek Myths
- The Statue of Liberty: A Gift From France

Fiction Books
- A Trip
- The Winning Point
- With a Twist

More Great Titles

Biography
- Extraordinary Athletes
- Great Women in U. S. History
- Thomas Hart Benton: Painter of Murals

Section 3 Matching Books and Readers

Connecting Science and Social Studies

Need more choices? Look back to Grade 2.

Grade 2 Leveled Readers

Science

Earth and Space Science

Nonfiction Books
- All About Astronauts
- An Astronaut Space Walk
- Desert Animals
- Deserts
- Hurricane!
- Look at Our Galaxy

Fiction Books
- Blizzard!
- Maggie's New Sidekick
- Rainbow Crow Brings Fire to Earth
- A Slice of Mud Pie

Life Science

Nonfiction Books
- Arachnid or Insect?
- Compost: Recycled Waste
- Farming Families
- How a Seed Grows
- How Can Animals Help?
- How Do Plants Grow?
- How to Grow Tomatoes
- Plants Grow Everywhere
- A Vet for All Animals

Fiction Books
- Annie Makes a Big Change
- Camping at Crescent Lake
- Growing Up
- Too Many Rabbit Holes
- Where Is Fish?

Physical Science

Nonfiction Books
- Many Types of Energy
- Sink or Float?

Fiction Books
- The Hummingbird
- Our School Science Fair

Grade 2 Leveled Readers

Social Studies

Citizenship

Nonfiction Books
- America's Birthday
- The Barn Raising
- Be Ready for an Emergency
- Everyone Can Make a Difference!
- Join an Adventure Club!
- Keeping Our Community Safe
- Protect the Earth
- The Rescue Dogs
- Service Workers
- Special Animal Helpers
- Using a Net
- What Can You Do?
- Working Dogs

Fiction Books
- Andrew's Mistake
- Camping with Pup
- Freda the Signmaker
- Hubert and Frankie
- Let's Work Together!
- Marty's Summer Job
- Sally and the Wild Puppy
- Stripes and Silver
- Too Many Frogs!
- Training Peanut

Culture

Nonfiction Books
- Celebrations and Family Traditions
- Living in Seoul
- Showing Good Manners
- Special Chinese Birthdays
- A World of Birthdays

Fiction Books
- Ana Is Shy
- The Camping Trip
- Country Friends, City Friends
- Dotty's Art
- The First People to Fly
- Glooskap and the First Summer: An Algonquin Tale
- Happy New Year!
- The International Food Fair
- Just Like Grandpa
- Living on a Ranch
- The New Kid in Bali
- Voting Day

Economics

Nonfiction Books
- Services and Goods

Fiction Books
- Country Mouse and City Mouse
- A Quiet Place
- Snakeskin Canyon

History

Nonfiction Books
- A Few Nifty Inventions
- The Hoover Dam
- Living in a Democracy
- Making Travel Fun
- Saint Bernards and Other Working Dogs
- Starting a New Life
- Women Play Baseball

Fiction Books
- At Home in the Wilderness
- A Class Play
- A Cowboy's Life
- Down on the Ranch
- Hank's Tortilla Factory

Government

Nonfiction Books
- Communicating Then and Now
- Let's Send a Letter!

More Great Titles

Biography
- American Revolution Heroes
- Baseball Heroes Make History
- Thomas Adams: Chewing Gum Inventor
- Three Great Ballplayers

Section 3 Matching Books and Readers

Connecting Science and Social Studies

Need more choices? Look ahead to Grade 4.

Grade 4 Leveled Readers

Science

Earth and Space Science

Nonfiction Books

- *Danger: The World Is Getting Hot!*
- *Darkness Into Light*
- *Day for Night*
- *Earth's Closest Neighbor*
- *Let's Explore Antarctica!*
- *Looking For Changes*
- *The Mysteries of Space*
- *One Giant Leap*
- *Orbiting the Sun*
- *Putting a Stop to Wildfires*
- *Severe Weather: Storms*
- *Storm Chasers*
- *Wondrously Wild Weather*

Fiction Books

- *Exploring the Moon*
- *Flash Flood*
- *Life on Mars: The Real Story*
- *Stuart's Moon Suit*
- *Surviving Hurricane Andrew*
- *To the Moon!*

Life Science

Nonfiction Books

- *Birds Take Flight*
- *Come Learn About Dolphins*
- *Dolphins: Mammals of the Sea*
- *Florida Everglades: Its Plants and Animals*
- *The Gray Whale*
- *How Does Echolocation Work?*
- *Migration Relocation*
- *Mini Microbes*
- *Mysterious Monsters*
- *Plants and Animals in Antarctica*
- *Saving Trees Using Science*
- *Sharing Our Planet*
- *What in the World Is That?*

Life Science

Fiction Books

- *The Missing Iguana Mystery*
- *Protecting Wild Animals*
- *The Salamander Stumper*
- *Top Hat Tompkins, the Detective*

Grade 4 Leveled Readers

Social Studies

Citizenship

Nonfiction Books
- *Equality in American Schools*
- *Danger! Children at Work*
- *Dogs on the Job*

Fiction Books
- *Mountain Rescue*
- *The Super Secret Surprise Society*

Culture

Nonfiction Books
- *The Black Ensemble Theater*
- *The Diné*
- *From Spain to America*
- *What It Takes to Stage a Play*

Fiction Books
- *A Book of Their Own*
- *A New Home*
- *Birthday Surprise*
- *Cheers for the Cheetahs*
- *The Grizzly Bear Hotshots*
- *Living with Grandpa Joseph*
- *The Show Must Go On!*
- *Something to Do*
- *To Be a Star*

Economics

Nonfiction Books
- *The Alaskan Pipeline*
- *Ranches in the Southwest*
- *Ranching in the Great American Desert*
- *Two Powerful Rivers*

Fiction Books
- *The Seahaven Squids Host a Pet Wash*

History

Nonfiction Books
- *Becoming a Melting Pot*
- *The Civil Rights Movement*
- *Code Breakers: Uncovering German Messages*
- *Let's Get to Know the Incas*
- *The Long Journey West*
- *Meet the Maya*
- *The Navajo Code Talkers*
- *Pompeii, the Lost City*
- *The Rosetta Stone: The Key to Ancient Writing*
- *The Sauk and Fox Native Americans*
- *Speaking in Code*
- *The Story of Libraries*
- *Thor Heyerdahl's Incredible Raft*
- *We Shall Overcome*
- *The Women's Movement*

History

Fiction Books
- *Bessie Coleman*
- *The Incredible Alexander Graham Bell*

Geography

Nonfiction Books
- *America's National Parks*
- *Maine, Now and Then*
- *A Trip to Capital Hill*
- *The Wonders of Western Geography*

Fiction Books
- *From Sea to Shining Sea*

Government

Nonfiction Books
- *The Power of the People*
- *The United States Government*

More Great Titles

Biography
- *Amazing Female Athletes*
- *Jim Thorpe*
- *John Muir*
- *The Legacy of César Chávez*
- *Lewis and Clark and the Corps of Discovery*

Planning Teacher Study Groups

Adventurous teachers often have good ideas for lessons. A teacher study group is a great way to share ideas and get feedback on the best way to connect content and students. Working with other teachers can provide you with the support and motivation you need to implement new teaching strategies. A teacher study group offers many opportunities to collaborate, support each other's work, share insights, and get feedback.

Think About It

A weekly or monthly teacher study group can help support you in developing your expertise in the classroom. You and a group of like-minded teachers can form your own study group. What can this group accomplish?

- Read and discuss professional articles by researchers in the field of education.

- Meet to share teaching tips, collaborate on multi-grade lessons, and share resources.

- Develop lessons to try out new teaching strategies. Meet to share experiences and discuss how to further improve your teaching approach.

Let's Meet!

Forming a study group is easy. Just follow these four steps:

1. **Decide on the size of the group.** A small group has the advantage of making each member feel accountable, but make sure that all people can make the same commitment!

2. **Choose teachers to invite to join your group.** Think about who you want to invite. Should they all teach the same grade? Can you invite teachers from other schools? Remember that the more diverse the group, the more it benefits from new perspectives.

3. **Set goals for the group.** In order to succeed, know what you want the group to do. Meet to set goals. Rank goals in order of importance and refer often to the goals to keep the group on track.

4. **Make logistical decisions.** This is often the most difficult. Decide where and when you will meet. Consider an online meeting place where group members can post discussion questions and replies if people are not able to meet.

What Will We Study?

Use the goals to help determine what your group will study. Consider what materials are needed to reach your goals, and how long you think is necessary to prepare for each meeting.

How Will It Work?

Think about how you structure groups in your classroom. Then use some of the same strategies.

- **Assign a group facilitator.** This person is responsible for guiding the meeting. This person comes prepared with discussion questions and leads the meeting. This could be a rotating responsibility dependent on experience with various topics. This person might be responsible for providing the materials.

- **Assign a recorder.** Have someone take notes during the meeting and record group decisions.

- **Use the jigsaw method.** Not everyone has time to be a facilitator. In this case, divide the text and assign each portion to a different person. Each person is responsible for leading the discussion on that particular part.

Meet Again

Make a commitment to meet for a minimum number of times. After that, the group can reevaluate and decide whether or not to continue.

> " Have some great teaching tips to share? Want to exchange ideas with your colleagues? Build your own professional community of teachers. **Customize Literacy** gets you started. "

Trial Lessons

Use your colleagues experience to help as you think about new ways to connect content and students. Use the following plan to create a mini-lesson. It should last twenty minutes. Get the support of your colleagues as you try something new and reflect on what happened.

Be Creative! As you develop a plan for a mini-lesson, use these four words to guide planning: *purpose, text, resources,* and *routine.*

- **Purpose:** Decide on a skill or strategy to teach. Define your purpose for teaching the lesson.

- **Text:** Develop a list of the texts you could use. Ask your colleagues for suggestions.

- **Resources:** Make a list of the available resources, and consider how to use those resources most effectively. Consider using the leveled readers listed on pages CL22–CL27 and CL34–CL39 of Customize Literacy.

- **Routine:** Choose an instructional routine to structure your mini-lesson. See the mini-lessons in Customize Literacy for suggestions.

Try It! Try out your lesson! Consider audio- or videotaping the lesson for later review. You may wish to invite a colleague to sit in as you teach. Make notes on how the lesson went.

How Did It Go? Use the self-evaluation checklist on page CL43 as you reflect on your trial lesson. This provides a framework for later discussion.

Discuss, Reflect, Repeat Solicit feedback from your teacher study group. Explain the lesson and share your reflections. Ask for suggestions on ways to improve the lesson. Take some time to reflect on the feedback. Modify your lesson to reflect what you have learned. Then try teaching the lesson again.

Checklist for Teacher Self-Evaluation

How Well Did I ...	Very Well	Satisfactory	Not Very Well
Plan the lesson?			
Select the appropriate level of text?			
Introduce the lesson and explain its objectives?			
Review previously taught skills?			
Directly explain the new skills being taught?			
Model the new skills?			
Break the material down into small steps?			
Integrate guided practice into the lesson?			
Monitor guided practice for student understanding?			
Provide feedback on independent practice?			
Maintain an appropriate pace?			
Assess student understanding of the material?			
Stress the importance of applying the skill as they read?			
Maintain students' interest?			
Ask questions?			
Handle student questions and responses?			
Respond to the range of abilities?			

Building Community

Books for Teachers

Students aren't the only ones who need to read to grow. Here is a brief list of books that you may find useful to fill your reading basket and learn new things.

A Professional Bibliography

Afflerbach, P. "Teaching Reading Self-Assessment Strategies." *Comprehension Instruction: Research-Based Best Practices.* The Guilford Press, 2002.

Bear, D. R., M. Invernizzi, S. Templeton, and F. Johnston. *Words Their Way.* Merrill Prentice Hall, 2004.

Beck, I. L., M. G. McKeown. *Improving Comprehension with Questioning the Author: A Fresh and Expanded View of a Powerful Approach.* Scholastic, 2006.

Beck, I., M. G. McKeown, and L. Kucan. *Bringing Words to Life: Robust Vocabulary Instruction.* The Guilford Press, 2002.

Blachowicz, C. and P. Fisher. "Vocabulary Instruction." *Handbook of Reading Research,* vol. III. Lawrence Erlbaum Associates, 2000.

Blachowicz, C. and D. Ogle. *Reading Comprehension: Strategies for Independent Learners.* The Guilford Press, 2008.

Block, C. C. and M. Pressley "Best Practices in Comprehension Instruction." *Best Practices in Literacy Instruction.* The Guilford Press, 2003.

Daniels, H. *Literature Circles.* 2nd ed. Stenhouse Publishers, 2002.

Dickson, S. V., D. C. Simmons, and E. J. Kame'enui. "Text Organization: Instructional and Curricular Basics and Implications." *What Reading Research Tells Us About Children with Diverse Learning Needs: Bases and Basics.* Lawrence Erlbaum Associates, 1998.

Diller, D. *Making the Most of Small Groups: Differentiation for All.* Stenhouse Publishers, 2007.

Duke, N. and P. D. Pearson. "Effective Practices for Developing Reading Comprehension." *What Research Has to Say About Reading Instruction,* 3rd ed. Newark, DE: International Reading Association, 2002.

Fillmore, L. W. and C. E. Snow. "What Teachers Need to Know About Language." Office of Educational Research and Improvement, U.S. Department of Education, 2000.

Fountas, I. C. and G. S. Pinnell. *Guiding Readers and Writers Grades 3–6: Teaching Comprehension, Genre, and Content Literacy.* Heinemann, 2001.

Guthrie, J. and E. Anderson. "Engagement in Reading: Processes of Motivated Strategic, Knowledgeable, Social Readers." *Engaged Reading: Processes, Practices, and Policy Implications.* Teachers College Press, 1999.

Harvey, S. and A. Goudvis. *Strategies That Work: Teaching Comprehension to Enhance Understanding.* 2nd ed. Stenhouse Publishers, 2007.

Keene, E. O. and S. Zimmerman. *Mosaic of Thought.* 2nd ed. Heinemann, 2007.

Leu Jr., D. J. "The New Literacies: Research on Reading Instruction with the Internet and Other Digital Technologies." *What Research Has to Say About Reading Instruction,* 3rd ed. International Reading Association, 2002.

McKeown, M. G. and I. L. Beck. "Direct and Rich Vocabulary Instruction." *Vocabulary Instruction: Research to Practice.* The Guilford Press, 2004.

McTighe, J. and K. O'Conner. "Seven Practices for Effective Learning." *Educational Leadership,* vol. 63, no. 3 (November 2005).

Nagy, W. E. *Teaching Vocabulary to Improve Reading Comprehension.* International Reading Association, 1998.

National Reading Panel. *Teaching Children to Read.* National Institute of Child Health and Human Development, 1999.

Ogle, D. and C. Blachowicz. "Beyond Literature Circles: Helping Students Comprehend Information Texts." *Comprehension Instruction: Research-Based Practices.* The Guilford Press, 2001.

Pressley, M. *Reading Instruction That Works: The Case for Balanced Teaching,* 3rd ed. The Guilford Press, 2005.

Stahl, S. A. "What Do We Know About Fluency?" *The Voice of Evidence in Reading Research.* Paul H. Brookes, 2004.

Taylor, B. M., P. D. Pearson, D. S. Peterson, and M. C. Rodriguez. "The CIERA School Change Framework: An Evidence-Based Approach to Professional Development and School Reading Improvement." *Reading Research Quarterly,* vol. 40, no. 1 (January/February/March 2005).

Valencia, S. W. and M. Y. Lipson. "Thematic Instruction: A Quest for Challenging Ideas and Meaningful Learning." *Literature-Based Instruction: Reshaping the Curriculum.* Christopher-Gordon Publishers, 1998.

Building Community

WEEK 4 Oral Vocabulary for

Let's Learn Amazing Words

Jalapeño Bagels

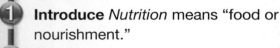

Amazing Words Oral Vocabulary Routine

DAY 1

nutrition

1. **Introduce** *Nutrition* means "food or nourishment."
2. **Demonstrate** We need to eat a variety of foods to get the right *nutrition*. There are many foods that give you good *nutrition*.
3. **Apply** Have students name some foods that they think are high in *nutrition*.

calorie

1. **Introduce** A *calorie* is a unit that measures the amount of energy a food contains.
2. **Demonstrate** Some foods are very high in *calories*. If we eat more *calories* than we use up, we will gain weight.
3. **Apply** Have students name foods they think may be high in *calories*.

DAY 2

nutmeg

1. **Introduce** *Nutmeg* is a spice used in cooking. It is the hard seed of a tree. It is dried and then grated or ground.
2. **Demonstrate** We grated the *nutmeg*. We put *nutmeg* and cinnamon in the cookies.
3. **Apply** Work with students to list recipes that might have *nutmeg* in them.

DAY 3

allergic

1. **Introduce** To be *allergic* to something means "you have an unpleasant reaction to it."
2. **Demonstrate** Some people are *allergic* to peanuts. Susan is *allergic* to cats.
3. **Apply** Have students name other things that they know of that people are *allergic to*.

DAY 4

grate

1. **Introduce** To *grate* something means "to break it into small pieces by rubbing it against a rough surface."
2. **Demonstrate** Mom showed us how to *grate* the lemon peel. We *grated* cheese for the tacos.
3. **Apply** Pantomime the act of *grating* something, such as cheese. Have students suggest things they may have seen their parents *grate* when cooking.

agent

1. **Introduce** An *agent* is something that produces an effect by its action.
2. **Demonstrate** Yeast is the *agent* that causes bread to rise. Insects like bees are *agents* of fertilization.
3. **Apply** Have students tell what the *agent* might be for the following effects: bread rising, clothes getting clean in the washer, ice melting.

Me and Uncle Romie

Amazing Words Oral Vocabulary Routine

DAY 1

scamper

1. **Introduce** To *scamper* means "to run or move quickly."

2. **Demonstrate** We watched the rabbit *scamper* across the yard. The squirrel *scampered* up the tree.

3. **Apply** Have students show how someone might *scamper.* Then have them use *scamper* in a sentence to describe someone or something moving.

scurry

1. **Introduce** To *scurry* means "to go or move in a hurry."

2. **Demonstrate** Let's *scurry* to our seats because the movie is about to start. The children *scurried* after their parents.

3. **Apply** Have students name another Amazing Word that is a synonym for *scurry.*

taxicab

1. **Introduce** A *taxicab* is an automobile that can be hired to take people where they want to go. A *taxicab* is also called a *taxi* or a *cab.*

2. **Demonstrate** Mom and Dad called a *taxicab* to take them to the airport.

3. **Apply** Have students who have ridden in a *taxicab* describe the ride. Have students tell when they might take a *taxicab* to go somewhere.

DAY 2

hurl

1. **Introduce** To *hurl* means "to throw something hard and fast."
2. **Demonstrate** Bob can really *hurl* the ball. We watched the pitcher as he *hurled* a strike.
3. **Apply** Have students name a synonym for *hurl.*

DAY 3

gutter

1. **Introduce** The *gutter* is a channel or ditch along the side of a street or road that carries off waste water.
2. **Demonstrate** The *gutters* in the streets were filled with water after the storm. The car wheels splashed water from the *gutter* onto the people standing on the corner.
3. **Apply** Have students tell why many streets have *gutters.*

DAY 4

ramble

1. **Introduce** To *ramble* means "to wander about, or to walk without any particular place to go.
2. **Demonstrate** I love to *ramble* through the woods. We *rambled* around the old farm.
3. **Apply** Have students name a synonym for *ramble.*

UNIT 5

Acknowledgments

Acknowledgments

Text

Grateful acknowledgment is made to the following for copyrighted material:

28: From *The Man Who Invented Basketball: James Naismith and His Amazing Game* by Edwin Brit Wyckoff. Copyright © 2008 by Enslow Publishers, Inc. From Enslow Publishers, Inc.

46: From *My Turn At Bat: The Story of My Life* by Ted Williams and John Underwood. Copyright © 1969, 1988 by Ted Williams and John Underwood. From Simon & Schuster, Inc.

49: "Ted Williams Timeline" from www.sportingnews.com/archives/williams/timeline.html. From *The Sporting News.*

51: "Baseball Hall of Fame Information and Baseball Card Statistics for Ted Williams" from http://www.baseballhalloffame.org/hofers/detail.jsp?playerId=124341. From National Baseball Hall of Fame (NBHOF)

62: From *Hottest, Coldest, Highest, Deepest* by Steve Jenkins. Copyright © 1998 by Steve Jenkins. Reprinted by permission of Houghton Mifflin Company. All rights reserved.

94: *Rocks in His Head* by Carol Otis Hurst. Text copyright © 2001 by Carol Otis Hurst. Illustrations © 2001 by James Stevenson. Used by permission of HarperCollins Publishers.

124: *America's Champion Swimmer: Gertrude Ederle*, text copyright © 2000 by David A. Adler, illustrations copyright © 2000 by Terry Widener, reprinted by permission of Harcourt, Inc.

126: From "Women in History: Wilma Rudolph biography." Lakewood Public Library. http://www.lkwdpl.org/wihohio/rudo-wil.htm. Reprinted by permission of Women in History, Lakewood, Ohio.

158: From *Fly, Eagle, Fly!* by Christopher Gregorowski, illustrated by Niki Daly. Text copyright © 2000 by Christopher Gregorowski, illustrations copyright © 2000 by Niki Daly. Reprinted with permission of Margaret K. McElderry Books, an imprint of Simon & Schuster Children's Publishing Division. All rights reserved.

176: *Purple Coyote* by Cornette, illustrated by Rochette. Copyright © 1997 by L'Ecole des Loisirs, Paris. First American edition 1999—Originally published in France by Pastel, 1997. English translation copyright © 1999 by Random House, Inc. Published by arrangement with Random House Children's Books, a division of Random House, Inc., New York, New York. All rights reserved.

185: "Written at the Po-Shan Monastery" by Hsin Ch'i-chi, translated by Irving Yucheng Lo, from *Sunflower Splendor: Three Thousand Years of Chinese Poetry* by Wu-Chi Liu (Author), Irving Yucheng Lo (Editor), published by Indiana University Press, 1990. Reprinted by permission of Indiana University Press.

186: "Me with apologies to Joyce Kilmer ("Trees")" from *Because I Could Not Stop My Bike* by Karen Jo Shapiro. Text copyright © 2003 Karen Jo Shapiro. Illustrations copyright © 2003 by Matt Faulkner. Used with permission by Charlesbridge Publishing, Inc. All rights reserved.

187: "By Myself" from *Honey, I Love* by Eloise Greenfield. Text copyright © 1978 by Eloise Greenfield. Used by permission of HarperCollins Publishers.

198: *Suki's Kimono*, written by Chieri Uegaki and illustrated by Stéphane Jorisch is used with the permission of Kids Can Press Ltd., Toronto. Text © 2003 Chieri Uegaki. Illustrations © 2003 Stéphane Jorisch.

230: From *I Love Saturdays y domingos* by Alma Flor Ada. Text copyright © 2002 by Alma Flor Ada. Reprinted with permission of Atheneum Books for Young Readers, an Imprint of Simon & Schuster Children's Publishing Division. All rights reserved.

250: From *Scott Foresman Social Studies Communities*, 2003. Copyright © 2003 Pearson Education, Inc. Reprinted by permission of Pearson Education, Inc.

262: Reprinted with permission of the National Geographic Society from *Good-Bye, 382 Shin Dang Dong* by Frances Park and Ginger Park. Copyright © 2002 Frances Park and Ginger Park. Illustrations © 2002 Yangsook Choi.

284: The Lois Lenski Covey Foundation, Inc., for "Sing a Song of People' from *The Life I Live* by Lois Lenski. Copyright © 1965 by The Lois Lenski Covey Foundation, Inc. Reprinted by Permission of Licensor. Copyright © Renewed 1993, no. RE 615-252.

296: From *Jalapeño Bagels* by Natasha Wing. Text copyright © 1996 by Natasha Wing. Reprinted with permission of Atheneum Books For Young Readers, an imprint of Simon &

552

Schuster Children's Publishing Division. All rights reserved.

314: Excerpts from *Viva Mexico! The Foods* by George Ancona (Benchmark Books). Copyright © 2002 by George Ancona. Reprinted with permission of Marshall Cavendish Corporation.

328: From *Me and Uncle Romie: A Story Inspired by the Life and Art of Romare Bearden* by Claire Hartfield, illustrated by Jerome Lagarrigue, copyright © 2002 by Claire Hartfield, text. Copyright © 2002 by Jerome Lagarrigue, illustrations. Used by permission of Dial Books for Young Readers, A Division of Penguin Young Readers Group, A Member of Penguin Group (USA) Inc., 345 Hudson Street, New York, NY 10014. All rights reserved.

360: "My Friend in School" from *Deshawn Days.* Text copyright © 2001 by Tony Medina. Permission arranged with Lee & Low Books, Inc., New York, NY 10016.

362: "Lunch Survey," from *Swimming Upstream: Middle Grade Poems* by Kristine O'Connell George. Text copyright © 2002 by Kristine O'Connell George. Reprinted by permission of Clarion Books, an imprint of Houghton Mifflin Company. All rights reserved.

363: "Saying Yes" by Diana Chang is reprinted by permission of the author.

374: *The Story of the Statue of Liberty* by Betsy C. Maestro, illustrations by Giulio Maestro. Text copyright © 1986 by Betsy Maestro. Illustrations copyright © 1986 by Giulio Maestro. Used by permission of HarperCollins Publishers.

390: From *Scott Foresman Social Studies:* Communities, 2003. Copyright © 2003 Pearson Education, Inc. Reprinted by permission of Pearson Education, Inc.

402: From *Happy Birthday Mr. Kang* by Susan L. Roth. Copyright © 2001 Susan L. Roth. Reprinted with permission of the National Geographic Society.

468: *Two Bad Ants* by Chris Van Allsburg. Copyright © 1988 by Chris Van Allsburg. Reprinted by permission of Houghton Mifflin Company. All rights reserved.

502: "Atlantis: The Legend of a Lost City" by Christina Balit. Atlantis copyright © 1999 by Frances Lincoln Limited. Text and illustrations copyright © 1999 by Christina Balit.

532: "Words Free as Confetti" from *Confetti: Poems for Children.* Text copyright © 1996 by Pat Mora. Permission arranged with Lee and Low Books, Inc., New York, NY.

535: "I Watched an Eagle Soar" from *Dancing Teepees: Poems of the North American Indian Youth* by Virginia Driving Hawk Sneve. Copyright © 1989 by Virginia Driving Hawk Sneve. Reprinted from *Dancing Teepees* by permission of Holiday House, Inc.

Every effort has been made to locate the copyright owner of material reproduced in this component. Omissions brought to our attention will be corrected in subsequent editions.

Illustrations

Cover: Leo Timmers
EI•1–EI•15 Mike Lester
80–82 James Madsen
113 Larry Jones
230–244 Claudia Degliuomini
284 Remy Simard
296–309 Antonio Castro
332–344 Jerome Lagarrigue
362 Laurie Keller
532 Stephen Daigle
W•2–W•15 Nomar Perez.

Photographs

Every effort has been made to secure permission and provide appropriate credit for photographic material. The publisher deeply regrets any omission and pledges to correct errors called to its attention in subsequent editions.

Unless otherwise acknowledged, all photographs are the property of Pearson Education, Inc.

Photo locators denoted as follows: Top (T), Center (C), Bottom (B), Left (L), Right (R), Background (Bkgd)

18 (C) ©Joel Sartore/Getty Images, (B) ©Rebecca Emery/Getty Images
20 (BR) ©Hans Neleman/zefa/Corbis, (BL) ©Yellow Dog Productions/Getty Images
26 (B) ©Roy Dabner/epa/Corbis, (C) ©Dennis Macdonald/PhotoLibrary Group, Ltd., (TL) Jupiter Images

553

Acknowledgments

27 (C) ©Stephen Wilkes/The Image Bank/Getty Images
30 (TC) ©Shironina Lidiya Alexandrovna/Shutterstock
46 (CL) ©Bettmann/Corbis, (B) ©Stockxpert
47 (TR) ©Bettmann/Corbis, (BR) Jupiter Images
48 (CC) Corbis
49 (BR) ©William McKellar /Jupiter Images
50 (TL) ©AP Photo, (CR) ©DK Images
54 (CR) ©Frans Lanting/Minden Pictures, (B) ©Robert Harding Picture Library Ltd/Alamy Images
55 (CC) ©Bill Draker/Rolfnp/Alamy Images
60 (C) Alamy Images, (T) ©Greg Vaughn/Alamy Images, (B) ©Nik Keevil/Alamy
86 (B,) ©Ariel Skelley/Corbis
87 (CR) ©Don Smetzer/PhotoEdit
92 (B) ©Markos Dolopikos/Alamy, (C) ©Paul Doyle/Alamy Images, (T) ©SW Productions/Getty Images
110 (T, BC) ©ZZ/Alamy, (B) Jupiter Images
111 (BR) ©ZZ/Alamy
112 (CR) ©ZZ/Alamy
113 (TR, BR, BL) ©ZZ/Alamy
116 (B) ©Pete Saloutos/Corbis
117 (BR) ©Bequest of Mrs. Benjamin Ogle Tayloe/Collection of The Corcoran Gallery of Art/Corbis, (TR) GRIN/NASA
122 (T) ©Annie Griffiths Belt/Getty Images, (C) ©David Madison/Jupiter Images, (B) ©Peter Adams/Corbis
144 (BC) ©George Silk/Time Life Pictures/Getty Images, (TR) ©Underwood & Underwood/Corbis
146 (CR) ©George Silk/Time Life Pictures/Getty Images
147 (CL) ©George Silk/Time Life Pictures/Getty Images, (CR) Bettmann/Corbis
150 (BL) ©David Shale/Nature Picture Library, (B) ©Joe McDonald/Corbis
151 (BR) ©Rick & Nora Bowers/Alamy Images
156 (C) ©Yann Arthus-Bertrand/Corbis, (B) ©Anne-Marie Weber/Getty Images, (T) ©Mireille Vautier/Alamy Images
188 (C) ©Jeremy Horner/Getty Images
190 (BC) ©Brian A. Vikander/Corbis, (B) ©Kayle M. Deioma/PhotoEdit
191 (BR) ©B&Y Photography/Alamy Images
196 (B) ©Goolia Photography/Alamy, (T) Philip Duff, (C) PhotoLibrary
216 (BC) ©Christie's Images/Peter Harholdt/Corbis, (BR) Art Resource, NY
217 (CR) ©Lynn Goldsmith/Corbis, (TR) Art Resource, NY
218 (TR) ©Historical Picture Archive/Corbis, (CR) ©Werner Forman/Corbis, (BR) Getty Images
219 (BR) ©Pavlovsky Jacques/Corbis, (TR) Corbis, (CR) Getty Images
222 (C) ©D. Hurst/Alamy Images, (BL) ©David-Young-Wolff/Alamy Images, (BC) ©Kevin Dodge/Corbis
228 (B) ©Demin Tony/PhotoLibrary Group, Ltd., (C) ©Richard Cooke/Alamy Images, (T) ©Stefan Sollfors/Alamy Images
250 (TR) Getty Images, (BR) ©Morton Beebe/Corbis
251 (BR) ©Steve Vidler/SuperStock, (TR) Getty Images
254 (BL) ©Tibor Bogner/Corbis, (B) ©Vince Streano/Corbis
255 (BR) ©Robert W. Ginn/PhotoEdit
260 (C) Corbis, (T) ©Elmari Joubert/Alamy, (B) ©Stephen Oliver/Alamy Images
288 (BC, B) Jupiter Images
289 (BR) ©foodfolio/Alamy Images
294 (B) Corbis, (T) ©Massimo Borchi/Corbis, (C) ©Vario Images GmbH & Co. KG/Alamy Images
314 (CR) George Ancona
315 (BC) George Ancona
316 (BR, B) George Ancona
317 (TR) George Ancona
320 (B) ©George Doyle/Getty Images, (TL) ©Rhoda Sidney/PhotoEdit
321 (BR) Getty Images
326 (C) ©Randy Faris/Corbis, (B) ©travelstock44/Alamy
354 (BR) ©David Zimmerman/Corbis, (TR) ©Terry W. Eggers/Corbis
355 (BR) AP/Wide World Photos
356 (BR) ©Duomo/Corbis
357 (CR) ©David Thomas/PictureArts/Corbis, (BR) ©Royalty-Free/Corbis
364 (C) ©Kevin Dodge/Corbis
366 ©Randy Faris/Corbis
372 (C) ©David Noble/Alamy Images, (B)

554

©Kai Wiechmann/Getty Images, (T) ©Taurus Taurus/PhotoLibrary Group, Ltd.
390 (CC) ©Jim Erickson/Erickson Productions, (TR) Corbis
391 (CR) ©Robert Holmes/Corbis
394 ©Canopy Photography/Veer, Inc.
400 (C) ©Foodcollection/Alamy, (T) Getty Images, (B) ©VStock/Alamy
424 (C) ©Joseph Sohm/ChromoSohm Inc./Corbis, (BC) Jupiter Images
425 (CR) ©Sandra Baker/Alamy Images
426 (BC) The Granger Collection, NY
427 (TR) ©Bill Howe/Alamy Images
430 ©David Young-Wolff/PhotoEdit, (BL) Getty Images
431 (B) ©David Young-Wolff/PhotoEdit, (BR) Jupiter Images
435 (TR) ©JM Labat/Photo Researchers, Inc.
436 (C) ©Don B. Stevenson/Alamy Images, (T) ©Ed Bock/Corbis, (BC) Getty Images, (B) ©Jim West/Alamy Images
438 (C) Meg Saligman
440 (CC) ©Ben Valenzuela
441 (B) ©Hector Ponce/Rich Puchalsky
442 (T) ©Hector Ponce/Rich Puchalsky
444 (C) *Reach High and You Will Go Far* ©2000 by Joshua Sarantitis. All Rights Reserved. Sponsored by the Philadelphia Mural Arts Program. Photograph ©2000 by Joshua Sarantitis. All rights reserved.
445 (CC) ©Paul Botello
447 (B) Getty Images
448 (B) ©Gianni Tortoli/Photo Researchers, Inc., (B) David Botello
449 (T) ©Gianni Tortoli/Photo Researchers, Inc., (BR) ©The British Museum/©DK Images, (BC) Courtesy of the U.S. Capitol Historical Society
450 (TL, B) Meg Saligman
460 (B) ©Purestock/Getty Images
461 (BR) ©Blend Images/Jupiter Images
466 (B) Alamy, (C) ©Matt Cardy/Alamy Images, (T) ©PhotosIndia LLC/Alamy
494 (B) ©David R, Frazier Photolibrary, Inc./Alamy Images
495 (TR) AP Images, (CC) Jupiter Images
499 (TR) ©Richard T. Nowitz/Corbis
500 (T) ©Franz Waldhaeusl/Alamy, (B) ©American Images Inc/Getty Images, (C) ©Pictor/Alamy
524 (T) Jupiter Images
525 (BR) Jupiter Images
527 (T) Jupiter Images
528 (CR) ©Stockxpert
529 (CR) ©Matt Carr /Jupiter Images.

555

Teacher's Edition

Text

KWL Strategy: The KWL Interactive Reading Strategy was developed and is used by permission of Donna Ogle, National-Louis University, Skokie, Illinois, co-author of *Reading Today and Tomorrow,* Holt, Rinehart & Winston Publishers, 1988. (See also the *Reading Teacher,* February 1986, pp. 564–570.)

Understanding by Design quotes: Wiggins, G. & McTighe, J. (2005). *Understanding by Design.* Alexandria, VA: Association for Supervision and Curriculum Development.

Illustrations

Cover Leo Timmers

Running Head Linda Bronson

Photographs

Every effort has been made to secure permission and provide appropriate credit for photographic material. The publisher deeply regrets any omission and pledges to correct errors called to its attention in subsequent editions.

Unless otherwise acknowledged, all photographs are the property of Pearson Education, Inc.

Teacher Notes

Teacher Notes

Teacher Notes

Teacher Notes

Teacher Notes

Teacher Resources

Looking for Teacher Resources and other important information?

In the **First Stop** on Reading Street

Teacher Resources

Looking for Teacher Resources and other important information?

In the **First Stop** on Reading Street